MASS CAPTURE

MASS CAPTURE

Chinese Head Tax and the Making of Non-citizens

LILY CHO

McGill-Queen's University Press
Montreal & Kingston | London | Chicago

ISBN 978-0-2280-0816-3 (cloth)
ISBN 978-0-2280-0932-0 (ePDF)
ISBN 978-0-2280-0933-7 (ePUB)
ISBN 978-0-2280-0934-4 (open access)

Legal deposit fourth quarter 2021
Bibliothèque nationale du Québec

Printed in Canada on acid-free paper

This book has been published with the help of a grant from the Canadian Federation for the Humanities and Social Sciences, through the Awards to Scholarly Publications Program, using funds provided by the Social Sciences and Humanities Research Council of Canada.

Funded by the Government of Canada | Financé par le gouvernement du Canada | Canada

Canada Council for the Arts | Conseil des arts du Canada

We acknowledge the support of the Canada Council for the Arts.

Nous remercions le Conseil des arts du Canada de son soutien.

Library and Archives Canada Cataloguing in Publication

Title: Mass capture : Chinese head tax and the making of non-citizens / Lily Cho.
Names: Cho, Lily, 1975- author.
Description: Includes bibliographical references and index.
Identifiers: Canadiana (print) 20210253649 | Canadiana (ebook) 20210253738 | ISBN 9780228008163 (cloth) | ISBN 9780228009320 (ePDF) | ISBN 9780228009337 (ePUB) | ISBN 9780228009344 (open access)
Subjects: LCSH: Chinese—Taxation—Canada—History. | LCSH: Immigrants—Canada—Identification—History. | LCSH: Identification photographs—Canada—History. | LCSH: Portrait photography—Political aspects—Canada—History. | LCSH: Ethnicity—Political aspects—Canada—History. | LCSH: Race discrimination—Canada—History. | LCSH: Canada—Emigration and immigration—Government policy—History.
Classification: LCC FC106.C5 C665 2021 | DDC 971.004/951—dc23

Set in 11/14 Minion Pro with Bison and Alliance 1
Book design and typesetting by Garet Markvoort, zijn digital

CONTENTS

FIGURES

Unless otherwise noted, all CI 9 documents reproduced herein are copyright of the Government of Canada and reproduced with the permission of the Minister of Public Works and Government Services Canada from the Library and Archives Canada/Department of Employment and Immigration fonds. Unless otherwise noted, all reproductions of CI 9 documents are those that have been re-photographed by the Mass Capture Project.

PREFACE
INSTITUTIONAL ADJACENCIES AND GENEALOGIES

I fell into *Mass Capture* because I wanted to know something about what it feels like to be racialized and severed from citizenship. These were research questions that came out of my previous work on race, affect theory, and Asian-Canadian literature and culture. Most of the Asian-Canadian literary work that I read dealt, in some way or another, with the grief of racial exclusion and exclusion from the sphere of citizenship. Just reading this literature, no matter how carefully, wasn't enough for the work I wanted to do. Especially not when I was confronted with an archive of grief and loss that was so enormous that it grabbed me and wouldn't let go.

It began in 2009 when, as an experiment, I presented a paper on the relationship between emotion and citizenship based on a reading of the photographs of Chinese-Canadian head tax certificates known as "Chinese Immigration 5s," or CI 5s. There was an archivist, Johanna Mizgala, in the audience. At the time, she worked at Library Archives Canada, an institution that I would end up collaborating, or conspiring, with – for the next decade.

After my paper, she came up and asked me if I knew about CI 9s. Well, no. A few weeks later, I received an envelope containing a CD-R (remember those?). On the top side of the disc, someone had used a Sharpie to scrawl two letters and a number: "CI 9." It read like a code to me. When I put the disc into my computer, I found 2,406 certificates unlike anything I had ever seen. For months, I carried the disc around, caught up entirely by the auratic value of the images. I didn't know what to do with them, or how to think about them. But, even then, I knew that they would change everything for me.

The CI 9s are so extraordinary. They are the most complete collection of Chinese head tax certificates in Canada. Library and Archives Canada (LAC) holds over 41,000 certificates. In contrast, LAC holds only a couple dozen CI 5s.

Between 1885 and 1923, every Chinese migrant to Canada had to pay a "head tax" under the terms of the Chinese Immigration Act. This legislation was periodically amended to increase the amount of the tax.

Initially, the tax was set at $50 per "head," but it was increased to $100 in 1900 and then again to $500 in 1903. The head tax remained at $500 until 1923, when the Chinese Immigration Act was further amended to exclude virtually all Chinese people from entering Canada. This final amendment led to the legislation becoming known colloquially as the "Chinese Exclusion Act." However, it is important to recognize both the head tax and this outright exclusion as policies rooted in the same legislation, belonging to a single continuum of restrictive immigration measures levelled at Chinese migrants to Canada. The exclusion of Chinese migrants from 1923 until 1947, when the Chinese Immigration Act was finally repealed, was part and parcel of the head tax system.

In order to track migrants entering Canada, as well as those who left, Canada implemented a vast protocol for acquiring detailed personal information about Chinese migrants in the country. The use of identification photographs was a key innovation of the repressive state apparatus that the Canadian government adopted in order to police and enforce the terms of the Chinese Immigration Act. Upon entry, Chinese migrants were issued a CI 5, which functioned as proof that they had paid the head tax. The CI 5s include the name of the migrant and their photograph. In contrast, the CI 9s contain a huge trove of information, including their date of birth, place of residence, occupation, identifying marks, known associates, and, significantly, identification photographs.

While the sheer number of CI 9 certificates held by LAC is notable, it is the demand for identification photographs on these certificates that underpins *Mass Capture*. The CI 9 photographs make up the largest photographic archive of images of Chinese migrants in Canada. Further, the CI 9s constitute the first mass use of identification photography in Canada. For the first time, the Canadian state attempted to track the identities of thousands of men, women, and children. Unlike any moment in its prior history, the government isolated one specific group of people, purely on the basis of race and ethnicity, in order to identify each individual member of that group through the creation of a massive apparatus that would systematically correlate their identity with a photographic image. What is more, this use of identification photography – what I identify as a technology of mass capture – was used to exclude people from the sphere of citizenship.

The argument of this book is that the CI 9s are a technology of mass capture that produces non-citizens. Citizenship functions through a series of exclusions. However, there is nothing simple about these exclusions. As the cumbersome apparatus of head tax certificates reveals, the state bent over backwards to police non-citizenship. It was an unwieldy system that generated a bewildering amount of paperwork. This paperwork had to be drafted, printed, completed, filed, cross-referenced, verified, filed again. It is a system that betrays state anxiety and the dynamism of non-citizenship.

The non-citizen is not a static figure. They must be constantly regulated and monitored. This project traces the concomitant rise of surveillance and citizenship by following one story of the construction of the non-citizen. The non-citizen is not simply there. They must be made and then made again. Every certificate filed, every form completed, constitutes another instance of their construction.

In order to do this work, I have had to work very closely – what I think of as adjacently – with a number of institutions. When I say that I have had to work adjacently, I mean that I have had to work in ways that recognize the limits and boundaries of the institutions that have been closest to the project. Namely, Library and Archives Canada (LAC), but also Canadiana.org, an organization that has since merged with other institutions to form the Canadian Research Knowledge Network (CRKN). Canadiana had been contracted by LAC to digitize much of its holdings, including the head tax certificates that are at the heart of my project.

One way to think about the institutional genealogy of mass capture is to think about the process of the digitization of the CI 9s.

When I began this project, these certificates had not been digitized. After a couple of years working with them on microfilm, I realized that I would have to digitize them. But just as I was about to do so, I learned that LAC had contracted with Canadiana to do this very thing, so I put the project on hold and waited for Canadiana to complete its work.

After the CI 9s had been digitized by Canadiana, I realized that the level of digitization was insufficient for my research. The resolution for the images that Canadiana had digitized, and which are now available through the LAC website, were far too low for the photographic and textual analysis that I needed to conduct. Even though the LAC version of these certificates is still the official version, it did not work for me. I had to re-digitize them.

Figures P.1–P.3 are a few examples of the difference between the digitizations completed for LAC and those that were completed for *Mass Capture*. The digitization of the certificates completed for my project (on the left) significantly differs from LAC's digitizations (on the right) because *Mass Capture* treats each certificate as a photographic object.

As I discuss at length in the coda, the original certificates were destroyed by order of microfilm authority M6-62 in 1963. Many of the images were of poor quality even before the destruction of the originals. However, as the work of my project reveals, treating each certificate as a photographic

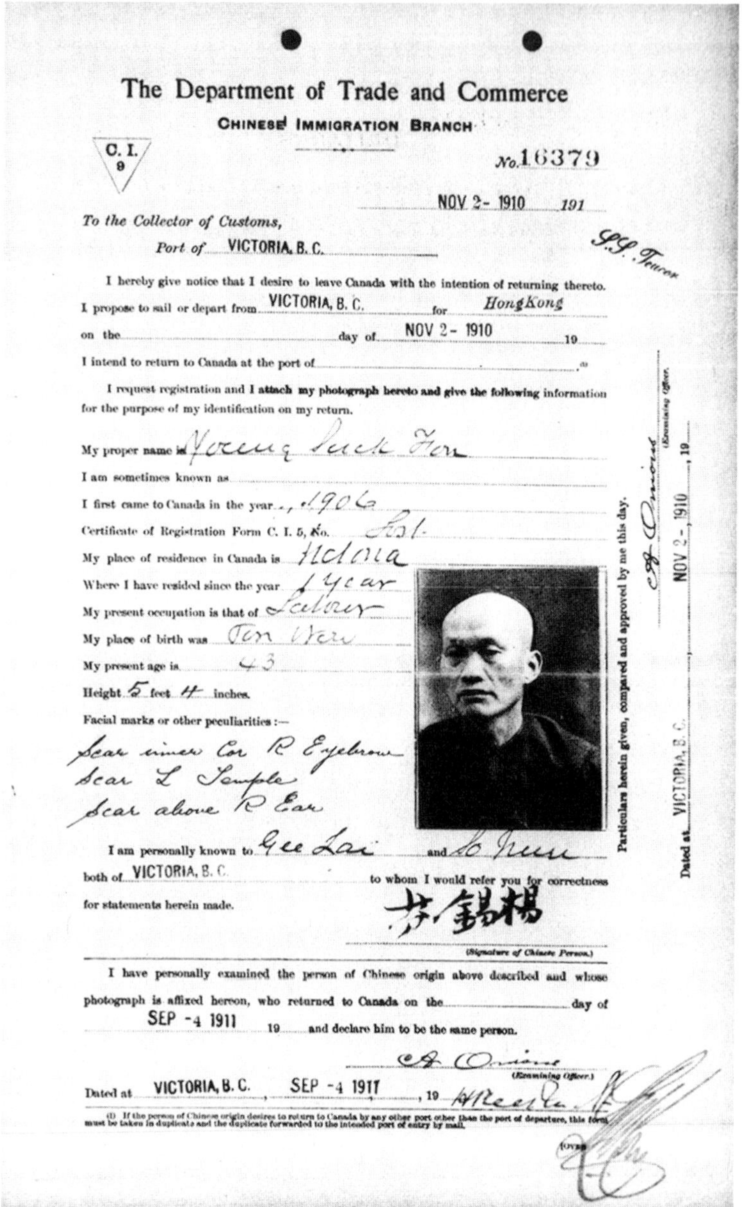

The Department of Trade and Commerce

CHINESE IMMIGRATION BRANCH

C. I. 9

No. 16379

NOV 2- 1910 191

To the Collector of Customs,

Port of VICTORIA, B. C.

S.S. Teucer

I hereby give notice that I desire to leave Canada with the intention of returning thereto.

I propose to sail or depart from VICTORIA, B. C. for HongKong

on the ...... day of NOV 2- 1910 19

I intend to return to Canada at the port of ......(1)

I request registration and I attach my photograph hereto and give the following information for the purpose of my identification on my return.

My proper name is Yoeng Suck Fon

I am sometimes known as

I first came to Canada in the year 1906

Certificate of Registration Form C. I. 5, No. Lost

My place of residence in Canada is Victoria

Where I have resided since the year 1 year

My present occupation is that of Labourer

My place of birth was Sun Wui

My present age is 43

Height 5 feet 4 inches.

Facial marks or other peculiarities:—

Scar inner Cor R Eyebrow
Scar L Temple
Scar above R Ear

I am personally known to Gee Lai and So ...

both of VICTORIA, B. C. to whom I would refer you for correctness for statements herein made.

苏錫榻

(Signature of Chinese Person.)

Particulars herein given, compared and approved by me this day.

Dated at VICTORIA, B. C. NOV 2- 1910, 19

(Examining Officer.)

I have personally examined the person of Chinese origin above described and whose photograph is affixed hereon, who returned to Canada on the ...... day of SEP -4 1911 19 and declare him to be the same person.

(Examining Officer.)

Dated at VICTORIA, B. C. SEP -4 1911, 19

(1) If the person of Chinese origin desires to return to Canada by any other port other than the port of departure, this form must be taken in duplicate and the duplicate forwarded to the intended port of entry by mail.

(OVER)

Fig. P.1
CI 9 No. 16379 [comparison: *Mass Capture* digitization above, LAC digitization opposite], Reel no. T-6038.

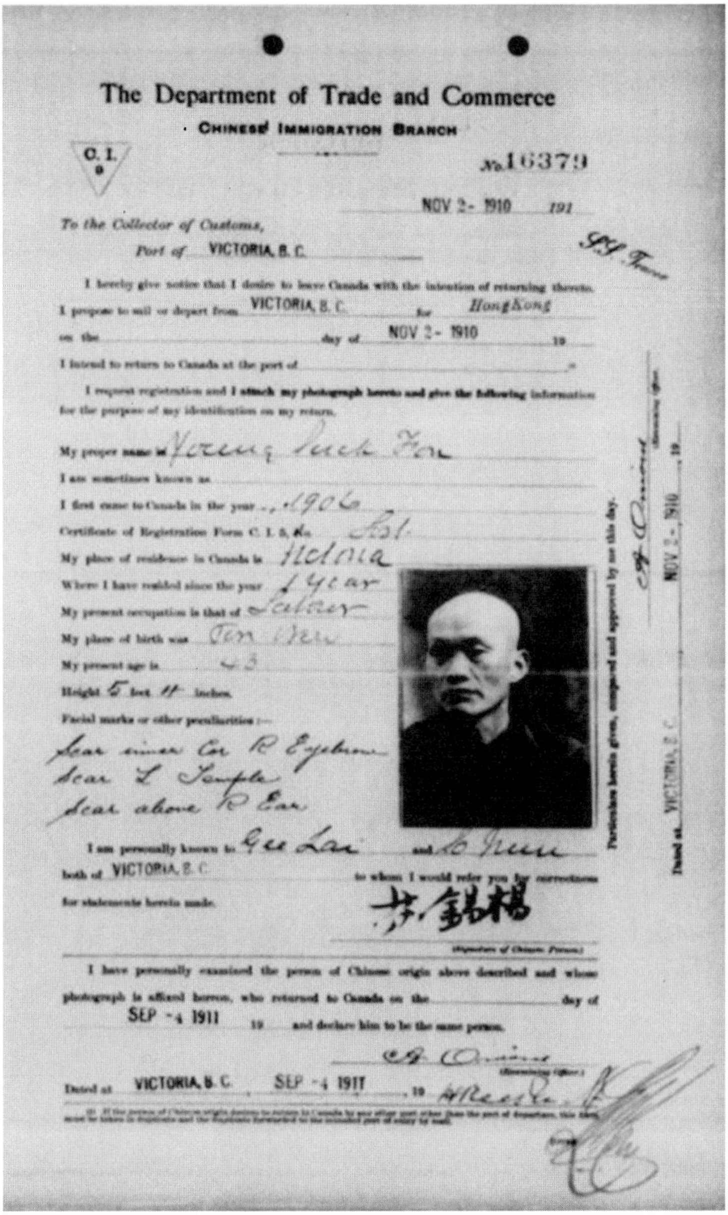

The Department of Trade and Commerce

CHINESE IMMIGRATION BRANCH

C. I. 9

No. 16379

NOV 2- 1910 191

To the Collector of Customs,

Port of VICTORIA, B. C.

S.S. Tenn

I hereby give notice that I desire to leave Canada with the intention of returning thereto.

I propose to sail or depart from VICTORIA, B. C. for HongKong

on the day of NOV 2- 1910 19

I intend to return to Canada at the port of

I request registration and I attach my photograph hereto and give the following information for the purpose of my identification on my return.

My proper name is Yoeng Suck Fon

I am sometimes known as

I first came to Canada in the year 1906

Certificate of Registration Form C. I. 5, No. Lost

My place of residence in Canada is Victoria

Where I have resided since the year 4 year

My present occupation is that of Laborer

My place of birth was Tin Wen

My present age is 43

Height 5 feet 11 inches.

Facial marks or other peculiarities :—

Scar inner Cor R Eyebrow
Scar L Temple
Scar above R Ear

I am personally known to Gee Lai and S Yuen

both of VICTORIA, B. C. to whom I would refer you for correctness for statements herein made.

(Signature of Chinese Person)

Particulars herein given, compared and approved by me this day.

Dated at VICTORIA, B. C. NOV 2 - 1910 19

(Examining Officer)

I have personally examined the person of Chinese origin above described and whose photograph is affixed hereto, who returned to Canada on the day of SEP -4 1911 19 and declare him to be the same person.

(Examining Officer)

Dated at VICTORIA, B. C. SEP -4 1911 19

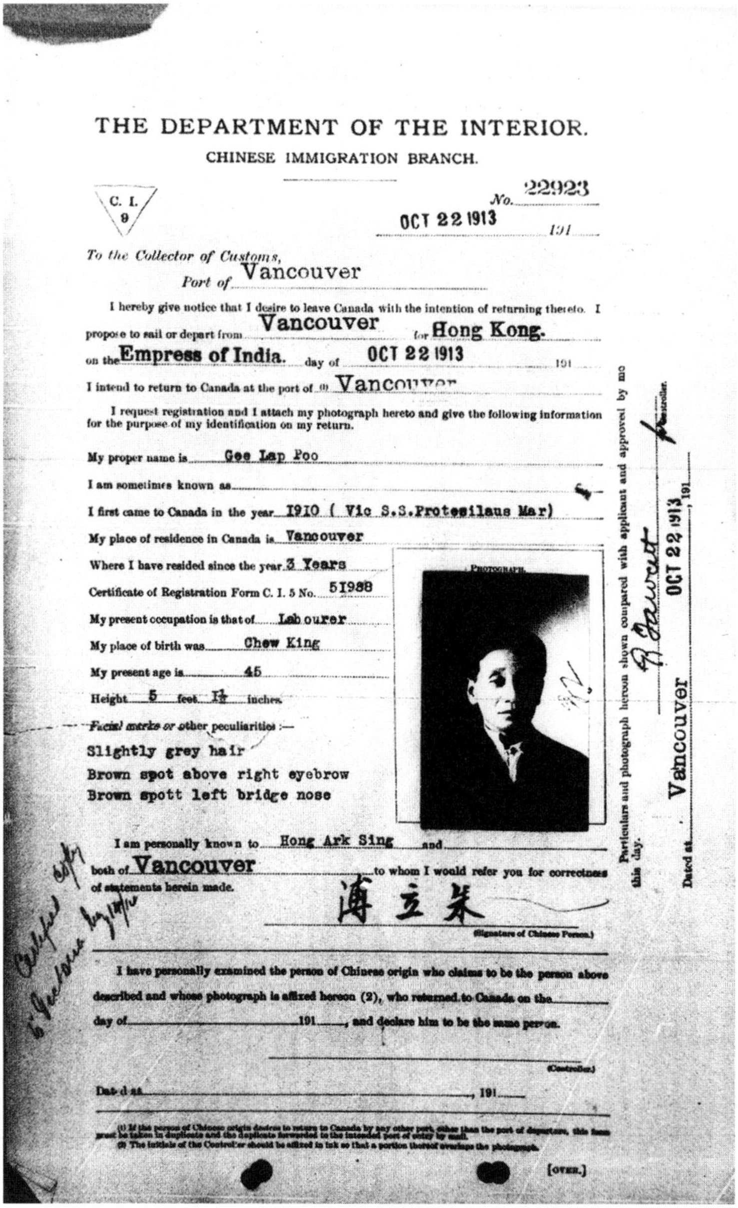

THE DEPARTMENT OF THE INTERIOR.

CHINESE IMMIGRATION BRANCH.

C. I. 9

No. 22923

OCT 22 1913 191

To the Collector of Customs,
Port of Vancouver

I hereby give notice that I desire to leave Canada with the intention of returning thereto. I propose to sail or depart from Vancouver for Hong Kong. on the Empress of India. day of OCT 22 1913 191

I intend to return to Canada at the port of (1) Vancouver

I request registration and I attach my photograph hereto and give the following information for the purpose of my identification on my return.

My proper name is Gee Lap Poo

I am sometimes known as

I first came to Canada in the year 1910 (Vic S.S.Protesilaus Mar)

My place of residence in Canada is Vancouver

Where I have resided since the year 3 Years

Certificate of Registration Form C. I. 5 No. 51988

My present occupation is that of Labourer

My place of birth was Chew King

My present age is 45

Height 5 feet 1½ inches.

Facial marks or other peculiarities:—
Slightly grey hair
Brown spot above right eyebrow
Brown spott left bridge nose

I am personally known to Hong Ark Sing and both of Vancouver to whom I would refer you for correctness of statements herein made.

溥立朱

(Signature of Chinese Person.)

Particulars and photograph hereon shown compared with applicant and approved by me this day.

Dated at Vancouver OCT 22 1913, 191

Controller.

I have personally examined the person of Chinese origin who claims to be the person above described and whose photograph is affixed hereon (2), who returned to Canada on the day of 191 , and declare him to be the same person.

(Controller.)

Dated at , 191

(1) If the person of Chinese origin desires to return to Canada by any other port, other than the port of departure, this form must be taken in duplicate and the duplicate forwarded to the intended port of entry by mail.
(2) The initials of the Controller should be affixed in ink so that a portion thereof overlaps the photograph.

[OVER.]

Fig. P.2
CI 9 No. 22923 [comparison: *Mass Capture* digitization above, LAC digitization opposite], Reel no. T-6049.

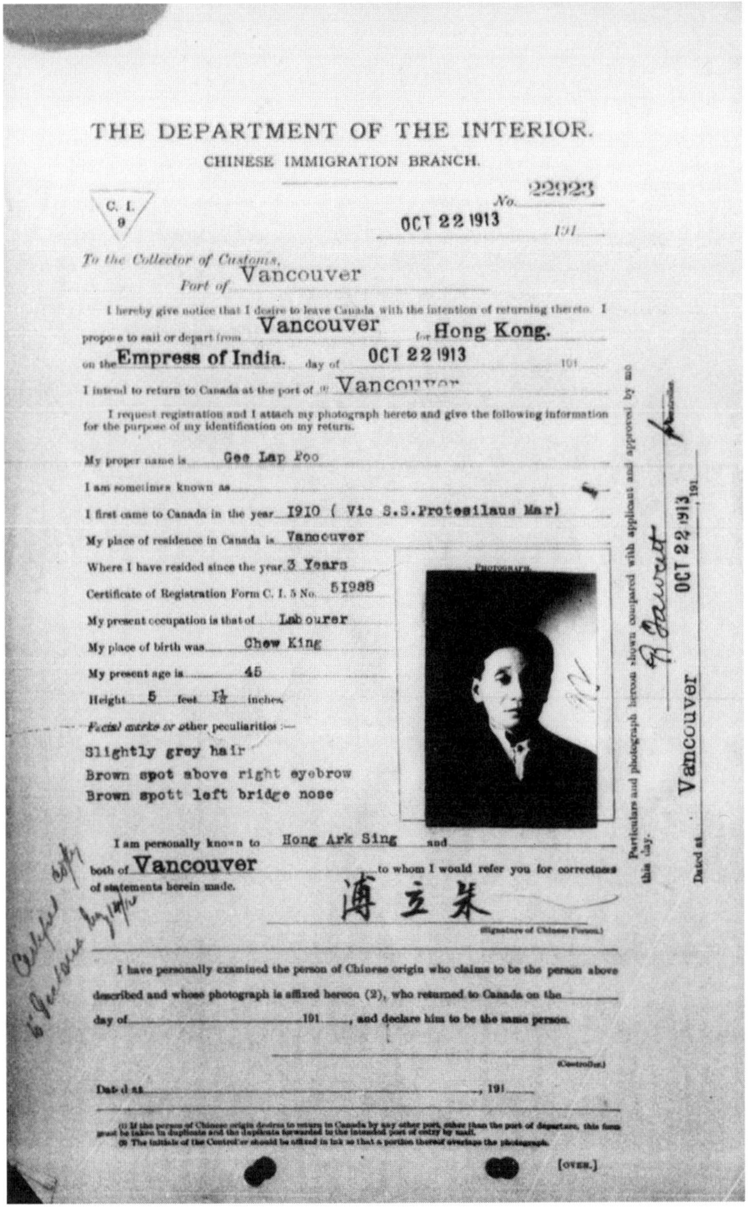

THE DEPARTMENT OF THE INTERIOR.

CHINESE IMMIGRATION BRANCH.

C. I. 9

No. 22923

OCT 22 1913 191

To the Collector of Customs,
Port of Vancouver

I hereby give notice that I desire to leave Canada with the intention of returning thereto. I propose to sail or depart from Vancouver for Hong Kong. on the Empress of India. day of OCT 22 1913 191

I intend to return to Canada at the port of (1) Vancouver

I request registration and I attach my photograph hereto and give the following information for the purpose of my identification on my return.

My proper name is Gee Lap Foo

I am sometimes known as

I first came to Canada in the year 1910 (Vic S.S.Protesilaus Mar)

My place of residence in Canada is Vancouver

Where I have resided since the year 3 Years

Certificate of Registration Form C. I. 5 No. 51988

My present occupation is that of Labourer

My place of birth was Chew King

My present age is 45

Height 5 feet 1½ inches.

Facial marks or other peculiarities :—

Slightly grey hair

Brown spot above right eyebrow

Brown spott left bridge nose

Photograph.

I am personally known to Hong Ark Sing and

both of Vancouver to whom I would refer you for correctness of statements herein made.

溥立朱

(Signature of Chinese Person.)

I have personally examined the person of Chinese origin who claims to be the person above described and whose photograph is affixed hereon (2), who returned to Canada on the day of 191 , and declare him to be the same person.

(Controller.)

Dated at , 191

(1) If the person of Chinese origin desires to return to Canada by any other port, other than the port of departure, this form must be taken in duplicate and the duplicate forwarded to the intended port of entry by mail.
(2) The initials of the Controller should be affixed in ink so that a portion thereof overlaps the photograph.

[OVER.]

Particulars and photograph hereon shown compared with applicant and approved by me this day.

Dated at Vancouver OCT 22 1913 , 191

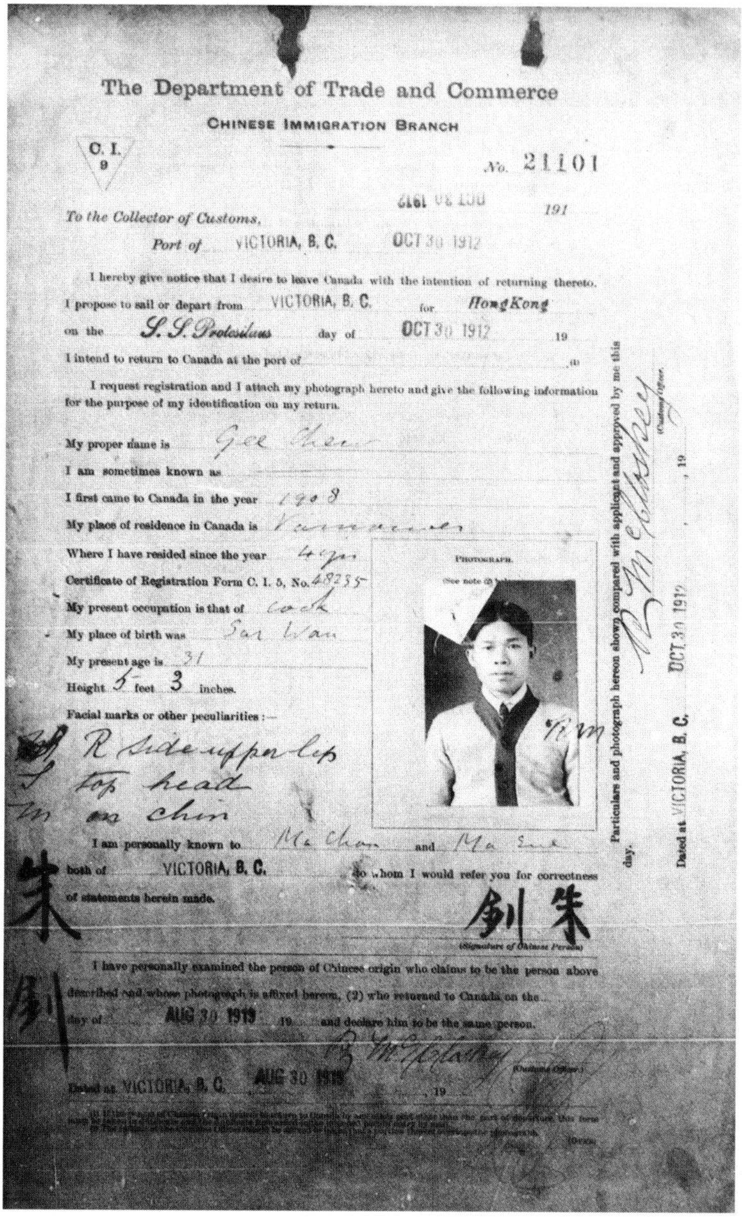

The Department of Trade and Commerce

CHINESE IMMIGRATION BRANCH

C. I. 9

No. 21101

To the Collector of Customs, 191

Port of VICTORIA, B. C. OCT 30 1912

I hereby give notice that I desire to leave Canada with the intention of returning thereto.

I propose to sail or depart from VICTORIA, B. C. for HongKong

on the S.S. Protesilaus day of OCT 30 1912 19

I intend to return to Canada at the port of (1)

I request registration and I attach my photograph hereto and give the following information for the purpose of my identification on my return.

My proper name is Gee Chew

I am sometimes known as

I first came to Canada in the year 1908

My place of residence in Canada is Vancouver

Where I have resided since the year 4 yrs

Certificate of Registration Form C. I. 5, No. 48235

My present occupation is that of cook

My place of birth was Sar Wan

My present age is 31

Height 5 feet 3 inches.

Facial marks or other peculiarities:—

R side upper lip

top head

on chin

PHOTOGRAPH. (See note (2))

I am personally known to Ma Chan and Ma Sue

both of VICTORIA, B. C. to whom I would refer you for correctness of statements herein made.

朱釗

(Signature of Chinese Person)

I have personally examined the person of Chinese origin who claims to be the person above described and whose photograph is affixed hereon, (2) who returned to Canada on the day of AUG 30 1919 19 and declare him to be the same person.

(Customs Officer.)

Dated at VICTORIA, B. C. AUG 30 1919 19

Particulars and photograph hereon shown compared with applicant and approved by me this day. (Customs Officer.)

Dated at VICTORIA, B. C. OCT 30 1912, 19

Fig. P.3
CI 9 No. 21101 [comparison: *Mass Capture* digitization above, LAC digitization opposite], Reel no. T-6040.

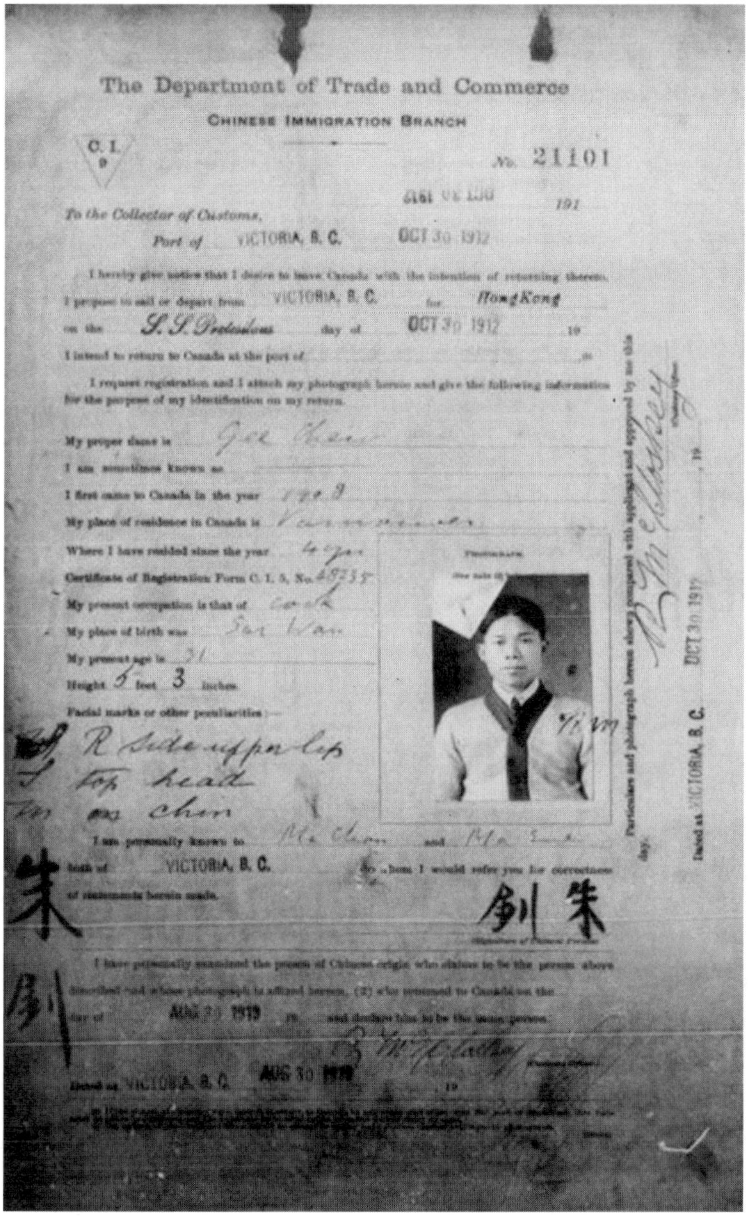

The Department of Trade and Commerce

CHINESE IMMIGRATION BRANCH

C. I. 9

No. 21101

191

To the Collector of Customs,

Port of VICTORIA, B. C. OCT 30 1912

I hereby give notice that I desire to leave Canada with the intention of returning thereto.

I propose to sail or depart from VICTORIA, B. C. for Hong Kong

on the S. S. Protesilaus day of OCT 30 1912 19

I intend to return to Canada at the port of

I request registration and I attach my photograph hereto and give the following information for the purpose of my identification on my return.

My proper name is Gee Chew

I am sometimes known as

I first came to Canada in the year 1908

My place of residence in Canada is Vancouver

Where I have resided since the year 4 yrs

Certificate of Registration Form C. I. 5, No. 48735

My present occupation is that of cook

My place of birth was Sun Wui

My present age is 31

Height 5 feet 3 inches

Facial marks or other peculiarities:—

R side upper lip

top head

chin

I am personally known to Ma Chow and Ma Sun

both of VICTORIA, B. C. to whom I would refer you for correctness of statements herein made.

朱釗

Signature of Chinese Person

I have personally examined the person of Chinese origin who claims to be the person above described and whose photograph is affixed hereto, (2) who returned to Canada on the day of AUG 30 1919 19 and declare him to be the same person.

Dated at VICTORIA, B. C. AUG 30 1919 19

Dated at VICTORIA, B. C. OCT 30 1912 19

object, deserving of the attention of a professional photographer who would be sensitive to the potential beauty of each certificate as an image in its own right, could and did produce startling results.

Before I could even study the CI 9s, I had to re-create the archive so that the certificates could be fully visible as objects worthy of photographic study. In this re-creation the CI 9s become "activated," to use Michelle Caswell's term for record-keeping's project of continual renewal and community (in the context of the Tuol Sleng archive in Cambodia): "From a records continuum perspective the reuses of the [Tuol Sleng] mug shots highlight the circular nature of the archive. The record isn't created just once but re-created (as the by-product of the act of witnessing), recaptured (as new records such as tribunal footage, documentary films, and magazine articles), recognized (in internal institutional systems), and repluralized (as it is published and viewed in the formation of collective memory) as it used again and again or 'activated' at various points in time and space" (2014, 132). The mugshots in Caswell's study have a different afterlife than that of CI 9s. They belong to a history of atrocity that has now become part of a physical space of memory, the Tuol Sleng Genocide Museum, as well as a virtual memory space through a digitization project. The CI 9 identification photographs no longer exist as original photographs. As the coda discusses, the CI 9 photographs have a different materiality because the originals were destroyed, and these images have been created and re-created many times. They will likely continue to be activated and re-created many times still. In re-creating the CI 9 archive by digitizing it, and by making these images freely available by depositing them in my university's institutional repository while also connecting them to another public repository (LAC), my project intends for the CI 9s to be records that are continually activated in the service of struggles for recognition and against the forms of discrimination that brought this archive into being in the first place.

This book also traverses disciplinary boundaries. It is adjacent to many fields of study, including history, museum studies, digital humanities, artificial intelligence, information and media studies, Asian-Canadian literary and cultural studies, and photography. It is the CI 9s themselves that have led me to the edge of every disciplinary adjacency in this book. A question about how these certificates were stored led me to consider the implications of the filing cabinet on the ordering of the people who were captured in the CI 9s. Another question about the language of the certificates led me into an investigation of diplomatics. In trying to understand how the identification photographs on these certificates function as a form of surveillance, I was particularly taken by the work of a pioneer in the field of artificial intelligence, Philip Agre, whose argument for distinguishing between surveillance and capture brought me to the entire theoretical underpinning of this book, as well as its title. I followed question after question about the photographs attached to each certificate, and found myself falling headlong into the study of vernacular photography, family photography, ancestor portraits, and conventions of Chinese portraiture.

The historical value of the CI 9s is readily apparent to anyone interested in Chinese-Canadian history, genealogy, citizenship, and labour. But their artistic value, their value as photographs and images, has been less apparent. As my commitment to re-digitizing each and every CI 9 should make clear, *Mass Capture* takes the photographic value, the aesthetics, of the CI 9s as its starting point. My analysis of these certificates moves across a number of disciplines and questions, but at the heart of each discussion in the book is a commitment to understanding the CI 9 as a photographic text. Before I could write, I had to find a way to really *see* these certificates, and to see past their seeming disposability. For this project, re-digitizing the CI 9s meant that each certificate had to be photographed frame by frame by an extraordinarily dedicated professional photographer, Helen Piekosweski, who attended to each one with painstaking detail.

The images in these pages, along with thousands more that could not be included but which were nonetheless essential for the project as a whole, were not generated through a microfilm scanner. Every image was individually photographed. Each one was attached to a lightbox using gaffer tape, the tape folded so that the adhesive would not touch the microfilm itself, and then captured using a Canon 5D Mark III camera with a Canon EF-S 60mm f/2.8 macro lens on a Manfrotto ball head tripod. This setup allowed Helen to take detailed close-ups of each certificate. After they were photographed, each image was put through a rigorous post-production process in Adobe Photoshop, where Helen adjusted the levels, sharpness, brightness, contrast, highlights, and shadows. She also inverted the colours to create a positive and added a black-and-white adjustment layer to make sure that there were no colour casts. These edits were tested and tweaked so that they were appropriate for the film slides as well. All of this had to be accomplished before my research assistants and I could zoom in on each one to study not only the identification photographs, but also the handwriting, the stamps, signatures, smudges, punch holes, and many other details that became crucial for the analysis of these certificates. From this base of images, *Mass Capture* examines how the CI 9 photographs function both as individual portraits of individual people, and as a collective portrait of an entire community that had been denied access to citizenship.

I am keenly aware of the moral dilemma involved in focusing this book on documents, rather than the people captured in these documents. I recognize that this difficult choice limits the capacity of the book to address the social histories of the people whose histories can be found in the CI 9s. Still, these documents themselves are, for me, very much alive. Throughout my research for this book, I have had the privilege of sharing my thinking with a range of communities and audiences. Every time, people have wanted to know more, to look for their own histories in the archive, and to look further and deeper into what the CI 9s might tell us about the people captured in them. I hope this book will bring about more engagements with the CI 9s that will extend and deepen the social histories connected to each photograph and certificate.

This book is the story of one historical archive and one decades-long historical moment. But mass capture is also a technology of the present. Because non-citizens continue to be a tragic feature of the current period, mass capture is also about our world now. The final years of my work on this book have seen an intensification of processes of mass capture as a technology of non-citizenship. From the internment of Uighur minority communities in the People's Republic of China, to the separation of migrant families in the United States, to the closure of international borders during the COVID-19 pandemic, the use of surveillance tools to track migrants for the purposes of excluding them from citizenship has become the de facto practice of a perpetually horrifying new normal.

Even though international charters and laws declare that all people have the right to citizenship, the mass capture of non-citizens continues apace. I write this book in the hope that its arguments will one day be obsolete because non-citizens no longer underwrite citizenship. I hope that mass capture will be an unfortunate feature of a past that is truly past.

ACKNOWLEDGMENTS

This book owes many debts.

To Johanna Mizgala, curator, House of Commons Heritage Collection, who told me about CI 9s in the first place, and trusted me to know what to do when she sent me a CD-R of 2,406 certificates.

To Émilie Létourneau, lead archivist, Archives Branch, Library and Archives Canada, who was so gracious to serve as my collaborator on the SSHRC grant that allowed me to pursue the primary research for this book.

To Julienne Pascoe, digital archivist, Library and Archives Canada, who understood the relationship of the CI 9s to Canadiana.org and the Canadian Research Knowledge Network, and who generously helped me to see the relationships between the documents and the metadata attached to them. Thank you also for your friendship during different moments of vulnerability as I was trying to wrap my head around things that sometimes felt too big.

To Helen Piekosweski, who photographed every single CI 9 that I had acquired, treated them with so much tenderness, and understood that each is a work of art.

To Jonathan Crago, who stayed with this manuscript for years. You did not laugh when I asked you how we could give the book away for free if I published with MQUP. You sent me unwaveringly supportive emails during low moments. You bring so much care and deep intelligence to this work and you saw better than I did what this book could be.

To Scott Howard for brilliant, sensitive, and deft copyediting.

To the anonymous peer reviewers of the manuscript. Your work may not be immediately visible to the world, but you changed this book with the depth of your engagement and the great sensitivity of your critiques.

To the tremendous team at York University Libraries for finding a home for the CI 9s that are at the core of this book, and for helping me understand what I wanted from an Open Access monograph: Kris Joseph, Andrea Kosavics, Lisa Slownioski, and Anna St Onge. Special thanks to Anna for telling me to go look up diplomatics.

To Janet Friskney who taught me that there is no room for hope in a successful research grant application. The principal investigator does not hope to do the work. The prinçipal investigator *does* the work thanks to research officers who help them find the funds to support the work.

To Alicia Filipowich who showed me how to spend the funds and was there at every step to make holding a research grant a truly rewarding experience. As a term, "post-award administration" does not do justice to the real pleasure and ease that Alicia brings to the bureaucracy of using grant funds to support research.

Alicia was also absolutely central to helping me put together an outstanding research team. It is my great privilege to acknowledge the contributions of so many brilliant undergraduate and graduate research assistants: Tiffany Phan, Shalika Sivathasan, Sara Rozenberg, Chloe (Rong) Shi, Rachel Wong, and Biwei Zhang.

To the members of the Toronto Photography Seminar. Particular thanks to Sarah Parsons and Thy Phu for reading early drafts of key chapters; to Laura Levin for insisting that I see myself in these conversations about photography; to Dot Tuer for asking me why I could write about my father and not my mother; to Deepali Dewan for telling me about her work with microfilm at the Royal Ontario Museum and showing me that digitally photographing microfilm was not only possible, but something that one of the best museums in the country had been doing for a long time; and huge special thanks to Gabrielle Moser and Sharon Sliwinski for agreeing to be joint guardians of the manuscript when I was scared of not being able to see it through all by myself.

To Tina Campt, Marianne Hirsch, and Brian Wallis for inviting me to see my research as part of much larger conversation about vernacular photography; and to Ali Behdad, Nicole Fleetwood, and Laura Wexler for having those conversations on stage with me at the "Imagining Everyday Life" symposium. Those conversations were central to allowing me to see how captivation is also a part of the work of capture.

To University College at the University of Toronto for the Canadian Studies Fellowship in 2010, which allowed me to begin my work on this book.

To Massey College at the University of Toronto and the Office of the Vice President for Research and Innovation at York University for the York-Massey Fellowship, which allowed me to complete a major part of the manuscript in 2016–17. To Amela Marin. To Elena Ferranti. To the incredible Junior Fellows who made me think harder about all the important things. Particular thanks to Principal Hugh Segal.

During the years when I worked on this book, I served in a number of academic administrative positions at York University: undergraduate program director for the Department of English, chair of the Department of English, and associate dean, Global and Community Engagement, for the Office of the Dean, Faculty of Liberal Arts and Professional Studies. There is no way I could have found time for research and writing while holding these positions if I had not had the benefit of outstanding academic support staff who found that time for me. For always protecting my research time and doing your jobs so well so that I could do mine, sincere thanks to Michelle Anacleto, Kathy Armstrong, Debra Bisram, Rose Crawford, Meaghan McCue, and Rameila Williams.

To the dean and the merry band of associate deans in the Faculty of Liberal Arts and Professional Studies at York University who made the work of navigating a big institution through the Before Times, and then through the pressures of a global pandemic, actually joyful: Peter Avery, Ravi de Costa, Roberta Iannacito-Provenzano, Michele Johnson, Sean Kheraj, Anita Lam, J.J. McMurtry, David Mutimer, and Sandra Whitworth. Administrative work can be consuming but it was Ananya Mukherjee-Reed who taught me that this work is also part of our life as researchers. I am grateful to have been able to do this work, to make it a part of my intellectual life, alongside such stellar decanal colleagues. To Kathryn McPherson who suggested that I enter this strange world of associate deanship in the first place.

To my *Hook & Eye* collaborators: Aimée Morrison, Melissa Dalgleish, and truly, deeply, especially, Erin Wunker, because fast feminism helped me to write slowly and thoughtfully.

To friends who have been a part of the journey of this book. It is a great gift to be in a profession where I can be surrounded by so many smart people. You may not have always known that you were talking about mass capture with me, but you were: Ian Balfour, Marcus Boon, Alexandra Boutros, Jessica Bucholz, Shannon Chace, David Chariandy, Mary Chapman, Katharine Charlton, David Clark, Alison Conway, Julia Creet, Andrea Davis, Kathyrn Doyle, Angela Failler, Joel Faflak, Lindsay Gonder, Eve Haque, Manina Jones, Martin Krieswirth, Sue Malley, Corey Mintz, Alex Panther, Saba Rafiq, Emma Rhodes, Emma Segal, Catherine Salole, Sarah Sharma, Katherine Skene, Sasha Torres, Bryce Traister, Pauline Wakeham, Deanne Williams, and Rinaldo Walcott.

To Jennifer Harris, who responded to my desperate social media plea on New Year's Eve, 2019, with her skills as a genealogy sleuth extraordinaire. In a matter of hours, I went from being unable to decipher the place of birth on James Ying Choury's CI 9, to looking in wonder at his wedding photographs because Jennifer was so generous with her time and expertise.

To Stephen Slemon, always and forever, thanks: I would not be here if you had not told me to go to graduate school when I did not know that graduate school existed.

To my family, especially to my father, who showed me how to carve out a life of grace and kindness in the aftermath of his own mass capture.

To Harriet Frances Green. You are my all and my everything.

Credits

A small portion of the introduction is published in "Mass Capture: The Making of Non-citizens and the Mainland Travel Permit for Hong Kong and Macau Residents," in "Migration Infrastructures and the Constitution of (Im)mobilities," special issue, *Mobilities* 12, no. 2 (2017): 188–98.

A portion of chapter 2 is published in "Mass Capture against Memory: Chinese Head Tax and the Making of Non-citizens," *Citizenship Studies* 22, no. 4 (2018): 381–400, doi:10.1080/13621025.2018.1462505.

The opening discussion of CI 9 nos. 20306 and 20307 in chapter 3 is published in the Champlain Society's blog *Findings/Trouvailles*, "A Family Torn Apart as Revealed by the 'Chinese Immigration 9 Form,'" 7 February 2019, https://champlainsociety.utpjournals.press/findings-trouvailles/2019/02/family-torn-apart-revealed-chinese-immigration-9-form.

A portion of chapter 5 is published in "Anticipating Citizenship: Chinese Head Tax Photographs," in *Feeling Photography*, edited by Elspeth Brown and Thy Phu (Durham, NC: Duke University Press, 2014), 159 80.

The research for this book has been generously supported by a SSHRC Insight Grant, the York University Faculty of Liberal Arts and Professional Studies Minor Research Grant, and the York Centre for Asian Research.

Preliminary versions of some of the arguments in this book have been presented at the following venues:

"Capture, Captivity, and Captivation in Migrant Labour Photograph Series." Columbia University and the Walther Collection, New York, NY, 2018.

“Mass Capture: Chinese Head Tax Certificates and the Making of Noncitizens.” McGill Institute for the Study of Canada, McGill University, Montreal, QC, 2016.

“Anticipating Citizenship: Chinese Head Tax Photographs.” Studies in International and National Development Colloquium, Queen’s University, Kingston, ON, 2010.

“Feeling and Citizenship: Chinese Head Tax Photographs.” Keynote address for “In Transit,” Comparative Literature graduate conference, University of Western Ontario, London, ON, 2010.

“Unsentimental Archive: Chinese Head Tax Photographs.” Critical Intimacies Speakers Series, McMaster University, Hamilton, ON, 2010.

I am very grateful to the organizers for giving me the opportunity to think out loud with so many brilliant audiences throughout the years while the arguments for *Mass Capture* were taking shape.

MASS CAPTURE

INTRODUCTION
MASS CAPTURE

Fig. I.1
CI 9 No. 15811 [cropped], Reel no. T-6038.

Here is the first identification photograph of a Chinese migrant in Canada. It was attached to a form known as a CI 9 (Chinese Immigration 9), issued by the Chinese Immigration Branch of the Department of Trade and Commerce. It is called CI 9 no. 15811 (fig. I.2).

Please, imagine over 41,000 more. When I first encountered the CI 9s, the scale of this archive took my breath away. Each certificate is bursting with so much information, and so many stories that are still untold. The CI 9s are the most complete collection of Chinese head tax certificates in Canada.

CI 9 no. 15811 inaugurates an era of identification photography in Canada. From this point forward, the use of identification photographs for the purposes of tracking migration and immigration becomes the norm. Beginning with this document, Canada embarks on the first large-scale use of identification photographs. Between 1910 and 1953, tens of thousands of Chinese people residing in Canada would submit their photographs to be filed by the Chinese Immigration Branch. These records constitute the most comprehensive archive of early twentieth-century Chinese immigration in Canada.

Because CI 9s were systematically collected and filed by the state, they form an astonishingly comprehensive collection. With very few exceptions, Library and Archives Canada (LAC) holds every CI 9 issued from Vancouver and Victoria between 1910 and 1953. In 1910, efforts were made to tighten policies and practices governing Chinese migrants' entry into Canada due to an immigration fraud scandal that led to the *Report of Mr. Justice Murphy, Royal Commissioner Appointed to Investigate Alleged Chinese Frauds and Opium Smuggling on the Pacific Coast, 1910–11*. The intensification of the surveillance of Chinese migrants, including the use of identification photographs, coincides with the work of this commission. Despite the loss of certificates issued before 1910, after 1910 there is a continuous sequence of every single certificate issued spanning forty-three years. The certificates are individually numbered, have been filed by port of entry, and kept in pristine numerical and chronological order.

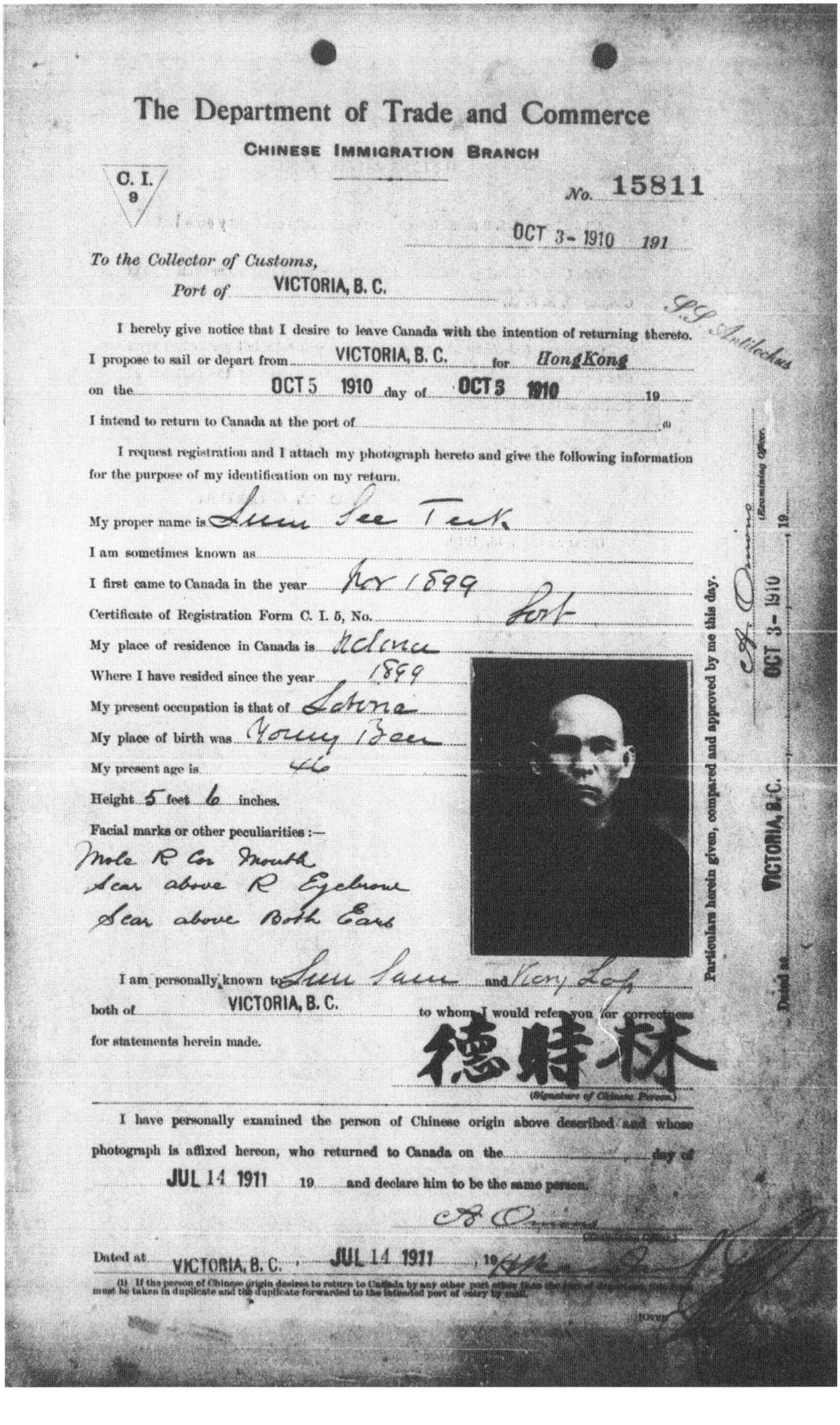

The Department of Trade and Commerce

CHINESE IMMIGRATION BRANCH

C. I. 9

No. 15811

OCT 3-1910 191

To the Collector of Customs,

Port of VICTORIA, B. C.

S.S. Antilochus

I hereby give notice that I desire to leave Canada with the intention of returning thereto.

I propose to sail or depart from VICTORIA, B. C. for HongKong

on the OCT 5 1910 day of OCT 3 1910 19

I intend to return to Canada at the port of (1)

I request registration and I attach my photograph hereto and give the following information for the purpose of my identification on my return.

My proper name is Lum See Teck

I am sometimes known as

I first came to Canada in the year Nov 1899

Certificate of Registration Form C. I. 5, No. Port

My place of residence in Canada is Nelson

Where I have resided since the year 1899

My present occupation is that of Laborer

My place of birth was Young Ben

My present age is 46

Height 5 feet 6 inches.

Facial marks or other peculiarities:—

Mole R Cor Mouth

Scar above R Eyebrow

Scar above Both Ears

I am personally known to Lum Sam and Yong Lop

both of VICTORIA, B. C. to whom I would refer you for correctness for statements herein made.

德時林

(Signature of Chinese Person.)

Particulars herein given, compared and approved by me this day.

Dated at VICTORIA, B. C. OCT 3-1910 19

A. Owens (Examining Officer.)

I have personally examined the person of Chinese origin above described and whose photograph is affixed hereon, who returned to Canada on the day of JUL 14 1911 19 and declare him to be the same person.

A. Owens

(Examining Officer.)

Dated at VICTORIA, B. C. JUL 14 1911 19

(1) If the person of Chinese origin desires to return to Canada by any other port other than the port of departure, this form must be taken in duplicate and the duplicate forwarded to the intended port of entry by mail.

Fig. I.2
CI 9 No. 15811,
Reel no. T-6038.

Beginning late in 1910, there is an identification photograph attached to every certificate. These photographs constitute an astounding visual archive. Images of Chinese people in Canada from this period are rare enough, but images of those not among the elite are even rarer. The CI 9s include photographs of people at the margins – farm hands, lumber camp workers, fisherman, vegetable peddlers, cannery workers, railway workers, and general labourers. What is more, because of the nature of these records, we know exactly who they are, or who they claimed to be. The people in these photographs are not anonymous. Far from it.

As with all identification photographs, the CI 9 photographs offer an indication of the identity of their subjects. However, as I will discuss in chapter 2, the name on the certificate can be more of a promise or a suggestion of the identity of its bearer than an absolute proof of identity. Any regime of identification risks misidentification. Such risks are magnified when the record necessarily involves some level of translation. The vast majority of Chinese migrants did not speak English. No agent assigned to the offices responsible for these records spoke Chinese. And then, of course, there was the practice of "paper sons," whereby Chinese-Canadians sold their immigration papers in order to allow other Chinese migrants to enter Canada using their names and identities. During the exclusion period (1923–47), this trade in paper identities offered the only route for Chinese migrants to enter Canada.

Until the repeal of the Chinese Immigration Act in 1947, and even for many years after the official end of this requirement, Chinese migrants who wished to temporarily leave Canada were required to "register out" with immigration authorities prior to departure. Under the auspices of the act, registers of all outward-bound Chinese migrants were kept at each port and every migrant was issued a "Certificate of Leave," later called an out-registration or CI 9 certificate. Such was the power of this demand that until 1953, six years *after* the repeal of the Chinese Immigration Act, many Chinese migrants continued to voluntarily register out before departing Canada. The name of the person travelling would be entered in an out-registration register located at the port of departure. At that point, they would also be issued a CI 9, valid for two years. Chinese migrants were additionally required to leave behind other identifying certificates (CI 5, 6, 28, 30, or 36 – see appendix A for the details of each type of certificate). Upon the migrant's return to Canada, the identifying certificates would be returned, and the CI 9 would be annotated with the date and port of re-entry. If the Chinese migrant did not return before the two-year time limit, the CI 9 would be marked as expired, and the other documents would be sent to Ottawa for cancellation. A migrant with an expired CI 9 lost their right of re-entry even if they had been born in Canada.

Before this book took shape, I had thought of the CI 9 as a kind of "proto-passport." Booklet-style passports were not used in Canada until 1921 (Wagner 2006, 163). It seemed to me that the CI 9s offered a unique view of a mobility infrastructure that was still in process. The state had not always needed to track the movements of its citizens. It did not always put so much faith in a positive correlation between a traveller's identity and the identity on their documents. The demand for documents betrays the anxieties of the state. Without uncertainty, there would be no demand. The passport is, in the first instance, a document of suspicion. Originally I argued that the CI 9s illustrate precisely the anticipation and formation of this suspicion.[1]

My thinking shifted when I came to terms with the fact that the people in these certificates were not citizens. Further, they had no reasonable hope of becoming citizens. From 1885 to 1923, the Chinese Immigration Act limited the entry of Chinese people into Canada through the levying of a series of "head taxes," which by 1903 cost $500 per person. Further, from 1923 to 1947, with very few exceptions for merchants, students, and diplomats, Chinese people were categorically barred from entering Canada. Families were separated. People were stranded. And throughout this time, Chinese people living in Canada were non-citizens.

To be Chinese in Canada prior to 1947 was to be denied the rights and privileges of citizenship. For one thing, there was no such thing as Canadian citizenship until 1947 when the Canadian Citizenship Act passed. Prior to its passage, those with the fullest access to citizenship were British subjects living in Canada. During the period of the Chinese Immigration Act (1885 to 1947), a period that encompasses both the levying of the head tax upon Chinese migrants until 1923 and the outright exclusion thereafter, Chinese migrants living in Canada could theoretically apply for naturalization and become British subjects, but very few were ever successful. As Julia Lum recognizes, "'citizenship,'" for Chinese Canadians before 1947, "is a term that has been used beyond its strict legal sense. Some historians, authors and community members refer to the exclusion period as a time when citizenship was denied to Chinese Canadians, even those born in Canada. The representations of Chinese bodies as foreign, alien bodies speak to their exclusion from participation in the body politic and an exclusion from images that constitute the official founding of the nation" (121).

1 Please see "Anticipating Citizenship" (Cho 2014, 158–80).

Most Chinese Canadians remained outsiders despite residing and working in Canada for decades. Catherine Clement outlines how, although the federal government was responsible for the Chinese Immigration Act, municipal and provincial governments across the country also implemented numerous anti-Chinese laws and policies:

> Other levels of government did their part to restrict and harass the Chinese community. They allowed or promoted segregation; forbid the Chinese access to public facilities, like swimming pools; prohibited entry into critical professions and public employment; denied Chinese born in Canada the right to vote; and enacted punitive business levies and by-laws to keep them out of commercial life. The racism carried over into the streets and into local business. It also found its way onto newspaper pages. Harassment; name calling; denial of service; derogatory editorials and cartoons; beatings; and damage to property was a common experience for early Chinese. (18)

Chinese people faced harassment and discrimination that affected every aspect of their daily lives. On a hot day, they could not use the local swimming pool to cool off. When they were able to start a business, in most provinces they were prevented from hiring white female staff members. When their children did well in school, they were not given access to professional opportunities. Their homes in Chinatown were constantly at risk of being razed due to complaints about sanitation and health standards. For Chinese migrants in Canada, non-citizenship encompassed a range of exclusions that had to be endured. Chinese people were both terribly present throughout the country, and utterly absented from the rights and privileges of citizenship.

As the cumbersome apparatus of head tax certificates reveal, the state bent over backwards to regulate and police the terms of non-citizenship. It was an unwieldy system that generated a bewildering amount of paperwork. There were dozens of different kinds of forms and certificates relating to the head tax alone (see appendix A). This paperwork had to be drafted, printed, completed, filed, cross-referenced, verified, and filed again. While the exclusion of Chinese migrants from Canadian life is clear cut, the mechanisms for enforcing this exclusion were anything but. There was confusion, anxiety, and a great deal of general incompetence in the way these exclusion laws were actually enforced. The excluded were themselves constantly changing and shifting. The non-citizen is not a static figure. They must be constantly regulated and monitored. They demand vigilance.

Mass Capture follows the story of this vigilance. This book tells the story of citizenship's entanglement with surveillance by studying one specific set of documents, the CI 9s. The non-citizen is generated again and again through state surveillance. The non-citizen persists through the documents that mark their exclusion. Every certificate filed, every form completed, constitutes another instance of their construction.

Non-citizenship is the verso of citizenship, and the existence of one depends on the other. Mass surveillance is also about the constant work of producing non-citizens. What is more, because citizenship emerges only in relation to non-citizenship, the latter functions as citizenship's perpetual other. Non-citizenship haunts citizenship.

Mass Capture is not a pre-history of mass surveillance. It does, however, investigate one specific instance of surveillance on a mass scale, leveraged against non-citizens in the name of perpetuating their alienation from the rights and privileges of citizenship. *Mass Capture* makes two arguments that are intimately connected. First, I argue that the head tax functions as a form of surveillance, and second, I argue that this surveillance is a process of mass capture by which non-citizens are made.

The CI 9s constitute an early and elaborate system of surveillance. These certificates reveal so much. But they are also telling in their function as negation. The people captured in these certificates are not immigrants. Their presence in Canada was handled by the Department of Trade and Commerce. They were not treated as settlers. Their presence was meant to be temporary. But they endured.

Photography and Vernaculars of Non-citizenship

CI 9 no. 15811 was issued on 3 October 1910. Before this date, before this exact certificate, there were no identification photographs of Chinese migrants on file. And then, suddenly, it starts. Like watching the hand of the clock tick past midnight, we can see the exact moment when this era of mass capture begins. Immediately before no. 15811, on CI 9 no. 15810, issued on 28 September 1910, for Louie You, sometimes known as Louie Peters, a merchant from Ottawa formally listed as a "commercial traveller," there is no photograph.

In the passage from CI 9 no. 15810 to 15811, we can see the beginning of a new era of identification practices. After CI 9 no. 15810, we enter an era of hyper-visibility for the non-citizen. Already singled out for discrimination and racist violence by the visuality of their difference, Chinese migrants would now enter the record caught in the persistent demand to show themselves, by producing photographs as proof of their identity.

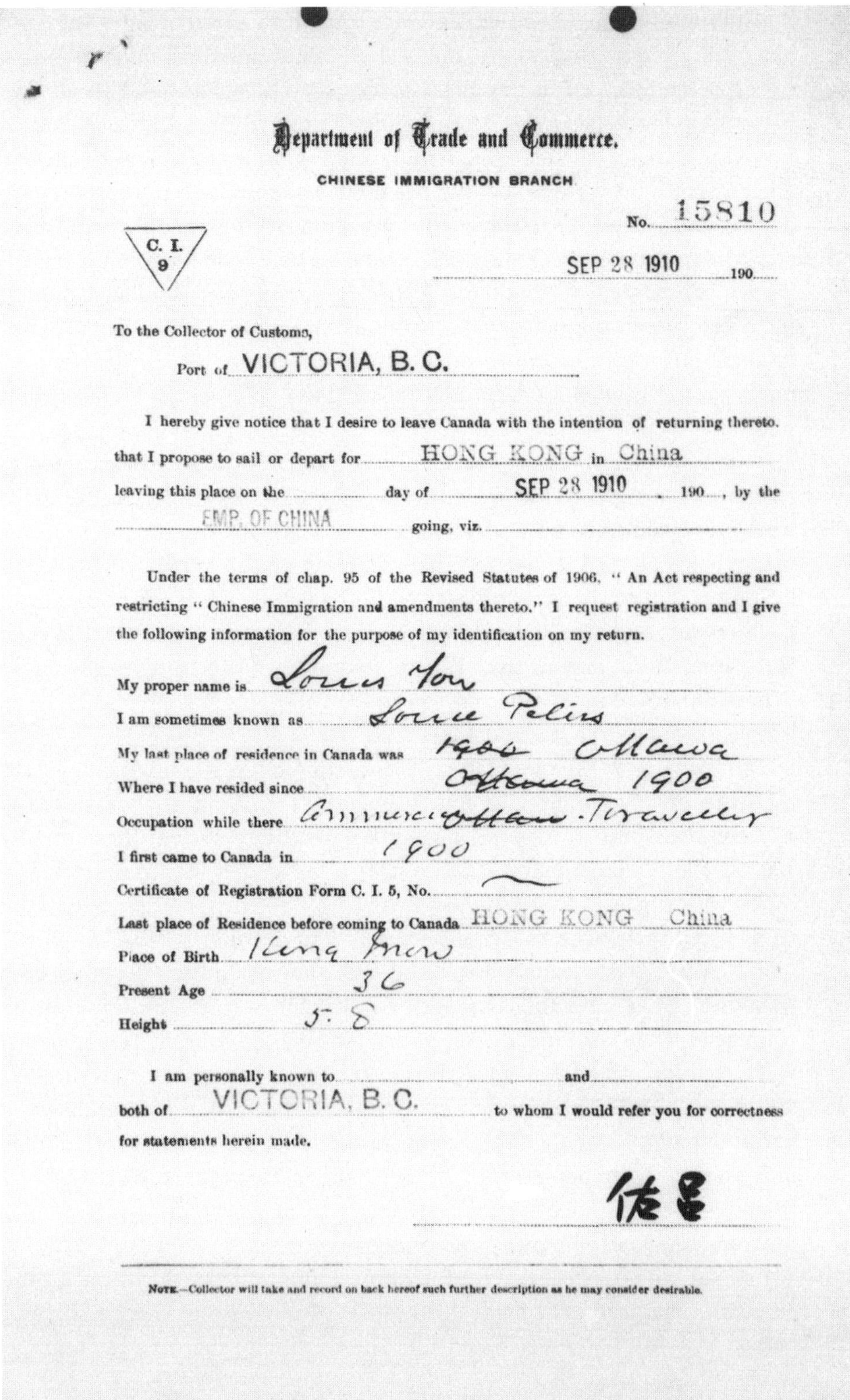
Department of Trade and Commerce.

CHINESE IMMIGRATION BRANCH

No. 15810

C. I. 9

SEP 28 1910 190

To the Collector of Customs,

Port of VICTORIA, B. C.

I hereby give notice that I desire to leave Canada with the intention of returning thereto. that I propose to sail or depart for HONG KONG in China leaving this place on the day of SEP 28 1910 190 , by the EMP. OF CHINA going, viz.

Under the terms of chap. 95 of the Revised Statutes of 1906. "An Act respecting and restricting "Chinese Immigration and amendments thereto." I request registration and I give the following information for the purpose of my identification on my return.

My proper name is Louis Yon

I am sometimes known as Louie Pelis

My last place of residence in Canada was ~~1900~~ Ottawa

Where I have resided since ~~Ottawa~~ 1900

Occupation while there Commercial ~~Ottawa~~ Traveller

I first came to Canada in 1900

Certificate of Registration Form C. I. 5, No. —

Last place of Residence before coming to Canada HONG KONG China

Place of Birth Keng Mow

Present Age 36

Height 5: 8

I am personally known to and

both of VICTORIA, B. C. to whom I would refer you for correctness for statements herein made.

佐昌

NOTE.—Collector will take and record on back hereof such further description as he may consider desirable.

Fig. I.3
CI 9 No. 15810,
Reel no. T-6038.

Although the men, women, and children on these certificates were not given the chance to speak for themselves in any way beyond responding to the demand to fill in the blank spaces on the certificates, this archive is not mute. What is more, the photographic turn that begins with CI 9 no. 15811 initiates an intensified volubility for non-citizens. Non-citizens are not silent. Even when they are not invited to speak, even when they are denied the rights of citizenship, the very forms of their capture produce a vernacular of presence. In the case of the CI 9s, the identification photographs constitute a distinct, and distinctly notable, vernacular. Although identification photographs are both "quiet and quotidian," as Tina Campt understands, they also transmit "suppressed forms of diasporic memory" (2017, 4, 6). Campt warns against conflating the quietness of identification photographs with silence because "quiet photography names a heuristic for attending to the lower range of intensities generated by images assumed to be mute" (6). Indeed, the identification photographs affixed to the CI 9s were presumed to be so mute, so silent, that the photographs were never meant to speak for themselves. Their function on this certificate of identification is that of silent corroboration to the textual demands of the form. Each response to the questions on the form (Who are you? What is your real name? What is your job? Where do you live? Who are your friends? Where did you come from and where are you going?) is an audible, and legible, response to a state demand.

The response to the question of "occupation" offers a small window into the social life of Chinese migrants throughout the duration of the head tax and exclusion period. Except for a handful of outliers such as the commercial traveller, Louie You, on CI 9 no. 15810 (fig. I.3), or the interpreter, Lee Mong Kow (fig. 4.5), that I discuss in chapter 4, the people captured on the CI 9s listed their occupation as "farmer," "laundryman" or just "laundry," "cook" or just "restaurant." Most frequently, they listed their occupation as "labourer." They gave their strength and resilience to the building of the country in whatever capacity was necessary, be it the construction of a railway or clearing land for agricultural use. These occupations are limited and also generic. There are only so many jobs that Chinese migrants were permitted to hold, and yet the lack of specificity of these occupational titles indicates the interchangeability of their labour. However, the existence of the accompanying identification photograph suggests the circulation of a different language of identity and presence.

I began with a photograph of a Chinese migrant that I cut out of the context of the head tax certificate because I wanted to see this person as a person (fig. I.1). I wanted to consider the possibility that this photograph might be a portrait, even though I first encountered it as an instance of what John Tagg (1988) and Allan Sekula (1986) identify as repressive photography. In the latter, the state uses photography instrumentally in order to identify and to enforce exclusion through photographic capture. It is, of course, crucial to read the photograph in the context of the certificate itself because the photograph alone cannot carry the burden of the work of identification. As Sekula understands, late nineteenth-century and early twentieth-century proponents of identification photography were some of the very first to recognize the limitations and unreliability of photography: "Contrary to the commonplace understanding of the 'mug shot' as the very exemplar of a powerful, artless, and wholly denotative visual empiricism, these early instrumental uses of photographic realism were systematized on the basis of an acute recognition of the inadequacies and limitations of ordinary visual empiricism" (1986, 18). In response to the recognition of these limitations, Sekula notes, there arose a "merger of optics and statistics" such as that of Alphonse Bertillon, inventor of "the first modern system of *criminal identification*" (ibid., emphasis original). Bertillon "combined photographic portraiture, anthropometric description, and highly standardized and abbreviated written notes on a single *fiche*, or card. Second, he organized these cards within a comprehensive, statistically based filing system" (ibid.). In chapter 1, I argue that this combination of the statistical and the photographic functions as a form of documentary mass capture. In chapter 2, I examine the particularity of filing, and systems of filing, as central to the ways in which mass capture fails. For now, let me return to where I began: the identification photograph taken out of its context, or the identification photograph as a potential portrait.

I will be the first to admit that it is not much of a portrait. According to the aesthetics and conventions of good portraiture, this photograph fails. The image quality is very poor. You can barely make out the subject's features. The lighting is so deficient that we cannot even see his eyes – they are dark hollows. Indeed, the contrast is so high and the lighting so bad that the man in the image is almost skeletal. There is a line across the photograph where the whole document, photograph included, had been folded. The photographic image has been bifurcated by this trace of bureaucratic indifference in the name of space-saving efficiency.

Filed, allowed to fade, and literally folded into the settler-colonial archive, this photograph might not be much of a portrait in any conventional sense. Yet, here is a man who was denied so much, who has, according to this form, spent at least eleven years in a country that did not permit him the right to be at home in it, whose very presence is questioned by the existence of this form itself, and who nonetheless makes a quiet demand to be seen, to be remembered, to be heard. We may not be able to look him in the eye, but he looks out at those who behold him. We may not be able to hear the story of his life, but, as I will argue in detail in chapter 4, there is in this image a refusal of silence.

Identification photographs are "conduits of an unlikely interplay between the vernacular and the state" (Campt 2017, 5). That is, they function as images of an ordinary life at the same time that they circulate as evidence produced for the state. Certainly, in the context of the CI 9 certificate, the identification photographs did serve the state. They are unquestionably repressive in precisely the terms that Tagg articulates in *The Burden of Representation*: "It is a portrait of the product of the disciplinary method: the body made object; divided and studied; enclosed in a cellular structure of space whose architecture is the file-index; made docile and forced to yield up its truth; separated and individuated; subjected and made subject" (1988, 76). The identification photographs at the heart of *Mass Capture* are undeniably the product of this system of representation. However, as I will show in the later chapters of this book, they also exceed and escape the repressive instrumentality to which they had been relegated. I track this excess, and this escape, by following Campt's injunction to listen to these images, and to hear in them the possibilities of a vernacular.

The CI 9 identification photographs are vernacular in form and, at the same time, they put into place a vernacular. It is a vernacular of refusal. As Campt observes with regard to passport photographs of Black British men claiming citizenship in the wake of the 1948 British Nationality Act, even though these photographs are "documents of permission, surveillance, and accountability, the fugitivity of these images exceeds this regulatory function" (2017, 32). We must, as Campt insists, move beyond merely looking at images: "To look at these images is to see genre and form" (45). Looking at the CI 9 photographs renders visible the scale of state repression and suspicion levelled at the non-citizen. But to learn to listen to them "is to be attuned to their unsayable truths, to perceive their quiet frequencies of possibility" (ibid.). These possibilities reside in the many ways through which these non-citizens refused the terms of their exclusion. They did so, as chapter 2 shows, by subverting the CI 9 system so profoundly that it would fail in its most basic objective of identification. Further, as chapter 3 uncovers, looking at representations of family in the CI 9 photographs reveals ways of making and remaking ideas of kinship. At the same time, the extremely rare photographs of women and children that can be found in the CI 9 archive vividly illustrate how the law separated families.

The non-citizens captured in these certificates demand forms of legibility, and audibility, that far exceed the limits of the certificates themselves. In this demand, and in the persistence of their refusal to be silent, these non-citizens practise a mode of agency anchored in anticipation, as I outline in chapter 5. In so doing, they shift the temporality of their presence away from histories of exclusion and towards the expectation of futures of "diasporic dwelling," or, "the right to come and go, to stay, as well as to arrive and return over and over again" (Campt 2017, 31). In short, the right to citizenship. As I will show in the final chapter, although they would not be granted citizenship, these non-citizens establish anticipation as a mode of agency where the line between citizen and non-citizen is not one of division, but of relation.

The CI 9 archive reveals the way in which citizenship and non-citizenship pivot on the photographic turn. There is a profound relationship between citizenship (and thus non-citizenship) and photography. For Ariella Azoulay, "Photography has directly interpellated the citizen – he or she can become the bearer of history, both as photographer and as photographed" (2008, 114). Azoulay's concept of "the civil contract of photography" outlines the complex array of relationships that come into play in the construction of citizens and non-citizens. In the civil space of photography, she asserts, the operator of the camera is not the only agent. We must contend also with the subject, the spectators, and presumably also darkroom technicians, photographic distributors, and all of the other people who affect, and are affected by, the photographic situation. The civil contract of photography "binds all individuals who take part in photography … The modern citizen has thus renounced the exclusive right to his or her image in favor of an economy of images that, in principle, includes the individual and all others" (116). In the case of the CI 9s, the civil contract of photography helps to illuminate the peculiar ways in which the migrant is bound to the customs agent, who is also bound to the photographer, who is also bound to the second customs agent co-signing the certificate upon the migrant's return, who is also bound to the persons identified on the certificate as those to whom the migrant is "personally known" (fig. I.2). Azoulay's concept goes a long way towards expanding the idea of the social relations mediated by photography in the service of the construction of contemporary citizenship. Still, despite the enormous productivity this concept, I share Thy Phu's departure from Azoulay with regard to the rehabilitation of citizenship encoded in the civil contract of photography. As Phu notes, the work of "suturing the seemingly irrevocable split between man and citizen" enshrined in the 1789 *Declaration of the Rights of Man and Citizen* is work that is still, in many ways, before us (2011, 19). Instead, as Phu suggests, "Before citizenship can be rehabilitated, its significance must be reconsidered" (19). For *Mass Capture*, the work of reconsidering the significance of citizenship lies in a rigorous examination of the practices and materiality of the construction of non-citizenship.

Non-citizenship and Its Others

Who or what is the non-citizen? The answer is at once obvious and strangely murky. A non-citizen is not a citizen. This statement verges on the tautological. Well, of course. However, it is the very circularity, the way in which this definition turns in on itself and falls apart upon that turning, where things get interesting. Can a non-citizen only be defined in terms of its opposite? Does that mean that non-citizens exist only in relation to citizens? Is it possible, then, to have citizenship without non-citizenship? Is the non-citizen human?

On this last point, the Office of the United Nations High Commissioner for Human Rights (UNHCHR), in the opening paragraph of *The Rights of Non-citizens*, attempts to obviate any ambiguity: "All persons should by virtue of their essential humanity, enjoy all human rights. Exceptional distinctions, for example between citizens and non-citizens, can be made only if they serve a legitimate State objective and are proportional to the achievement of that objective" (UNHCHR 2006, 5). The UNHCHR proceeds in the next paragraph to offer a definition of citizenship as that which can be acquired through *jus soli* (law of place), or *jus sanguinis* (birth to a parent who is a citizen of a country), or naturalization. Finally, in the third paragraph, there is a definition of the non-citizen: "A non-citizen is a person who has not been recognized as having these effective links to the country where he or she is located. There are different groups of non-citizens, including permanent residents, migrants, refugees, asylum-seekers, victims of trafficking, foreign students, temporary visitors, other kinds of non-immigrants and stateless people" (ibid.). The non-citizen is thus many things, but, first and foremost, they are indeed human and definitely not a citizen. Both these limits – the humanity of the non-citizen and their exclusion from citizenship – signal a seemingly limitless aporia at the heart of non-citizenship. The multiple ways of being, or becoming, a non-citizen contrast sharply with the clarity of citizenship acquisition. Non-citizenship remains curiously under-theorized.

Even more than the citizen, the non-citizen is a densely complex figure occupying a dynamic and problematically transient state of being. Non-citizens are not meant to remain non-citizens. Their status is defined by impermanence. Permanent residents are only permanent insofar as they are on their way to becoming citizens. Migrants are not meant to be perpetually migrant. Refugees, asylum-seekers, and victims of trafficking are looking for safe haven. Foreign students are expected to graduate, and temporary visitors are meant to return home. Theorizing non-citizenship demands an engagement with a figure that is, by definition, in flux and on the move. In addition, it calls for an approach to non-citizenship that understands how it is routed through citizenship and the subject of human rights.

No small task.

There is still more. While there is universal agreement on the process by which one becomes a citizen (it bears repeating not least because of its simplicity: *jus soli, jus sanguinis*, or naturalization), there is a striking lack of clarity about the process, or processes, by which one becomes a non-citizen. And even though it may not be a desirable state, it is certainly not one arrived at by accident.

As the case of the thousands of Chinese people tracked by the CI 9 system reveals, the construction of non-citizens is a deliberate process of exclusion and discrimination exercised by the state in the name of safeguarding citizenship. In order to define who or what a citizen is or ought to be, the state must also identify its other, the non-citizen.

Scholarship on citizenship recognizes that citizenship is defined through the identification of non-citizens. For example, as Engin Isin recognizes in his study of the genealogies of citizenship, "citizenship and its alterity always emerged simultaneously in a dialogical manner and constituted each other. Women were not simply excluded from ancient Greek citizenship, but were constituted as its other as an immanent group by citizens. Similarly, slaves were not simply excluded from citizenship, but made citizenship possible by their very formation" (2002, 2). Isin identifies categories of people (women, slaves) whose status as non-citizens at different points in history and geography secures the existence of citizens. Similarly, Leti Volpp's (2007, 2014, 2015) work in legal scholarship examines the ways in which citizenship is imbricated with dominant culture as it is defined through and against minority cultures. In terms of Canadian citizenship specifically, Ayelet Shachar's (2009) research on citizenship focuses on the way in which the acquisition of citizenship in Canada is bound by policies that privilege birthright (being born on Canadian soil, or to Canadian parents, or naturalized – etymologically derived from Latin to connote being born again), instead of connection to a particular country of residence.

That is, Canadian citizens emerge out of a process of differentiation that depends not only on identifying who and what a citizen is, but also who and what they are not.

Throughout this book, I refer to Chinese migrants captured in the CI 9s as non-citizens because, quite simply, they were not citizens. Nor did they have any hope of becoming citizens. Prior to 1947, Chinese migrants could petition to become naturalized as British subjects residing in Canada, and a handful of people did make successful petitions. However, overwhelmingly, Chinese migrants were not meant to access the rights and privileges of citizenship in a settler-colonial state "that relies on the settlement of select individuals for the express purpose of securing control over people and territory" (Madokoro 2016, 12). As the 1902 *Report of the Royal Commission on Chinese and Japanese Immigration* declared, "there was entire unanimity" on the idea that Chinese migrants in Canada are "unfit for full citizenship" and that the Chinese migrants "are so nearly allied to a servile class that they are obnoxious to a free community and dangerous to the state" (278). A few lines down, the commissioners lay the groundwork for what would become the outright exclusion of Chinese immigrants: "This class of immigration falls short of the standard so essential to the well-being of the country. From a Canadian standpoint it is injurious, and in the interest of the nation any further immigration ought to be prohibited" (278). In the first half of the twentieth century, emigrants were wanted, immigrants were not desirable, and Chinese immigrants were the least desirable of all.

The language of emigration marked those who were desired for Canadian settlement. Under the auspices of the Department of Agriculture, beginning in 1869, "Emigration Agents" were stationed "in various ports and central towns in Great Britain (with a few strategic European locations) to inspect immigrants embarking for Canada and to publicize Canada as a place of settlement" (LAC 2020). In contrast, according to the minister of the interior at that time, Frank Oliver, the 1906 Immigration Act had only one purpose: "to enable the Department of Immigration to deal with undesirable immigrants" (Kelley and Trebilcock 2010, 138). In short, in Canada prior to 1947, emigrants were desirable and immigrants were not. The Chinese Immigration Act (1885) precedes the Immigration Act (1906), and both pieces of legislation were geared towards regulating and limiting the entry and settlement of those who were deemed undesirable. Chinese migrants were not intended to be settlers. They were not considered to be emigrants. They were certainly not meant to be immigrants in the contemporary sense: "Neither the Chinese migrants recruited through the indentured labour schemes in the mid-1800s nor the later generations who moved to *gam saan* were desired as citizens by governing officials. Their labour was valued but their permanent membership in white settler societies was not" (Madokoro 2016, 11). For this reason, this book understands the people governed by the Chinese Immigration Act as Chinese migrants who were never intended to be given the rights and privileges of citizens and who were meant to live as perpetual non-citizens throughout their time in Canada.

Mass Capture as a Technology of Non-citizenship

Just as citizens emerge out of a series of social, cultural, and political movements, non-citizens also emerge out of a complex process. It is not the case that non-citizens just happen to be there as women, slaves, refugees, immigrants, and Indigenous peoples. In this book I argue that non-citizens are made. Further, they are not simply made; they are captured.

Specifically, non-citizens are constructed out of a specific process that I call mass capture. Legal writing on the large-scale collection of personal data conducted by private corporations and the state uses "mass capture" to refer to this practice (Lynch 2012a; 2012b). In chapter 1, I extend this usage and theorize mass capture as a technology for the production of non-citizenship. Mass capture is a practice that is both corporeal and documentary. That is, it depends upon the capture of bodies and information about those bodies. Mass capture is not solely about data collection. And it is not only about the bodies of migrants amassed in the hold of a ship or the barracks of an immigration detention centre. It is about how these two processes work together to produce the non-citizen.

Mass capture occurs through the process of data collection related to the members of a large group. The record for each member of the group will include such information as identification photographs and the assemblage of personal data, such as name, place of residence, occupation, migration history, and biometric data such as the recording of facial scars and fingerprints. Throughout the years of the Chinese Immigration Act (1885–1947), and for many years after, Chinese people entering and exiting Canada were systematically tracked in ways that were entirely novel. The head tax certificate that has received the most public and academic attention is the certificate formally titled Chinese Immigration 5 (CI 5). As the language of the CI 5 suggests, these certificates were essentially receipts, or proof of payment, showing that the bearers had paid the initial tax permitting their entry into Canada.

The CI 5s were kept by individual migrants. Because the state did not keep them, relatively few survive. Still, they have been particularly important

Fig. I.4
CI 5 No. 87231, MG55/30-N0116, R12115-0-5-E.

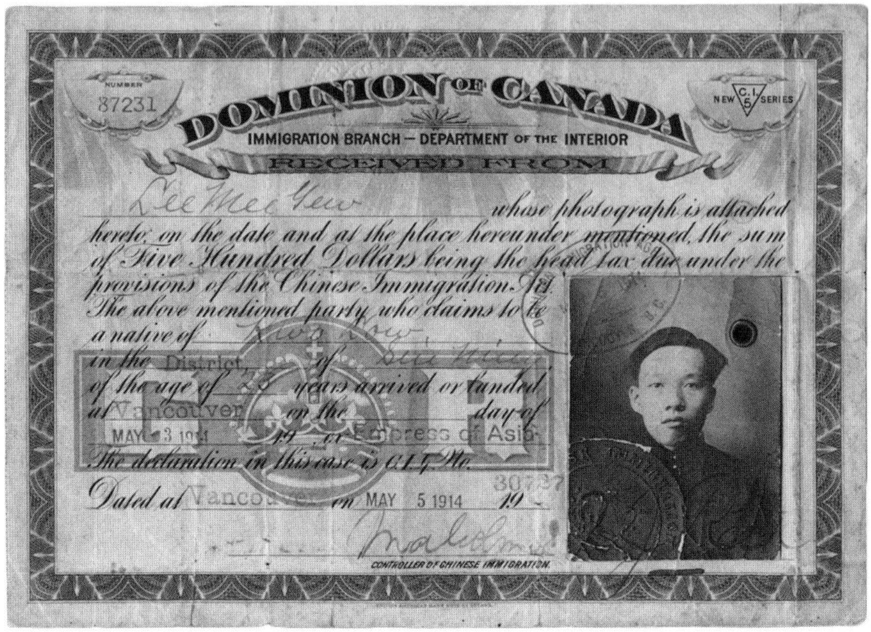
NUMBER 87231

DOMINION OF CANADA

NEW C.I. 5 SERIES

IMMIGRATION BRANCH – DEPARTMENT OF THE INTERIOR

RECEIVED FROM

Lee Mee Yew whose photograph is attached hereto, on the date and at the place hereunder mentioned, the sum of Five Hundred Dollars being the head tax due under the provisions of the Chinese Immigration Act. The above mentioned party who claims to be a native of in the District of of the age of years arrived or landed at Vancouver on the day of 19 Empress of Asia. The declaration in this case is C.I. 4 No.

Dated at Vancouver on MAY 5 1914 19

CONTROLLER OF CHINESE IMMIGRATION.

for activism and scholarship on Chinese head tax redress (Mawani 2010; 2011; 2014; Moran and Dyzenhaus 2005). These certificates also become part of the way in which Chinese families document their lives in Canada: "For many families whose roots in Canada go back to the days of the head tax and the exclusion period, the discriminatory identification documents also become a part of family lore, as a point of contrast to measure family progress and the decline of racism. It is also a strange outcome that many of these documents have earned prominent places in the family album as both evidence of state-sponsored discrimination *and* a family's Canadian origin story" (Lum 2017, 121).

Even though many documents were kept by Chinese families and passed down as part of a family history, the vast majority of the documents pertaining to the head tax, including photographs of individual migrants and the accompanying identification documents, were kept by the government. The tracking of these immigrants under the terms of the Chinese Immigration Act generated substantial documentation and a significant archive of materials. This legislation "created Canada's first policy to closely screen individual immigrants, and it set precedents that would have a lasting impact on national policy" (Mar 2010, 16). Much of the documentation generated by this legislation is now known collectively as "head tax certificates."

However, there were actually a number of different types of documents grouped under that name. In fact, as appendix A shows, there were fifty different types of head tax certificates. Although the purpose of many of these certificates is no longer known, each certificate was distinct and played a part in the immense bureaucracy that emerged out of the implementation and enforcement of the Chinese Immigration Act. In addition to all of these different types of head tax certificates, there was also the General Register of Chinese Immigration, which the University of British Columbia digitized in 2011. This register recorded detailed information in a series of columns (fig. I.5). Taken together, the vast array of certificates, combined with the information collated in the General Register, reveals a complex system put into the ostensible service of limiting and regulating the movements of Chinese people in Canada.

The CI 9s stand out not only because of their sheer numbers (in contrast, there are only a few dozen CI 5s held at various archives and in private collections), but also because of the depth of information on each certificate. Each one is the story of a life. It may not, as my discussion in chapter 2 will show, be the life of the person named and pictured on that document,

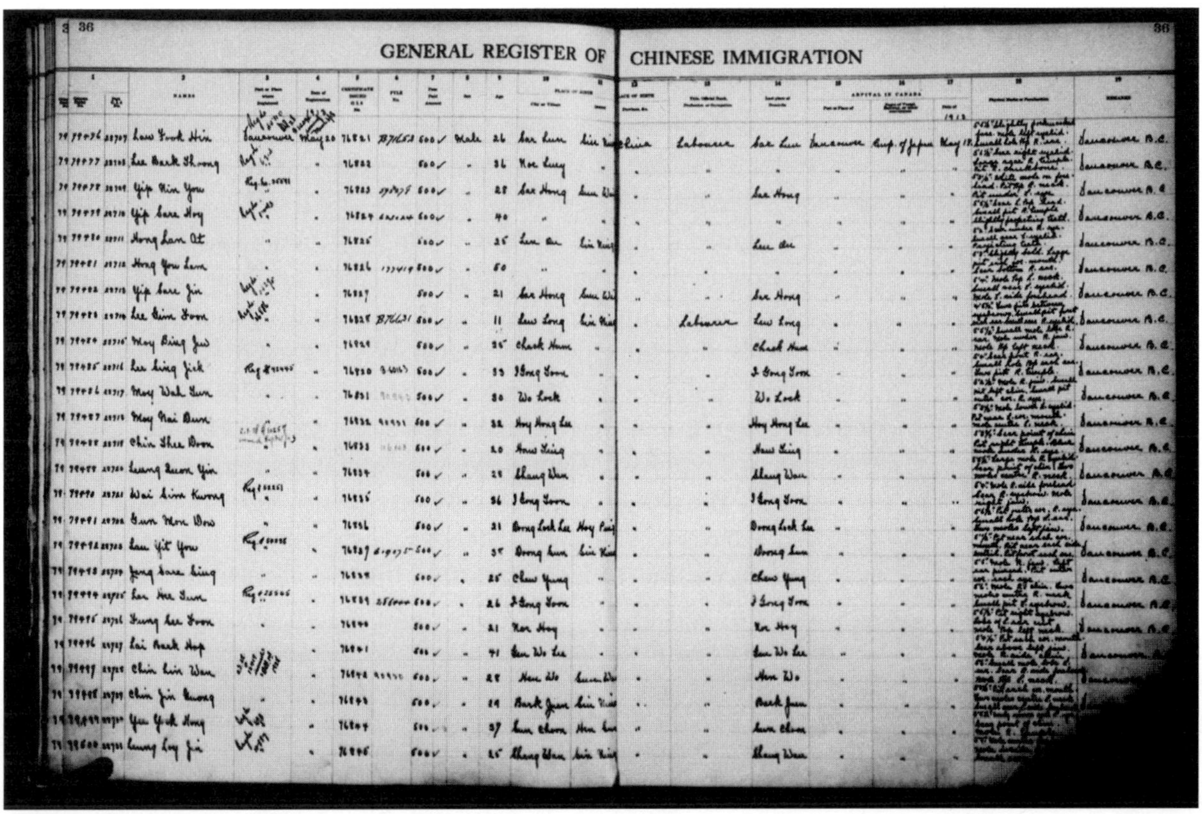

Fig. I.5
General Register of the Chinese Immigration, T-3484.

but it is nonetheless a detailed glimpse into the life of a migrant. Although the number of CI 9s that we have today vastly outnumber the surviving CI 5s, very few scholars have seen or worked with CI 9s. While the CI 5s proved that the bearer had paid the head tax, the CI 9s were essential for surveilling the mobility of Chinese migrants and were explicitly instated as an exit-entry system for this particular group of non-citizens. In order to do so, the CI 9s, unlike the CI 5s, collected a range of biographical and biometric data in addition to identification photographs.

CI 9s were also used to in attempts to thwart immigration fraud (Mar 2010, 27). These certificates contain a substantial amount of information about the immigrant, including their name and age; their year of arrival in Canada; the name of the arrival vessel; their profession in Canada; any identifying marks; their signature in Chinese, English, or, in some cases, a thumbprint; and their place of residence. These immigrants were not considered citizens, but they were given the right to return to Canada. Typically, the right to return to a "home" country, not that of entering a "host" one, is the defining function of a passport (Cho 2014a; Robertson 2010; Salter 2007). The CI 9s thus occupy a curious and richly ambiguous place: travel documents that offer non-citizens one of the rights of citizenship.

Notably, Chinese immigrants were not the only group whose mobility was placed under surveillance during this period. From 1885 until 1941, Indigenous people in Canada were subject to a pass system that attempted to track and restrict their movements (Barron 1988; Bennett 1974). As Danielle Taschereau Mamers argues in *Settler Colonial Ways of Seeing*, the pass system was one of the "seemingly more benign forms of disciplinary and biopolitical governance" (2017, 75) that replaced the militarized violence against Indigenous peoples with bureaucratic processes that were no less violent. This system caused enormous suffering within Indigenous communities. Initially implemented as a security measure to "prevent further resistance after the 1885 North West Rebellions, the pass system required that all reserve residents register and receive approval for any travel through Indian Agents" (Mamers 2017, 75), and was supposed to be enforced by the NWMP (North West Mounted Police, the predecessor of the RCMP). The pass system was never made into legislation and was thus enforced arbitrarily and inconsistently, leaving Indigenous peoples at the mercy of the whims of local agents and police entities and exacerbating the pain wrought by the system. As Keith Smith observes in *Liberalism, Surveillance, and Resistance*, "the pass system was part of a coercive and flexible matrix meant to restrict Indigenous movement in the interests of White settlers and it must be seen in that light … Even though Canada never had the capacity to forcibly restrict all off-reserve movement, the will of both the police and the DIA [Department of Indian Affairs] to do what they could in this regard is evident, even if some in the upper echelons of the former were sometimes uncomfortable" (2009, 67).

The pass system could only be enforced through intimidation: "Indian Affairs simply assumed an air of authority" through means such as the illegal arrest of First Nations individuals who were found off the reserve without passes. "The whole system … rested on very shaky grounds" and was undermined both by the refusal of First Nations communities to recognize the system, and by the reluctance of the NWMP to enforce a system that was not based in legislation (Barron 1988, 35–6). Indeed, the DIA and the NWMP were at odds. DIA agents sought the enforcement of the system, but could only do so at the behest of the NWMP, which was often not eager to enforce a policy that even Prime Minister John A. Macdonald, himself a keen supporter of the pass system, knew "could not be legally enforced" (Smith 2009, 64). As Macdonald's own handwritten notes in the margins of a memo admit: "The system should be introduced in the Loyal Bands as well & the advantage of the change pressed upon them. But *no punishment for breaking bonds could be inflicted & in case of resistance on the grounds of Treaty rights should not be insisted on*" (quoted in Smith 2009, 64, emphasis mine). Indeed, bureaucrats such as Hayter Reed, the assistant to the Indian commissioner in 1885, complained in his own memos that "unless one is at their heels Police duties here are done in a half hearted manner" (ibid.). Despite this lacklustre approach to enforcement, the devastation of the pass system was real and painful.

The pass system was used by local officials to intimidate and restrict the movements of Indigenous peoples, preventing them from accessing opportunities for commerce and family reunion. Perhaps most devastatingly, as Alex Williams illustrates in his meticulously researched 2015 documentary *The Pass System*, passes were used to prevent parents from visiting children who had been sent to residential schools. The pass system allowed the Canadian government to transform reserves into what James Daschuk calls "centres of incarceration" (2013, xxii). Until 1895, when changes to Section 14 of the Indian Act explicitly prohibited most Indigenous religious ceremonies, the pass system already "served to curtail broad participation" (171) in such ceremonies. These prohibitions on movement thus affected multiple aspects of social, spiritual, and economic life for Indigenous peoples.

The system ended in 1941 upon the circulation of a letter to all western reserves that "requested the return of all remaining books of pass documents to be returned to DIA headquarters for destruction" (Mamers 2017, 75). A handful of pass documents remained with individual people, but the attempt to systematically destroy the documents – though not the considerable trove official memoranda containing evidence of the system – results in the loss of what would have been a significant visual archive of identification photographs of Indigenous peoples. As with the CI 9s, this archive would have been problematic in that it emerges from a system of policing movement that contributed to the devastation resulting from the Indian Act. Still, given the paucity of images of Indigenous peoples from this era, the possibility for using these documents in ways that counter their original intent is now lost.

The pass system was different from the CI 9s in many ways. It was not passed into legislation, and its goals were to control movement in the name of preventing rebellion, to restrict participation in Indigenous religious ceremonies such as the Ghost Dance, and to severely limit the possibilities for trade for Indigenous communities. However, it still offers an important corollary. Unlike the pass books, CI 9s were filed and stored by the state. Even when the originals were destroyed, copies were kept in a virtually indestructible format: microfilm.

Another major difference lies in the enforceability of the CI 9 system. The Chinese head tax certificate system as a whole was definitively part of Canadian legislation under the auspices of the Chinese Immigration Act. During the periods of the head tax (1885–1923) and the ban on Chinese immigrants to Canada (1923–47), Chinese migrants were explicitly overseen by the Department of Trade and Commerce, and not by the Departments of Agriculture, Immigration, Citizenship and Immigration, and External Affairs. That is, prior to the repeal of the Chinese Immigration Act in 1947, the entry of Chinese migrants to Canada was the purview of a federal department that had no responsibility for settling people in an ostensibly under-populated nation. Governed by what historian Robert Bothwell identifies as "a marginal ministry," Chinese labour was central to national industries such the building of the Canadian Pacific Railway, but Chinese migrants were explicitly non-citizens (1994, 60). Securing the status of non-citizens demanded a painstaking and elaborate process of data collection and corporeal capture.

Biometrics, Social Networks, and Anticipation as a Mode of Agency

The process of capture turns on photographic technology and its imbrication with biometric and biographical information. Photographic identification was not the only means by which the state captured these non-citizens. Indeed, the process of mass capture depends upon an intricate interplay between text and image. A cursory glance at any CI 9 issued after 28 September 1910 reveals the lockstep nature of the relationship between the words on the page and the identification photograph itself. In this instrumentalization of photography, the image and text are supposed to offer a perfect correspondence. The photograph is useless as a mechanism of identification, without, at minimum, the name of the photographic subject. The introduction of a demand for identification photographs in 1910 ushers in an era of identification technology whereby textual and visual markers, together, would be used to track the mobility of persons. In addition to an identification photograph, these certificates contain a substantial amount of information about the immigrant, including:

- Port of departure
- Intended destination
- Ship upon which they travelled
- Name
- Years and place of residence in Canada
- Occupation
- Place of birth
- Age of the migrant
- Facial marks or peculiarities
- Other people who personally know the bearer
- Signature of the migrant
- Signature of the immigration agent
- Date of and port of re-entry

Each field of information on the CI 9 works to build on the other. The point of departure is tied to port of re-entry. The name is connected to the signature. Occupation is bound to the years and place of residence. All of this information works to construct a detailed and complex dossier of information that is itself entwined with the photographic portrait. This information was assembled and put into place in order to entrench a system of identification and verification. In this sense, the CI 9 is very much a biometric system as defined by Joseph Pugliese, in that "biometrics does not only refer to contemporary, computer-automated technologies that authenticate or identify enrolled subjects. Rather, taking the term in its most literal sense, it refers to a cluster of technologies that have all been preoccupied with the measurement of the body in order to identify, classify, evaluate and regulate target subjects" (2010, 10). Of course, in the case of the CI 9s, the forms of measurement extend beyond the body and into the social life of the "target subjects" – where they live, what they do, where they have been, where they intend to go.

What is more, this form of biometric capture extended into a process of what we now know as social network analysis. Nearly a century before the rise of social media and its eventual use as a tool of state and corporate surveillance, the CI 9 system sought to identify migrants not only through documenting facts about them, but also who they knew. The part of the certificate where each migrant is asked to identify those to whom they are known foreshadows our present moment. We are now made known not only by documents that identify us as individuals (e.g., passports and driver's licences), but also across a wide range of platforms where our identities are tied to our social networks.

As a systemic approach to identifying individuals through a combination of identification methods, the CI 9s presage the recent rise of the "smart" border, the intensifying securitization of national borders, and the increasing use of biometrics for the purpose of differentiating the non-citizen from the citizen (Bhandar 2004; Browne 2005; Btihaj 2012; Merolli 2016; Pugliese 2007 and 2010; Salter 2007). As Ajana Btihaj observes, "biometrics is not without a history" (2012, 864). This history is deeply racialized. Building on the work of Pugliese on biometrics, Btihaj suggests, "It is as though these non-white subjects are ghosts in the biometric machine whose presence is an absent presence and whose appearance is a non-appearing appearance" (865). For Btihaj and Pugliese, biometrics depends upon an occlusion of race whereby the white body functions as a norm, thus resulting in failures to "see" racialized bodies even though these very bodies suffer the consequences of misrecognition. As Simone Browne excavates in *Dark Matters*, surveillance practices have always been deeply racialized. *Mass Capture* builds on these discussions by examining how the CI 9s illuminate the intersection of biometrics and race depends upon the hyper-visibility of the racialized body.

In the case of the Chinese migrants tracked by the CI 9 system, it was not that there was a system premised on the normative white body which thereby jeopardized the identification of the racialized other, but rather that the racialized body *anticipates* the ways in which non-citizens, and then also citizens, would be identified and tracked. As I will show in chapter 5, this anticipation is itself a mode of agency. I am not attaching potentially anachronistic terms such as biometrics and social network analysis to a body of historical documents only for the sake of pointing to the compelling ways in which they connect the past and present. Certainly, that is part of the work of this book: to borrow Pugliese's term, there is a sense in which the CI 9s function as a "proto-biometric system" (2010, 2). However, more than this, the CI 9s document the workings of anticipation on the part of its subjects. The people in these certificates were constantly reading the world around them, translating it, and trying to position themselves in advance of the demands that would be made of them. As anyone who has ever lived in precarity will know, anticipation is a key mode of survival and resistance. Those who occupy positions of uncertainty and powerlessness must be keenly attuned to the currents of repression and exclusion. They must try to see ahead. They cannot afford to be caught off-guard. All of this vigilance constellates into anticipation as a mode of agency.

For the mass captured of the CI 9 system, it was imperative to understand in advance that they would bear the burden of looking and acting like a citizen long before they would be granted the rights and privileges of citizenship. In chapter 5, I will take up the ways in which Chinese migrants modelled citizenship even though they were not themselves citizens. Giorgio Agamben notes of what he calls "biopolitical tattooing": "History teaches us how many such practices, initially reserved for foreigners, are soon applied to every citizen alike" (2008, 202). It is not just that biometric systems of mobility control like the CI 9 predate the current use of technologies such as iris scans, gait analysis, facial recognition, and so on, but that they are also omens of the mutability of the differentiation of the citizen from the non-citizen.

Although current discussions of the use of biometrics in relation to citizenship focus overwhelmingly on biometrics as a way to distinguish the citizen from the non-citizen (Bhandar 2004; Merolli 2016; Müller 2004; Salter 2007), the CI 9s show the necessity of understanding these categories as constitutive rather than oppositional. For example, both Davina Bhandar and Benjamin Müller identify 11 September 2001 as a key moment that marks this increasing securitization of citizenship and what Müller calls the turn from citizenship to identity management, or the shift from identification to authorization, where the primary question is no longer whether you are who you claim to be, but rather whether you are authorized to be where you are (Müller 2004, 287). However, such a process of distinction risks obscuring the constitutive role of the non-citizen in the construction of citizenship. The emphasis on distinction suggests an either/or, and yet, as Merolli's (2016) discussion of naturalization reveals, the non-citizen remains integral to the citizen. In Merolli's case, it is about the failure of naturalization processes to rid the newly re-born citizen of her residual non-citizenship identities and practices; but this failure can also be read as a trenchant reminder that the non-citizen is part of the citizen, and that one constitutes the other. Identifying the citizen is not so much about a binarizing process of distinction (Are you, or are you not?), but rather about stifling and managing the non-citizen whose very existence makes citizenship possible.

Practising Refusal

The legislation and regulation of Chinese migrants through processes of mass capture instigates a series of unintended effects. In the annals of colonial governance, there is a long history of this double movement of regulatory intention complicated by unintended consequences generated by recalcitrant subjects. This book follows the story of one instance of the gap between intention and consequence. Although the purpose of the CI 9 system was that of identifying Chinese migrants for the purposes of preventing immigration fraud, it is not at all clear that the system actually did so.

The first chapter of this book theorizes and outlines mass capture as a technology of exclusion. In attempting to follow Ann Laura Stoler's injunction to read "along the grain" of the archive, to pay attention to the "archive's granular rather than seamless texture" (2008, 43), this book begins with a careful look at how this system worked, and what about it actually did work. But the real story of mass capture does not end with the production of thousands of non-citizens through the CI 9 system. That is just a beginning. There is another much more interesting story of mass capture that lies in the refusals and resistances enacted by the mass captured. All the remaining chapters of this book are dedicated to unfolding this other story.

The system for tracking the comings and goings of Chinese migrants was both elaborate and curiously useless. As this book shows, CI 9s illuminate a larger history of the failure of the state to capture, contain, and limit Chinese migrants in Canada. Each certificate contains the potential of its own form of unknowing, and most of this book is devoted to the ways in which the CI 9s are evidence both of the un-making of knowledge, and of the leveraging of unspoken or quiet knowledge as forms of resistance and agency.

In the CI 9s, there are what Campt identifies as "*practices of refusal* – nimble and strategic practices that undermine the dominant" (2017, 32). These documents persistently complicate the forms of knowledge that they instantiate. At first glance, they seem to be identity documents that were generated to regulate the mobility and movements of a specific group of people. And yet, as chapters 2 and 3 will show, there is nothing straightforward about the knowledge that they purport to contain. The names of the vast majority of the migrants are unreliably recorded, translated, or transcribed. There is, as I discuss in chapter 1 and in more detail in chapter 4, a grammar embedded in the language of the CI 9 certificates themselves that demands to be read and which absolutely refuses an easy reading.

Even though the certificates are supposed to use a formulaic template that would capture each migrant's identity, the language of the certificate, and the tension between that language and the migrant's responses, makes for a "tense grammar" (Campt 2017, 50). Between the system's attempts at stasis, at pinning down and making constant the identity of a particular non-citizen, and the variances of that non-citizen's positioning throughout the certificate, there is a practice of refusal anchored in what Agre calls a "grammar of action" (1994, 102). The concept of mass capture as having a grammar, and the connection between grammar and capture, owes a debt to Agre that chapters 1 and 4 will detail.

The CI 9s generated far more information than could be processed during the period of its existence. Even now, it is hard to do justice to the sheer amount of information that each certificate contains. There are the signatures or initials of the custom agents that were often, but not always, scrawled across the photographs. There is the question of how each migrant chose to portray themselves in their photographs, how they wore their hair, and what clothes they chose to wear. Some wore European clothes such as suits and neckties. Others kept their hair queues plainly in sight. And then there are the many layers of institutional handling that can be traced and read on each document. For example, there are the checkmarks that some, but not all, immigration agents made on each line of a certificate, presumably as part of a process of verifying the answers received from the migrant upon their return to Canada.

And there is still much more. These documents are so textured. I have been examining them for many years now and it is hard for me to stop looking, to feel as though I have seen fully all that there is to see, and to hear all that these documents have to say. In this sense, this book is not only about capture, but also about the possibilities of captivation. In the concluding chapter and the coda, I will turn to the relationship between these documents and art. In doing so, I am guided, in part, by Rey Chow's thinking on captivation as a "deranged remainder" of competing social forces (2012, 52). In Chow's investigation, those forces are economic (the contest between consumerist capitalism and socialist revolution). For *Mass Capture*, they are what remains between repression and resistance, and the imperative to keep looking at these images.

The CI 9s are not solely documents of a repression animated by racism. Nor are they only representations of the many forms of agency carved out of repressive conditions by people who had so little power but who nonetheless did so much with what little they had. As the book charts, the CI 9s are both of these things. Yet in between those two poles, there is something else. I hesitate to call it beauty, but there is much about these certificates

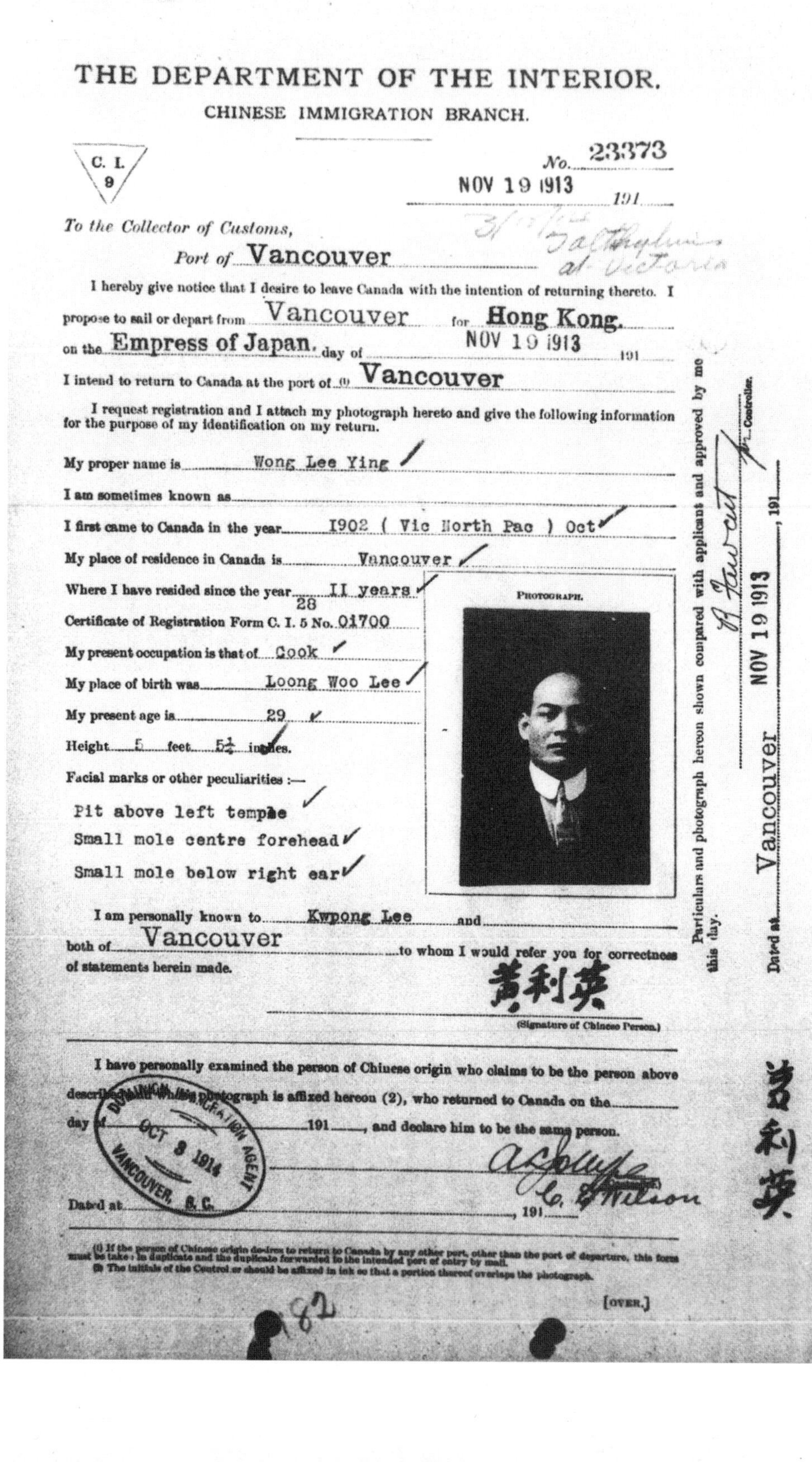

THE DEPARTMENT OF THE INTERIOR.

CHINESE IMMIGRATION BRANCH.

C. I. 9

No. 23373

NOV 19 1913 191

To the Collector of Customs,

Port of Vancouver

3/12/15 Saltcoglu at Victoria

I hereby give notice that I desire to leave Canada with the intention of returning thereto. I propose to sail or depart from Vancouver for Hong Kong. on the Empress of Japan. day of NOV 19 1913 191

I intend to return to Canada at the port of (1) Vancouver

I request registration and I attach my photograph hereto and give the following information for the purpose of my identification on my return.

My proper name is Wong Lee Ying

I am sometimes known as

I first came to Canada in the year 1902 (Vic North Pac) Oct

My place of residence in Canada is Vancouver

Where I have resided since the year II years

Certificate of Registration Form C. I. 5 No. 28 01700

My present occupation is that of Cook

My place of birth was Loong Woo Lee

My present age is 29

Height 5 feet 5½ inches.

Facial marks or other peculiarities :—

Pit above left temple
Small mole centre forehead
Small mole below right ear

PHOTOGRAPH.

I am personally known to Kwpong Lee and

both of Vancouver to whom I would refer you for correctness of statements herein made.

黃利英

(Signature of Chinese Person.)

Particulars and photograph hereon shown compared with applicant and approved by me this day. [signature] Controller.

Dated at Vancouver NOV 19 1913, 191

I have personally examined the person of Chinese origin who claims to be the person above described and whose photograph is affixed hereon (2), who returned to Canada on the day of 191, and declare him to be the same person.

DOMINION IMMIGRATION AGENT OCT 3 1914 VANCOUVER, B.C.

[signature] C. G. Wilson

Dated at , 191

黃利英

(1) If the person of Chinese origin desires to return to Canada by any other port, other than the port of departure, this form must be taken in duplicate and the duplicate forwarded to the intended port of entry by mail.
(2) The initials of the Controller should be affixed in ink so that a portion thereof overlaps the photograph.

[OVER.]

182

Fig. I.6
CI 9 No. 23373,
Reel no. T-6049.

that is, for me, beautiful. There is the quiet dignity of the people in these photographs, and the way in which their self-positioning within the very limited frame of the identification photograph offers so much that exceeds those limits. I have been captivated by this archive. You might be too.

In demanding to be looked at, and to be heard, the CI 9s also put into circulation the possibility of captivation as agency. They capture their beholders and demand an attentiveness, and a response, that is deeply felt. To study these certificates and these images is to think about the lives behind them. Look at the faces of one worker after another and think about how exhausting their labours would have been. Read the unending list of "peculiarities," noting how many times a scar on the face or the head has been recorded, and think about the forms of violence to which these migrants were subjected. If we allow it, there is something there for us in these certificates that captivates and captures the aftermath and excess of repression and resistance.

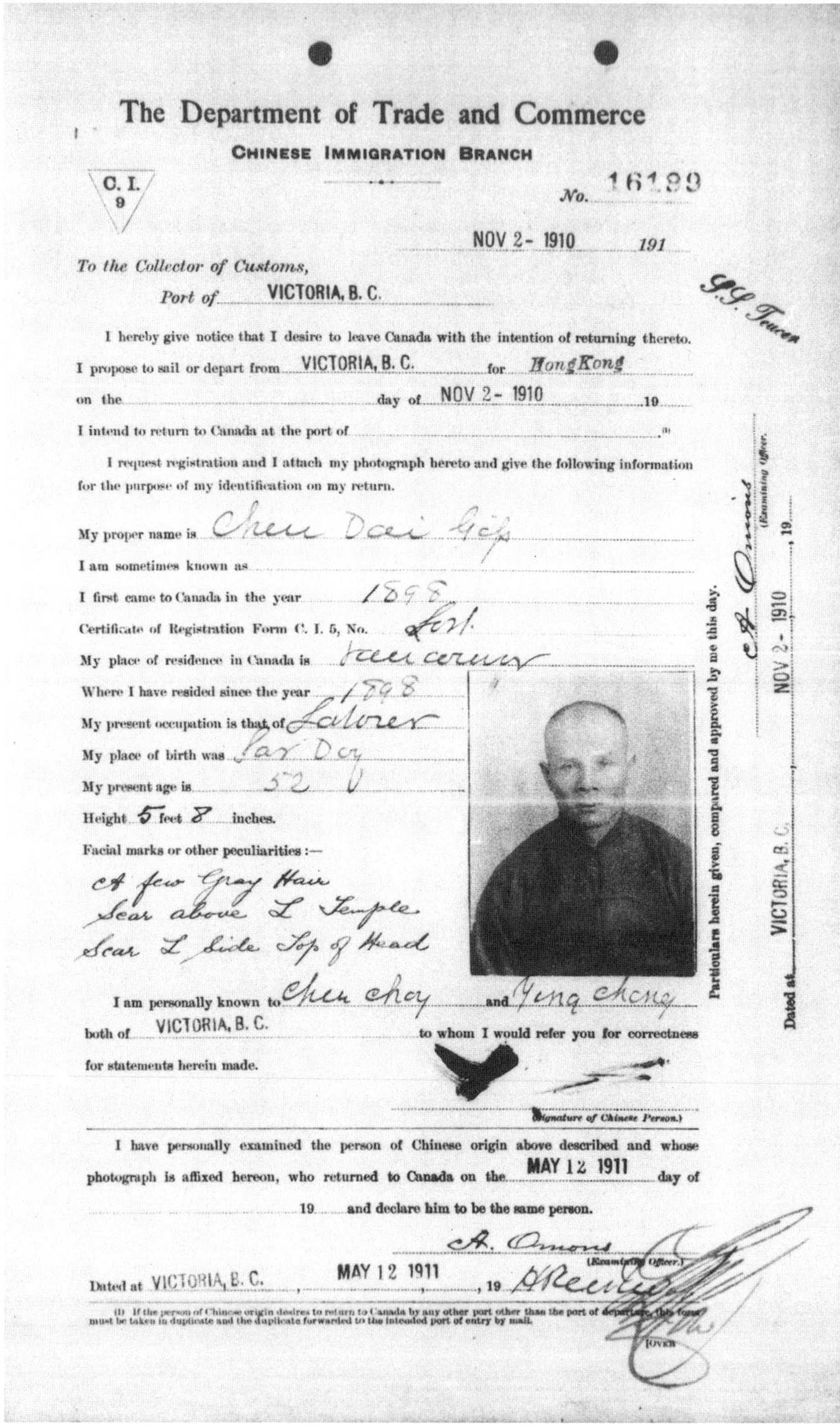

The Department of Trade and Commerce

CHINESE IMMIGRATION BRANCH

C. I. 9

No. 16199

NOV 2- 1910 191

To the Collector of Customs,

Port of VICTORIA, B. C.

I hereby give notice that I desire to leave Canada with the intention of returning thereto.

I propose to sail or depart from VICTORIA, B. C. for HongKong

on the .... day of NOV 2- 1910 19

I intend to return to Canada at the port of ....(1)

I request registration and I attach my photograph hereto and give the following information for the purpose of my identification on my return.

My proper name is Chew Dai Gip

I am sometimes known as

I first came to Canada in the year 1898

Certificate of Registration Form C. I. 5, No. Lost

My place of residence in Canada is Vancouver

Where I have resided since the year 1898

My present occupation is that of Laborer

My place of birth was Sar Dey

My present age is 52

Height 5 feet 8 inches.

Facial marks or other peculiarities :—

A few Gray Hair
Scar above L Temple
Scar L Side Top of Head

I am personally known to Chew Chay and Ying Cheng

both of VICTORIA, B. C. to whom I would refer you for correctness for statements herein made.

(Signature of Chinese Person.)

Particulars herein given, compared and approved by me this day.

Dated at VICTORIA, B. C. NOV 2- 1910, 19

A. Omons (Examining Officer.)

I have personally examined the person of Chinese origin above described and whose photograph is affixed hereon, who returned to Canada on the MAY 12 1911 day of 19 and declare him to be the same person.

A. Omons (Examining Officer.)

Dated at VICTORIA, B. C. MAY 12 1911, 19

(1) If the person of Chinese origin desires to return to Canada by any other port other than the port of departure, this form must be taken in duplicate and the duplicate forwarded to the intended port of entry by mail.

[OVER]

Fig. 1.1
C.I. 9 No. 16199,
Reel no. T-6038.

CHAPTER ONE
MASS CAPTURE AS A TECHNOLOGY OF NON-CITIZENSHIP

On 2 November 1910, Chew Dai Gip was a labourer residing in Vancouver, BC, when he applied for a CI 9 in order to sail on the SS *Teucer* bound for the Port of Hong Kong. He had been in Canada since 1898 and was fifty-two years old. He had lost his CI 5 certificate. He measured five feet eight inches tall and was noted as having "a few grey hairs," a scar about the left temple, and another scar on the left side at the top of the head. We don't know how he got these scars. But we do know that he was known to Chin Choy and Ying Chong. We know that he did not know how to write his name, because unlike the majority of men who boarded the SS *Teucer* with him, he could only make a swipe of ink where his signature should have been. He returned to Canada on 6 July 1911. We know these things from CI 9 no. 16199 (fig. 1.1). He was among thousands who applied for permission to temporarily leave Canada in 1910, and among the more than 41,000 who made this same application, identification photograph in hand, between 1910 and 1953. What is the relationship between this man and the other migrants who applied in this way? What is their relationship to these documents and to the state that produces them? Each certificate can be read on its own, but each one is also connected to thousands of others, and to a system of identification and discrimination. Thinking about the whole of the CI 9 archive as more than just a series of individual parts, as more than just one certificate after another, means thinking about it as a system. It is this systemic nature that marks the CI 9s as a technology.

Mass capture, manifested in the CI 9 system, is anchored in the earliest etymologies of the technology. Emerging from post-classical Latin *technologia* and Hellenistic Greek τεχνολογία, "technology" refers to a "systematic treatment," and in particular, "a systematic treatment of grammar" (OED). Grammar maps the relationships between words. Technology systemizes those relationships. To understand mass capture as technology is thus to take up how mass capture systemizes the relationships between units of articulation. The CI 9 is an expression, repeated over and over again, of a systematic relationship of exclusion premised on hyper-visibility. The non-citizen is anything but invisible. They must remain always within the view of the state. This visibility is systematized. It is a technology precisely in that it systematizes the rules of relation.

The system of identification generated by the CI 9s ordered relationships between migrants and the state, and between one migrant and another. It made one migrant known by demanding to know who else knew them, thus implicating others in the project of identification while also creating an elaborate map of social networks between migrants. This project of ordering is a grammar. Mass capture is not divorced from contemporary forms of technology, but it is first and foremost a system – a treatment of something that is systematic and rooted in grammar. Indeed, even though it may seem far removed from contemporary technologies of surveillance, grammar is actually central to the latter. Thus, at the heart of Philip Agre's pivotal theorization of surveillance and capture in computing sciences are what he identifies as "grammars of action" (1994, 102). For Agre, grammars of action allow systems of capture to be replicable such that human activities form "lexical units" that can be sequenced and ordered (108–9). I will discuss grammars of action in more depth later in this chapter, but for now, it is important to note that, as Agre writes, "the practice of constructing systematic representations of organizational activities is not at all new, nor is it inherently tied to computer systems development … it can be valuable in itself, even without any computers" (108). That is, capture, as a technology bound to a grammar, does not need computers. But it does need bodies.

Before there can be grammars, there are bodies through which these grammars are expressed. Further, the grammar of mass capture only works on bodies that are already captive. This chapter theorizes mass capture as a double formation that is both documentary and corporeal. In current scholarship, there are two existing uses of the term "mass capture," and both are central to how this book understands the ways in which non-citizens are produced. First, in work on privacy and new media, mass capture has been used as a term to describe the ways in which personal data is stored and manipulated for corporate or state interests. I call this *documentary mass capture*. Second, in the biological sciences, particularly in the study of wildlife management, techniques for capturing large numbers of animals – such as fencing, nets, traps, and so on – are described as mass capture. This scholarship focuses on mass capture as a form of physical entrapment.[1] I call this *corporeal mass capture*. Although there has not been

1 See, for example, Gooch (1953), "Techniques for Mass Capture of Flightless Blue and Lesser Snow Geese"; Smuts, Whyte, and Dearlove (1977), "A Mass Capture

any overlap between the two uses of this term, in my project they are entwined. Together, documentary and corporeal forms illuminate the workings of mass capture as a technology for producing non-citizens.

Before turning to detail these two formations of mass capture, I want to emphasize that Chinese migrants were indeed non-citizens. In thinking through the experience of pre-1947 Chinese migrants in Canada as one of mass capture, it is crucial to remember that the legislation that put the head tax system into place was not simply about restricting immigration. It is a mistake to understand the Chinese migrants governed by the Chinese Immigration Act as *immigrants* in the sense that we would use that term now. As I note in the introduction, Canada explicitly identified desirable immigrants as "emigrants." Emigration agents (*not* immigration agents) were stationed throughout Britain and in "strategic" parts of Europe beginning from at least 1869 (LAC 2020). Emigrants were seen as future settlers. In contrast, immigrants were clearly marked as undesirable. Indeed, the 1906 Immigration Act was unambiguous in its objective: to give the Department of Immigration the tools it would need to regulate the entry of "undesirable immigrants" (Kelley and Trebilcock 2010, 138). Thus, a quirk of settler-colonial terminology obscures the truth of the Chinese Immigration Act as legislation dedicated to the project of refusing Chinese migrants permanent entry into Canada.

Insofar as it was more restrictive, punitive, and focused, the Chinese Immigration Act is an intensification of the Immigration Act. Where the latter was more broad and less specifically racialized in terms of its target, the former was explicitly directed at one racial group. This specificity owes something to the related contingencies of the settler-colonial state's clear desire to import substantial numbers of labourers from China, and the fact that China, unlike India, was not part of the British Empire and thus not afforded the dubious niceties of Commonwealth membership. As revealed by Radhika Mongia's work on the crisis engendered by the arrival of Indians on the *Komagata Maru*, the fact that Indians were technically British subjects meant that Canada could not simply exclude them in the way that they could Chinese migrants: "the discourse of the liberal state made it exceedingly difficult to distinguish among subjects of the British Empire" (2003, 208). Excluded from the only form of citizenship available to Canadians at this time, that of being subjects of the empire, Chinese migrants presented a crisis of a different sort.

Technique for Lions"; Marshall (1987), "Maori Mass Capture of Freshwater Eels"; Bamford, Monadjem, and Diekmann (2009), "Development of Non-explosive-Based Methods of Mass Capture of Vultures."

It was a crisis of presence, in which Chinese migrants were actively recruited to come to Canada, but deeply unwelcome as potential settlers. Chinese migrants were necessary for the work of settlement: building the railways, but also a range of other labour-intensive undertakings including fisheries, canneries, bush clearing, and, on the domestic front, laundry and cooking in remote work camps. As one of the commissioners of the 1885 *Report of the Royal Commission on Chinese Immigration*, Sir Joseph-Adolphe Chapleau, makes clear in his submission: "cheap labour in a new country is absolutely necessary, and we should have the cheapest labour we can get" (Canada 1885, cii). Five years after this report, in June 1900, the House of Commons sat through a sweltering Ottawa summer night debating amendments to the Chinese Immigration Act that would result in raising the amount of the head tax. After several hours, William Cameron Edwards, member of Parliament for the riding of Russell in Ontario, asked a simple question: "Now what is the purpose of this legislation? Is it for the purpose of excluding Chinese from Canada, or is it for the purpose, in an indirect way, of collecting taxes from them?" (Canada, Parliament, *Debates* 1900, 8166). The response came from Uriah Wilson, member of Parliament for the riding of Lennox, Ontario: "It is to keep them out" (ibid.). Twenty-three years later, Wilson's statement would finally be realized.

When the Chinese Immigration Act was amended in 1923 so that Chinese immigrants were excluded from entering Canada altogether, the true objectives of this legislation were revealed. Although it may seem obvious now, I wish to reiterate: the Chinese Immigration Act was never intended to enable Chinese migrants to settle in Canada. The act legislated a tax for the ostensible purpose of discouraging Chinese migrants from coming to Canada. From 1885 to 1923, it allowed Chinese migrants to come to Canada for a fee. This amount was initially set at $50 per "head" and was increased through subsequent amendments such that it rose to $500 by 1904. Although the increase in the fee was supposed to curb the number of migrants entering, as I argue in "Rereading Head Tax Racism" (2002), it is not at all obvious that limiting Chinese migrants was the true intention of the head tax either. Importantly, Canada's head tax legislation, unlike Australia's, dropped a clause on tonnage (stipulating the number of Chinese passengers per tonne of cargo on any given ship). The lack of a tonnage clause suggests that this legislation may have been a savvy political move, whereby working-class voters would be pacified by the appearance of government action even though there would be no practical effect on the number of Chinese migrants entering Canada. The census numbers show that the number of Chinese migrants to Canada rose throughout the head tax years (ibid., 73). What is more, despite surges in the emigration of white Europeans to Canada throughout this period, "the ratio of Chinese to the total population did not decrease. In 1881 out of a total population of 49,459 in British Columbia, there were some 4,350 Chinese. In 1901 the population of the province totaled 177,272, of whom 15,942 were Chinese" (Campbell 1923, 51). Thus, for a time, the Canadian government had it both ways: the state relied on inexpensive Chinese migrant labour in order to construct the railway and a few other major projects, while at the same time claiming to be restricting that very influx of migrants. However, once those projects were completed, the migrants were no longer a benefit, just a political liability. The outright exclusion of 1923 reveals not only a callous attempt to exploit and then discard Chinese migrants through successive amendments of the Chinese Immigration Act, it also illuminates the tragedy of mass capture. These men, women, and children remained caught in a state system that sought to deny their presence by constantly drawing attention to the fact of their exclusion from citizenship.

Denying citizenship to a specific population necessitates an elaborate structure of capture. Capture is central to exclusion. The state cannot exclude those it does not apprehend. The state has to make knowable the Chinese migrants residing within its borders. To do so, it must document them.

Documentary Mass Capture

As the sheer quantity of information collected on the CI 9s makes plain, the state obsessively documented the lives of individual Chinese migrants on a level that was, at that point, entirely unparalleled in the history of Canada. Here, there are over 41,000 people whose individual photographic, biographical, and physiological features have been extracted and recorded. In contrast, throughout the head tax years, there are no parallel records of citizens residing in Canada and certainly no system that compares with the CI 9s for tracking the comings and goings of British citizens. There are a handful of individual passport applications, but there is no systematic record of each and every citizen. The enormous scale of the records we have of non-citizens set against the paucity of the records we have of citizens reveals a paradox of the technology of non-citizenship: the state must capture those it wishes to keep out.

This capture takes both physical and documentary forms. Documentary mass capture turns on the acquisition of vast quantities of information.

In understanding individualized personal information as a site of mass capture, I draw from legal and activist work on mass surveillance. Specifically, Jennifer Lynch, senior staff attorney for the Electronic Frontier Foundation (EFF), has consistently used the phrase "mass capture" in her writing on the FBI's use of a massive facial recognition database that draws on identification photographs submitted by US citizens for the purposes of acquiring a driver's licence, passport, or visa. This database is part of the FBI's Next Generation Identification (NGI) biometrics database. In no small part because the database tracks citizens who have not been suspected, much less convicted, of a crime, the EFF continues to push for greater transparency and oversight in terms of the construction and uses of this information. Lynch refers to the acquisition of these photographs as mass capture. For example, in her testimony for the US House Committee on Government Oversight and Reform Hearing: Law Enforcement's Use of Facial Recognition Technology, she states, "Facial recognition allows for covert, remote, and mass capture and identification of images – and the photos that may end up in a database could include not just a person's face but also how she is dressed and possibly whom she is with" (Lynch 2012b, 15–16). Although "mass surveillance" is the phrase most commonly used in relation to concerns over privacy and its breaches, I hang on to Lynch's phrasing because it evokes a specific logic of capture that ties back to pioneering work on the intersection of computing and surveillance by Philip Agre.

The logic of capture, as theorized by Agre, lies at the heart of my thinking on mass capture as a documentary practice. In a groundbreaking article published in 1994, "Surveillance and Capture: Two Models of Privacy," Agre differentiated between conventional approaches to surveillance, which rely on visual models and metaphors stemming largely from the panopticon, and surveillance as capture. For Agre, the work of capture is underpinned by "grammars of action" that break down a series of activities into discrete and replicable units. Agre notes that "capture" is a "term of art" amongst AI researchers and "refers to a representation scheme's ability to fully, accurately, or 'cleanly' express particular semantic notes or distinctions, without reference to the actual taking in of data" (106). As Wendy Chun explains, "an AI program has successfully 'captured' a behavior when it can mimic an action – like a typical retail transaction – without having to sample the actual movement. It works, in other words, when it can 'pass on' data because data is not necessary" (2016, 59–60). Agre gives a number of examples of grammars of action: accounting systems; toll highway collection schemes; waiters in a restaurant using automated systems in order to convey orders to the kitchen; and so on (1994, 109).

These are systems where human activities can be represented as specific and replicable units so that the data itself moves cleanly across the system. Long before the creeping normalization of social media, "smart borders," and phones that we turn on and unlock with the touch of our fingertips, Agre understood that surveillance was about data and that data was about capture. Furthermore, capture for Agre is not a form of surveillance that relies on seeing something. Rather, it attends to a pattern of behaviour and the systems whereby these patterns can be codified.

For Agre, the capture model is deeply informed by linguistic metaphors. He notes that "the verb 'to capture'" is "employed as a common term of art among computing people" (1994, 106), and extends this use to understanding the idea of grammars of action. Grammars of action treat human activity "as a kind of language … for which a good representation scheme provides an accurate grammar" (108). Capture is a grammar governing the relations between actions rather than words. Capture understands discrete actions as functioning like words in a sentence. Each word has a function but each one is also replicable and coded as a part of a sentence. *Mass Capture* builds on this work by using Agre's theory to understand a historical instance of capture and its implications for understanding citizenship.

The CI 9s are a grammar of action. They reveal a system of information capture governing the relationship between one non-citizen and another, and between non-citizens and citizens. Each step of the process is a unit in a grammar of action: getting an identification photograph taken at a studio; cropping that photograph so that it will fit onto the form; going to the office of the immigration agent; completing the form through an interview with an immigration agent through a translator; signing one's name on the form; tucking that form into one's belongings and taking care while travelling so as not to damage or lose it; returning to Canada with it; requesting re-entry by convincing the agent that you really are the person the form declares you to be. Every one of these actions is governed by rules of relation. Together, these rules are, precisely in Agre's conception, "a kind of language … a good representation scheme" that provides an "accurate grammar" that produces the Chinese migrant as a non-citizen (1994, 108).

In this representation scheme, the state captures the non-citizen through methods that are derived from the treatment of criminals. Beginning in the late nineteenth century, as Allan Sekula and John Tagg track, the advent of identification photographs, imbricated with the collection of statistical information on their subjects, produced a system of criminal identification that models most of the identification apparatuses that are still in use today. For Tagg, the use of identification photographs coincided with the introduction of British police services and was central to "the complicity of photography in this spreading network of power" (1988, 74). In form and content, the criminal records of Tagg's study are similar to the CI 9s that would be produced thirty years later in Canada. Like the records for criminals, the CI 9s were forms that bound the identification photograph together with a range of biographical and biometric information. The photograph alone was not sufficient, and could not be entirely believed: it needed to be reinforced through complementary statistical knowledge. Sekula observes that the instrumentalization of photography, particularly for policing, offers "plentiful evidence of a crisis of faith in optical empiricism." Instead of a purely "optical model" there emerges a "truth-apparatus" where the "camera is integrated into a larger ensemble: a bureaucratic-clerical-statistical system of 'intelligence'" (1986, 16). This system or apparatus was imported almost wholesale into the tracking of Chinese migrants in Canada in the CI 9 system.

Although it is not surprising that the CI 9 system criminalizes migrant bodies, recall that none of the migrants were captured in this system because the state believed them to be criminals. They had not yet committed any crime. They were merely attempting to cross a border and to travel from where they lived and worked to where they were born or had family and friends. Put this way, such a trajectory of movement could describe the travel itineraries of the vast majority of diasporic peoples. The value of observing the similarity between a prison record and a travel record lies in seeing how we have normalized the repressive methods that are now part of cross-border mobility for citizens and non-citizens alike. As I will discuss in the next chapter, such repressive systems are, not surprisingly, doomed to vulnerabilities and failure. Nonetheless, it is important to recognize the forms of state repression and the ways in which they ostensibly work to differentiate varying categories of criminality and citizenship, even though they also conflate these very distinctions. These systems break down not only because people cannot be perpetually and constantly tied to their documents, but also because they expand outward in order to capture larger and larger groups of people. That is, the bureaucratic-clerical-statistical system of intelligence that Sekula tracks in terms of criminal identification is also the same system that is leveraged against Chinese migrants in the CI 9 system, which is itself the same system that captures any passport holder today.

Part of the value of Agre's theorization lies in the way it denaturalizes a series of actions that may now seem completely unexceptional. In the twenty-first century, so much cross-border travel has been routinized. The presentation of standardized documents, manufactured under the terms specified by international bodies such as the International Civil Aviation Organization (ICAO), which determines the standard for international passports, may now be taken for granted. But in 1910, when the first CI 9s with attached identification photographs were sent out into the world, this system was relatively novel. It was part of a long process of inventing the systems and rules that would govern how different kinds of bodies would be permitted across different kinds of borders. The notion of difference is, of course, key. If all bodies were equal, and if all borders were equal, then this system would be unnecessary.

The demand for documents of identification at a national border has a long history of being unevenly applied to those who are considered foreign. In his study of the invention of the passport, John Torpey follows the rise of increasingly stringent border controls issued by the Constituent Assembly in post-revolutionary France. In 1791, the Assembly passed legislation that "upheld a ban on departures from the country and enjoined those who had left after 1 July 1789, to return within one month" (2000, 27). Although the law was weak and nullified after a month, "the revolutionary leadership regarded the emigres as potential enemies of the revolution in league with the King, reactionary priests and nobles, and foreign powers – as a profound threat to its survival" (ibid.). The consolidation of the passport as a document of border control in eighteenth-century France thus emerges at the same time as the idea of the foreigner. As Torpey is careful to point out, because of the Constituent Assembly's fears of political instability, "the term 'foreigners' therefore applied as much to those who opposed the revolution, regardless of their 'national' origins, as it did to persons not of French birth" (28). The subjection of those who are considered foreign, no matter how their foreignness is defined, becomes more and more rigorous with the stabilizing of the French republic. Thus, in 1912, the French parliament passed a new law that "focused on control of 'nomads' (itinerant persons and groups) and the vagaries of their existence. While the law ignored the question of nationality and theoretically applied to all 'nomads,' it was in fact directed at foreigners" (108). The new law required those identified as nomads to acquire identity documents that used biometric information including fingerprints and photographs. These documents, "'*carnet des nomades*,'" target "the mobile non-national, the inscrutable outside within," and "helped to constitute people of different countries as mutually exclusive 'nationals'" (ibid.). The passport comes into being because of fears of foreignness and becomes a durable convention once foreignness itself is identified as distinguishable by race and ethnicity.

Unlike the *carnet des nomades*, the CI 9 system was leveraged against only one specific group of foreigners, Chinese migrants. And unlike passports, which articulate a relationship between one citizen and another, the CI 9 captures the relationship between a non-citizen and the nation where he or she lives and works, for decades, without the rights and privileges of citizenship. Agre's theory of capture shows how the CI 9 system was not just about differentiating one migrant from another. Rather, it was a system of identification premised upon the logic of capture.

While Agre's theory comes out of a meditation on contemporary technology (computers), his model of capture, and in particular its manifestation as a grammar of action, is a very useful way to understand the implications of mass data collection in an era that predates modern computing systems. I do not dismiss the importance of computing technology to Agre's thinking. But I propose that we can understand technologies that precede the advent of modern computing as conceptually related to it. As the idea of grammars of action suggests, capture is not just about machines recording and storing data, but also a complex negotiation of replicating and representing a range of human activity.

Further, the concept of "information processing" emerges at precisely the same historical period as that of the introduction of the identification photograph requirement on the CI 9s. Agre identifies the rise of information processing as connected to the changes in workplace efficiencies in the era just prior to the First World War: "The first methods for representing human activities on computers were derived from the work-rationalization methods that industrial engineers had been developing since the 1910s. Hence the phrase 'information processing': the idea was that computers automate a kind of factory work whose raw material happens to be information rather than anything physical or tangible" (1998, 33). Processing information was a human activity arising out of the use of information as something that could be shaped, sorted, and managed.

The technology of capture is not simply a matter of having the necessary hardware and software, but also one that is imbricated within the social world that uses it. As David J. Phillips contends, "Technology is culture made obdurate. It embodies, fixes, and stabilizes social relations" (1998, 248). Phillips further argues that "technological systems not only secure and fix social relations; they are products of social relations" (ibid.). Technology is not abstracted from the social and cultural world that produces and uses it, and neither is the information that this technology processes. "Information is not an industrial material or a mirror of a pre-given reality," writes Agre. "It is, quite the contrary, something deeply bound up with the material practices by which people organize their lives. Computer systems design will not escape its associations with social control until it cultivates an awareness of these material practices and the values they embody" (1998, 57–8). Systems embody material practices, but they also carry within them a history of their emergence. Even though computing systems may seem perpetually new and constantly updated, Agre argues that it is crucial to recognize that they have specific histories. He understands computing as a "representational practice": "At stake is the sense in which a technical field has a history: what it inherits from past practice, how this inheritance is handed down, the collective thinking through which the field evolves, and how all this is shaped by the institutional contexts within which the work occurs" (57). Indeed, before the kind of information processing that Agre examines, there were the elaborate management and accounting systems used by US and British colonial slaveholders, which converted labouring bodies into forms of data for tracking and reporting. "Slaveholders left behind thousands of volumes of account books," revealing, Caitlin Rosenthal observes, an "obsession with data" (2018, 2). Technological systems are deceptive in their seemingly perpetual newness: they should also be understood as habitually old and palimpsestic, in that they retain the traces and structures of that which precedes them.

Part of this history attends to the connection between computing and surveillance. Even though, as Simone Browne (2015) makes clear, surveillance must be understood as fundamentally shaped by race and this racialization precedes the rise of computer, computing itself is bound to surveillance from its inception: "Ever since the rise of organizational computing in the 1950s, social imagination has always associated computing with surveillance. The reasons for this association are clear enough: computer systems analysis and design promptly took up and generalized the methods of rational administration that organizations had developed throughout the modern era [Clement 1988]. The technical aspect of 'algorithm' was assimilated to the bureaucratic concept of 'procedure,' and the technical concept of 'data' was assimilated to the bureaucratic concept of 'files'" (Agre 1998, 31). Following the provocations of Agre's genealogy of computing language, there is a way in which the CI 9s could easily be understood as data (files) developed and acquired for the purposes of creating an algorithm (procedure) whose objective was to screen and track every Chinese migrant arriving and departing the country. My point is not that we should read backwards and look for a kind of pre-history of computing in the CI 9 system. It may or may not be there, but the line between what counts as computational is mutable. Taking this mutability seriously makes visible the kinds of institutional impulses driving a seemingly bland bureaucratic system of data entry and filing. These are the workings of documentary mass capture.

As Agre recognizes,[2] especially in relation to capture and the tracking of individuals and information, computers are not the only part of the mechanism of capture: "The … technology of "tracking is not a simple matter of machinery: it also includes the empirical project of analysis, the ontological project of articulation, and the social project of imposition" (1994, 113). Thus, for *Mass Capture*, the capture of non-citizens, in the form of large-scale information collection, demands an engagement with the empirical project of analyzing their subjectivity, the ontological project of articulating their status within the nation, and the social project of imposing and securing their status as non-citizens.

Corporeal Mass Capture

Despite the overwhelming mass of the documents that make up the CI 9 system, we must not forget that capture is corporeal in the first instance. Before the non-citizen can be captured in a document or series of documents, they must first endure the physical capture of the ship's hold, the

2 I want to pause to meditate on invisibility and disappearance in relation to Agre himself. Agre disappeared sometime between 2008 and 2009. The story of his disappearance appears near the top of the results of any internet search of his name. He had abandoned his apartment and his job as a tenured professor of computing science at the University of California, Los Angeles. His sister filed a missing person's report. On 16 January 2010, the Los Angeles County Sheriff's Department reported finding him in "good health and self-sufficient." But his family remained concerned and were not convinced by this report. Found and not found, safe and not safe, Agre's disappearance is full of contradiction and irresolution. In working with his writing, it has been increasingly difficult to separate the intellectual legacy from this biographical information. I am not advocating a biographical approach to Agre's writing. But his disappearance continues to raise questions for me about the unknowable implications of his thinking.

In Agre's disappearance, there is a lesson that I am still trying to learn about what it means to test the limits of knowability and visibility. He left a whole life behind when he disappeared. As an early theorist of the connection between data and capture, Agre's life and disappearance shine a light on the importance of remembering the bodies that are behind the data. In the case of the CI 9s, this work demands a turn to considering more than the information captured on the forms; a turn to considering the physical bodies that are subject to mass capture, as well.

cantonment, or the camp. The body must first be captured before it can be disciplined by documentation.

My understanding of mass capture as corporeal process is indebted to Christina Sharpe's theorizing of the ship's wake and "wake work." Sharpe outlines the continuing violence of the holding spaces (capture, incarceration) and the holding pattern of historical returns: "We are positioned in the knowledge that we are living in the afterlives of slavery, sitting in the room with history, in a lived and undeclared state of emergency" (2016, 100). The afterlives of this devastation reverberate. The spaces of containment and capture do not disappear with their dismantlement. This wake work demands thinking "through containment, regulation, punishment, capture, and captivity" and the ways in which the hold of the slave ship repeats in the contemporary US prison industrial complex (21). In articulating this wake work, Sharpe asks for more than understanding the painful ways in which the past lives on in the present. She asks for a turn to the future where the violence of the hold can be transformed into acts of "beholden-ness": "Across time and space the languages and apparatus of the hold and its violences multiply; so, too, the languages of beholding. In what ways might we enact a beholden-ness to each other, later-ally? … How are we beholden to and beholden of each other in ways that change across time and place and space and yet remain?" (100–1). What does it mean to be a later-ally? To be allied in the aftermath means, for *Mass Capture*, to find the connections between Blackness and the subjectivity of non-citizenship, and to locate in those connections the intersections and resonances between captured Black and Asian bodies.

Falling historically after and figuring later than slavery, Asian labour offers a site of later-alliance. While "slavery was not singular [but] rather a singularity" (Sharpe 2016, 106), indenture is beset by multiplicity. It ranges from textbook indenture to what I think of as "near-indentured" labour, such as railway workers who were technically free but also contractually obligated in ways that left them so deeply indebted for the costs of passage and materials that their debts were nearly impossible to pay off. As such, the conditions of Asian labour vary, and the countries from which indentured labourers were drawn are also diverse. The history and experience of South Asian indenture varies significantly from that of East Asian indenture. Likewise, the experience of Asian labourers working on the Canadian Pacific Railway was significantly different from that of Asian labourers digging in the guano in Peru. And yet, as Lisa Lowe outlines in *The Intimacy of Four Continents*, there were "often obscure connections between the emergence of European liberalism, settler colonialism in the Americas, the transatlantic slave trade, and the East Indies and China trades in the late eighteenth and early nineteenth century" (2015, 1). Such intimacies do not erase differences, but rather insist upon the power of those differences to make visible the violence of colonial erasure.

Although there is little evidence to suggest that the Chinese migrants who travelled to Canada were subject to the same brutal conditions as those who were bound for Peru, it is also the case, as the example of the *Bald Eagle* below shows, that differently bound groups of Chinese workers are not completely divorced from one another. They share something in their treatment at the hands of settler-colonial societies that demanded their labour but refused to grant them citizenship. I think of what they share as trans-oceanic intimacy that hinges on the complexity of the Chinese migrant labourer's relationship between freedom and unfreedom. Despite the elaborate taxonomies that differentiated one Chinese labourer from another – taxonomies that are intent on separating migrants from each other – I do not want to lose sight of the relationship between those labourers who were, for example, bound for Canada, and those bound for Peru. The Chinese "coolie" remains a densely complex figure. It is a mistake to simplify and flatten this complexity by taking at face value the system of differentiation and regulation put into place by settler-colonial states insistent that they were no longer in the business of slavery. As Persia Crawford Campbell's exemplary overview of Chinese labour migration throughout the British Empire reveals, there were a number of variations and differences in the conditions of the labour to which Chinese migrants were subjected. For example, in the British West Indies (British Guiana), Malaysia, and South Africa, Chinese labourers worked under a contract system where they held individual contracts with the state (Campbell 1923, 6, 86, 165). In Canada, Australia, New Zealand, and the US, Chinese migrants worked under the credit-ticket system in which the migrants were indebted to brokers who recruited them, supervised their work assignments, and monitored and enforced repayment (26–59). It was a system of "debt-bondage" that allowed people such as Colonel Bee, the attorney for the Six Chinese Companies, who were the main brokers of Chinese labourers, to say, "There is not a Chinaman here who comes under a servile contract" (29). Potentially free in theory, the migrants existed in a state of "long-term indebtedness" to their brokers (ibid.). As W. Pember Reeves observes in his preface to Campbell's book, the credit-ticket system offers only a veneer of virtue: "At first sight a system under which passage-money was advanced to labourers in Chinese ports and repaid by them out of their earnings in the Colonies seems innocent enough. But managed as it was, chiefly by Chinese middlemen, crimps and compradores, it became largely a veiled slave-trade. Labourers were decoyed into barracoons and virtually sold. They were induced to gamble and lose money. They were kept in confinement, not only at points of departure, but at points of arrival" (xii).

The credit-ticket system was innocent of the horrors of the contract system in name only. In practice, many of the abuses of the indenture system continued.

One point of trans-oceanic intimacy lies in the apparatus of the hold. Following, literally, from slavery, ships carrying Chinese indentured labourers were designed to mimic the slave ship. Overcrowding on such vessels was a persistent problem. The British parliament attempted to address this issue by regulating the space required for each Chinese labourer with the passage of the Chinese Passengers Act in 1855, which was subsequently folded, entirely intact, into the 1894 Merchant Shipping Act, thus preserving these regulations throughout the period of the head tax. This act identified any ship carrying "more than 20 passengers of Asian ethnicity aboard" as "'Chinese passenger ships' in law" (Choi 2017, 177). Regarding space for Chinese passengers, Section 4 (2) specifies "that the space appropriated to passengers 'tween decks contains at the least 12 superficial and 72 cubical feet of space for every adult on board; that is to say, for every passenger above 12 years of age, and for every two passengers between the age of one year and 12 years." Setting aside for the moment the definition of adulthood as beginning at twelve years of age, let me simply focus on spatial regulations. Seventy-two cubic feet is about the space of two average kitchen refrigerators. That was the regulated ideal, and in practice, these laws were not observed. Meagher cites Don Aldus's eyewitness account of the outfitting of a coolie ship in the 1860s (long after the Chinese Passenger Act had been passed):

> The bunks for the emigrants consist of two rows of shelves running the whole length of the ship both sides, as well as down the center. These shelves are six feet wide with an eight inch footboard … After the shelves and footboards are completed the next operation is to measure and number each bedspace, allowing each man a [space] … of from twenty to twenty-four inches, the latter being the legal allowance, but it would appear they are not over particular in this matter as they seldom exceed twenty one inches. There is no kind of division between the sleepers – in short each shelf simply represented one hundred and fifty in a bed. (Meagher 2008, 153)

Meagher turns to two other eyewitness accounts that corroborate Aldus and goes on to note that "this arrangement of space per passenger was the norm, at least during the 1860s and 1870s" (ibid.). Long after the contract labour system was replaced with the credit-ticket system (in itself not necessarily a significant improvement, as noted above) and the so-called era of the coolie trade was supposedly ended, the overcrowding of Chinese passengers continued to be a problem.[3] Stowed by being literally shelved, and frequently locked down under the hatches, Chinese passengers were bound by the forced intimacy of the ships' holds.

Given the conditions aboard, rebellions on these ships were common. Only one month after the start of the Indian Mutiny of 1857, Karl Marx wrote in the *New York Daily Tribune* about indentured labourer rebellions that seemed to be occurring on every ship: "The very coolies emigrating to foreign countries rise in mutiny, and as if by concert, on board every emigrant ship, and fight for its possession, and, rather than surrender, go down to the bottom with it, or perish in its flames" ("Persia and China," 5 June 1857). In these flames, Marx points to a history of brutality where rebellious "cargo" was frequently locked in the hold and left to perish. Such was the history of the *Bald Eagle*.

In a collection of sea yarns published at the end of the nineteenth century, a sailor named Herbert Elliott Hamblen (using the pseudonym Frederick Benton Williams) tells of a fellow sailor, an Irishman named Mike Cregan, who conveyed to him the fate of the *Bald Eagle*, a US clipper ship under the helm of a Portuguese captain and a largely Portuguese crew. Five hundred miles off the coast of Manila, its cargo, several hundred Chinese men destined to become coolies in Peru, made a desperate attempt to take the ship by rushing at the hatch ladders. The crew quickly closed the hatches and shot at the men below, creating piles of bodies four or five deep, but leaving many still alive. However, a spark from a revolver caught fire on the clothes of the dead men, and half an hour later, smoke began pouring out of the fore and main hatches. Through the smoke of burning bodies and the oncoming darkness, the crew got the ship hove to and eventually abandoned the *Bald Eagle* for their longboats. The hatches were never lifted, and the crew, including Mike Cregan, sailed away with the cries of those burning alive echoing in their ears.

3 Choi notes, for example, that the British consul in Chefoo reported in 1893 a case of a ship overcrowded with Chinese passengers. The ship's owners, Jardine, Matheson, and Co., "were responsible for the coolie business, [and] protested against the consul's report as unfair to British trade" (178). Thus, the persistence of the coolie trade, and of overcrowding, is only visible because the owners of the ship protested a consular report about their own violation of the law.

This is not the whole story.[4] I have re-told it only in its barest form. There are many details we do not know, such as exactly when this happened, or how many people were in the hold when the ship was abandoned. It may have even happened on a different ship – perhaps the *Norway*, or the *Sea Witch*, or the *White Falcon*, or the countless others that burned and disappeared in the years of the coolie trade.[5] Even when we do know the names of ships, we usually do not know the names of all the people who made up their cargo. The general registers of immigration only note those who arrived, but not those who perished. We know that there were countless reports of events like this one. We know that the *Bald Eagle* was not the only ship that perished in this way.

In order to understand the corporeality of mass capture, this book takes what we do know in order to understand the beholden-ness of the entwined demands of memory and for justice that reverberate in the cries of the captive dead. For, as Eduardo Cadava exhorts, "in order to speak in the name of freedom, in the name of justice, we must speak of the past we inherit and for which we remain answerable, we must speak of the ghosts, of generations of ghosts – of those who are not presently living, whether they are already dead or not yet born" (2004, 140). Theorizing mass capture means, in the first instance, dwelling in the discomfiting and haunting space of these deaths, not in order to put these ghosts to rest, but in order to understand how it is that we live with them, and to think through their restlessness as central to the formation of the subjectivity

4 This story is published as the eighth chapter of *On Many Seas: The Life and Exploits of a Yankee Sailor* (1896). Hamblen/Williams claims to have overhead Cregan tell the story one night as a reason for his inability to sleep. The structure of the chapter where one sailor tells the story of the bad dreams of another signals the way in which this story circulates as a nightmare that repeats.

5 The British experimented first with using Chinese and East Indian labourers in Trinidad in 1806, not coincidentally during the first year that they ended the slave trade. While the experiment was a failure, by the late 1830s thousands of East Indian and Chinese labourers had been transported to the West Indies. The coolie trade, or *la trata amarilla*, in Latin America thrived largely between the years of 1847 and 1874, although coolie labour was still in use in the region until the late nineteenth century. In 1904, spurred on by the "Rand crisis," the British reopened the transportation of Chinese contract labour, this time to South Africa. After a series of horrific abuses, an act was passed in 1907 to terminate the contracts. However, still under the administration of the British, coolie labour was in use in the South Pacific islands of Western Samoa and Nauru until the first decades of the twentieth century. See Campbell (1923), Hu-DeHart (1994), and Look Lai (2004) for further details regarding the historical data of this trade.

of non-citizenship. Subjectivities do not form in isolation. Any theory of mass capture must emphasize the relationality of diasporic formations. In the nightmares of an Irish sailor about a burning US ship crewed by Portuguese sailors with a cargo of Chinese labourers on their way to Peru to supplant the lost labour of newly "freed" African slaves, we cannot but come to terms with the problem of relation.

The unjust deaths of those murdered in captivity, as Ian Baucom recognizes in his reading of Édouard Glissant's *Poetics of Relation*, are not an ending, but the beginning of a memory that stretches across the depths of the Atlantic – and, as I will suggest in this chapter, the Pacific as well. For Baucom and Glissant, the *Zong* ship is the site of this beginning and this common history.[6] For *Mass Capture*, the *Bald Eagle* enables an understanding of the articulation of the poetics of relation in two modes: as an enunciation of subjectivity, and as the forming of a joint that allows movement. Understanding the corporeality of mass capture means exploring the joints, the connections, between the migrant ship and the slave ship that facilitate movement between and across these oceanic histories. This articulation draws out the ways in which the transpacific is not divorced from the transatlantic. In extending a sense of what is shared beyond the waters of the Atlantic towards the Pacific, we can risk seeing the ways in which relation does not mitigate difference, and attend to the claims of those whose cries of terror have not been stifled by the indifference of history.

The wake work of corporeal mass capture is marked by the underwater graves of the thousands of migrants who have perished in ocean crossings across the centuries. It is in the ashes that have become part of the sea. It is in the screams of those burning in the hold that have never been silenced. It is in the waves that return. It is in what Sharpe names the "maximal wake":

> Waves that occur in the wake of the ship move at the same speed as the ship. From at least the sixteenth century onward, a major part of the ocean engineering of ships has been to minimize the bow wave and therefore to minimize the wake. But the effect of trauma is

6 As will be discussed in chapter 3, in 1781 the *Zong*'s captain, Luke Collingwood, attempted to compensate for steering his ship off course and facing supply shortages by ordering drowned over 130 slaves in order to guarantee profit through the collection of insurance money. The insurers refused to pay and the ship's Liverpool owners sued the insurance company, thus recording in the judicial archives the details of this massacre.

the opposite. It is to make maximal the wake. The transverse waves are those waves that run through the back; they are perpendicular to the direction of the motion of the ship. Transverse waves look straight but are actually arcs of a circle. And every time, every instant that the boat is moving through water it has the potential to generate a new wave. (2016, 40)

In Sharpe's metaphor, wake work cuts across and behind the forward motion of the hold. Even though the hold of corporeal mass capture seems to move inexorably forward, it leaves behind a series of movements that resonate, that cut transversally, so that its residue refuses the linearity of the ship's motion.

In the Wake of the *Teucer*

In the final part of this chapter, let me follow the wake of one particular ship. I began this chapter with a man, Chew Dai Gip, who sailed from Vancouver to Hong Kong on the SS *Teucer* in 1910. Nearly seven years later, in February 1917, four Chinese passengers were charged with mutiny on this same ship. In the ship's log for the *Teucer*, the captain notes on 8 February: "four of the Chinese labourers of the 1st Chinese Labour Corps were this day put in irons under lock and key, for insubordination inciting to mutiny" (BT 165/1663). As archivists at the UK National Archives have uncovered, the Chinese Labour Corps consisted of approximately 50,000 Chinese men who were contracted to serve in Noyelles Sur Mer near Abbeville in southern France during the First World War (Kumlertsakul 2017). The *Teucer* carried the first contingent of 1,086 men, suffering what were often "extremely rough" crossings and taking part in major battles including the Flanders offensive in 1917, even while enduring significant losses during attacks such as the air attack on Dunkirk in 1917 (ibid.). The story of the Chinese labourers sent to work on the front lines of a war that was not their own reveals the extent of British colonial reliance on contract labour. The *Teucer* carried some men home, at least temporarily, and then turned around and carried others to war under the guise of labour. In the transport of that labour, in the story of the hold that emerges in a few faint lines in a ship's log, there is also the wake of resistance.

This mutiny was not a singular event. Nearly half a century before four Chinese men were put into irons in the hold for attempting to secure their freedom, a different mutiny resonated throughout the British colonial bureaucracy. In 1871, the Chinese labourers on the *Nouvelle Penelope* rebelled and killed the captain and the officers of the ship, but spared the rest of the crew, claiming that they were merely trying to secure their freedom from conditions akin to slavery.[7] Kwok A Sing, a purported leader of the mutiny, was caught and tried in Hong Kong. He made a *habeus corpus* application. In a celebrated decision, Justice John Jackson Smale, then the chief justice of Hong Kong, ordered Kwok A Sing released and noted in his decision: "A man under unlawful restraint of his personal liberty at sea, as well as on shore, has the right to take life to free himself from such constraint" (quoted in Meagher 2008, 175). Although Smale's decision was challenged and overturned on appeal by the attorney general of Hong Kong, it was ultimately upheld by the Privy Council. It was a decision that recast mutiny and piracy as rebellion and resistance by ripping away the veneer of freedom that had obscured the true conditions of Chinese contract labour.

There is a line of connection between the rebellions on the *Nouvelle Penelope* and the *Teucer* that extends beyond that of ships and the crimes themselves and into story of Teucer as a figure in Greek mythology. Teucer was the half-brother of Ajax. A renowned archer, he fought alongside Ajax in the Trojan War against Troy, and was one of the Danaans chosen to lie in wait in the belly of the famous Trojan horse that allowed the Greeks to win the war. Despite all that he has done, the Greeks refuse to consider him a true hero. In the *Iliad*, he is mocked by Agamemnon for the cowardice of fighting with a bow and arrow instead of engaging in close combat with a spear or sword – even though Teucer kills far more Trojans than other warriors. What is more, he is considered *nothos*, or illegitimate, because his mother is a Trojan slave-concubine instead of a Greek. In Sophocles's play, *Ajax*, Teucer demands a burial for Ajax despite the prohibition against it rendered by Menelaus. In this demand, Teucer dissents and resists Menelaus's authority. As Elton Barker notes, the play democratizes the idea of dissent through the figure of Teucer, who "demonstrates the necessity and desirability of dissent as a democratic prerogative" (2009, 14). Refusing the legitimacy of authority that is anchored in cruelty and the persistent silencing of the non-citizen, Teucer models the forms of agency that can be carved out even in the face of terrible loss.

Teucer is not just a dissenting figure, but also one who is denied speech in the political arena because his illegitimate birth renders him, under the Periclean rules of citizenship, a non-citizen. As Mary Ebbott notes, both Menelaus and Agamemnon connect Teucer to non-citizenship when they mock his inability to speak for himself in the assembly: "The taunt that

7 For a summary of the case, please see Norton-Kyshe, *History of the Laws and Courts of Hong Kong* (1898, 186–7).

Teucer needs to find a free man to plead his case points to not only the slavery connection but also to restrictions on the right to speak freely (*parrhêsia*) for *nothoi* in Athens. Excluded from the political assembly, where the freedom to speak is symbolized by the extension of the right to "whoever wishes" (*ho boulomenos*), *nothoi* would easily be associated with a lack of free speech and with the agency with which citizens were endowed. All of these categories can be lumped together as non-citizens" (2003, 46). Teucer has fought for the Greeks, but he is denied the rights and privileges of Greek citizenship. Here, the wake of Teucer's predicament flows over the Chinese workers who found themselves on a ship bearing Teucer's name, pressed into serving in a war for a nation in which they have no rights because they are not citizens. Their dissent, a failed mutiny, gestures towards a different kind of silence. Without any right or recourse, they were held below decks, detained in a hold where the only release was to sacrifice their bodies as labourers on a battlefield.

In this state of capture, their resonance with Horace's depiction of Teucer is also reinforced in the context of Teucer's displacement. Exiled by his own father for failing to bring back the body of Ajax, he can only return to the sea. Cast away from his only home, he tells his ship brothers:

> Wherever fortune may bear us, kinder than my father,
> We shall go, o men and comrades!
> Do not despair with Teucer as your leader and as protector,
> Surely resolved Apollo has promised uncertain
> Future to Salamis in a new world.
> O men, who with me often have endured
> Worse fortunes, now, banish cares with wine;
> Tomorrow we shall set out upon the boundless sea! (*Odes*)

Despite being silenced and exiled, Teucer is not a pure figure of abjection. After his exile, he goes on to become king of Salamis, a small island near Athens. As Maria Bittarello observes, as a king, Teucer becomes an important mediating figure between the Greeks and the Cypriots:

> Extant sources clearly show how Athenian politicians and the Cypriot king Evagoras used the myth of Teucer ingeniously in order to serve their own political interests. Athens needed to secure in Evagoras a precious ally who was going to be useful in her commercial relations with the East as well as in the city's political relations with the Persian empire. As for Evagoras, he claimed to be a direct descendant of Teucer to gain a privileged position in Athens. Moreover,

> Evagoras's claim allowed him to keep his prerogatives as king of Cyprus and satrap of the Persian empire while maintaining a certain degree of independence from the Persian "king of kings." (2007, 5)

Further signalling the complexity of Teucer's position, Bittarello follows Teucer's depiction in Euripides's *Helen*, where Teucer is identified as "*metoecus* (i.e., *metic*), a term that indicated those who were free people but not full Athenian citizens. *Metics* lived in Athens, paid an annual tax, and had (limited) civil rights, although they were not allowed to participate fully in political life" (3). Ostensibly free but left without speech or political participation, Teucer as *metic* illuminates something of the complex position of the Chinese labourers who would be borne "upon the boundless sea" on a ship that bears his name.

Bound and unbound, unfree yet free, the Chinese labourers aboard the *Teucer* speak through the violence of failed resistance and mass capture. Caught in the hold, and again in the documentary systems (head tax certificates and ships' logs) that record the fact of their capture, Chinese migrants were subject to forms of capture that were both modern and ancient. Mass capture is a double formation that is documentary and corporeal. It emerges out of captive bodies and the systemic capture of information about those bodies. Working in tandem, corporeal and documentary mass capture make manifest the non-citizen. However, the mass captured do not remain captive. They dissent. They escape. In the next chapter, I will follow how the mass captured unsettle discourses of memory, and manufacture one form of escape.

CHAPTER TWO
MASS CAPTURE AGAINST MEMORY

In order to exclude Chinese migrants from the sphere of citizenship, the Canadian state laboured to remember these migrants through an elaborate system of capture that relied on an identification certificate known as a CI 9, which was demanded of each and every migrant who wished to temporarily leave Canada. The state sought to be able to recall each migrant who left the country in order to determine the validity of their right to return. In so doing, it created a vast archive for the purposes of exclusion. Yet, the mass capture of Chinese migrants to Canada in the first part of the twentieth century reveals the limits of conflating memory with storage.

As large and as complete as this archive is, it also offers a glimpse into the difficulty of accessing its contents. It is a difficulty that is both a problem of the present and the past. The discrepancy between the objectives of the CI 9 system of immigration control, and its effectiveness in achieving them, is a perfect demonstration of what Wendy Chun understands as the mutual exclusivity of memory and storage – or, as she puts it, how memory does not equal storage. Chun observes that computers have "erased the difference between memory and storage: users now store things in memory, rather than storing memory traces" (2016, 52). As she goes on to elaborate in a wonderful footnote, "Memory and storage are not the same things … Storage or stocks always look forward to the future. Memory is not static, but rather is an active process: a memory must be held – constantly recalled – in order to keep it from fading" (191). Although Chun refers to computational practices in the present, the conceptual distinction she makes between memory and storage is particularly pertinent for a system such as the CI 9. This system is premised on the ability to remember a particular migrant by storing their identity in a fixed location. Its use as a system fails precisely because it cannot accommodate the kind of dynamism that is central to the work of memory. This chapter investigates the ways in which mass capture works against memory in order to uncover the agential possibilities of persistent unknowability. Even though the state attempted to make each migrant knowable, its failure to do so illuminates how certain forms of forgetting are also a form of resistance.

Storage

Mass capture, in the form of CI 9s, is bound to questions of storage. How these certificates have been stored – both during the time of their circulation as active immigration files, and throughout their sequestration as records of a historical process of distinction and discrimination – tells us how they were used, how useful they were, and how they might be used now. On every certificate there are hole punch marks. Usually, there are two holes at the top. Sometimes, there are three or four along the sides.

These are, of course, the punch marks left by the filing system used to store the certificates. The CI 9s were kept in the most advanced document storage system of their time: the binder. First manufactured in Germany by Louis Leitz in 1871, the loose-leaf binder was perfected with the addition of a finger pull hole in 1911. This system of collecting slips of paper into a tidy whole was a "miraculous, order-creating contraption" wherein "the whole of the state emerges" through a "trinitarian formula of bureaucracy: 'The state, the bureau, and the file'" (Vismann 2008, 133). Neatly stacked, one on top of the other, threaded through by a metal clamp, and bound together, every CI 9 was stored in this way for future reference.

This system of physical storage extends the idea of documentary mass capture as a grammar of action in the previous chapter. The mass capture of non-citizens through the documentation of their identity is characterized by a replicability of actions that is at the core of Philip Agre's theory of surveillance as a form of capture. The form of the documents, which I will discuss shortly, as well as the way in which they were physically stored, signals how orderliness is intrinsic to the automation of this storage system. As Cornelia Vismann observes, the binder enforces its own order: "The old goal of avoiding the conflict that arises from scraps of paper lying around everywhere is replaced by an instrument, the self-binder. It puts an end to instructions on how to handle records. The file itself prescribes the necessary activities. Starting with the punch, its individual physical parts predetermine a clear order: *punch, open, fix, insert, close*" (2008, 137). Neatly bound by a clearly prescribed order of activity, the CI 9s were punched through and filed for a future where they could easily be retrieved and put to use.

This process of copying and filing is a form of control and owes a debt to systems of accounting developed in US and British colonial slave plantations. "The word 'control' itself comes from an accounting document:

the *countreroulle* or counter-roll, a duplicate of a roll or other document, which was kept for purposes of cross-checking" (Rosenthal 2018, 2–3). The issuance of two CI 9s – one for the migrant, one for the state, so each certificate could be checked against the copy on file – is an example of immigration control grounded in the power of the file to police the movements of Chinese migrants. Indeed, as Caitlin Rosenthal points out, the idea of cross-checking first meant "'verification,' but by the late sixteenth century it had come to encompass the direction, management, and surveillance that verification required" (2018, 3). The CI 9s that were kept on file by the state to enable this system of cross-checking are the counter-roll of an elaborate visual and textual record of control rendered through the technological innovation of ringed binders and filing cabinets.

It is because of the miracle of this filing system that researchers like you and me, more than a century after the creation of these documents, can consult this archive confident in its coherence. The camera alone is not sufficient. It must, as John Tagg recognizes via Gilles Deleuze and Félix Guattari, be tethered to a larger apparatus of capture: "This is how the machinery of capture works. To the magical capture of the image is harnessed the mechanics of subjection of a bureaucratic system, comes joined to the storage and retrieval system of the filing cabinet: the One-Eyed Man and the One-Armed Man, the two modalities of power that join in the technical-mechanic enslavement of the modern State" (Tagg 2009, 3). This hybrid creature works to expand the reach of the camera and to make sense of its processes. Merely having an image is not enough. The state had to be able to corroborate that image with a range of other information. What is more, merely putting image and text together is nothing without also having a system of storage that would make retrieval efficient and accessible. For the CI 9s, the Canadian government settled on a system in which the certificate number, above all the other information collected on each CI 9, would guide the filing and storage of this archive.

As I have noted, each CI 9 has been kept in meticulous order, sequenced by the certificate number and, following from that, the date of issue. However, this impressive legacy of orderliness also betrays a weakness. The dependency of the system upon the certificate number at the expense of any other information on the certificate indicates a problem of ordering, and, consequently, a problem of memory.

There is no question that the certificate number rules supreme in the organization of these certificates. The certificates' arrangement by number not only dictates the way they were physically filed in the moment of their creation, but also how they were preserved on microfilm reels in the middle of the twentieth century. This organization of the materials constitutes a problem of memory in that it would not have been possible to find a certificate by any attribute other than the certificate number and its physical place in the binder or on the microfilm reel. Despite the promise and premise of retrievability, this information is not particularly useful for finding anyone, even though the very existence of an identification document seems to suggest the ability to do just that. Think about someone you know well. Do you know their passport number or driver's licence number? We tend to remember people by their names, where they came from, what they do for a living, or what they look like. This remembering is itself a form of intimacy. The state does not require such an intimate level of recollection and so we are issued numbers for our identity documents. But, as I have been arguing, that process, on a mass scale, begins with the desire to identify those who do not belong, those who should be excluded. The ordering of these migrants by certificate number reduces them to these numbers. However, this reduction of a person to a number does not, in the end, result in practical efficiency. It is a show of efficiency, yes, but as this chapter will demonstrate, reducing memory to an act of storage is to risk the failure of memory. Such a reduction of a person to a number, of memory to storage, leaves this system of state memory vulnerable to failure. Indeed, memory falls apart at the level of storage.

Part of the failure of storage as memory in the case of the CI 9s lies in the resistance of Chinese names to alphabetical order. In her consideration of the rise of the binder as the preeminent system of document storage, Vismann notes, "Two worlds coincide in the binder: the mechanized world of the ordering apparatus and the alphabetical world of letters" (2008, 132). In the case of the CI 9s, the certificates certainly submitted to mechanical ordering – to being punched, fixed, inserted, and filed – but they were resistant to alphabetical sequencing. Although each migrant's name was recorded twice (and sometimes thrice in the case of aliases), in English and in Chinese, this information was not part of the system for filing and ordering these documents.

Each name, twice or thrice recorded, escapes the world of the binder as storage. Names are irrelevant to the ordering of these certificates and the way in which they have been filed and stored. Even though names are putatively central for identifying a person, they are not the primary mode by which the Chinese migrants in the CI 9 archive have been remembered. Knowing a name is, and would have been, insufficient for locating the identification certificate connected to that name.

Although this insistence upon identification by number is dehumanizing in effect, it is also indicative of the way in which these names, and thus these identities, overwhelmed the system designed to capture them.

The filing of identification photographs by number instead of name was not unique to immigration processes. Mugshots, organized into various "rogues' galleries" as police exhibits or albums, were also filed by number. Thomas Byrnes's famous 1895 book of criminal mugshots, *Professional Criminals of America*, featured mugshots set into grids of nine photographs per page (in rows of three) and were organized by numbers assigned to each criminal. It was easier to collect mugshots than it was to organize them in such a way that the identification information they provide could be easily retrieved. "The deployment of photography to document the criminal therefore posed a central problem: as the numbers of records increased, the utility of the collection decreased" (Finn 2009, 10). There were 204 mugshots in Byrnes's collection, and by the end of the nineteenth century, "rogues' galleries had grown in size from the hundreds … to the thousands, leather-bound books had given way to filing cabinets, and the resultant archives required the assistance of three attendants" (ibid.). Even though these mugshots may have been filed by number, like the CI 9s, the names of each criminal continued to matter in the way in which these files circulated.

Reference to criminals tended to privilege their names over their criminal identification numbers. As Lourdes Delgado argues in her study of the criminal mugshot as a site of a semantic history of guilt, even with the introduction of identification numbers for detainees, the number is listed almost as an afterthought or a way of lending administrative heft to the organization of police records: "From 1878, when referring to a criminal, the *New York Times* began to include a number, referring to the police archive, where the records of detainees were held, with the subsequent suggestion of scientific, or at least administrative, certainty that the numbers provided" (2017, 223). Thus, for example, the *Times* would report on "James Williams, alias John Lestrange, a pickpocket, (no. 1, 132 in the Rogues' Gallery)" (quoted in ibid.). This emphasis upon the name of each criminal as part of their identity was part of a larger effort to make the individual criminal familiar and knowable. One of the reasons why Byrnes assembled the albums for public circulation was to address the challenge of making the photographic records useful by "enlist[ing] the public in the practice of policing" (Finn 2009, 10). Although the mugshots are organized by number, their circulation is meant to make them more, not less, indexed to a person whose identity could be differentiated and distinguished by those who would put in the effort to look at them closely.

In contrast, the CI 9 system favoured differentiation and distinction through an identification number first and foremost. Upon returning to Canada and requesting re-entry, the migrant would present their certificate and it would have to match the one on file before they were readmitted. The filed certificate was retrieved via its place in the numerical sequence. Filing and storing each certificate by number rather than name displaces the burden of proof of identity onto the documents themselves. In relying so heavily on a specific document and document number, at the expense of all the other identification information, the state invests in the reading of documents rather than the reading of bodies.

The information about these bodies is certainly collected, but it is not used as the principal method for differentiating one migrant from another. All of the other information, recorded and kept with such diligence, merely corroborates what the certificate already tells: that this person is who their documents claim them to be. The representation of the racialized subject in an identification photograph calls attention to the dangers of misrecognition and the instability of the connection between the photograph and its subject. For the viewer, any identification photograph poses the silent question: Is that you? To request an identification photograph is to question someone's identity.

These are images that the law both demands and rejects. It demands the photograph as proof of the subject's identity. But it rejects it as questionable evidence at best. For there is a curious logic to demanding photographs to identify racialized migrants when another, contrary logic declares that they all look the same. Anna Pegler-Gordon notes that Congressional representative Thomas Geary, the primary sponsor of the United States' Chinese Exclusion Act (1892) and its amendment in 1893, argued in support of supplementing repetitive textual descriptions with photographic documentation of Chinese immigrants because "all Chinamen look alike, all dress alike, all have the same kind of eyes, all are beardless, all wear their hair in the same manner" (quoted in Pegler-Gordon 2009, 35). Like Sir James Herschel in India, whose reliance on fingerprinting I will discuss in chapter 4, Geary found textual descriptions to be inadequate for distinguishing between racialized subjects, but unlike Herschel, Geary turned to photographic identification as a way of resolving this problem. However, Geary's belief in the power of the identification photograph to distinguish between racialized subjects highlights the contradictory logic behind the demand for identification photographs from supposedly indistinguishable racialized subjects.

In this way, the document, the certificate, comes to stand in for the noncitizen. The body is secondary. It is further proof, a form of corroboration, but it is not the first site of examination. Files not only come to stand in for the body at the site of inspection, but also begin resembling bodies. Vismann herself begins to think of files as being like people: "Once files act like people by staying overnight and spending extended time in corridors, that is, once files take on the habits of their users, a new time has begun – the time of files" (2008, 139). Vismann's whimsical anthropomorphization of paper files is particularly poignant given the role and use of files during the Weimar Republic. To have a file, to be filed, also had horrific consequences for those who were persecuted by the Third Reich. Think of the chill experienced by those who realize that state intelligence services might have a file or dossier devoted to them. For Vismann, the time of the files is one of increased automation in terms of the management of information. But Vismann's provocative formulation can be easily extended to fall within the ambit of mass capture.

To imagine the files as people who spend the night in the binders and cabinets of their storage is to begin to see how these seemingly innocuous office supplies offer a way into understanding the files as an extension of the hold of the ship and the barracks of the migration detention centre. Bodies must be processed and housed just as the information about those bodies must be acquired, transcribed, and then punched through, inserted, and filed. Vismann's contemplation of files that act like people calls to mind Allan Sekula's engagement with the body and the archive, or the way in which "the camera is integrated into a larger ensemble: a bureaucratic-clerical-statistical system of 'intelligence.' This system can be described as a sophisticated archive. The central artifact of this system is not the camera but the filing cabinet" (1986, 16). As Sekula understands, given the sheer mass of information that the photograph provides, the photograph must be "tamed" through an apparatus, the filing cabinet, that will allow it to be retrieved (17–18). In the case of identification documents such as the CI 9s, the state does not just want the files to *act* like people, it wants them to *be* like people. For the state to make non-citizens, the capture and containment of these files, files threaded through the metal clamp of the binder, is coextensive with corporeal mass capture.

Yet these bodies and these files remain stubbornly resistant to recall. Stacked one upon the other in containers that dictate the precise dimensions of the space that they are permitted to occupy, the files that come to stand in for the bodies that they represent offer a promise of order and containment. However, files are not bodies. They may sometimes act like them; they may even, as in the case of the CI 9s, stand in for them. But the representation of the person is very clearly never the person as a whole. Nonetheless, the CI 9 system continually mistakes the file for the person. In so doing, it misunderstands storage as memory.

This investment in files and numbers over language not only fetishizes the document over the person it represents, it also attempts to reduce the act of reading a body to that of matching one number with one another. Through faith in numbers, the turn is not just away from language itself, but specifically away from Chinese names and the Chinese language. It might have been disdain for Chinese and its perceived archaism. As Thomas Mullaney observes in his study of the invention of the Chinese typewriter, among Western thinkers (most notably Hegel), ideographic languages such as Chinese, Incan, and Egyptian were "understood as being stuck in a state of arrested development that, in turn, froze in time those who spoke and thought in, with and through these languages" (2018, 66). Even well into the late twentieth century, "concepts of alphabetic supremacy and Chinese linguistic unfitness were not so easily dispelled" (69) such that "questions of Chinese linguistic unfitness … moved out of the politically untenable realm of race, and into the sanitized realm of technological devices like the typewriter" (70–1). Against the technological backwardness of the ideographic script, the CI 9s conflate an identification number (the certificate number) with the identity of the person. It goes without saying that a person is far more than the number to which they have been indifferently assigned. But, in refusing to engage in the complexity of Chineseness by reducing Chinese identities to thousands of five-digit numbers, the state fails to remember the very people it seeks to track.

Failed Memory

Memory is not storage. To think of one as interchangeable with the other is to risk the failure of memory. For mass capture, failed memory means the failure to accurately identify people who are represented on the CI 9 certificates. This system is premised entirely on the ability to remember a particular migrant by storing their identity in a fixed location. Its use as a system fails precisely because it cannot accommodate the kind of dynamism that is central to the work of memory. The CI 9s unsettle memory not least because even the most basic attempt to use these certificates for identification illuminates the ways in which they completely foil the identification process. The CI 9 system, for all its complexity and insistence on detail, could not handle the peculiarities of Chinese names.

Each migrant's Chinese name was anglicized by the immigration agent, with the help of a translator, at the time the certificate was issued. This process of anglicization was, at best, improvisational. At the time, there were no conventions for anglicizing Chinese names. A surname as common as "黃" (Wong) could be written in English as Huang, Wang, Wong, or Weng. Chinese migrants spoke a range of dialects including Cantonese,

Sze Yip, Toisanese, and Fujianese. To further complicate things, another very common surname, "王" (Wong), is a homonym for "黄" in Cantonese. Each dialect could have lent a different inflection to the anglicization of that particular name. Further, there was no distinction between surnames and proper names in the certificates. Following Chinese naming conventions, some agents entered surnames first; some did not.

All of these differences lead not only to the problem of accessing this history in the present, but also in the past. As the confusion over something as straightforward as names suggests, the CI 9s are also a testament to the ways in which massive projects of identification are so vulnerable to failure. See, for example, the certificate that inaugurates this new era of identification, certificate number 15811 (fig. P.1). Here, so this document claims, is Luie Lee Teck. Maybe? The handwriting is hard to decode. He has written his name in Chinese closer to the bottom of the certificate. But somehow this additional information only makes things more confusing. The Chinese writing is clearer, but the sound of the characters does not correspond in any way with the English transliteration on the form. In Cantonese, these characters would sound something like *dak shi lum*. Even if the man in this certificate spoke a dialect other than Cantonese, the opening consonants of each character of his name would not be that different. But then something twigs. That first part of the transliterated name might be "Lum." Perhaps, then, the name has been phonetically transcribed so that the surname has been replaced by a character in the given name? Still, there is uncertainty.

We do not even know his name. Or rather, we have two names and we cannot know if one, or both, or neither, might be correct. The textual material is in contradiction with, or belies, the claims of the visual evidence or photograph. In *The Disciplinary Frame*, John Tagg highlights the ways in which repressive state photography, such as identification photography, was pointless without a coherent system of storage: "It was no use accumulating records if the storage system did not make it possible to retrieve them, cross-reference them, or compare them" (2009, 13). Tagg's point converges with the skepticism of scholars of memory studies regarding the idea of memory as storage. Notably, Paul Connerton (2008, 65) identifies a surfeit of information as a key form of forgetting. Even though the state attempted to remember individual Chinese migrants by creating an apparatus of information capture in the form of the CI 9, the actual result was less an active process of remembering than an imperfect system of information storage. It was imperfect not least because the system of retrieval could not keep up with the sheer scale of the information that had been captured and stored. As Nancy Van House and Elizabeth Churchill (2008) emphasize, the design of systems of storage and retrieval fundamentally shapes the memories that can be retrieved. For example, there was no retrieval system for names in Chinese. The certificates made a point of capturing both the anglicized and Chinese name of each migrant, but this information was useless for the purposes of retrieval because the certificates were stored by number.

Not only was it difficult to recover information from these certificates (without a certificate number), but my research team found that significant mismatches between the English and Chinese names on the certificates reveals a strong possibility that the names themselves were practically useless for identifying migrants. In an analysis of 112 certificates issued in 1913, my team found considerable differences between the Chinese names that the migrants provided, and the names as they were anglicized by the immigration agent.

Figure 2.1 provides a summary of our findings. As you will see, there were very few cases (less than 1 per cent) where the Chinese name and the anglicized name corresponded. Sometimes there were slight differences (what we term "low difference"). A third of the time, we found moderate differences. And, in a finding that I still find surprising even though I suspected that there would be many such cases, almost 60 per cent of the Chinese names significantly differed from the anglicized ones on each certificate. Each certificate was examined and transcribed by at least two research assistants working under my direction. Wherever there were major differences in transcription, we consulted each other and worked together to arrive at the most likely name. We took into account the fact that the certificates did not differentiate between surnames and given names, that

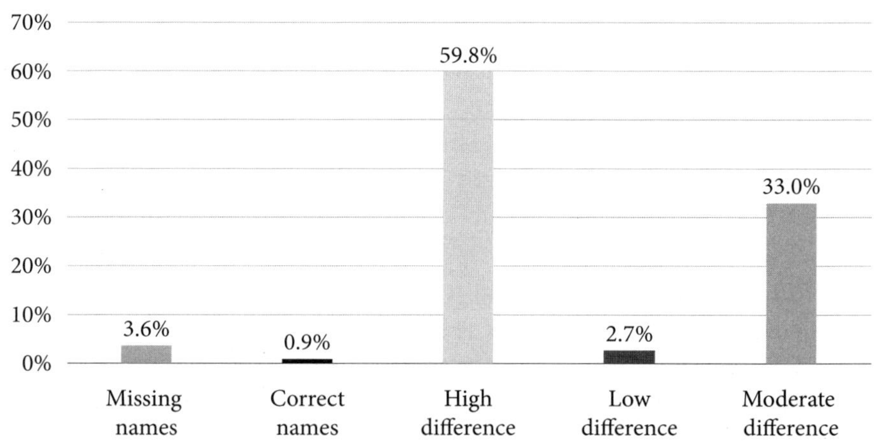

Fig. 2.1
Name correlations in CI 9 certificates numbered 23500 to 23355.

Chinese surnames are often written and given first, and that the Chinese names were often written according to the linear protocols of Chinese script so that the written Chinese names must be read from right to left. We also converted the names to Cantonese pinyin and tried variations of other regional dialects including Toisanese. Even after taking all of this into account, we found an enormous number of discrepancies between Chinese names and anglicized names on the certificates we examined.

For this chapter, we chose to work with a sample of certificates from 1913 because the iteration of the CI 9 system requiring photographs began in 1910; we wanted to examine certificates that were produced a few years after the inauguration of this system in order to see how it functioned after it had a chance to stabilize. The fact of the differences, the scale of them, is telling. If nothing else, these certificates suggest that the identities of the men, women, and children on these certificates could not be taken for granted. These identities certainly circulated differently depending upon the linguistic register.

That Chinese migrants sometimes used false documents in order to gain entry into Canada, particularly during the period of exclusion (1923–47), will come as no surprise to any observer of immigration history. Chinese migrants avoided exclusion by sharing head tax papers in order to be "re-admitted" to Canada when in fact they were entering for the first time. Contemporary Chinese-Canadian fiction such as Wayson Choy's *The Jade Peony*, Sky Lee's *Disappearing Moon Cafe*, and Judy Fong Bates's *Midnight at the Dragon Cafe*, as well as nonfiction work such as Choy's *Paper Shadows*, have made the idea of the "paper son" part of the parlance of Chinese immigration. My research supports the stories told by these writers and indicates that paper sons, and from them entire paper families, are not exceptional. These are not singular or occasional incidents. It was not just one or two people declaring themselves to be someone they very likely were not.

That we still have tens of thousands of perfectly ordered CI 9s, all filed neatly by number and date of issue, each bursting with a wealth of information, is a credit to the extensive reach of this system. However, as I have been arguing, this system of collection was only as effective as the system of retrieval – and here, the system fails. The expectation was that each migrant would return to the intended port of re-entry where their certificates would be kept on file for cross-referencing. That, of course, was the first obstacle. Entry and re-entry, while ostensibly dependent on an easily filed and retrieved CI 9, also depended on the immigration agents. Fraud could be enabled by the shortcomings of port guards who were invariably patronage appointments, including, as the 1910 *Royal Commission to Investigate Alleged Chinese Frauds and Opium Smuggling on the Pacific Coast* details:

> W.A Kent, aged 48, given to drink and unreliable.
> T. Physick, aged 63, physically unfit and service unsatisfactory.
> H.H. Warburton, 50, cripple and unfit.
> J. McPherson, given to drinking and unreliable. (Mar 2010, 43)

As Lisa Mar observes, "Even the immigration officials' measuring stick for height was discovered to be inaccurate, with one foot being only eleven inches" (114). Thus, this system of identification, information retrieval, and cross-referencing depends upon a series of agents who were themselves susceptible to a wide range of human errors. Despite these weaknesses, there was much hope placed in the potential of photographic technology. Mar notes that the "absence of photographic documentation [prior to 1910] encouraged fraud" (ibid.). And yet, as I have been suggesting, even the turn to photographic identification could not prevent fraud. If anything, the systematic investment in the indexicality of the identification photograph, the idea that the image presented would correspond seamlessly with the text on the page which could then be unproblematically indexed to the bearer of the certificate, makes this system even more vulnerable. In this system of mass capture, the photographic turn exacerbates the failures of relying on the indexical. Mass capture manufactures non-citizens by making them hyper-visible to the state, but this process is also deeply vulnerable to failure.

Bodies beyond the Archive

What emerges out of the failures of mass capture? In the first part of this chapter, I have shown that mass capture as a technology of non-citizenship fails. It fails because so many of its subjects remained elusive and largely invisible. This failure lies not only in the unwieldiness of the system, nor even in the incompetence of those charged with executing its grammars of action. Of course, these are factors. But the failure of the CI 9 system poses its greatest threat to the ideological underpinnings of surveillance: the CI 9s persistently undermine the idea that a photograph of a person can necessarily be counted upon to be a representation of that person.

As a collection and a specific archive, taken together, the CI 9 photographs tell us that identification photographs cannot simply be read as such; that repressive photography, as tracked by Sekula and Tagg, might also serve as a site of escape. Recall that Tagg sees in identification photographs the "traces of power, repeated countless times, whenever the photographer prepared an exposure" and that the "repetitive pattern" is central to the repression of the subjects of identification photography: "the body isolated; the narrow space; the subjection to an unreturnable gaze; the scrutiny of gestures, faces and features; the clarity of illumination and the sharpness of focus; the names and number boards" (1988, 85). Still, as Sekula notes, proponents of identification photography were well aware of its limitations. Their response to these limitations, as shown by Sekula's now canonical overview of the methods of Francis Galton and Alphonse Bertillon, were to imbricate the photographic representation with the statistical. What these responses fail to account for is the possibility that there might not be *any* correspondence between the photographic subject and the biographical, biometrical, and statistical information collected to correspond with that subject.

The body in the archive is not necessarily the body that the archive believes it to be. Certainly, there is a body. But whose? In the CI 9 archive, the bodies belonging to these names have moved far out of the disciplinary frame. What is more, they have used the frame itself as a cover for their escape. Take, for example, Wong Lin Foon, CI 9 number 22711 (fig. 2.2). According to this CI 9, he registered to leave Canada on the SS *Cyclops* on 1 October 1913. Given Tagg's observation of the machinery of capture as being akin to man with a single eye and arm, how fitting it is that he should have shipped out on a ship named after a mythical, one-eyed creature. In so doing, he gave the apparatus of mass capture the slip. Filed just in front of his certificate is a letter (fig. 2.3).

Exploiting the vulnerabilities of the system, Wong Lin Foon claimed to have lost his identity documents. Those documents were located and found to have belonged to someone else entirely, but by the time this ruse was uncovered, he had sailed on the SS *Cyclops*. He successfully registered out using CI 9 no. 22711, and thereby not only engineered his own exit with false documents but also seemingly allowed at least one other migrant to leave with documents that were not his own.

In a further twist, there is *another* CI 9 no. 22711 (fig. 2.4). This one appears to belong to a man named Ing Yon Lan. Let us read the story of these three documents: the two CI 9s claiming to be no. 22711, and the letter that is filed with the one belonging to Wong Lin Foon. First, the chronology.

On 1 October 1913, Wong Lin Foon departs on the *Cyclops* from Victoria, British Columbia, Canada, by registering his outward-bound migration on CI 9 no. 22711. On that same day, he claims to have lost his CI 5 no. 39222 and applied for a CI 28, which is an affidavit detailing his identifying information used to replace the lost CI 5.

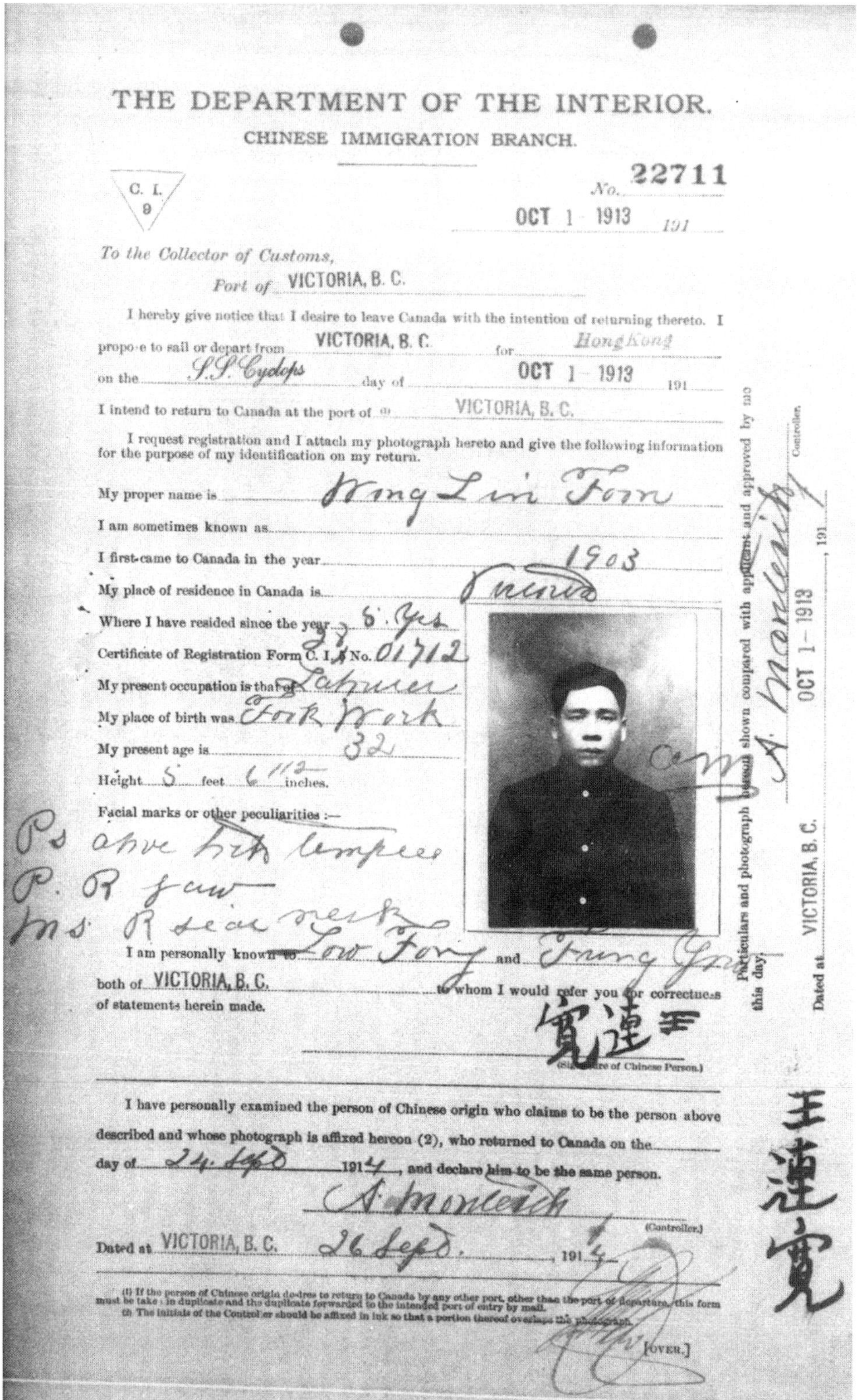

THE DEPARTMENT OF THE INTERIOR.

CHINESE IMMIGRATION BRANCH.

C. I. 9

No. 22711

OCT 1 1913 191

To the Collector of Customs,

Port of VICTORIA, B. C.

I hereby give notice that I desire to leave Canada with the intention of returning thereto. I propose to sail or depart from VICTORIA, B. C. for HongKong on the S.S. Cyclops day of OCT 1 1913 191

I intend to return to Canada at the port of (1) VICTORIA, B. C.

I request registration and I attach my photograph hereto and give the following information for the purpose of my identification on my return.

My proper name is Wong Lin Foon

I am sometimes known as

I first came to Canada in the year 1903

My place of residence in Canada is Vernon

Where I have resided since the year 8 yrs

Certificate of Registration Form C. I. 5 No. 01712

My present occupation is that of Labourer

My place of birth was Fook Work

My present age is 32

Height 5 feet 6 1/2 inches.

Facial marks or other peculiarities :—

Ps above left temples

P. R jaw

Ms R side neck

I am personally known to Low Fong and Fung Gar

both of VICTORIA, B. C. to whom I would refer you for correctness of statements herein made.

寬連王

(Signature of Chinese Person.)

I have personally examined the person of Chinese origin who claims to be the person above described and whose photograph is affixed hereon (2), who returned to Canada on the day of 24 Sept 1914, and declare him to be the same person.

A. Monteith

(Controller.)

Dated at VICTORIA, B. C. 26 Sept. 1914

(1) If the person of Chinese origin desires to return to Canada by any other port, other than the port of departure, this form must be taken in duplicate and the duplicate forwarded to the intended port of entry by mail.

(2) The initials of the Controller should be affixed in ink so that a portion thereof overlaps the photograph.

[OVER.]

Particulars and photograph of person shown compared with applicant and approved by me this day, A. Monteith Controller.

Dated at VICTORIA, B. C. OCT 1 - 1913 191

王連寬

Fig. 2.2
CI 9 No. 22711,
Reel no. T-6040.

Fig. 2.3 (opposite)
Letter filed in
front of Wong Lin
Foon's certificate,
Reel no. T-6040.

Victoria, B.C., 11th Sept., 14.

Sir,

I am in receipt of yours of the 4th instant -File No. 884985 Imm.- re Wong Lin Foon, C.I.28 No. 1712, who claims that he has lost his certificate C.I.5, No. 39222, which has now turned up, and which evidently belongs to a party in Vancouver. I beg to state that Wong Lin Foon has left here for China by the S.S. Cyclops on October 1st, 1913, being registered out under C.I.9 #22711, but he has not yet returned. I will investigate this case when he comes back, and if you wish him to be detained, please wire me. I retain the file sent by you, and will return same when the matter has been settled.

I have the honour to be,

Sir,

Your obedient servant,

Controller of Chinese Immigration.

W. D. Scott, Esq.,
Chief Controller of Chinese Immigration,
OTTAWA.

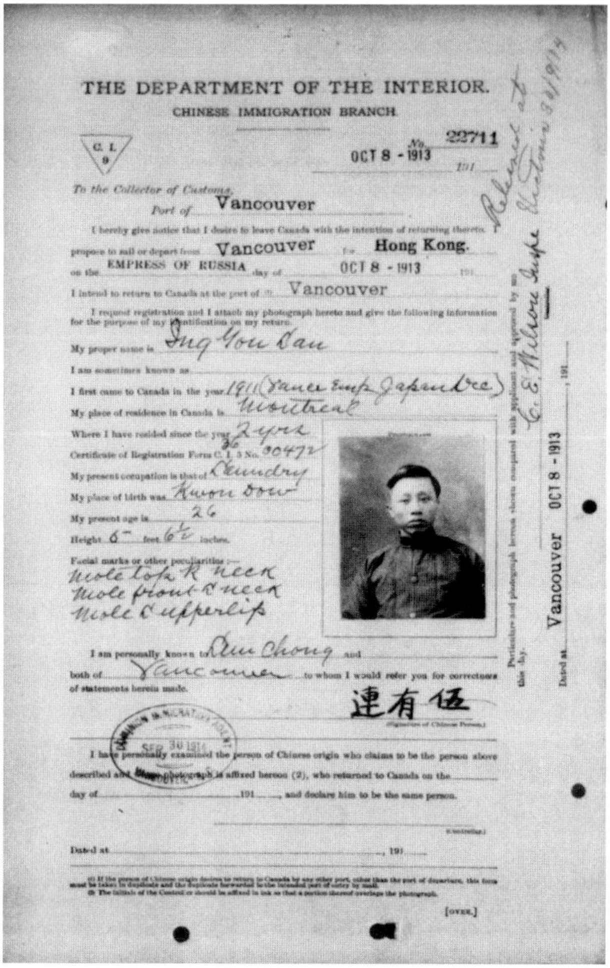
THE DEPARTMENT OF THE INTERIOR.
CHINESE IMMIGRATION BRANCH

C. I. 9

No. 22711

OCT 8 - 1913

To the Collector of Customs,
Port of Vancouver

I hereby give notice that I desire to leave Canada with the intention of returning thereto. I propose to sail or depart from Vancouver for Hong Kong. on the EMPRESS OF RUSSIA day of OCT 8 - 1913

I intend to return to Canada at the port of (1) Vancouver

I request registration and I attach my photograph hereto and give the following information for the purpose of my identification on my return.

My proper name is Ing Yon Lan

I am sometimes known as

I first came to Canada in the year 1911 (Vanc Emp Japan Dec)

My place of residence in Canada is Montreal

Where I have resided since the year 2 yrs

Certificate of Registration Form C. I. 5 No. 36 90472

My present occupation is that of Laundry

My place of birth was Kwon Dow

My present age is 26

Height 5 feet 6½ inches.

Facial marks or other peculiarities :—
mole top R neck
mole front R neck
mole R upperlip

I am personally known to Lum Chong and both of Vancouver to whom I would refer you for correctness of statements herein made.

連有伍
(Signature of Chinese Person.)

SEP 30 1914

I have personally examined the person of Chinese origin who claims to be the person above described and whose photograph is affixed hereon (2), who returned to Canada on the day of 191 , and declare him to be the same person.

(Controller.)

Dated at , 191

Particulars and photograph hereon shown compared with applicant and approved by me this day.
C. E. Wilcox Inspr

Dated at Vancouver OCT 8 - 1913

Released at Victoria 30/9/1914

[OVER.]

Fig. 2.4
CI 9 No. 22711, Reel no. T-6048.

On 8 October 1913, Ing Yon Lan departs Vancouver, British Columbia, on the *Empress of Russia*. In lieu of a CI 5, he has filed a CI 36 which was issued to replace CI 5s that had been issued prior to 1912 when there were no photographs attached to these certificates.

On 11 September 1914, the chief controller of Chinese immigration, William Duncan Scott, responds to a query from an immigration agent in Victoria dispatched on "the 4th instant," or 4 September 1914. In this letter, Scott uncovers a lie. Wong Lin Foon is not who he claims to be. Or, he has not lost the head tax certificate he was issued upon entering Canada, CI 5 no. 39222. That document, Scott reveals, "evidently belongs to a party in Vancouver." Although Scott does not disclose how he came to know this information, one gathers that the owner of CI 5 no. 39222 did not board the *Cyclops*. At the time of his missive, according to Scott, Wong Lin Foon has not yet returned from China. Scott assures the agent in Victoria that an investigation will follow upon this man's return and that the agent should wire Scott should he wish Wong Lin Foon to be detained.

On 24 September 1914, less than two weeks after Scott's letter was dispatched, Wong Lin Foon returns to Canada. Seemingly, he has done so with little fanfare. The agent at the port attests, as the form dictates, that he has "personally examined the person of Chinese origin who claims to be the person above described and whose photography is affixed hereon … and *declare him to be the same person*" (emphasis mine). Wong Lin Foon, or someone claiming to be Wong Lin Foon, countersigns the CI 9 on the lower right-hand corner. And that is that.

On 30 September 1914, Ing Yon Lan returns to Canada by landing at Victoria. His return date is noted and stamped, and scrawled across the top right corner of this CI 9 are written the words: "Released at Victoria 30/9/14."

It does not seem that either man was detained upon entry. The best indication of the unproblematic nature of their re-entry into Canada can be found on the CI 9s themselves: both certificates look, more or less, like every other one in the archive. True, Wong Lin Foon's was counter-signed by both the re-entering migrant and the controller at the port. In contrast, Ing Yon Lan's was not. Still, nothing indicates a problem with the identification photograph itself. In the case of Wong Lin Foon's, it has been neatly initialled by the controller. It does not seem to have been tampered with, and moreover, the photograph had been on file all this time, so the original could not have been swapped out with another. Neither certificate was cancelled, crossed out, ripped up, or treated with any kind of exceptionality.

And yet, Scott's letter was eventually filed with this certificate so that I would find it there, tucked neatly away, alongside the certificate question. At some point, someone knew that these two documents belonged together. But not on 24 September 1914, when Wong Lin Foon returned.

Once again, it is unclear that the officials have captured the names of the migrants correctly. In the case of Ing Yon Lan, the Mandarin pinyin of the characters he writes on his form, 連有伍, would be "Lian You Wu," and the Cantonese pinyin would be "Lin Jau Ng." In the case of the Cantonese pinyin, the differences are not so enormous between the name as it might have been pronounced and as it is transcribed. But even minor differences reveal the challenges faced by this system. In the case of Wong Lin Foon, his signature upon departure places the character for Wong (王) last even though it is written in English first. To complicate things further, when he returns, he writes his name vertically and this time Wong comes first. Given the overwhelming popularity of Wong as a surname, it seems likely that Wong is the surname intended for this document. That is: it seems likely, but we don't really know.

So, someone claiming to be Wong Lin Foon departed Canada. And someone claiming to be him, or someone who looks enough like him to resemble the identification photograph on CI 9 no. 22711, returned to Canada a little less than a year later. In light of Scott's letter, the man claiming to be Wong Lin Foon was probably not Wong Lin Foon. There are now already two bodies attached to one identification certificate (CI 5 no. 39222). The man claiming on his return to be Wong Lin Foon on CI 9 no. 22711 might or might not have been the same person who departed Canada using that certificate. Thus, there might be a third additional body attached to this certificate.

And then, just as importantly, there is Ing Yon Lan, who is, according to his photograph and the biographical information provided, an entirely different man. A man who may or may not have been him certainly left Canada in 1913, and a man who may or may not have been the man who left entered Canada in 1914 on the basis of that certificate. Have you been counting? I am beginning to lose track. The evidence found in the two CI 9 nos. 22711 indicate that the possibility that as many as four different men could have travelled to and from Canada using a single certificate number.

CI 9 no. 22711 gives us as the stories of at least two men. Wong claims to be thirty-six years old and a labourer in British Columbia. Ing claims to be a launderer who is twenty-six years old and living in Montreal. Both happen to be the same height, 5'6 ½", but their photographs reveal their facial differences. Somewhere, in between one certificate and another, between one set of a details and another, there might be the truth of one or another identity.

There is one more element of CI 9 no. 22711 to take up. It is not the only double. There are actually thousands of doubles. In a move that remains astonishing to me, this duplication is deliberately built into the system. Note that Wong Ling Foon departed from the Port of Victoria. Now look and note that Ing Yon Lan left via the Port of Vancouver. The CI 9 system used one set of numbers for certificates of migrants departing from Vancouver, and then used the same numbers all over again for those leaving from Victoria. Here is a breakdown of the CI 9 numbers for each port of departure and the LAC reel numbers in which each certificate can be found:

Vancouver departures
T-6047 – Sept 1910 to Jan 1912 – CI 9 no. 17286 to 20110
T-6048 – Jan 1911 to Oct 1913 – CI 9 no. 20111 to 22899
T-6049 – Oct 1913 to July 1916 – CI 9 no. 22900 to 27772
T-6051 – Nov 1917 to July 1919 – CI 9 no. 28650 to 31399
T-6052 – June 1915 to Sept 1929 – CI 9 no. 1 to 03240

Victoria departures
T-6038 – Sept 1910 to Oct 1911 – CI 9 no. 15701 to 18099
T-6039 – Oct 1911 to Oct 1912 – CI 9 no. 10100 to 21100
T-6040 – Oct 1912 to March 1914 – CI 9 no. 21101 to 23800
T-6041 – March 1914 to Dec 1914 – CI 9 no. 23801 to 26500
T-6042 – Dec 1914 to Oct 1915 – CI 9 no. 26501 to 29200
T-6043 – Oct 1915 to Nov 1916 – CI 9 no. 24201 to 31700
T-6044 – Nov 1916 to Oct 1918 – CI 9 no. 31701 to 34400
T-6045 – Oct 1918 to April 1920 – CI 9 no. 34401 to 37100
T-6046 – May 1913 to July 1952 – CI 9 no. 00001 to 2375

As you can see, there are two CI 9s sharing one certificate number, starting with CI 9 17286 and going up to 31399.

The CI 9 system presumed that migrants would return from the same port from which they departed. Certificates could thus be kept on file at

Vancouver and Victoria, matched with the returning migrant, and the certificates that had expired after two years would be sent to Ottawa for filing. But, as any traveller whose plans have had to change between departure and return can tell you, even those who intended to return to the same port from which they'd left did not always do so. The archive of CI 9s is full of certificates where migrants returned to Canada via a port different from the one through which they departed. Figures 2.5 to 2.12, for example, show eight men who left Canada on the SS *Bellerophon* through the Port of Victoria and were subsequently noted as having returned to Canada through the Port of Vancouver.

In each of these examples, the migrants left Victoria on the same day, 1 November 1911, but they returned at different times and to a different port. The stamp on the lower right-hand corner of each certificate, reading "Admitted at Vancouver, B.C. as per letter dated ______," does not simply indicate that their return to Vancouver was verified through a letter (presumably from an agent in Vancouver to one in Victoria), but also that this was a frequent occurrence. It was frequent enough for a stamp to have been made and yet another system (letters of verification) put into place to further refine the one already constructed (CI 9s). Keep in mind that in the case of each of the certificates pictured, there is another one that is numbered exactly the same but for an entirely different migrant who left from Vancouver instead of Victoria.

Figures 2.13 to 2.20 are the Vancouver doubles of the *Bellerophon* certificates I discuss above. Each one of these certificates shares a number with another. They are differentiated by the ports of departure, either stamped or written into the first blank space on the form. Given the primacy of the certificate number on these certificates, it is surprising to say the least that the entire archive holds thousands of these doubles – certificates that share one number but were issued in different cities to different migrants. Threaded throughout the archive, these doubles were not considered a deficiency in the system. The Department of Trade and Commerce seems very confident that having one set of certificates issued from Victoria, and another set issued from Vancouver using the very same numbers, would not pose any kind of problem for the management of these files. Still, even if the certificates from Vancouver and Victoria were always perfectly siloed, even if they never crossed or mixed, these doubles suggest that the primacy of the certificate number as a central part of document retrieval is flawed. The number alone does not suffice. It never did.

In addition to the problems attendant upon relying on certificate numbers, there is also the issue of the names themselves. At least in the case of Wong Lin Foon, the characters correspond to the transliteration. As I

The Department of Trade and Commerce

CHINESE IMMIGRATION BRANCH

C. I. 9

No. 18434

NOV 1 1911 191

To the Collector of Customs,

Port of VICTORIA, B. C.

I hereby give notice that I desire to leave Canada with the intention of returning thereto.

I propose to sail or depart from VICTORIA, B. C. for Hongkong on the S.S. Bellerophon day of NOV 1 1911 19

I intend to return to Canada at the port of (1)

I request registration and I attach my photograph hereto and give the following information for the purpose of my identification on my return.

My proper name is Wong Lun

I am sometimes known as —

I first came to Canada in the year 1900

My place of residence in Canada is Vancouver

Where I have resided since ~~the year~~ 8 yrs

Certificate of Registration Form C. I. 5, No. 26862

My present occupation is that of merchant

My place of birth was Pong Won

My present age is 40

Height 5 feet 4½ inches.

Facial marks or other peculiarities:—

Scar inner corner R eye. Scar above both ears. Scar on chin

I am personally known to Gee Lai and Sum Mon both of VICTORIA, B. C. to whom I would refer you for correctness of statements herein made.

倫黃

(Signature of Chinese Person)

Particulars and photograph hereon shown compared with applicant and approved by me this day. A. [illegible] (Customs Officer.) Dated at VICTORIA, B. C. NOV 1 1911, 19

I have personally examined the person of Chinese origin who claims to be the person above described and whose photograph is affixed hereon, (2) who returned to Canada on the day of 19 and declare him to be the same person.

(Customs Officer.)

Dated at VICTORIA, B. C. , 19

Admitted at Vancouver, B. C. as per letter dated 17/9/12

(1) If the person of Chinese origin desires to return to Canada by any other port other than the port of departure this form must be taken in duplicate and the duplicate forwarded to the intended port of entry by mail.
(2) The initials of the Customs Officer should be affixed in ink so that a portion thereof overlaps the photograph.

(OVER)

Fig. 2.5
CI 9 No. 18434, Reel no. T-6039.

Fig. 2.6 (opposite)
CI 9 No. 18445, Reel no. T-6039.

The Department of Trade and Commerce

CHINESE IMMIGRATION BRANCH

C. I.
9

No. 18445

NOV 1 1911 191

To the Collector of Customs,

Port of VICTORIA, B. C.

I hereby give notice that I desire to leave Canada with the intention of returning thereto.

I propose to sail or depart from VICTORIA, B. C. for HongKong

on the S.S. Bellerophon day of NOV 1 1911 19

I intend to return to Canada at the port of (1)

I request registration and I attach my photograph hereto and give the following information for the purpose of my identification on my return.

My proper name is # Wong How

I am sometimes known as

I first came to Canada in the year 1908

My place of residence in Canada is Winnipeg

Where I have resided since ~~the year~~ 3 yrs

Certificate of Registration Form C. I. 5, No. lost

My present occupation is that of Laundry

My place of birth was Nam Chun

My present age is 37

Height 5' feet 4½ inches.

Facial marks or other peculiarities :—

mole between eyes.
Pit. L. side neck
mole R side neck

PHOTOGRAPH.
(See note (2) below.)

I am personally known to Ying Shong and Ying Dor

both of VICTORIA, B. C. to whom I would refer you for correctness of statements herein made.

WONG HOW
(Signature of Chinese Person)

Particulars and photograph hereon shown compared with applicant and approved by me this day. NOV 1 1911, 19 A. Monteith (Customs Officer.) Dated at VICTORIA, B. C.

I have personally examined the person of Chinese origin who claims to be the person above described and whose photograph is affixed hereon, (2) who returned to Canada on the day of 19 and declare him to be the same person.

(Customs Officer.)

Admitted at Vancouver, B. C. as per letter dated 17/7/1912

Dated at VICTORIA, B. C. , 19

(1) If the person of Chinese origin desires to return to Canada by any other port other than the port of departure, this form must be taken in duplicate and the duplicate forwarded to the intended port of entry by mail.
(2) The initials of the Customs Officer should be affixed in ink so that a portion thereof overlaps the photograph.

(OVER)

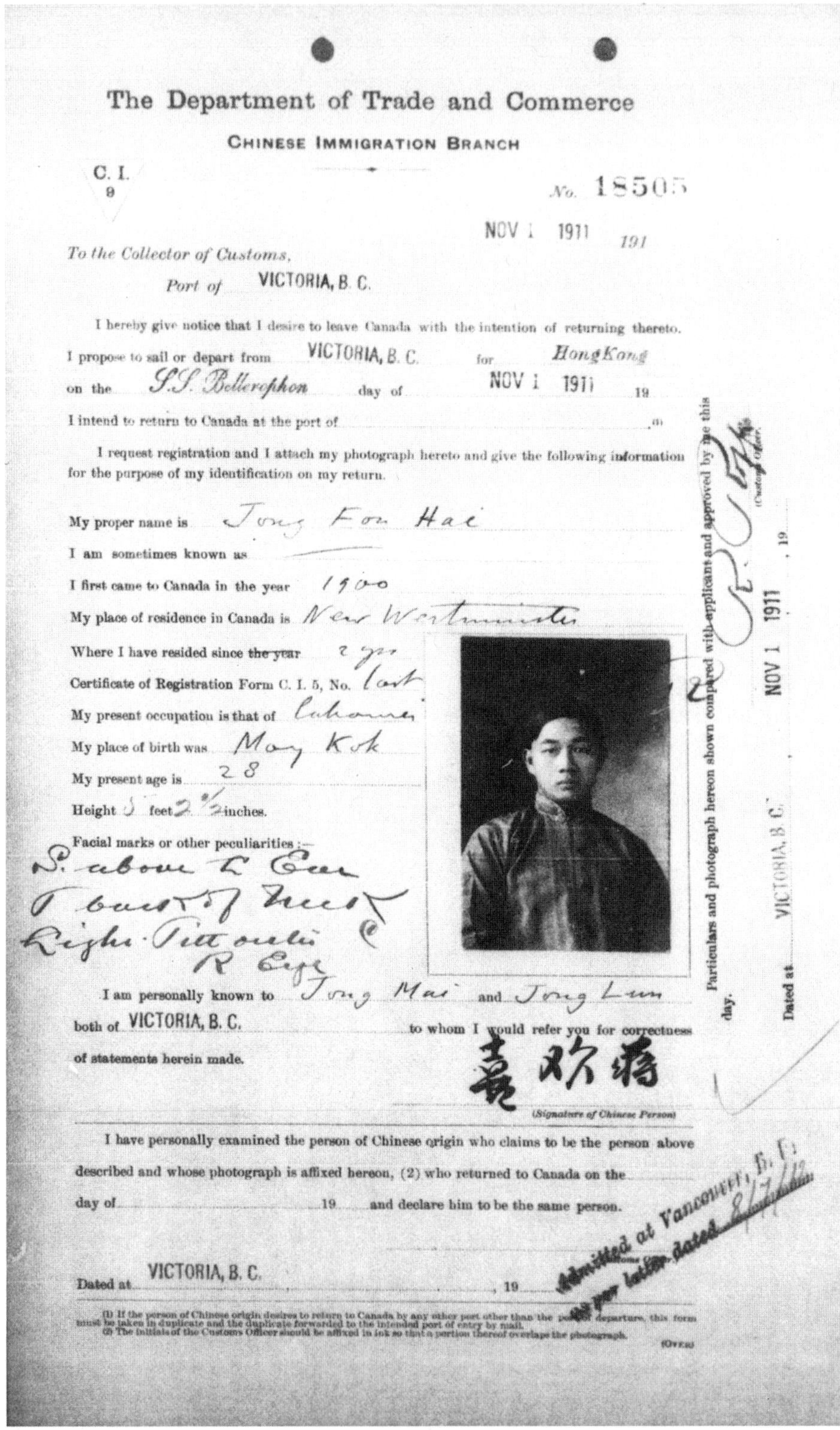
The Department of Trade and Commerce

CHINESE IMMIGRATION BRANCH

C. I.
9

No. 18505

NOV 1 1911 191

To the Collector of Customs,

Port of VICTORIA, B. C.

I hereby give notice that I desire to leave Canada with the intention of returning thereto.

I propose to sail or depart from VICTORIA, B. C. for HongKong

on the S.S. Bellerophon day of NOV 1 1911 19

I intend to return to Canada at the port of (1)

I request registration and I attach my photograph hereto and give the following information for the purpose of my identification on my return.

My proper name is Jong Fon Hai

I am sometimes known as —

I first came to Canada in the year 1900

My place of residence in Canada is New Westminster

Where I have resided since ~~the year~~ 2 yrs

Certificate of Registration Form C. I. 5, No. lost

My present occupation is that of Laborer

My place of birth was Moy Kok

My present age is 28

Height 5 feet 2 1/2 inches.

Facial marks or other peculiarities:

I am personally known to Jong Mai and Jong Lum

both of VICTORIA, B. C. to whom I would refer you for correctness of statements herein made.

(Signature of Chinese Person)

I have personally examined the person of Chinese origin who claims to be the person above described and whose photograph is affixed hereon, (2) who returned to Canada on the day of 19 and declare him to be the same person.

Dated at VICTORIA, B. C. , 19

Admitted at Vancouver, B. C. per letter dated

Particulars and photograph hereon shown compared with applicant and approved by me this day. Dated at VICTORIA, B. C. NOV 1 1911, 19

(Customs Officer)

(1) If the person of Chinese origin desires to return to Canada by any other port other than the port of departure, this form must be taken in duplicate and the duplicate forwarded to the intended port of entry by mail.
(2) The initials of the Customs Officer should be affixed in ink so that a portion thereof overlaps the photograph.

(Over)

Fig. 2.7
CI 9 No. 18505, Reel no. T-6039.

Fig. 2.8 (opposite)
CI 9 No. 18577, Reel no. T-6039.

The Department of Trade and Commerce

CHINESE IMMIGRATION BRANCH

C. I.
9

No. **18577**

NOV 1 1911 191

To the Collector of Customs,

Port of VICTORIA, B. C.

I hereby give notice that I desire to leave Canada with the intention of returning thereto.

I propose to sail or depart from VICTORIA, B. C. for HONG KONG,

on the *S.S. Bellerophon* day of NOV 1 1911 19

I intend to return to Canada at the port of .(1)

I request registration and I attach my photograph hereto and give the following information for the purpose of my identification on my return.

My proper name is *Chin Ming Yin*

I am sometimes known as

I first came to Canada in the year *1899*

My place of residence in Canada is *Nanaimo*

Where I have resided since ~~the year~~ *6 yrs*

Certificate of Registration Form C. I. 5, No. *Cft.*

My present occupation is that of *Labourer*

My place of birth was *Yok Wai*

My present age is *38*

Height *5* feet *4* inches.

Facial marks or other peculiarities :—

Pitts both C mouth
S front of neck
Pitts under L jaw

I am personally known to *Chin Chee* and *Chin Yan*

both of VICTORIA, B. C. to whom I would refer you for correctness of statements herein made.

陳明現

(Signature of Chinese Person)

Particulars and photograph hereon shown compared with applicant and approved by me this day.

Dated at VICTORIA, B. C. NOV 1 1911, 19

[illegible] (Customs Officer.)

I have personally examined the person of Chinese origin who claims to be the person above described and whose photograph is affixed hereon, (2) who returned to Canada on the day of 19 and declare him to be the same person.

(Customs Officer.)

Dated at VICTORIA, B. C. , 19

Admitted at Vancouver, B.C. as per letter dated 17/9/12

(1) If the person of Chinese origin desires to return to Canada by any other port other than the port of departure, this form must be taken in duplicate and the duplicate forwarded to the intended port of entry by mail.
(2) The initials of the Customs Officer should be affixed in ink so that a portion thereof overlaps the photograph.

(OVER)

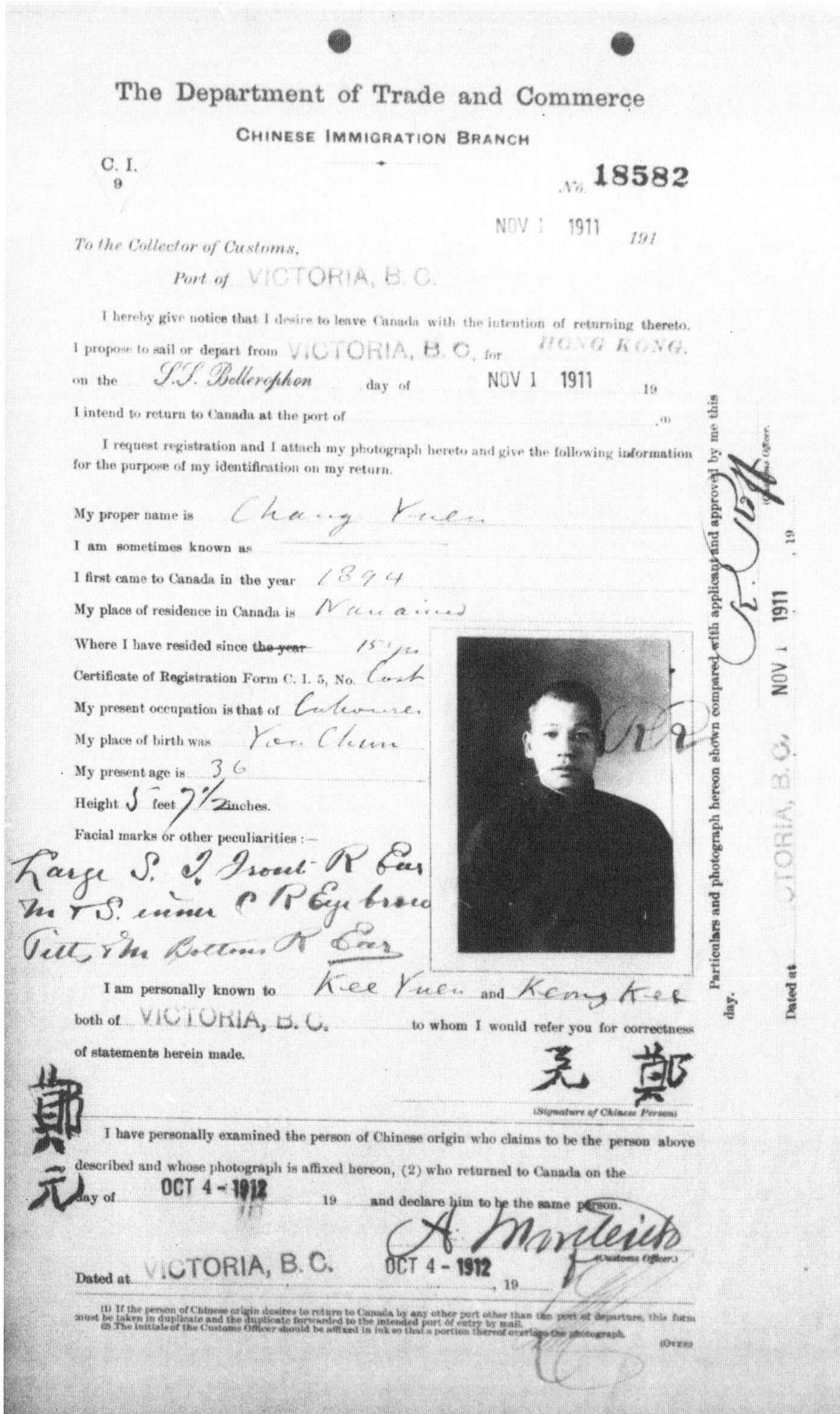

The Department of Trade and Commerce

CHINESE IMMIGRATION BRANCH

C. I. 9 No. 18582

NOV 1 1911 191

To the Collector of Customs,

Port of VICTORIA, B. C.

I hereby give notice that I desire to leave Canada with the intention of returning thereto. I propose to sail or depart from VICTORIA, B. C. for HONG KONG, on the S.S. Bellerophon day of NOV 1 1911 19

I intend to return to Canada at the port of ,(1)

I request registration and I attach my photograph hereto and give the following information for the purpose of my identification on my return.

My proper name is Chang Yuen

I am sometimes known as

I first came to Canada in the year 1894

My place of residence in Canada is Nanaimo

Where I have resided since ~~the year~~ 15 yrs

Certificate of Registration Form C. I. 5, No. Lost

My present occupation is that of [illegible]

My place of birth was [illegible]

My present age is 36

Height 5 feet 7½ inches.

Facial marks or other peculiarities: — [illegible]

I am personally known to Kee Yuen and Kong Kee both of VICTORIA, B. C. to whom I would refer you for correctness of statements herein made.

元 鄭

(Signature of Chinese Person)

Particulars and photograph hereon shown compared with applicant and approved by me this day. Dated at VICTORIA, B. C. NOV 1 1911, 19 (Customs Officer.)

I have personally examined the person of Chinese origin who claims to be the person above described and whose photograph is affixed hereon, (2) who returned to Canada on the day of OCT 4 - 1912 19 and declare him to be the same person.

A. Monteith (Customs Officer.)

Dated at VICTORIA, B. C. OCT 4 - 1912, 19

(1) If the person of Chinese origin desires to return to Canada by any other port other than the port of departure, this form must be taken in duplicate and the duplicate forwarded to the intended port of entry by mail.
(2) The initials of the Customs Officer should be affixed in ink so that a portion thereof overlaps the photograph.

(OVER)

Fig. 2.9
CI 9 No. 18582, Reel no. T-6039.

Fig. 2.10 (opposite)
CI 9 No. 18583, Reel no. T-6039.

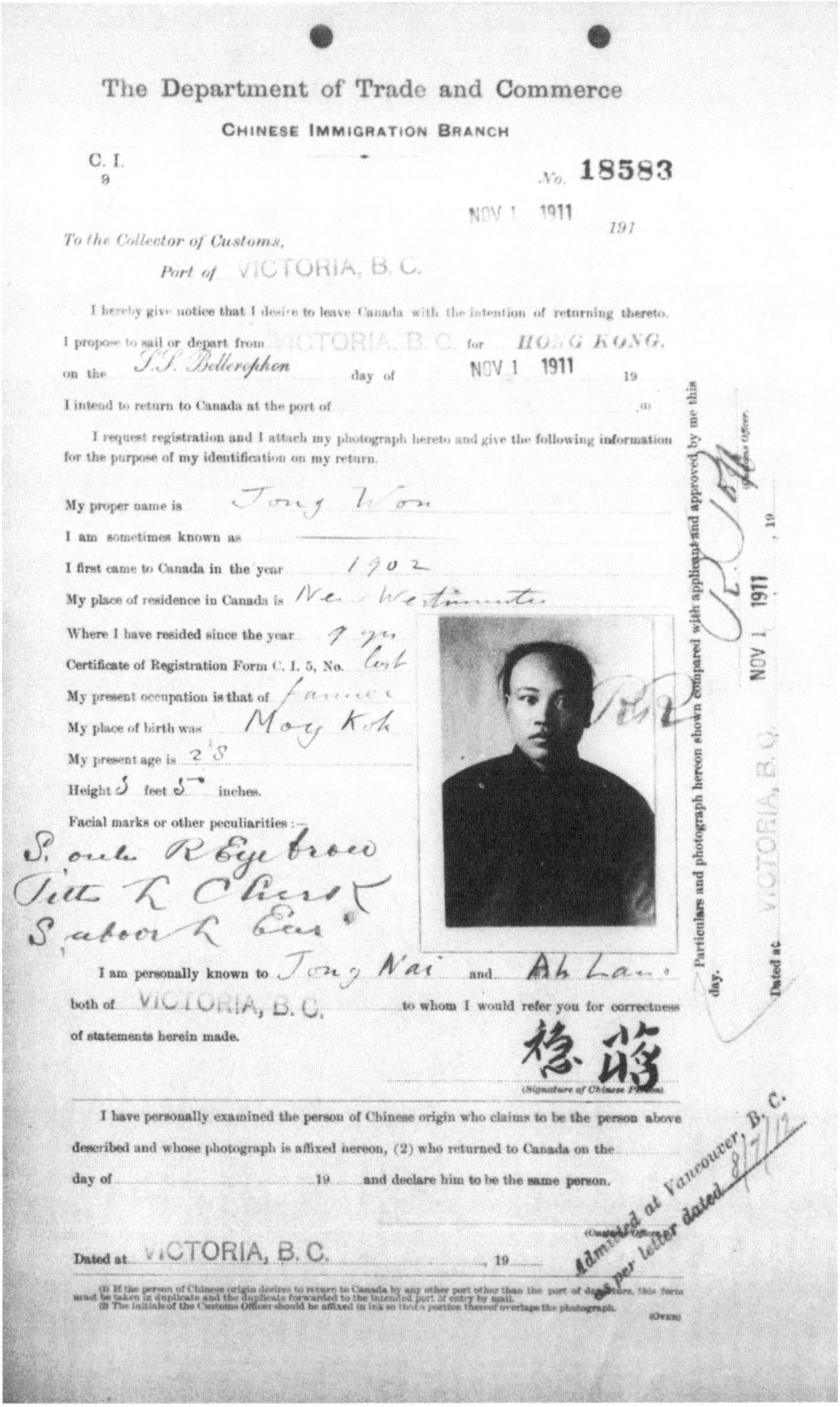

The Department of Trade and Commerce

CHINESE IMMIGRATION BRANCH

C. I.
9

No. 18583

NOV 1 1911 191

To the Collector of Customs,

Port of VICTORIA, B.C.

I hereby give notice that I desire to leave Canada with the intention of returning thereto. I propose to sail or depart from VICTORIA, B.C. for HONG KONG, on the S.S. Bellerophon day of NOV 1 1911 19

I intend to return to Canada at the port of (1)

I request registration and I attach my photograph hereto and give the following information for the purpose of my identification on my return.

My proper name is Tong Won

I am sometimes known as

I first came to Canada in the year 1902

My place of residence in Canada is New Westminster

Where I have resided since the year 9 yrs

Certificate of Registration Form C. I. 5, No. Lost

My present occupation is that of farmer

My place of birth was Moy Kok

My present age is 28

Height 5 feet 5 inches.

Facial marks or other peculiarities :—

S. outer R Eyebrow
Pitt L Cheek
S. above L Ear

I am personally known to Tong Nai and Ah Lan
both of VICTORIA, B.C. to whom I would refer you for correctness of statements herein made.

穩蔣

(Signature of Chinese Person)

I have personally examined the person of Chinese origin who claims to be the person above described and whose photograph is affixed hereon, (2) who returned to Canada on the day of 19 and declare him to be the same person.

(Customs Officer)

Dated at VICTORIA, B.C., 19

(1) If the person of Chinese origin desires to return to Canada by any other port other than the port of departure, this form must be taken in duplicate and the duplicate forwarded to the intended port of entry by mail.
(2) The initials of the Customs Officer should be affixed in ink so that a portion thereof overlaps the photograph.

(OVER)

Particulars and photograph hereon shown compared with applicant and approved by me this day. NOV 1 1911, 19

Customs Officer.

Dated at VICTORIA, B.C.

Admitted at Vancouver, B.C. as per letter dated 8/7/12

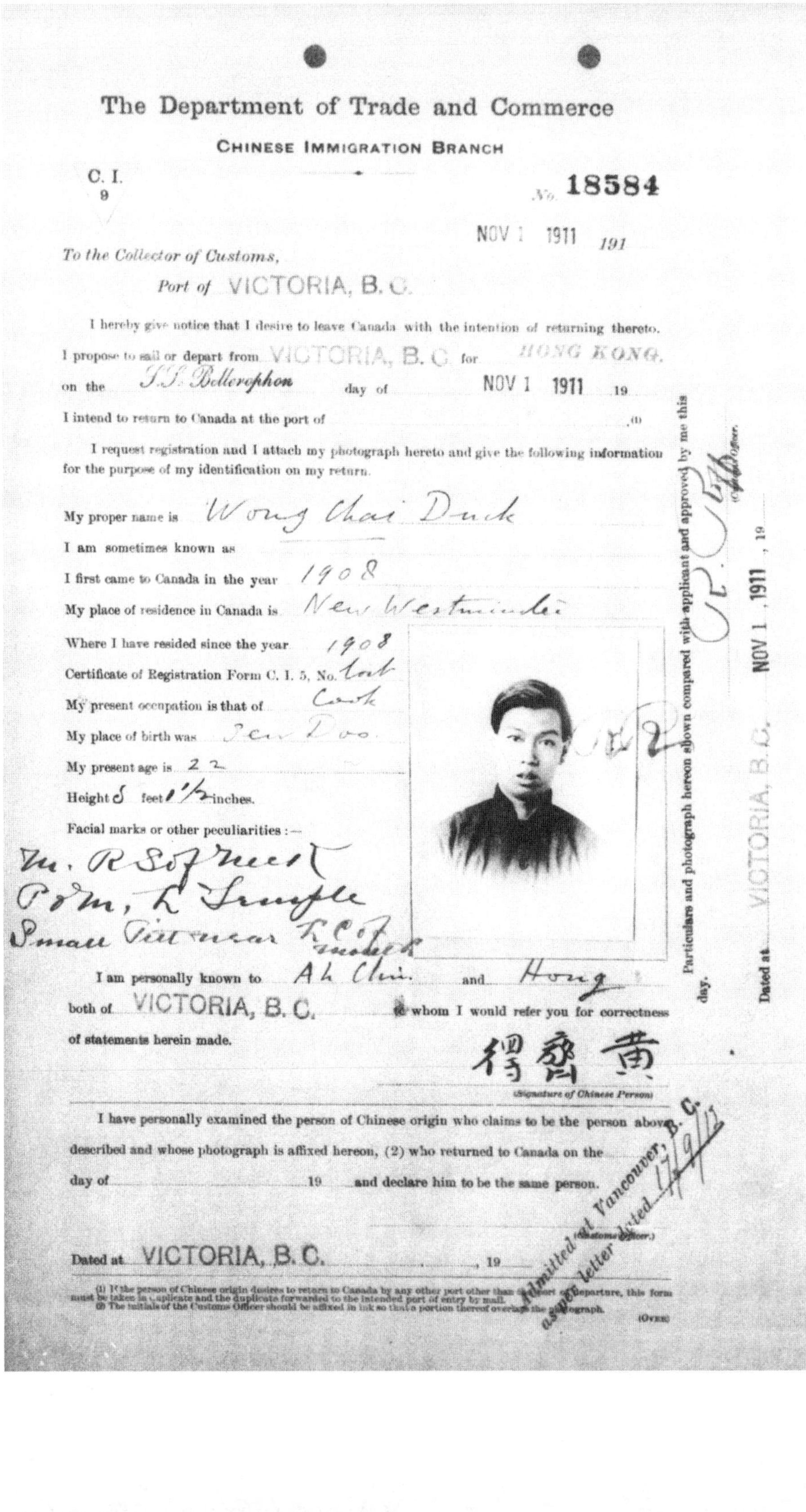

The Department of Trade and Commerce

CHINESE IMMIGRATION BRANCH

C. I. 9

No. 18584

NOV 1 1911 191

To the Collector of Customs,

Port of VICTORIA, B. C.

I hereby give notice that I desire to leave Canada with the intention of returning thereto. I propose to sail or depart from VICTORIA, B. C. for HONG KONG. on the S.S. Bellerophon day of NOV 1 1911 19

I intend to return to Canada at the port of (1)

I request registration and I attach my photograph hereto and give the following information for the purpose of my identification on my return.

My proper name is Wong Chai Duck

I am sometimes known as

I first came to Canada in the year 1908

My place of residence in Canada is New Westminster

Where I have resided since the year 1908

Certificate of Registration Form C. I. 5, No. Cat

My present occupation is that of Cook

My place of birth was Sen Doo

My present age is 22

Height 5 feet 1½ inches.

Facial marks or other peculiarities :—

M. R S of neck

P & m, L temple

Small Pitt near R C of mouth

I am personally known to Ah Chin and Hong

both of VICTORIA, B. C. to whom I would refer you for correctness of statements herein made.

得齊黄

(Signature of Chinese Person)

Particulars and photograph hereon shown compared with applicant and approved by me this day. NOV 1, 1911, 19

(Customs Officer.)

Dated at VICTORIA, B. C.

I have personally examined the person of Chinese origin who claims to be the person above described and whose photograph is affixed hereon, (2) who returned to Canada on the day of 19 and declare him to be the same person.

(Customs Officer.)

Dated at VICTORIA, B. C. , 19

Admitted at Vancouver, B. C. as per letter dated 17/9/13

(1) If the person of Chinese origin desires to return to Canada by any other port other than the port of departure, this form must be taken in duplicate and the duplicate forwarded to the intended port of entry by mail.
(2) The initials of the Customs Officer should be affixed in ink so that a portion thereof overlaps the photograph.

(OVER)

Fig. 2.11
CI 9 No. 18584, Reel no. T-6039.

Fig. 2.12 (opposite)
CI 9 No. 18596, Reel no. T-6039.

The Department of Trade and Commerce

CHINESE IMMIGRATION BRANCH

C. I.
9

No. **18596**

NOV 1 1911 191

To the Collector of Customs,

Port of VICTORIA, B. C.

I hereby give notice that I desire to leave Canada with the intention of returning thereto.

I propose to sail or depart from VICTORIA, B. C. for HONG KONG, on the S.S. Bellerophon day of NOV 1 1911 19

I intend to return to Canada at the port of .... (1)

I request registration and I attach my photograph hereto and give the following information for the purpose of my identification on my return.

My proper name is Wong Foo

I am sometimes known as

I first came to Canada in the year 1902

My place of residence in Canada is Montreal

Where I have resided since ~~the year~~ 8 yrs

Certificate of Registration Form C. I. 5, No. Lost

My present occupation is that of Laundry

My place of birth was Kee Boy

My present age is 38

Height 5 feet 2 inches.

Facial marks or other peculiarities :—

S. L Eye Lid
P both Cheek Bone
m. under R Jaw

PHOTOGRAPH.

I am personally known to Ma Chan and Ma Sen both of VICTORIA, B. C. to whom I would refer you for correctness of statements herein made.

富黃

(Signature of Chinese Person)

I have personally examined the person of Chinese origin who claims to be the person above described and whose photograph is affixed hereon, (2) who returned to Canada on the day of .... 19 ...... and declare him to be the same person.

Admitted at Vancouver, B. C. as per letter dated 8/10/12

(Customs Officer.)

Dated at VICTORIA, B. C. ...., 19......

Particulars and photograph hereon shown compared with applicant and approved by me this day.

Dated at VICTORIA, B. C. NOV 1 1911, 19

(Customs Officer.)

(1) If the person of Chinese origin desires to return to Canada by any other port other than the port of departure, this form must be taken in duplicate and the duplicate forwarded to the intended port of entry by mail.
(2) The initials of the Customs Officer should be affixed in ink so that a portion thereof overlaps the photograph.

(OVER)

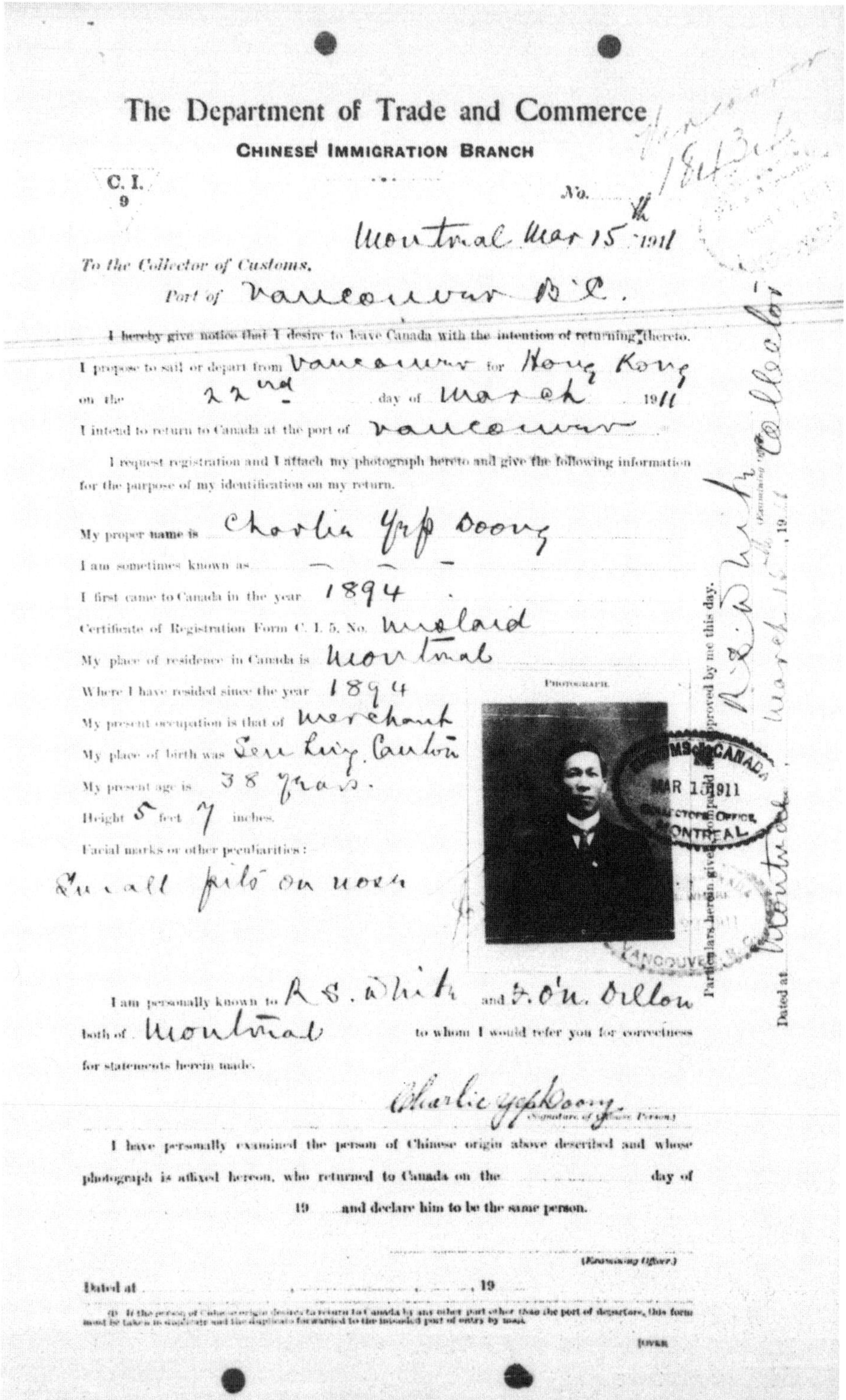

The Department of Trade and Commerce

CHINESE IMMIGRATION BRANCH

C. I. 9

No. ......

Montreal Mar 15th 1911

To the Collector of Customs,

Port of Vancouver B.C.

I hereby give notice that I desire to leave Canada with the intention of returning thereto.

I propose to sail or depart from Vancouver for Hong Kong on the 22nd day of March 1911

I intend to return to Canada at the port of Vancouver

I request registration and I attach my photograph hereto and give the following information for the purpose of my identification on my return.

My proper name is Charlie Yip Doong

I am sometimes known as — — –

I first came to Canada in the year 1894.

Certificate of Registration Form C. I. 5, No. inland

My place of residence in Canada is Montreal

Where I have resided since the year 1894

My present occupation is that of merchant

My place of birth was Sun Ling Canton

My present age is 38 years.

Height 5 feet 7 inches.

Facial marks or other peculiarities:

Small pile on nose

PHOTOGRAPH.

CUSTOMS CANADA MAR 15 1911 COLLECTOR'S OFFICE, MONTREAL

I am personally known to R S. White and J. O'N. Dillon both of Montreal to whom I would refer you for correctness for statements herein made.

Charlie Yip Doong (Signature of Chinese Person.)

Particulars herein given approved by me this day.

Dated at Montreal March 15th 1911 R S White Collector

I have personally examined the person of Chinese origin above described and whose photograph is affixed hereon, who returned to Canada on the .... day of .... 19 ...... and declare him to be the same person.

(Examining Officer.)

Dated at .... 19 ......

(1) If the person of Chinese origin desires to return to Canada by any other port other than the port of departure, this form must be taken in duplicate and the duplicate forwarded to the intended port of entry by mail.

(OVER)

Fig. 2.13
CI 9 No. 18434, Reel no. T-6047.

Fig. 2.14 (opposite)
CI 9 No. 18445, Reel no. T-6047.

The Department of Trade and Commerce

CHINESE IMMIGRATION BRANCH

C. I.
9

No. 18445

Vancouver ... 191

To the Collector of Customs,

Port of Vancouver

I hereby give notice that I desire to leave Canada with the intention of returning thereto.

I propose to sail or depart from ... for Hong Kong.

on the ... day of APR 19 1911 19

I intend to return to Canada at the port of ...

I request registration and I attach my photograph hereto and give the following information for the purpose of my identification on my return.

My proper name is Chan Soone

I am sometimes known as

I first came to Canada in the year 1909 (Victoria Aug. Empress - a face)

Certificate of Registration Form C. I. 5, No. Lost

My place of residence in Canada is Vancouver

Where I have resided since the year 2 years

My present occupation is that of Actor

My place of birth was Sun Ning

My present age is 26

Height 5 feet 5 inches.

Facial marks or other peculiarities:

Pit on each temple
Scar left side forehead
Scar front right ear

Particulars herein given, compared and approved by me this day.

(Examining Officer.)

Dated at ... 1911, 19

I am personally known to Sue Lai Cheng and

both of Vancouver, B.C. to whom I would refer you for correctness for statements herein made.

順陳

(Signature of Chinese Person.)

I have personally examined the person of Chinese origin above described and whose photograph is affixed hereon, who returned to Canada on the ... day of ... 19 and declare him to be the same person.

(Examining Officer.)

Dated at ..., 19

(1) If the person of Chinese origin desires to return to Canada by any other port other than the port of departure, this form must be taken in duplicate and the duplicate forwarded to the intended port of entry by mail.

(OVER)

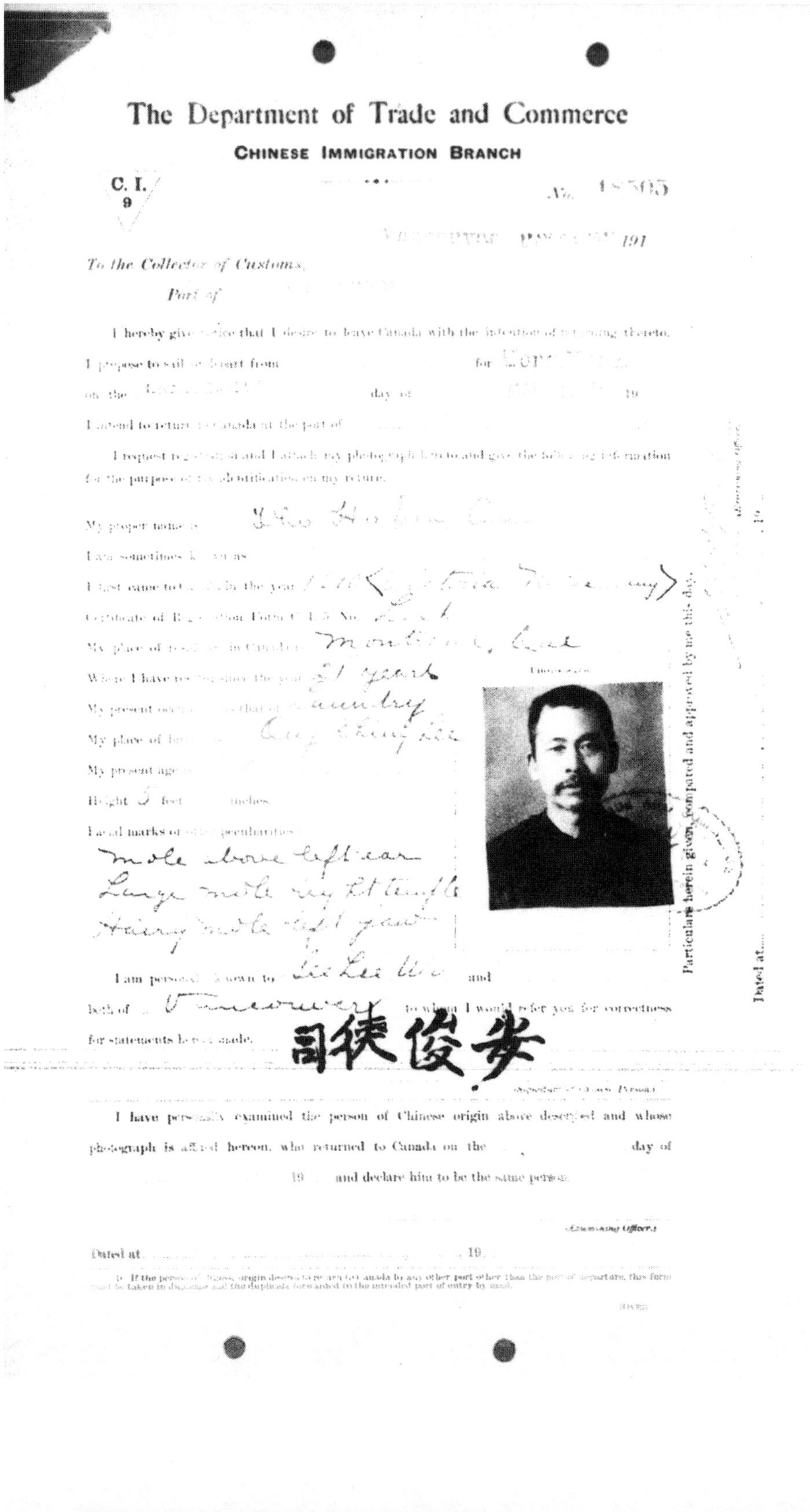

The Department of Trade and Commerce

CHINESE IMMIGRATION BRANCH

C. I. 9

No. 18505

To the Collector of Customs,

Port of

Hereby give notice that I desire to leave Canada with the intention of returning thereto.

I propose to sail or depart from for

on the day of 19

I intend to return to Canada at the port of

I request registration and I attach my photograph hereto and give the following information for the purpose of my identification on my return.

My proper name is

I am sometimes known as

I first came to Canada in the year

Certificate of Registration Form C.I. 5 No.

My place of residence in Canada: Montreal, Que

Where I have resided since the year: 21 years

My present occupation: Laundry

My place of birth

My present age

Height 5 feet inches

Facial marks or other peculiarities:

Mole above left ear

Large mole right temple

Hairy mole left jaw

I am personally known to and

both of Vancouver to whom I would refer you for correctness for statements herein made.

司徒俊安

Signature of Chinese Person

I have personally examined the person of Chinese origin above described and whose photograph is affixed hereon, who returned to Canada on the day of 19 and declare him to be the same person.

Examining Officer

Dated at 19

Particulars herein given compared and approved by me this day.

Dated at

Fig. 2.15
CI 9 No. 18505, Reel no. T-6047.

Fig. 2.16 (opposite)
CI 9 No. 18577, Reel no. T-6047.

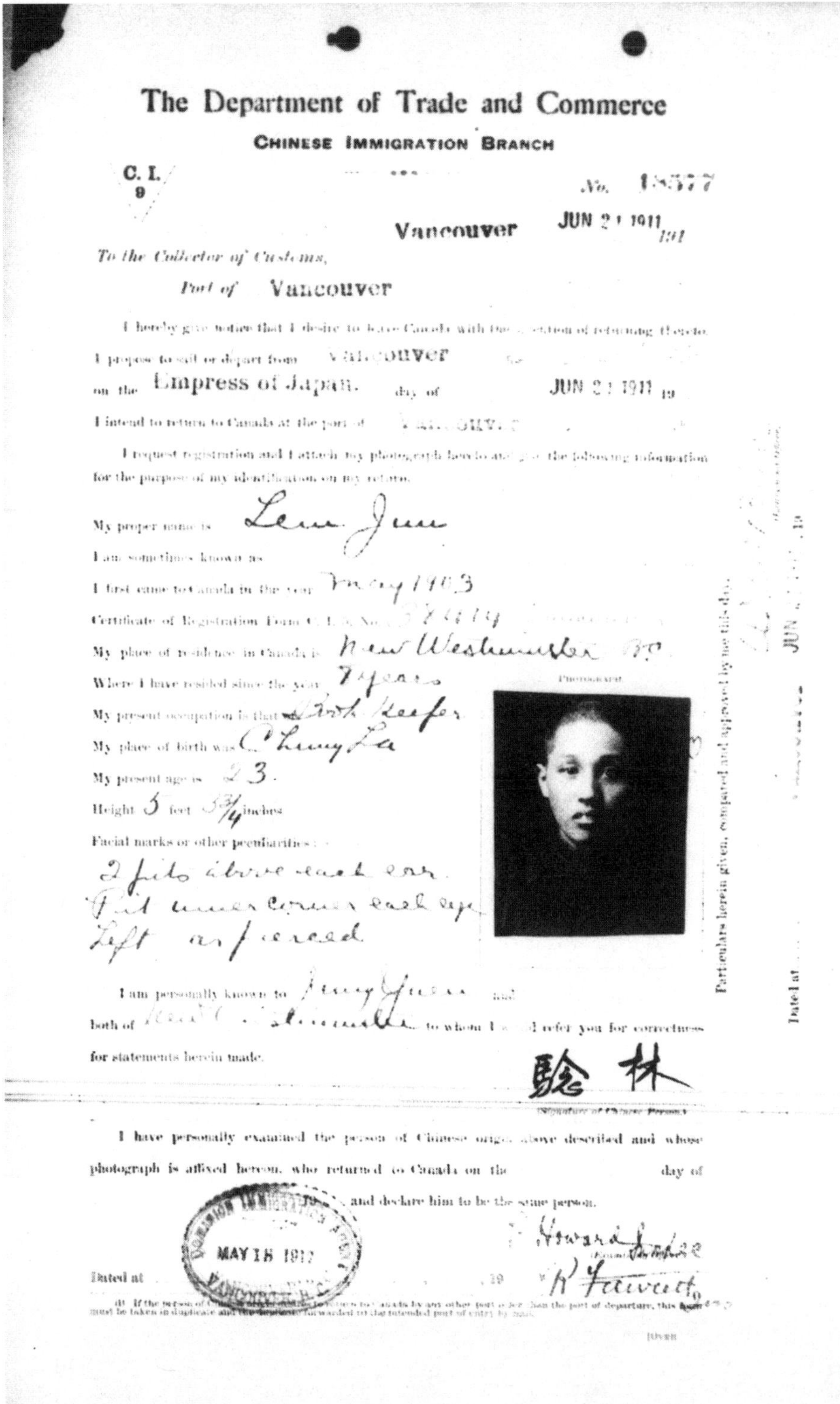

The Department of Trade and Commerce

CHINESE IMMIGRATION BRANCH

C. I. 9

No. 18377

Vancouver JUN 21 1911

To the Collector of Customs,

Port of Vancouver

I hereby give notice that I desire to leave Canada with the intention of returning thereto.

I propose to sail or depart from Vancouver

on the Empress of Japan. day of JUN 21 1911

I intend to return to Canada at the port of Vancouver

I request registration and I attach my photograph hereto and give the following information for the purpose of my identification on my return.

My proper name is Lem Jun

I am sometimes known as

I first came to Canada in the year May 1903

Certificate of Registration Form C.I. 5, No. 78414

My place of residence in Canada is New Westminster B.C.

Where I have resided since the year 7 years

My present occupation is that Book keeper

My place of birth was Chung La

My present age is 23.

Height 5 feet 3¾ inches

Facial marks or other peculiarities:

2 pits above each ear.
Pit inner corner each eye
Left ear pierced

Photograph

I am personally known to Jung Juen and

both of New Westminster to whom I would refer you for correctness for statements herein made.

林驗

(Signature of Chinese Person)

I have personally examined the person of Chinese origin above described and whose photograph is affixed hereon, who returned to Canada on the day of 19 , and declare him to be the same person.

Dominion Immigration Agent
MAY 18 1912
Vancouver, B.C.

Howard Loder

Dated at 19

R Fawcett

Particulars herein given, compared and approved by me this day

Dated at JUN 19

(1) If the person of Chinese origin returns to Canada by any other port or her than the port of departure, this form must be taken in duplicate and the duplicate forwarded to the intended port of entry by mail.

[OVER]

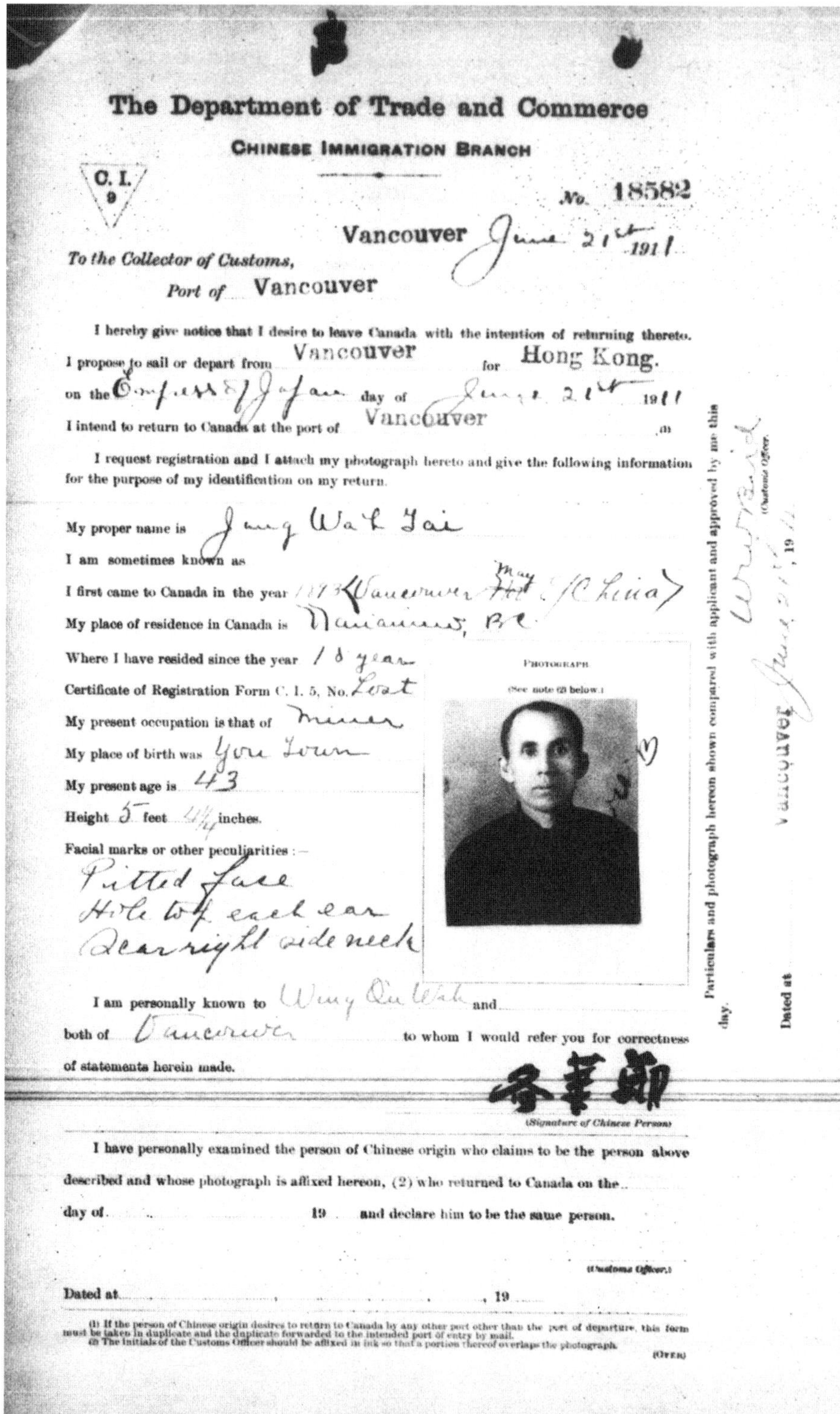

The Department of Trade and Commerce

CHINESE IMMIGRATION BRANCH

C. I. 9

No. 18582

Vancouver June 21st 1911

To the Collector of Customs,

Port of Vancouver

I hereby give notice that I desire to leave Canada with the intention of returning thereto.

I propose to sail or depart from Vancouver for Hong Kong.

on the Empress of Japan day of June 21st 1911

I intend to return to Canada at the port of Vancouver (1)

I request registration and I attach my photograph hereto and give the following information for the purpose of my identification on my return.

My proper name is Jung Wah Tai

I am sometimes known as

I first came to Canada in the year 1893 (Vancouver May ... China)

My place of residence in Canada is Nanaimo, B.C.

Where I have resided since the year 18 years

Certificate of Registration Form C. I. 5, No. Lost

My present occupation is that of Miner

My place of birth was You Loun

My present age is 43

Height 5 feet 4¼ inches.

Facial marks or other peculiarities :—

Pitted face
Hole top each ear
Scar right side neck

PHOTOGRAPH (See note (2) below.)

I am personally known to Wing Ou Wah and

both of Vancouver to whom I would refer you for correctness of statements herein made.

(Signature of Chinese Person)

I have personally examined the person of Chinese origin who claims to be the person above described and whose photograph is affixed hereon, (2) who returned to Canada on the day of 19 and declare him to be the same person.

(Customs Officer.)

Dated at , 19

(1) If the person of Chinese origin desires to return to Canada by any other port other than the port of departure, this form must be taken in duplicate and the duplicate forwarded to the intended port of entry by mail.
(2) The initials of the Customs Officer should be affixed in ink so that a portion thereof overlaps the photograph.

(OVER)

Particulars and photograph hereon shown compared with applicant and approved by me this day.

(Customs Officer.)

Dated at Vancouver June 21, 1911

Fig. 2.17
CI 9 No. 18582, Reel no. T-6047.

Fig. 2.18 (opposite)
CI 9 No. 18583, Reel no. T-6047.

C. I. 9

The Department of Trade and Commerce

CHINESE IMMIGRATION BRANCH

No. 18583

Vancouver June 21st 1911

To the Collector of Customs,

Port of Vancouver

I hereby give notice that I desire to leave Canada with the intention of returning thereto.

I propose to sail or depart from Vancouver for Hong Kong.

on the Empress Japan day of June 21st 1911

I intend to return to Canada at the port of Vancouver (1)

I request registration and I attach my photograph hereto and give the following information for the purpose of my identification on my return.

My proper name is Leung Wong

I am sometimes known as

Sept 1910 I first came to Canada in the year 1910 (Victoria Blue Funnel Aug)

My place of residence in Canada is Vancouver

Where I have resided since the year 10 months

Certificate of Registration Form C. I. 5, No. 56248

My present occupation is that of Laborer

My place of birth was Bok Gin

My present age is 33

Height 5 feet 5 3/4 inches.

Facial marks or other peculiarities :—

Small scar centre forehead
Mole behind right ear
Mole inside left ear

PHOTOGRAPH

(See note (2) below.)

I am personally known to Lee On and

both of Vancouver to whom I would refer you for correctness of statements herein made.

(Signature of Chinese Person)

Particulars and photograph hereon shown compared with applicant and approved by me this day.

W. W. Bird (Customs Officer.)

Dated at Vancouver June 21st, 1911

I have personally examined the person of Chinese origin who claims to be the person above described and whose photograph is affixed hereon, (2) who returned to Canada on the .... day of .... 19 .... and declare him to be the same person.

(Customs Officer.)

Dated at ...., 19 ....

(1) If the person of Chinese origin desires to return to Canada by any other port other than the port of departure, this form must be taken in duplicate and the duplicate forwarded to the intended port of entry by mail.
(2) The initials of the Customs Officer should be affixed in ink so that a portion thereof overlaps the photograph.

(OVER)

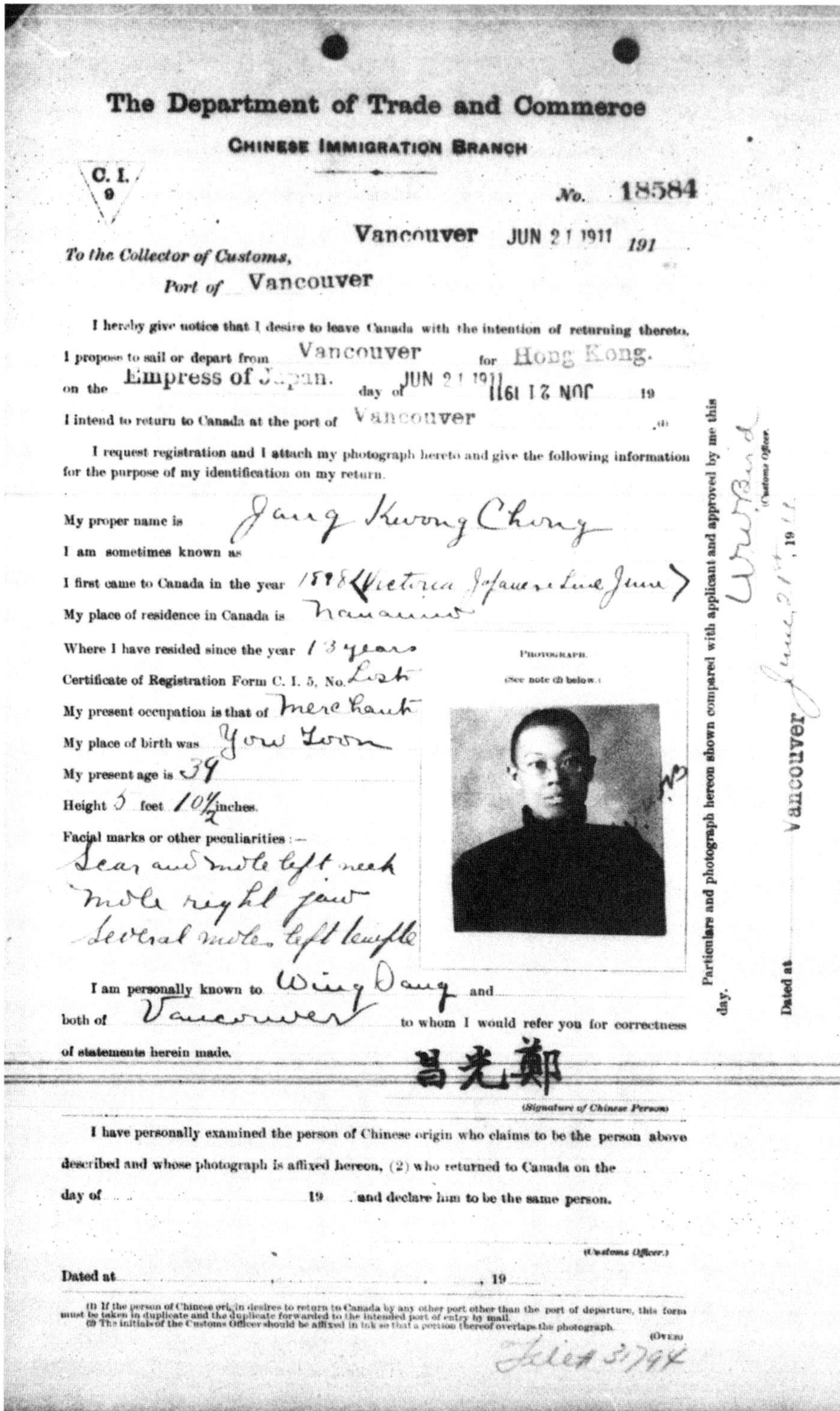
The Department of Trade and Commerce

CHINESE IMMIGRATION BRANCH

C. I. 9

No. 18584

Vancouver JUN 21 1911 191

To the Collector of Customs,

Port of Vancouver

I hereby give notice that I desire to leave Canada with the intention of returning thereto.

I propose to sail or depart from Vancouver for Hong Kong.

on the Empress of Japan. day of JUN 21 1911 19

I intend to return to Canada at the port of Vancouver

I request registration and I attach my photograph hereto and give the following information for the purpose of my identification on my return.

My proper name is Jang Kwong Chung

I am sometimes known as

I first came to Canada in the year 1898 (Victoria Japanese Line June)

My place of residence in Canada is Nanaimo

Where I have resided since the year 13 years

Certificate of Registration Form C. I. 5, No. Lost

My present occupation is that of Merchant

My place of birth was Yow Loon

My present age is 39

Height 5 feet 10½ inches.

Facial marks or other peculiarities:—

Scar and mole left neck

Mole right jaw

Several moles left knuckle

PHOTOGRAPH.

(See note (2) below.)

I am personally known to Wing Dang and

both of Vancouver to whom I would refer you for correctness of statements herein made.

鄭光昌

(Signature of Chinese Person)

Particulars and photograph hereon shown compared with applicant and approved by me this day.

W. R. Bird (Customs Officer.)

Dated at Vancouver June 21st, 1911

I have personally examined the person of Chinese origin who claims to be the person above described and whose photograph is affixed hereon, (2) who returned to Canada on the day of 19 and declare him to be the same person.

(Customs Officer.)

Dated at , 19

(1) If the person of Chinese origin desires to return to Canada by any other port other than the port of departure, this form must be taken in duplicate and the duplicate forwarded to the intended port of entry by mail.

(2) The initials of the Customs Officer should be affixed in ink so that a portion thereof overlaps the photograph.

(OVER)

File # 3194

Fig. 2.19
CI 9 No. 18584, Reel no. T-6047.

Fig. 2.20 (opposite)
CI 9 No. 18596, Reel no. T-6047.

The Department of Trade and Commerce

CHINESE IMMIGRATION BRANCH

C. I. 9

No. 18596

Vancouver JUL 1 1911 191

To the Collector of Customs,

Port of Vancouver

I hereby give notice that I desire to leave Canada with the intention of returning thereto.

I propose to sail or depart from Vancouver for Hong Kong.

on the Empress of China day of 19

I intend to return to Canada at the port of Vancouver (1)

I request registration and I attach my photograph hereto and give the following information for the purpose of my identification on my return.

My proper name is Lee Quon

I am sometimes known as

I first came to Canada in the year 1899. Summer. Vancouver. Emp. Asia

My place of residence in Canada is Winnipeg

Where I have resided since the year 1907

Certificate of Registration Form C. I. 5. No. Lost

My present occupation is that of Laundryman

My place of birth was Shin Soon

My present age is 36

Height 5 feet 2 inches 3/4

Facial marks or other peculiarities:—

hairy mole left chin
Pit right corner mouth
Mole left neck

PHOTOGRAPH.

(See note (2) below.)

I am personally known to Wong Sang and

both of Vancouver to whom I would refer you for correctness of statements herein made.

李焜

(Signature of Chinese Person)

I have personally examined the person of Chinese origin who claims to be the person above described and whose photograph is affixed hereon, (2) who returned to Canada on the day of 19 and declare him to be the same person.

DOMINION IMMIGRATION AGENT JUN 3 1912 VANCOUVER, B.C.

P. Howard Insp.

(Customs Officer.)

Dated at 19

R. Fawcett Insp.

(1) If the person of Chinese origin desires to return to Canada by any other port other than the port of departure, this form must be taken in duplicate and the duplicate forwarded to the intended port of entry by mail.
(2) The initials of the Customs Officer should be affixed in ink so that a portion thereof overlaps the photograph.

(OVER)

Particulars and photograph hereon shown compared with applicant and approved by me this day.

Dated at Vancouver JUL 1 1911 19

(Customs Officer.)

noted earlier, there is often no correspondence between the name in English and the Chinese name. For example, there is CI 9 no. 23413 (fig. 2.21). His name is given in English as “Yee Chan Kam.” He writes his name in Chinese as “奎贊余.” The Mandarin pinyin for these characters is “Kui Zan Yu.” The Cantonese pinyin (and it is much more likely that he spoke Cantonese or a dialect more closely connected to Cantonese) is “Fuk Chan Yu.” What are we to do with this riot of difference? The lack of correspondence between the anglicized name and the one in Chinese script is an indication, as I have been noting throughout this chapter, of one of the many ways in which the CI 9 system fails to capture Chinese migrants. But there is more here than just the fumblings of a state system that could not get a lot of names right. There is the possibility of agency on the part of non-citizens.

I do not wish to overstate the forms of agency available to the subjects of the CI 9s. As Michelle Caswell cautions, in the context of reading mug shots produced at Tuol Sleng or S-21 prison in Cambodia, “we must tread carefully for fear of conferring a false sense of agency on the part of the victims” (2014, 59). I recognize that the conditions under which the CI 9s were produced are hugely different than the conditions at Tuol Sleng, where “the subjects of these mug shots did not choose to be photographed, they did not have any ownership over the way they were depicted, they were acted upon against their will” (59). The CI 9 system is a far cry from the “total institution” Caswell describes (52). Still, Caswell’s caution against a “concept of co-creatorship [as] a fallacy that grants too much agency to the subjects of these photos” remains important when attempting to find agency in oppressive photography (59). The Chinese migrants in the CI 9 photographs were not agents or co-creators of the CI 9 archive. However, as the discrepancy between Chinese and anglicized names indicates, there is the possibility of small acts of refusal.

Understanding that a significant portion of the head tax certificates in this archive are, at some level, fictional, given the scanty correspondence between the Chinese name and its anglicized counterpart, the CI 9 certificates are not so much an archive of state repression as of subaltern ingenuity. I am not necessarily suggesting that migrants deliberately sought to delude the controllers. Certainly, some might have. However, I am interested in the possibilities of more passive forms of dissimulation. A lapse here; a decision not to correct a mistake there. A shrug of the shoulders when one realizes that the bureaucrat on the other side of the table has bungled one’s name beyond all recognition. These are small resistances

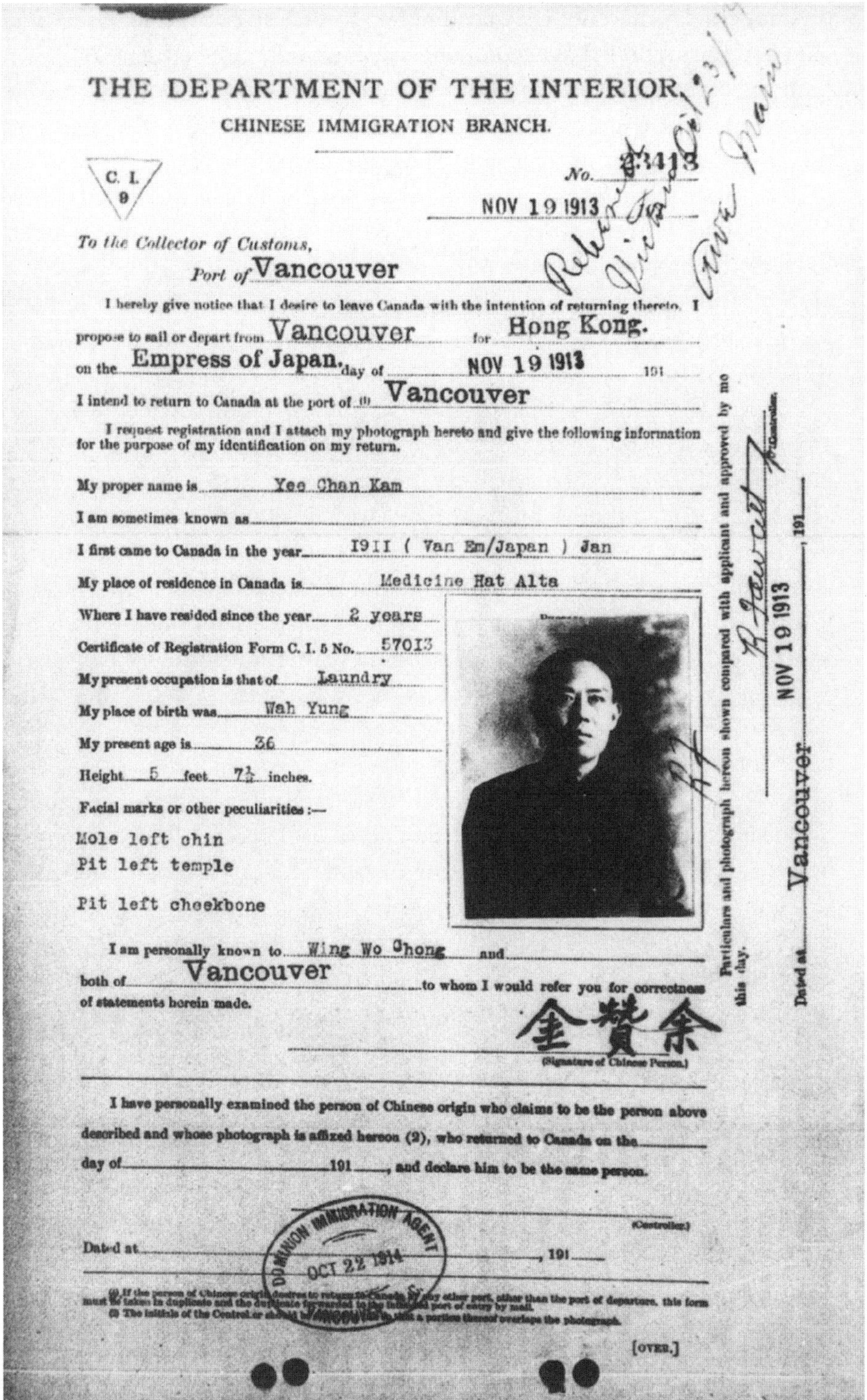

THE DEPARTMENT OF THE INTERIOR.

CHINESE IMMIGRATION BRANCH.

C. I. 9

No. 23413

NOV 19 1913

To the Collector of Customs,

Port of Vancouver

I hereby give notice that I desire to leave Canada with the intention of returning thereto. I propose to sail or depart from Vancouver for Hong Kong. on the Empress of Japan. day of NOV 19 1913 191

I intend to return to Canada at the port of (1) Vancouver

I request registration and I attach my photograph hereto and give the following information for the purpose of my identification on my return.

My proper name is Yee Chan Kam

I am sometimes known as

I first came to Canada in the year 1911 (Van Em/Japan) Jan

My place of residence in Canada is Medicine Hat Alta

Where I have resided since the year 2 years

Certificate of Registration Form C. I. 5 No. 57013

My present occupation is that of Laundry

My place of birth was Wah Yung

My present age is 36

Height 5 feet 7½ inches.

Facial marks or other peculiarities :—

Mole left chin

Pit left temple

Pit left cheekbone

I am personally known to Wing Wo Chong and

both of Vancouver to whom I would refer you for correctness of statements herein made.

余贊金

(Signature of Chinese Person.)

Particulars and photograph hereon shown compared with applicant and approved by me this day.

Dated at Vancouver NOV 19 1913 191

I have personally examined the person of Chinese origin who claims to be the person above described and whose photograph is affixed hereon (2), who returned to Canada on the day of 191 , and declare him to be the same person.

(Controller.)

Dated at , 191

DOMINION IMMIGRATION AGENT OCT 22 1914 VANCOUVER

(1) If the person of Chinese origin desires to return to Canada by any other port, other than the port of departure, this form must be taken in duplicate and the duplicate forwarded to the intended port of entry by mail.
(2) The initials of the Controller should be so placed that a portion thereof overlaps the photograph.

[OVER.]

Fig. 2.21
CI 9 No. 23413, Reel no. T-6049.

that nonetheless accrue. They accumulate so that, over time, an entire system, and the archive that accompanies it, can no longer be trusted.

In the cases of Wong Lin Foon and Yee Chan Kam, at least as they are known in the CI 9 archive, the photographs do not index the men that the certificates claim to represent. They, along with many others, undo the bind between identification photograph and the person identified. These photographs put into question not only the claims of the individual certificates themselves, but also those of the entire project of photographic identification. By injecting so much uncertainty into this system of mass capture, the subjects of the CI 9 photographs insistently undermine the work of capture.

Again and again, certificate after certificate, Chinese people in this archive refused the demand to be made known and knowable for the purposes of being excluded from the sphere of citizenship. The CI 9s are evidence of unknowability as one form of agency in the face of the deprivations of non-citizenship. If mass capture as a technology of non-citizenship is premised on making the non-citizen knowable to the state, this study uncovers instead a project of mass misrecognition and invisibility. In the CI 9 archive, thousands of Chinese migrants hide in plain sight.

It is not clear whether or not the state had a sense of the scope of the failure of this project of capture. It is not only the state that invested some belief in the truth-claims of head tax certificates. For example, as suggested by projects such as the Chinese Head Tax Searchable Database, developed by a team at the University of British Columbia, head tax information has been seen as one way of conducting ancestry research. That database is based on the Chinese Head Tax Register, which is similar to a ledger book that contains information on Chinese migrants transcribed from various certificates, but it does not contain the certificates themselves. Therefore, there are no identification photographs, and, given that the information in the register is copied from individual certificates, there is an even greater chance of errors than on the CI 9s.

Given the results of my research, I would caution against relying too heavily upon materials such as the head tax register as a site for genealogical research. Certainly, the CI 9s are an incredibly important and rich source of genealogical information. I do not want to take away from the importance of this information. What is more, for Chinese-Canadian people who are searching for family, given the histories of racism and persecution that these families survived, the CI 9s offer more information about individual Chinese migrants in Canada than any other set of documents. People have found their families through the CI 9s. Still, although there are many names, and many identities, it is not always the case that these are real names attached to real people. Rather, these identities should be read along a broad continuum with truth on one end and necessary fictions on the other. That there was fraud is not in doubt, and the kinds of fictions that are the basis of these frauds should be a celebrated part of the story of the CI 9s. For *Mass Capture*, these fictions are instances of the kind of ingenuity and creativity exercised by people who often had very few resources for escaping the strictures of this discriminatory system of capture and exclusion.

Of course, the state had some sense that its attempts to prevent fraud were not successful. As Laura Madokoro observes, "From the late 19th century, fake identity documents and elaborate coaching papers enabled Chinese migrants to adopt new personas and gain admission under false pretexts. Officials in white settler societies were well aware of the practice, but in the face of language barriers and brokers who benefited financially from the schemes (such as translators whose services could be purchased to facilitate entry), authorities found themselves at a loss as to how to effectively combat these practices" (2016, 98). While the Canadian government was stymied in its attempts to prevent fraud, it did attempt to punish the fraudulent. In the late 1950s, the Royal Canadian Mounted Police (RCMP) began investigating immigration fraud committed by Chinese people in Canada. "Upon confirmation of fraud in Hong Kong, the RCMP, aided by plain clothes officers from the Royal Hong Kong Police Force, raided Chinese homes and businesses across Canada. Their targets included the Chinese Benevolent Association in Vancouver, which the RCMP alleged was overseeing the paper son scheme" (119). However, this attempt at punishment was limited. Chinese community leaders lobbied intensely against what they saw as forms of discrimination based solely on race. Further, "the costs of enforcement were politically and economically high enough and the phenomenon of illegal entry sufficiently widespread to convince Canadian authorities that prosecution and deportation were not viable solutions to the problem of illegal entry. Instead of punishing paper families, the Canadian government introduced a Status Adjustment Program in 1960 whereby all those who had moved to the country illegally could confess and then apply to be naturalized, receiving all the rights of other naturalized Canadians, including family sponsorship" (ibid.). This program was, as Madokoro points out, consciously modelled after the Chinese Confession Program in the United States.

After decades of legislated discrimination and exclusion, thousands of Chinese people living in North America overcame their fears of exposure and deportation and identified themselves as illegal migrants. They did so through a formal process of confession. However, amnesty was not a guaranteed outcome, given that "the state-proffered solution" left Chinese migrants "susceptible to the subjective operation of power: they were accused and interrogated and their possible futures in the United States and Canada ultimately depended on the discretion of immigration officials" (Madokoro 2016, 121). Madokoro reports that 13,865 people in the US took part in the confession program. There was also a significant number of participants in the Canadian program. "By late 1966," notes Patricia Roy, "10,533 Chinese had applied for adjustment, 9,962 had been processed, and the department expected to clear the backlog in a few months" (2007, 298). But there is a difference between applying, being processed, and being made a citizen. It is not clear how many of those who had been "processed" were granted citizenship.

Even though there appeared to be widespread participation in these programs, we do not know "how many hundreds or thousands of other migrants never came forward to have their legal status adjusted, or more accurately, readjusted by the state" (Madokoro 2016, 121). The necessarily voluntary nature of the confession programs, and the inevitable failure of such programs to capture every non-citizen, signals ways in which many bodies in this archive remain inscrutable. The confession programs undoubtedly went a long way towards remediating and normalizing a number of fugitive subjects and fugitive families. However, we will never know the full extent of the failure of the head tax system, and in particular the CI 9 system.

How, then, to understand the failure of mass capture in terms of the making of non-citizenship subjects? I have been suggesting that mass capture is a technology that produces non-citizens. I have identified the CI 9 certificates as a prime instance of mass capture. Now, we are faced with a broken or corrupt technology. The archive is not a machine of repression, but rather, to recall the magical one-eyed and one-armed creature invoked by Tagg, a beast that is half-blind and maimed. These thousands of bodies that have moved well beyond the archive indicate not simply a failure of mass capture. Rather, and more importantly, they show how mass capture is productive of forms of agency and subjectivity. Non-citizens are not wholly figures of abjection and loss. They are not necessarily the subjects of repression and state capture. These thousands of mismatched names and bodies suggest that the non-citizen can be a figure of refusal and resistance. Even without the tenuousness of the connection between the textual information and the photographic material on each certificate, the CI 9s offer a powerful testament to the refusal of the demand to be documented.

Constructing Inclusion out of Exclusion

Although the CI 9s were a technology put into place for the purposes of excluding Chinese migrants from citizenship, in the many instances of evasion and refusal that emerge out of this archive, I also see a demand for inclusion. In the final part of this chapter, I will outline the workings of refusal and resistance in terms that understand the photographs attached to these certificates as part of a different cultural formation: a Chinese view of photography, and the traditions of Chinese portraiture. As I have noted throughout this chapter, identification photography is never simply functional. Indeed, as Karen Strassler suggests in her discussion of identification photography's use during the New Order in Indonesia, "the identity photograph became a widespread visual idiom for legitimate belonging within the state-authorized national community, but the state's fetishization of 'proof' of identity also gave rise to doubt and irreverence about documentary truths. Moreover, when appropriated for popular use – circulated among friends, incorporated into personal albums, or reframed as memorial images – identity photographs enter into spheres of social relations and identifications that challenge the state's claim to be the sole agent of recognition within the nation" (2010, 21). It is not only the state that has the power to bestow identity via the photograph. These photographs carry a power that exceeds that of their supposed utility. They were used by their subjects outside the frame of the CI 9 as sites of self-representation, and as a form which could be suffused with an entirely different set of cultural norms and visual cues.

Outside the Mass Capture Frame

The CI 9 photographs were not simply captured and filed. They travelled. Chinese migrants brought their own photographs to be affixed to the CI 9s. At least one other copy of the photograph, the one held by the migrant who departed, would have been outside the confines of the binder and the file. But it is important to also imagine how they might circulate detached from the certificates. Freed from the textual context of the immigration certificate, these identification photographs offer the possibility of other uses and forms of circulation. Taken out of the frame of state documentation, many of these head tax images could certainly function within the tradition of honorific or bourgeois portraiture. As Christopher Pinney notes in his introduction to *Photography's Other Histories*, "A greater sense of the fragility and instability of the relationship between images and their contexts might allow the exploration of why certain images prove capable of recoding while others are more resistant, and many others are completely intractable" (2003, 4). Unfixed from the strictures of the head tax certificates, these photographs could very easily have been disseminated among families and friends.

The size of the photographs also indicates the possibility that they were used for purposes other than identification. The photographs measure approximately 2½ inches to 2⅜ inches by 3 inches. The CI 9 forms allowed for a space of 2½ inches by 4 inches. These measurements suggest that many of these photographs could have been taken with standard *carte de visite* cameras, which allowed for up to eight exposures. The cameras that produced such images were inexpensive, popular, and thus readily available. The *carte de visite* cameras also promoted the construction of images of their subjects as prosperous and confident through the use of props and costumes. As Mary Warner Marien notes, these cameras "encouraged sitters to construct an image of self-satisfaction and financial prosperity" through the use of "fancy furniture and painted backdrops" (2002, 84). The possibility that these identification photographs could have been taken inexpensively while offering elaborately constructed forms of self-representation, and multiple exposures, strongly suggests that many of the photographs affixed to the head tax certificates would also have circulated as portraits used for private consumption. Indeed, given that the state would have required only one or two images, it seems entirely likely that there were surplus images in circulation.

It would be a mistake to think of these photographs merely as responses to a governmental demand for identification. Identification photographs are rarely simply functional. They move across spaces and genres. Jennifer Bajorek, with reference to national photography in Senegal, writes of "the impossibility of deciding on and maintaining distinctions between genres" (2010, 159). A Senegalese photographer tells Bajorek, "'We all did ID cards, and we all did portraits'; 'All of us who did portraits also did ID cards'" (ibid.). The distinction between the portrait and the identification photograph is both maintained and collapsed in this photographer's declaration. He did both. In doing both, he suggests that the contrast between one and the other is a matter of degree rather than absolute difference. As the work of Bajorek, Finn, and Strassler shows, the identification photographs, once they have been liberated from their textual markers, suggest the possibility of other uses, other forms of circulation that exceed the repressive demands of the state.

Self-representations

Indeed, though they were used to fulfill the demands of the state, the CI 9 photographs nevertheless trouble the distinction between the honorific portrait and the identification photograph. While the former is intended

The Department of Trade and Commerce

CHINESE IMMIGRATION BRANCH

C. I. 9

No. 17829

SEP 6 - 1911 191

To the Collector of Customs,

Port of VICTORIA, B. C.

I hereby give notice that I desire to leave Canada with the intention of returning thereto.

I propose to sail or depart from VICTORIA, B. C. for HongKong

on the S.S. Keemun day of SEP 6 - 1911 19

I intend to return to Canada at the port of (1)

I request registration and I attach my photograph hereto and give the following information for the purpose of my identification on my return.

My proper name is Chong Dan

I am sometimes known as

I first came to Canada in the year 1901

Certificate of Registration Form C. I. 5, No. Lost

My place of residence in Canada is Toronto

Where I have resided since the year 1901

My present occupation is that of Laundry

My place of birth was Shong Lou

My present age is 34

Height 5 feet 5 inches.

Facial marks or other peculiarities: —

3 Scars L Side Neck

Mole on F Head

Scar above L Ear

I am personally known to Jing Chow and Jing Yeu

both of VICTORIA, B. C. to whom I would refer you for correctness for statements herein made.

進 鍾

(Signature of Chinese Person.)

I have personally examined the person of Chinese origin above described and whose photograph is affixed hereon, who returned to Canada on the day of 19 and declare him to be the same person.

(Examining Officer.)

Dated at VICTORIA, B. C. , 19

Admitted at Vancouver, B. C. as per letter dated 17/7/1912

(1) If the person of Chinese origin desires to return to Canada by any other port other than the port of departure, this form must be taken in duplicate and the duplicate forwarded to the intended port of entry by mail.

[OVER

Particulars herein given, compared and approved by me this day.

(Examining Officer.)

Dated at VICTORIA, B. C. SEP 6 - 1911 19

Fig. 2.22
CI 9 No. 17829,
Reel no. T-6038.

for private circulation, the latter is produced in response to a state demand. The repressive or instrumental portrait renders its subject powerless. It uses the power of the camera to capture its subject for scientific or criminalizing purposes. In contrast, the honorific portrait represents its subject in light of the traditions of bourgeois portraiture. Such images are destined to be kept in family albums, or mementos passed between friends. The subjects pose with props and costumes that indicate the positions they aspire to, even if they do not necessarily occupy them in the moment the photograph was taken.

Thus, Cheng Dau wears a tailored suit and reclines in a chair as he places his hands on the hat resting on his lap. Neither the suit, nor the hat, nor his posture betrays the fact that he has laboured in Canada for a decade as a laundryman. It is only the accompanying text that contradicts the posture of bourgeois comfort he adopts in the photograph. While some of these photographs portray their subjects in plain, dark clothing, many of them feature subjects in carefully tailored Western-European-style dress. The men wear stiffly starched collars, carefully knotted ties, and suits. These are photographs of subjects who actively participated in the way they would be represented. They convey a dignity and respectability that confounds the very stereotypes that have led to their subjection to this form of state scrutiny. In this photograph, Cheng Dau turns away, quite literally, from the visually flat and symmetrical pose that is typical of identification photography. As Pegler-Gordon understands, "Chinese immigrants played a role in shaping their representations of themselves" as a means of negotiating and contesting their racial marginalization (2009, 42). While Pegler-Gordon's work is focused on the archives of Chinese immigration to the United States, her suggestion that variations in identity photographs constitute a form of contestation and resistance remains pertinent to Chinese-Canadian identity photographs.

The CI 9 photographs illustrate the way in which Chinese immigrants had a strong role in shaping how they would be identified by the state. As the photography historian Roberta Wue observes, "as much as the photographer may have posed and directed each photograph, each client inevitably brought his or her own preferences and expectations to the making of the portrait." Posing for the camera for the CI 9 photographs, Chinese immigrants take a repressive state measure and transform it through an existing honorific visual tradition. As Strassler points out, state-imposed identification measures continually "rub up against competing local, familial, and religious forms of identity and sources of recognition" (2010, 129). The line between the honorific and the repressive remains blurred in the CI 9 photographs.

Formally, even though most of these head tax photographs can be located within the protocols of repressive photography, these images are also entirely self-aware and consciously styled portraits. It is clear from the use of backdrops, props, lighting, and the oval shapes of some of the prints that these photographs were taken in a professional photographer's studio. This commercial backdrop is itself an indication of the connection between instrumental and bourgeois photography manifested in these photographs. The backdrops and props strongly suggest that these portraits circulated further than an identification photograph on a government document. The images show that there are modes of responding to the demands of the state that transform this repression into an occasion for self-representation.

The arguments for a more agential approach to identification photography made by Pegler-Gordon and Strassler mark a departure from the Foucauldian protocols for reading portraiture developed by Tagg. Nonetheless, Pegler-Gordon does allow that there are significant differences between honorific portraits taken as a form of self-representation and repressive photography taken "for the purposes of criminal identification or scientific observation" (2009, 42). As Tagg suggests, honorific portraits often include identifying props, soft lighting, and what he calls "cultivated asymmetries" (1988, 36). In contrast, repressive photography strips its subject of distinguishing props, uses harsh lighting, and places its subject in the centre of the frame. These instances of repressive photography follow in the tradition of the mug shot as delineated by critics such as Finn. However, as Sekula notes of modernist photography in the works of photographers like August Sanders and Walker Evans, the model of the archive – for example, the police photographs that inspired Evans – informs the work of art photography. Indeed, it is not at all coincidental that images of racialized subjects reveal a moment prior to the polarization of affect between honorific and repressive portraits.

Further, the connection between a cultivated asymmetry and the honorific does not hold when we turn to Chinese traditions of portraiture.

Chinese Traditions of Portraiture

Instead of assuming that the Chinese migrants who posed for these identification photographs were contorting themselves in order to conform to a repressive demand based on Western European modes of representation, it is also possible to read the CI 9 photographs as taking part in, and injecting into the archive of Western repressive photography, non-Western modes of photography, specifically portraiture. As Yi Gu recognizes, "By the time the Chinese encountered photography, portraiture had already reached an expanded and democratized market" (2013, 121). Relatedly,

Roberta Wue demonstrates that Chinese portrait traditions have a long history of precisely the same kind of visual format associated with standard identification photographs. Early photography in China was dominated by portraiture. "After its arrival in Hong Kong in the 1840s," Wue notes, "photography was almost primarily used to make portraits" (2005, 262). She points to the close relationship between traditions of Chinese portraiture painting, particularly ancestor portraits, which have been in use since the Song Dynasty (960–1279), and early Chinese photographic practices.

As Wue recognizes, there is an emphasis on flatness in both Chinese painting and photographic portraits: "In ancestor portraits, the face is nearly reduced to its constituent components, with every feature emphatically and clearly represented, including both ears, and with profile and partial views of the face avoided. Something of this approach to likeness carried over into photography. In fact, photographers even powdered the sitter's face or later retouched the face in the photograph in order to eliminate unwanted shadows or marks" (269). Chinese portraiture's emphasis upon uniformity and visual flatness went directly against "two assumptions of nineteenth-century Western portraiture in general and American portraiture in particular: that the individual and his or her inner life could be understood through telling physical idiosyncrasies and that conveying the sitter's individuality was crucial to a successful portrait" (261). In contrast, Chinese demands for portraiture emphasized a completely different set of visual desires. Wu Hung reports that, around the late 1860s and 1870s, "the Chinese 'peculiarities' in portrait taking also became a recurrent topic of ridicule in Western accounts: a local sitter always demands a full frontal view with both ears showing, always looks straight into the camera lens in a confrontational manner … always hates shadows on his face, always wears his best clothes" (2010, 80). Understanding the visual history of portraiture in China allows for a recasting of the identification photographs in the CI 9 archive where the very elements that make these photographs seem like superlative examples of repressive photography are the same elements that Chinese portrait sitters sought out.

I am not the first to see some connection between identification photographs and ancestor portraits. Jan Stuart writes, "The ancestor portrait is reductionist – much like an unflattering modern ID photograph that aims to reproduce key features of a face clearly, without trying to arouse an emotional response from the viewer. Western artists trying to balance the desire to capture a key kernel of personality while also projecting a faithful likeness of a person often turn to a three-quarter view as the most satisfactory, but that view was unacceptable in Chinese ancestor portrait with its desire to hide nothing in the face" (2005, 224). Stuart rejects a Foucauldian approach to the genre and argues instead that interpreting the subjects of these images "as effigies that fulfill socially constructed roles" results in a failure to see the ways in which these images produce "fidelity to personal appearance" that results in a "misrepresent[ion of] the genre" (201). Further extending her analysis to the ways in which these images might be consumed by non-Chinese viewers, Stuart suggests that the West's interest in portraits as offering psychological insight into their subjects actually distorts the ability of Westerners to portray and see these images as physically accurate in their representations of their subjects:

> The tendency of foreigners to read Chinese ancestor likeness as homogenous images may stem, at least in part, from the unconscious application of standards used in the West to judge portraits since the Renaissance. From the late fifteenth century in Europe, so-called humanistic portraits that reveal a nugget of the sitter's personality have been appraised as naturalistic regardless of the manipulations the painter indulged in to lay bare the soul of the sitter. This desire to privilege psychological insight over clinically accurate and emotionally detached description of physical features reveals priorities diametrically opposed to those underlying Chinese ancestor portraits. (ibid.)

Stuart's claim indicates a way in which the supposed flattening of features found in Chinese ancestor portraits might actually be more accurate, more attuned to representing the individual, than supposedly natural or humanistic portraits emerging out of the European Renaissance tradition.

The Western emphasis on individuality, and the faith in photographic portraiture as a direct line to that individuality, runs counter to a different understanding of portraiture in Chinese photography studios. Discussing an anonymous report in an 1875 edition of *Anthony's Photographic Bulletin* on Chinese photography, Yi Gu notes that the report is "laden with racial bias," but it also records a common phenomenon: photography studios without cameras. Instead, the observer reports, "You could go in at any hour of the day, providing you were a Chinaman, and get a portrait executed in a very short time … The heathen Chinese had merely acquired a large collection of portrait negatives, and when a customer came, he took his measure mentally, looked through all the stock, and chose the picture most like. As all Chinese heads are pretty similar, and their pigtails much about the same length, it was never difficult, apparently, to make a match, for the public were quite content with what they got for their money" (2013, 120). As Gu recognizes, the story is ostensibly humorous because of “the sharp contrast between photography’s supposed faithful reference to reality and Chinese clients’ alleged acceptance of generic images as their own likeness. ‘All Chinese heads are pretty similar’ echoes the contemporaneous Western complaints about the formulaic nature of Chinese portraiture” (ibid.). More than just an indication of Chinese approaches to portraiture that pull away from naturalism and realism, in the context of identification photography, this anecdote also reveals a different way of relating to indexicality. In addition to the racism of the anecdote, let us rest for a moment on what it reports: at least as early as 1875, Chinese people frequently went to photography studios in China, and, after perusing a number of pre-existing portraits, would select the one they felt most resembled themselves, and purchase copies of that image to be used as a self-portrait. This practice of using a generic image as a self-portrait points at an entirely different approach to identification photography. Here, there is a pre-existing practice of portraiture that claims verisimilitude through broadly defined forms of likeness. The body in the photograph does not have to be the body that claims that photograph as its own likeness.

Look, for example, at an exceptional instance of this practice in the CI 9 archive. Here, there are two bodies posed together to represent one. The body in either photograph does not have to be the body that claims to be represented on the certificate. But, as the multiple signatures and countersignatures make clear, both were accepted as representations of the person attached to the certificate.

Departing from Victoria on the *Bellerophon* on 1 November 1911, alongside the migrants I discuss earlier in this chapter, Ma Chow Lai’s CI 9 contains not one but two identification photographs. Look carefully at them both. Although they share some generic likeness – both of the photographs depict a person with little hair at the crown even though it is unclear if this person is balding or has fashioned their hair into a queue – it is not at all obvious that they are images of the same person. The shape of the face is distinctly different. The lips do not seem to be the same. The eyes and eyebrows also appear to be quite different from one image to the next. And yet, at one point, both photographs were accepted as representing the same person. Here, a generic likeness suffices not once, but twice, as an identification photograph. Not only did Ma Chow Lai, or the person or people claiming to be Ma Chow Lai, insist upon the correctness of both portraits by deploying them on the CI 9, he (or they) also convinced the immigration agent to accept these versions of likeness. In an echo of the custom of choosing a likeness from a pre-existing selection outlined by Yi Gu, Ma Chow Lai’s doubled portrait poses a challenge to the outlandish idea that one image should suffice as an index to a single identity.

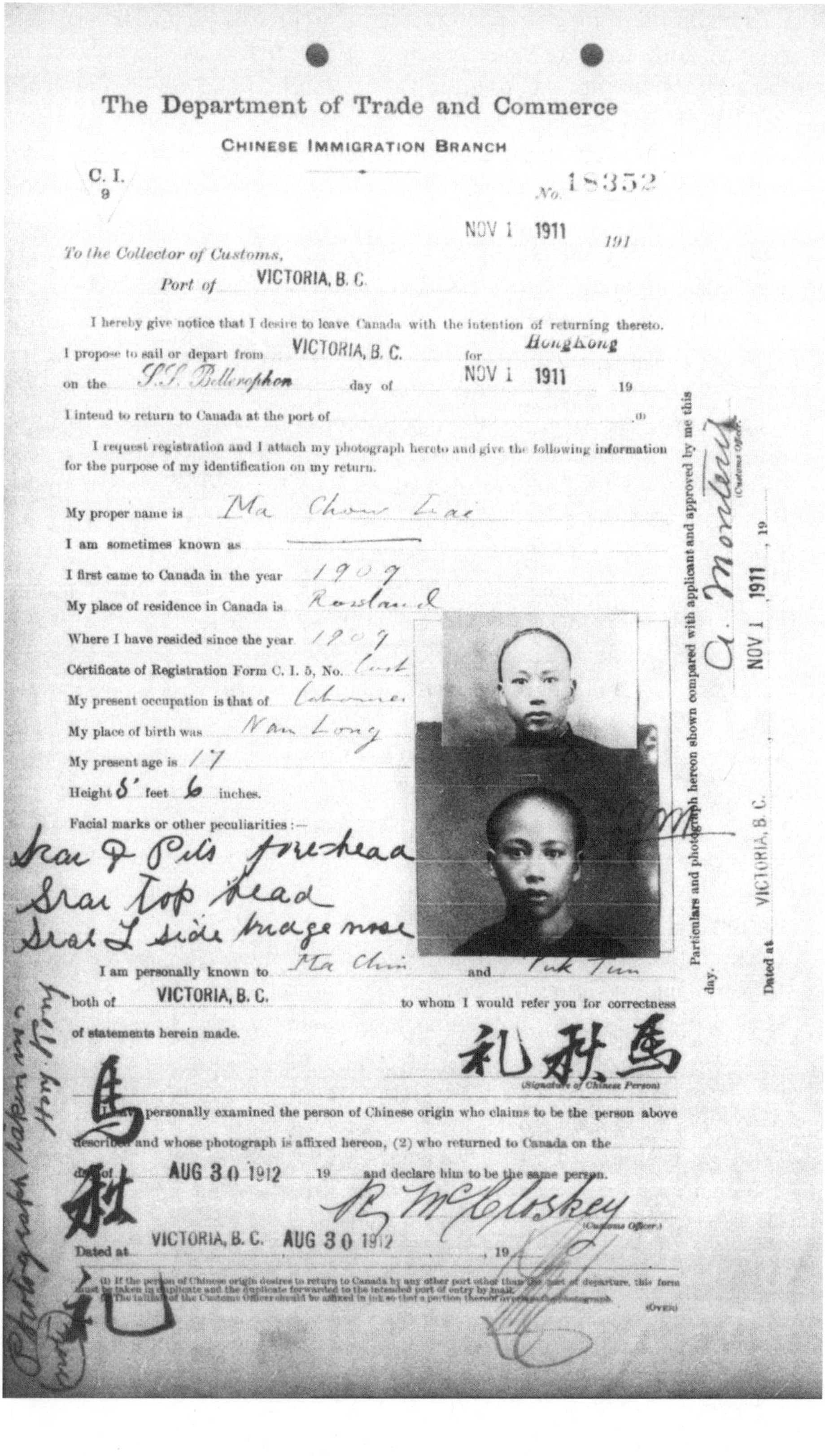

The Department of Trade and Commerce

CHINESE IMMIGRATION BRANCH

C. I. 9

No. 18352

NOV 1 1911 191

To the Collector of Customs,

Port of VICTORIA, B. C.

I hereby give notice that I desire to leave Canada with the intention of returning thereto.

I propose to sail or depart from VICTORIA, B. C. for HongKong

on the S.S. Bellerophon day of NOV 1 1911 19

I intend to return to Canada at the port of (1)

I request registration and I attach my photograph hereto and give the following information for the purpose of my identification on my return.

My proper name is Ma Chow Lai

I am sometimes known as ——

I first came to Canada in the year 1907

My place of residence in Canada is Rossland

Where I have resided since the year 1907

Certificate of Registration Form C. I. 5, No. Lost

My present occupation is that of Laborer

My place of birth was Nan Long

My present age is 17

Height 5' feet 6 inches.

Facial marks or other peculiarities :—

Scar & Pits forehead
Scar Top head
Scar L side bridge nose

I am personally known to Ma Chin and Puk Tum

both of VICTORIA, B. C. to whom I would refer you for correctness of statements herein made.

馬秋礼
(Signature of Chinese Person)

Particulars and photograph hereon shown compared with applicant and approved by me this day.

C. Montero
(Customs Officer.)

Dated at VICTORIA, B. C. NOV 1 1911, 19

(1) I have personally examined the person of Chinese origin who claims to be the person above described and whose photograph is affixed hereon, (2) who returned to Canada on the day of AUG 30 1912 19 and declare him to be the same person.

R. McCloskey
(Customs Officer.)

Dated at VICTORIA, B. C. AUG 30 1912, 19

(1) If the person of Chinese origin desires to return to Canada by any other port other than the port of departure, this form must be taken in duplicate and the duplicate forwarded to the intended port of entry by mail.
(2) The initials of the Customs Officer should be affixed in ink so that a portion thereof appears on the photograph.

(OVER)

馬秋礼

Photograph taken in Hong Kong (note)

Fig. 2.23
CI 9 No. 18352, Reel no. T-6039.

How this need for both photographs arises on this particular certificate remains a mystery. We have only the evidence before us: the material on the certificate itself. According to the certificate, Ma Chow Lai returned to Victoria less than a year after departing and was admitted back into Canada on 30 August 1912. Did the admitting agent check for the facial marks and peculiarities noted on the form? Did the man who returned in 1912 also have a scar and pits on his forehead, a scar on the top of his head, and a scar on the left side of the bridge of his nose? These marks are not visible in either photograph.

One photograph, the one on top, is pasted over the bottom one. It is possible that the bottom one was original to the certificate, and the top one was appended as a form of further verification. In this deployment of a doubled image, CI 9 no. 18352 is unique. I have not come across any others that contain two photographs purporting to identify one person. In its exceptionality, it both reveals a number of singularities specific to this certificate, and also illuminates the obverse, the practices and norms that regulate the vast majority of the other certificates.

Not least, its singularity suggests that the majority of identification photographs were taken in Canada. Scribbled in the lower left-hand corner of the certificate are the words: "Photograph taken in Hong Kong." There are no other notes about the origins of the photographs in any of the CI 9s that I have encountered. How a photograph originating in Hong Kong might explain the need for two distinct photographs is not at all clear. Perhaps it was an explanation for the change in appearance between the man who departed and the one who returned. Perhaps it suggests that the first photograph was inadequate. Whatever the explanation, that note in the corner does imply that it was unusual for a photograph to be taken in Hong Kong and used on a CI 9.

This doubled identification photograph also shows the way in which a single image was almost always expected to serve as a sufficient tool of identification. Indeed, not unlike our contemporary passport photographs, the CI 9 system's reliance on one photograph does not account for how a person might change over the passage of time. As I will discuss in the next chapter, even where there are photographs of children who return many years later, and thus presumably would have changed a great deal, the single original image of the child is still sufficient proof of identity for readmittance.

Ma Chow Lai's Hong Kong photograph is the most visible evidence of the way in which Chinese photographic and portraiture practices and customs became threaded into the CI 9 system. Even though this system was put into place to capture Chinese migrants on a massive scale for the purposes of excluding them from citizenship, the system did not merely impose a Western European mode of surveillance upon its Chinese subjects. The system was also susceptible to the ways in which Chinese migrants imposed on it a different set of codes and values. Not only was the CI 9 system ill-equipped to remember those it captured on the basis of their given names, it also possessed no bulwark against different ways of seeing and being seen that Chinese migrants inserted into each certificate with each photograph.

I want to be cautious and resist claiming that there is an easily distinguishable and homogenous Chinese tradition to which we can ascribe so much of the visuality of the identification photographs on the CI 9 certificates. Of course, China was and is a deeply diverse site of photographic practices, and there is no single, continuous, uncontested photographic tradition. What is more, I take seriously Wu Hung's cautions against the almost too-neat dichotomies of Western and non-Western visualities that can be drawn from these contrasts between Chinese and Western portraiture. Or, as Gu notes, the story of the photography studio without cameras "neatly embodies the dichotomies – Western versus Chinese, naturalistic versus fanciful, realistic versus formulaic – that beset Chinese visual culture after its head-on encounter with Western imagery, ideas, and techniques" (2013, 120). Wu Hung challenges the idea that there was a distinct divide between Chinese and Western portrait styles:

> As Régine Thiriez summarizes, after having scrutinized hundreds of old portraits from the nineteenth and twentieth century, generally speaking there are no radical differences between products of Chinese and Western studios. Chinese studios adopted Western formulas in setting up the backdrop and arranging the sitters' poses, whereas many works by Western studios nicely fit the aforementioned Chinese conventions. Her conclusion is supported by Cody, Terpak, and Fraser in their catalog essays and by my own study of photo archives in China and abroad. Rather than confirming the sharp divide reported in the Western accounts, an empirical study of primary data reveals instead an abrupt split between practice and discourse. (2010, 81)

This skepticism over any kind of intrinsic East-West aesthetic divide is warranted. At the same time, though, it is absolutely the case that Chinese portraiture has a long and robust tradition that did influence the rise of photography in China. As Gu notes, "While we may downplay the emphasis on 'Chinese peculiarity' as a mere reflection of colonial anxiety, traces of stylistic distinction *were* manifested in a good many photographs of Chinese sitters" (2013, 122). Gu attempts to recognize the specificity of Chinese photography, without falling into an easy East-West binary, through a rigorous investigation of the Chinese names for photography, their evolution, and the implications of these names for illuminating an approach to photography that could be identified as specifically Chinese.

Through her investigation, Gu draws attention to the intimate relationship between painting and photography in China. "The first names for photography in Chinese – *yingxiang, xiaoxiang, xiaozhao* – were all preexisting terms for portrait painting" (2013, 121). For Gu, China's encounter with photography needs to be understood as part of a broader complex of visual practices where painting and photography are not diametrically opposed but, in fact, synchronous. "If there are antinaturalistic traits in Chinese photography, they neither indicate a lack of understanding by the Chinese of photography's media specificity nor demonstrate a conscious resistance to it. The fact that the names first used for photography were all preexisting words for portrait painting highlights a historical moment in China when photography belonged to a rapidly changing and expanding field of visual practice that was conveniently dubbed 'painting'" (ibid.). Gu's interventions break down the divide between photography and painting in Chinese visual practices. Indeed, as she shows in her discussion of photography studios in nineteenth-century China and in her engagement with the work of early photography critics such as Wang Tao and Du Jiutian, from the inception of photography in China, there was an intimate connection between painting and photography.

While Gu's analysis focuses on Chinese photographers in nineteenth-century China, Catherine Clement's *Chinatown through a Wide Lens: The Hidden Photographs of Yucho Chow* shines a light on how photographic portraiture – and its connection to painting – was practised in early twentieth-century Canada. Yucho Chow operated a photographic studio in Vancouver's Chinatown from 1907–49. As Clement notes, Chow operated this studio during a period of intense change and turmoil for Chinese Canadians: "He started photographing during the time of escalating head taxes and the famous 1907 Race Riot. His camera operated through the First World War; the 1923 Chinese Exclusion Act [the Chinese Immigration Act was amended in 1923 to exclude virtually all Chinese immigration until its repeal in 1947]; the Great Depression; the Second World War; and finally, the repeal of the Chinese Exclusion Act and the granting of voting rights in 1947 to several communities, including the Chinese" (2019, 25). In this mapping of the historical period of Chow's studio, Clement draws attention to the connection between Chow's photographic work and Chinese Canadians' trajectory from exclusion to citizenship. Chow's studio focused almost entirely on portraiture. Aside from a handful of images of Chinese businesses and Sikh temples, the archive of Chow's photographs is overwhelmingly made up of portraits of people in the Vancouver community: "Over the course of four decades, he captures photos of people across the arc of life's journey: from newborn babies to the recently deceased. (These 'death' photos were often sent back to family in China and Europe and served as a form of death certificate for grieving relatives)" (33). His studio moved at least four times within Chinatown, but it was, as Clement points out, one of the very few places that welcomed people of all races and classes. Thus, Chow captured portraits not only of Chinese Canadians, but also those from South Asian and European communities. Although the majority of his images were taken in his studio, Chow would also "haul his heavy equipment down to Vancouver's central train station where he regularly took head and shoulders shots of bleary-eyed, newly-arrived European immigrants. Ironically, these were the very immigrant groups that the federal government was inviting to Canada even as his own community was increasingly stigmatized and unwelcome" (ibid.). Chow's studio portraits involved carefully chosen props to connote wealth and status, such as area rugs, distinctive backdrops, faux marble pedestals, intricately carved furniture, and porcelain vases.

The connection between painting and portraiture in Yucho Chow's portraits can be found not only in the composition of the portraits, but also in his backdrops and use of hand colouring. His portraits were distinctive for the backdrops he constructed and painted himself. Practised photographic historians such as Clement can quickly spot a Yucho Chow portrait by looking at the backdrop alone. Chow's portraits were also particularly notable for their hand-painted embellishments. Chow's daughter Jessie (1916–1999) "learned to hand paint the photos using oils. She became so skilled that some photographs look as if they were originally shot on colour film" (Clement 41). While many photographers, whether they are Chinese or not, deploy some combination of all of these painterly practices (compositions, backdrops, hand colouring), Chow's use of them in this early period of Canadian photographic portraiture offers a bridge between the period of Chinese portraiture that Yi Gu examines, and the CI 9s in my analysis. Although there is no clear indication that Yucho Chow took photographs for use on CI 9 identification photographs, his focus on portraiture indicates that a Chinese-Canadian photographer from this period did indeed bring knowledge of Chinese portraiture traditions into early Canadian photographic practice.

As Yi Gu argues, for Chinese photographers, the distinction between painting and photography was mutable. One was not opposed to the other and they shared practices and techniques. These visual traditions not only break down the binaries between photography and painting and between East and West, but they also show how the migrants in the CI 9 photographs might have used these photographs to mediate a refusal of the protocols of identification photography where one body was to be so insistently indexed to one image affixed to one certificate. Instead, these photographs attest to a range of refusals: to be identified; to be fixed; to be cut off from honour and dignity.

Even though the stipulations of identification photographs might read as repressive, they are also evocative of an alternative visual history of Chinese portraiture. Viewed from within a continuum of visual practices that connect photography and painting, the CI 9 photographs offer a representational through line connecting ancestor portraits and identification photography. The very characteristics that indicate the repressive measures of the state – visual flatness, full-frontal exposure of the face, minimization of light and shadow – are also the characteristics of successful, honorific portraiture in China.

Punched through, filed, and stored, the CI 9s are a testament of the failure of memory when it is conflated with storage. They are a tribute to the multiple possibilities for evasion and escape. Hiding while still inhabiting the technology of mass capture, Chinese migrants manufactured forms of inclusion for themselves that far exceeded the limits of non-citizenship.

CHAPTER THREE
ENVISIONING KINSHIP IN MASS CAPTURE

This chapter looks for ways to envision kinship in mass capture. Because the photographs in this archive are almost always of men, posed singularly in what we now understand as the generic form of the identification photograph, photographs of women and children, and sometimes even of whole families, stand out as breathtaking exceptions. And yet, the reprieve that these photographs offer from the overwhelming loneliness captured in the others is itself problematic. Not least, of course, because they are, in their exceptionality, evidence of the way in which the Chinese Immigration Act prevented the vast majority of Chinese migrants from being with their families. Because there is so much loneliness wound through this archive, it is hard not to look for relations, for evidence of kinship and family, for something more than the devastation of people separated from their loved ones. Thus, in this chapter, I will take up how kinship can be envisioned in, and despite, mass capture. I argue that the CI 9 photographs offer a different route to seeing Chinese families, in spite of the separations they endured. In so doing, I suggest trying to look at the CI 9 images as a series of collective portraits and as a different kind of family portraiture.

Looking for families by only examining conventional family portraits, where all members are grouped together in one image, risks missing the families present in this archive, even when their members are never pictured together. Some images of intact families pictured together are included in this archive due to the privileges of class. Only merchant families can be found in the same CI 9 photographs, and even then such images are very rare. To dwell only upon these atypical photographs would be to ignore the ways in which the CI 9 photographs demand looking for relation in ways that embrace what Hortense Spillers and David Eng, in different capacities, call "a feeling of kinship" (Spillers 1987, 76; Eng 2010, 196). As Spillers argues, the feeling of kinship is not divorced from material conditions, but rather is deeply tied to those conditions: "the *feeling* of kinship is *not* inevitable … it describes a relationship that appears 'natural,' but must be 'cultivated' under actual material conditions" (1987, 76). Under slavery, "'kinship' loses meaning *since it can be invaded at any given and arbitrary moment by the property relations*" (74, emphasis original). Spillers makes clear the pain of what it means to make family, to find kinship, out of material conditions in which the "connection between 'kinship' and 'property'" enforces a perpetual logic of possible loss (75). The mass captured Chinese migrants on the CI 9s are not enslaved. And yet, the lesson of Spillers's argument is one that has resonance for this book. Chinese migrant families endured forms of separation, and a very limited view of that separation can be glimpsed in the CI 9 archive. The separation of Chinese migrants from their families, of children from their parents, was systemic. Out of this system, I have tried to look for feeling, for the places and moments where kinship might still be found. For Eng, long histories of race and racism are central to the formation of what we call family, and making these histories visible means looking at how kinship is an affective formation that is deeply tied to the complex relation between history and memory. Although I was unable to trace visual evidence of alternative and queer forms of kinship in the CI 9 archive, I have tried to at least consider how something like a "ship brotherhood" or "ship sisterhood" might be a way of seeing kinship beyond that of the conventional family.

Mass Capture envisions kinship by looking for relations formed out of the grief of historical racism, and at the recuperative possibilities of relations formed out of the bonds of diasporic passage – as I will show through the images of the migrants aboard the SS *Oanfa*. In this exploration, I take a cue from the titular question of kinship and heterosexuality posed by Judith Butler in her 1994 essay, "Is Kinship Always Already Heterosexual?" Butler questions the "hypostatized heterosexuality … [that] has been the basis of the claim that kinship is always already heterosexual" (1994, 34). Instead, Butler suggests, "kinship loses its specificity as an object once it becomes characterized loosely as modes of enduring relationship. Obviously, not all kinship relations last, but whatever relations qualify for kinship enter into a norm or a convention that has some durability, and that norm acquires durability through being reinstated time and again" (37). The CI 9 archive offers a view into the ways that kinship as an enduring relationship – whether that relationship is founded in hypostatized heterosexuality or loosened from it, such as in a shipboard brotherhood or sisterhood – is undercut by visual and bureaucratic practices. These practices include the handling and filing of identification photographs for family members and the refusal to recognize the intimacies of a bachelor society of men torn away from their biological families. To see kinship in the

CI 9 archive, we also have to look at how conventional and unconventional forms of kinship were ruthlessly curtailed and denied.

Looking for this denial means unlearning the impulse to look for kinship relations when they are not there. Consider CI 9 nos. 20306 and 20307 (figs. 3.1 and 3.2). This pair of certificates is a major finding. There is no more than a handful of images of multiple people in a photograph in the entire CI 9 collection. Children, even babies, were most often photographed following the conventions of the identification photograph: alone. There are very few images of people photographed together, and these two photographs are the only ones I have found of a woman and a child together.

At first, it was hard for me to resist the desire to see these photographs as portraits of a mother and child. Setting aside for a moment the violence of the pen marks that cross out the face of the woman and then the child, what I initially missed in this pair of photographs is the violence of family separation that it records. In her discussion of family photographs from communities of people who have been persecuted, Kirsten McAllister writes of the "performative scripts" that family photographs elicit (2018, 169). I engaged in my own version of this scripting when looking at these photographs for the first time. For me, the photographs on CI 9 nos. 20306 and 20307 seemed like a reprieve, a welcome break from the pattern of single men in the centre of the frame. I was looking for relationships, for families, for signs that not everyone was alone. But I was also tripped up in this desire. It took me a long time to critically engage with these two photographs. I had to unlearn the desire to immediately presume that I was seeing an image of a mother and her child.

Looking again, and looking more closely, it becomes unlikely that these photographs depict a mother and her child. In CI 9 no. 20307 Mrs See declares her age to be forty-one years old. She came to Canada in 1887 when she was sixteen. Before she embarked on the *Panama Maru* for a trip to China, she was a housewife living in Victoria. She could not write her name in either Chinese or English and instead her signature is marked with an "x." The certificate was issued on 4 September 1912. It is highly improbable that she is the child's mother. She does not share a surname with the child. The certificate is stamped "expired." There is no evidence Mrs See returned to Canada. If she did, it would have been after a prolonged sojourn of more than two years.

The baby in Mrs See's lap is "Miss Wong Louie Youe." She is one year old. She was born in Victoria. She also did not return to Canada before her CI 9 expired after two years. As the certificate declared, the child is "personally known" to Wong Ma and Wong Wai. Perhaps these are her parents. We cannot know. The mystery around this dramatic departure endures.

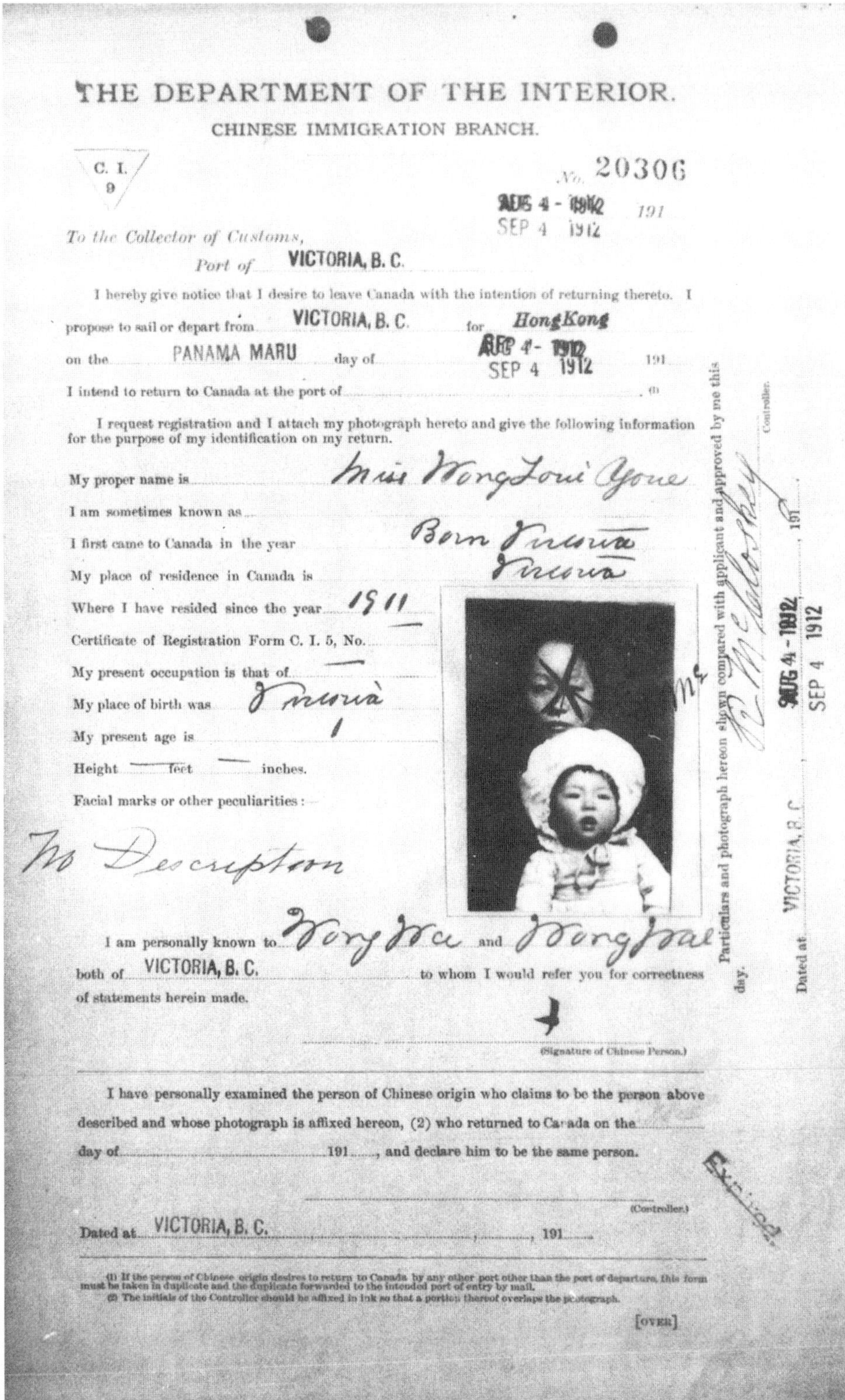

THE DEPARTMENT OF THE INTERIOR.

CHINESE IMMIGRATION BRANCH.

C. I. 9

No. 20306

AUG 4 - 1912 191
SEP 4 1912

To the Collector of Customs,

Port of VICTORIA, B. C.

I hereby give notice that I desire to leave Canada with the intention of returning thereto. I propose to sail or depart from VICTORIA, B. C. for HongKong on the PANAMA MARU day of AUG 4 - 1912 SEP 4 1912 191

I intend to return to Canada at the port of .... (1)

I request registration and I attach my photograph hereto and give the following information for the purpose of my identification on my return.

My proper name is Miss Wong Louie Yone

I am sometimes known as

I first came to Canada in the year Born Victoria

My place of residence in Canada is Victoria

Where I have resided since the year 1911 —

Certificate of Registration Form C. I. 5, No.

My present occupation is that of —

My place of birth was Victoria

My present age is 1

Height — feet — inches.

Facial marks or other peculiarities:

No Description

I am personally known to Wong Wa and Wong Yoal both of VICTORIA, B. C. to whom I would refer you for correctness of statements herein made.

(Signature of Chinese Person.)

Particulars and photograph hereon shown compared with applicant and approved by me this day. AUG 4 - 1912 SEP 4 1912 191

R McCloskey Controller.

Dated at VICTORIA, B. C.

I have personally examined the person of Chinese origin who claims to be the person above described and whose photograph is affixed hereon, (2) who returned to Canada on the ...... day of .... 191....., and declare him to be the same person.

Expired

(Controller.)

Dated at VICTORIA, B. C. ...., 191......

(1) If the person of Chinese origin desires to return to Canada by any other port other than the port of departure, this form must be taken in duplicate and the duplicate forwarded to the intended port of entry by mail.
(2) The initials of the Controller should be affixed in ink so that a portion thereof overlaps the photograph.

[OVER]

Fig. 3.1
CI 9 No. 20306,
Reel no. T-6040.

Fig. 3.2 (opposite)
CI 9 No. 20307,
Reel no. T-6040.

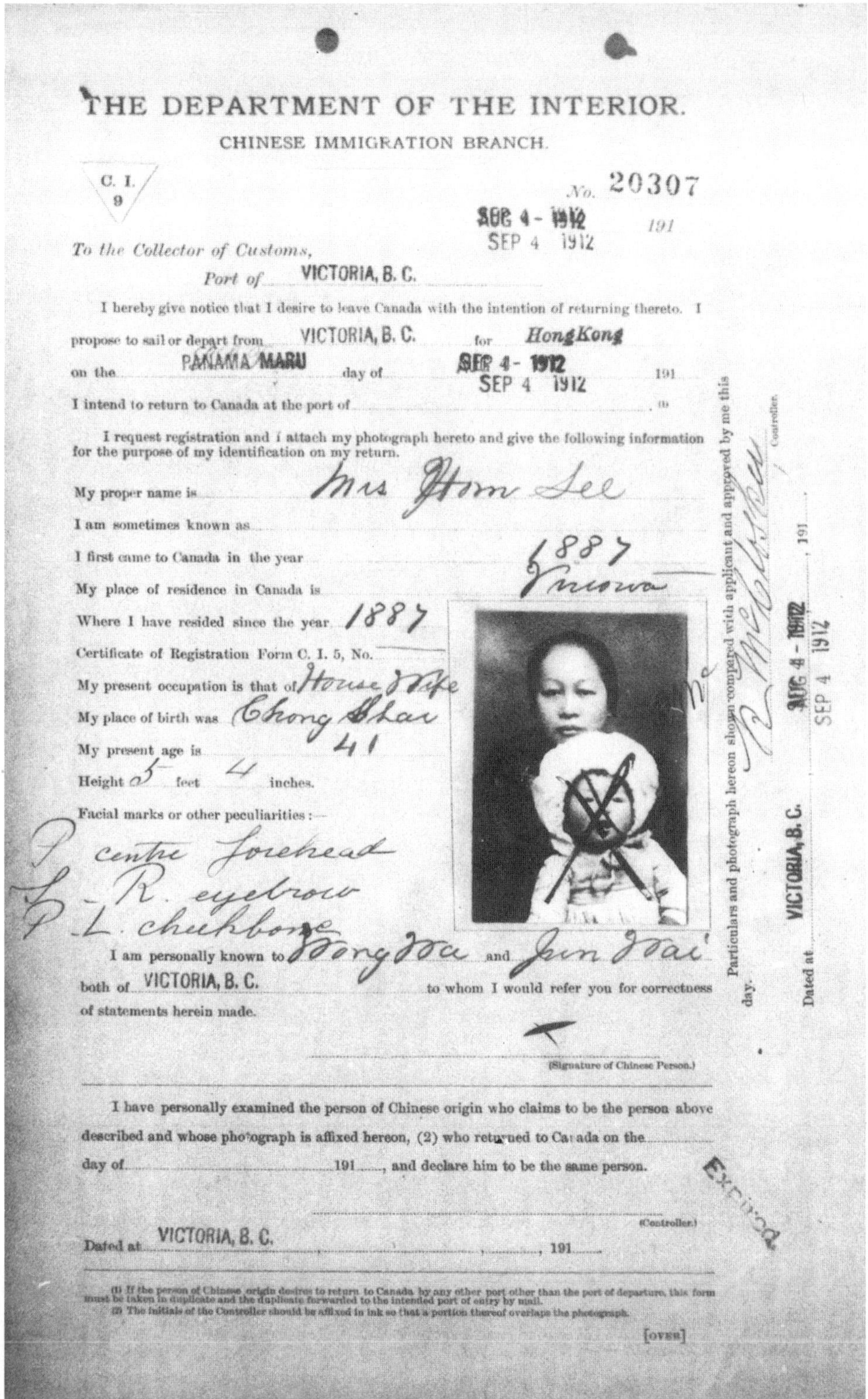

THE DEPARTMENT OF THE INTERIOR.

CHINESE IMMIGRATION BRANCH.

C. I. 9

No. 20307

AUG 4 - 1912 191
SEP 4 1912

To the Collector of Customs,

Port of VICTORIA, B. C.

I hereby give notice that I desire to leave Canada with the intention of returning thereto. I propose to sail or depart from VICTORIA, B. C. for HongKong on the PANAMA MARU day of AUG 4 - 1912 SEP 4 1912 191

I intend to return to Canada at the port of .... (1)

I request registration and I attach my photograph hereto and give the following information for the purpose of my identification on my return.

My proper name is Mrs Hom See

I am sometimes known as

I first came to Canada in the year 1887

My place of residence in Canada is Victoria

Where I have resided since the year 1887

Certificate of Registration Form C. I. 5, No. —

My present occupation is that of House Wife

My place of birth was Chong Shan

My present age is 41

Height 5 feet 4 inches.

Facial marks or other peculiarities:—

P centre forehead
S – R. eyebrow
P L. cheekbone

I am personally known to Wong Wa and Jun Wai

both of VICTORIA, B. C. to whom I would refer you for correctness of statements herein made.

X

(Signature of Chinese Person.)

Particulars and photograph hereon shown compared with applicant and approved by me this .... day. ...., 191

R McLeese, Controller.

Dated at VICTORIA, B. C. AUG 4 - 1912 SEP 4 1912

I have personally examined the person of Chinese origin who claims to be the person above described and whose photograph is affixed hereon, (2) who returned to Canada on the .... day of .... 191...., and declare him to be the same person.

EXPIRED

.... (Controller.)

Dated at VICTORIA, B. C. ...., 191....

(1) If the person of Chinese origin desires to return to Canada by any other port other than the port of departure, this form must be taken in duplicate and the duplicate forwarded to the intended port of entry by mail.
(2) The initials of the Controller should be affixed in ink so that a portion thereof overlaps the photograph.

[OVER]

In this pair of certificates, kinship is formed and reformed. While the conventions of photographic portraiture would lead a casual observer to see these photographs as being of a mother and her child, they reveal instead a child who left Canada without her mother and in the care of a relative stranger. The baby is bound to Mrs See both by the sequential numbering of their certificates, indicating that they travelled together, and by being photographed with her. But these photographs on CI 9 nos. 20306 and 20307 are of a family torn apart.

The CI 9s are a form of record-keeping that memorializes the tragedy of separating a baby from her family without ever having to acknowledge the fact of this separation. Citing Hannah Arendt, Michelle Caswell connects the work of record-keeping to the willful ignorance necessary for perpetuating systems of injustice: "Records are the media through which procedures are routinized; records enable repetition, which leads to 'the nearly universal ability to make any activity into a routine that deadens the awareness of what is to be done'" (2014, 53). In CI 9 nos. 20306 and 20307, folded into the routine and repetition of recording is a difficult personal history. McAllister argues that there are "social and ethical considerations of working with photos of families from persecuted communities" and that these considerations mean that "family photographs need to be understood not just as problematic normative scripts, but also as practices that families use to affirm their social relations and identities, in other words, to survive" (2018, 169–70). The photographs on these two certificates capture something of what survival might have meant for the child, if not also the woman. Surely, the decision to send Miss Wong Louie Youe away was based on a desire for a better life for the child. Thus, an image that might seem at first like a portrait of a familial relation is actually one of family separation. The image encodes a child's separation from her mother.

This pair of photographs, CI 9 nos. 20306 and 20307, offers a poignant counter to an image of a woman and a child discussed by LiLi Johnson in her examination of Chinese head tax photographs in the United States. Johnson's essay examines what are known as the Chinese Exclusion Act Case Files, created by the Immigration and Naturalization Service and held at the New York City National Archives at Bowling Green in Manhattan. Among the files that Johnson examines, there is one of Eleanor Sing Yee (fig. 3.3).

Here, a mother with her child: the very thing I wanted to see in CI 9 nos. 20306 and 20307. Johnson describes it as "a more conventional family photograph of a mother and daughter," and goes on to note how this photograph "challenged the standards of the immigration bureaucracy" (2017, 111). Johnson notes that the need to identify the baby posed a challenge

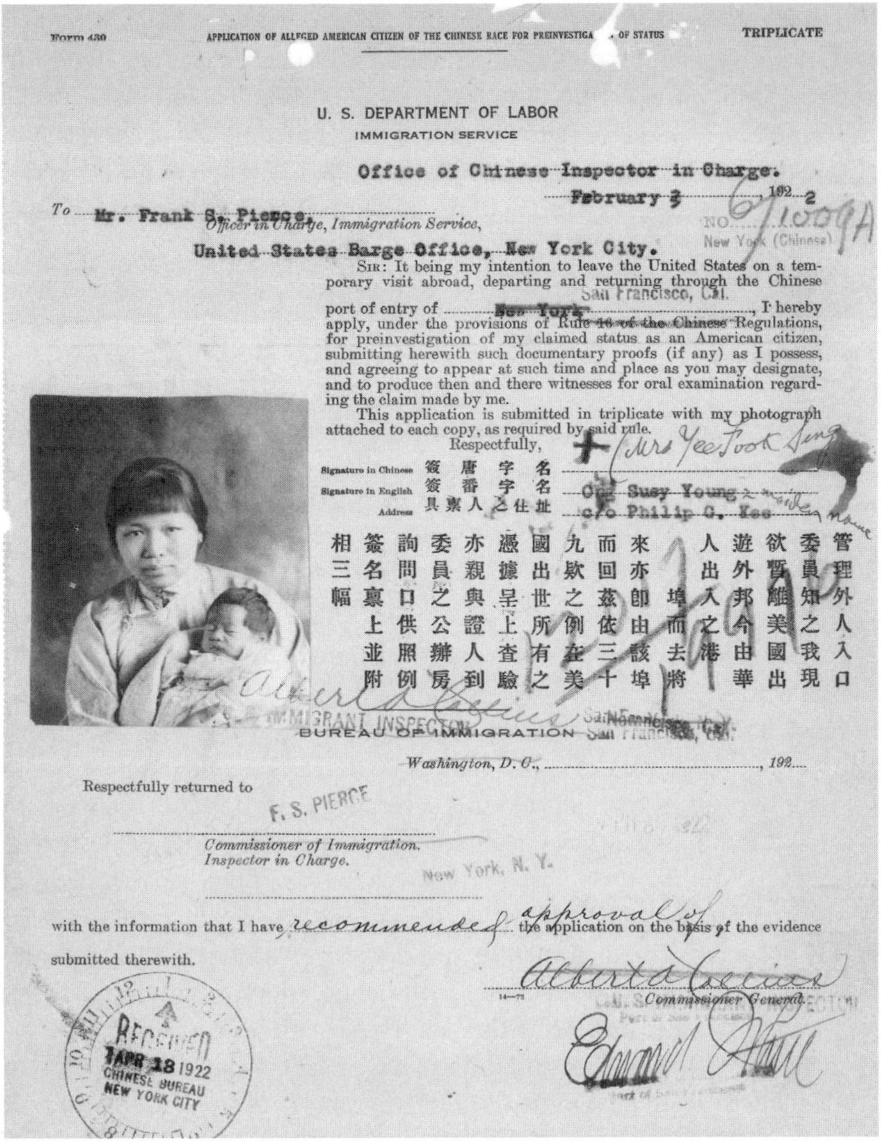
Form 430 APPLICATION OF ALLEGED AMERICAN CITIZEN OF THE CHINESE RACE FOR PREINVESTIGA[TION] OF STATUS TRIPLICATE

U. S. DEPARTMENT OF LABOR
IMMIGRATION SERVICE

Office of Chinese Inspector in Charge.
February 3, 1922

NO. 6/1009A
New York (Chinese)

To Mr. Frank S. Pierce, Officer in Charge, Immigration Service,
United States Barge Office, New York City.

SIR: It being my intention to leave the United States on a temporary visit abroad, departing and returning through the Chinese port of entry of ~~New York~~ San Francisco, Cal., I hereby apply, under the provisions of ~~Rule 16 of the Chinese~~ Regulations, for preinvestigation of my claimed status as an American citizen, submitting herewith such documentary proofs (if any) as I possess, and agreeing to appear at such time and place as you may designate, and to produce then and there witnesses for oral examination regarding the claim made by me.

This application is submitted in triplicate with my photograph attached to each copy, as required by said rule.

Respectfully,

Signature in Chinese 簽唐字名 + (Mrs Yee Fook Sing)
Signature in English 簽番字名 Ong Suey Young
Address 具禀人之住址 c/o Philip C. Yee

管理外人入口
委員知之我現
欲暫離美國出
遊外邦今由華
人出入之港
埠而去將
來亦即由該埠
而回茲依三十
九欵之例在美
國出世之所有
憑據呈上查驗
亦親與證人到
委員之公辦房
詢問口供照例
簽名稟上並附
相三幅

IMMIGRANT INSPECTOR San Francisco, Cal.
BUREAU OF IMMIGRATION
Washington, D. C., ..., 192...

Respectfully returned to F. S. PIERCE
Commissioner of Immigration.
Inspector in Charge.
New York, N. Y.

with the information that I have recommended approval of the application on the basis of the evidence submitted therewith.

Albert a ...
Commissioner General.

RECEIVED APR 18 1922 CHINESE BUREAU NEW YORK CITY

Fig. 3.3
Form 430, File 6/1848
Ong Suey Young
(Mrs Yee Fook Sing),
13 April 1922.

to the limits of the identification form in that "the logistical obstacles of photographing [the baby] alone" seem to allow for "the bureaucratic officials to make an exception" (114). How is it, she asks, that this "mother and daughter, disenfranchised by their racial identity gender, can represent the mounting anxieties of a bureaucratic system? In the case of Eleanor and her mother, Ong Suey Young, the identification photo was not created to accommodate infants. To have a photograph of two people used as duplicates of the same photo was outside the expected practice" (ibid.). But in the case of Mrs Hom See and Miss Wong Louie Youe, the CI 9 system had no trouble with a duplicate photograph. It needed only to engage in defacing both photographs in order to make the duplication work. While the Canadian head tax system often took its cues from the US approach to Chinese migrants, as this chapter will show, the treatment of the portrayal of kinship was often more cruel in the systemic denial and erasure of families and kinship relations.

At the most basic level, the CI 9 certificates refused to recognize kinship. There are blank spaces for so many details about each person on these certificates – age, occupation, CI 5 number, place of birth, facial marks – but a howling silence when it comes to family connection. These certificates deny family as a route to identity. The families that are not pictured, and the families that have been separated and broken by legislation and poverty, are also central to envisioning kinship under mass capture.

Families Ruptured, Kinship Interrupted

Mass capture is a technology of non-citizenship not only because it tracked migrants for the sole purpose of excluding them from citizenship, but also because it illuminates how these exclusions work at the level of families and kinship relations. We know that the head tax broke up families. In the CI 9 archive, we can actually see this severance at work. More than a mere record of families that have been separated and destroyed, or destroyed through separation, the CI 9s are the mechanisms of this separation. That is, the archive is a record, but it is also the means by which these separations occurred. The document is not a passive witness to this violence, but its active tool. Without these documents, migrants could not travel to see their families outside of Canada. Because the vast majority of Chinese migrants from this period did not have families in Canada, the CI 9s regulated when and how most Chinese migrants could be with their loved ones. The CI 9 is therefore a way to see processes of isolation and loss at work. As I will argue below, each individual certificate and each identification photograph, filed and sequestered from the others, is a portrait of isolation. The very form of the identification document and photograph are manifestations of the social and communal isolation that so many migrants had to live through.

In the CI 9 archive, there are two primary ways in which we can see the breakup of the family. First, the archive is made up almost exclusively of men. Second, when children, women, and families are pictured, these representations are themselves exercises in negation and excision. The treatment of the photographs of Mrs See and Miss Wong Louie Youe are stark in the deliberate and graphic way they negate the presence of the woman and then the baby girl. The agent could have differentiated the woman from the baby in so many other ways. Indeed, he need not have done anything to the photographs: anyone reading the certificate could immediately grasp the difference between the forty-one-year-old woman and the one-year-old baby. As my discussion of the Jung and Chong families later in this chapter shows, images of merchant families were not subjected to this disfigurement. There is a callousness to the marking up of the photographs on CI 9 nos. 20306 and 20307. It was not necessary. The decision to do it was arbitrary. It is a record of disregard and contempt, through a literal defacement of a woman and a child. There is something especially cruel about the treatment of these photographs given the scarcity of Chinese women and children in this archive.

That almost all of the people pictured in the CI 9s are men is not surprising. Still, seeing photograph after photograph after photograph, thousands upon thousands of Chinese men who lived and worked in Canada for decades, gives an inexorable visual weight to the loneliness of their experiences. Through her engagement with Allan Sekula's arguments about the body in the archive, McAllister notes that "what archives lack in specific details about each photograph insofar as they have been torn from their social context of use, they are rich in potential for identifying patterns and relations" (2018, 179). The pattern that emerges out of the CI 9 photographic archive is one of immense isolation and the persistent deprivation of familial and kinship relations.

It has long been accepted that early Chinese migrants to Canada formed a "bachelor society" because the restrictions imposed by the head tax, and outright exclusion after 1923, meant that it was nearly impossible for any Chinese person, much less Chinese women and children, to migrate to Canada. As Arlene Chan recognizes in her entry on the Chinese Immigration Act for *The Canadian Encyclopedia*, the effect of exclusion in terms of diminishing the community was stark: "During the exclusionary period, fewer than 50 Chinese immigrants were allowed entry. The population decreased by 25 per cent, from 39,587 in 1921 to 32,528 by 1951." The decline of the Chinese community in Canada emerges not only out of the fact of exclusion, but also out of the significant gender imbalance within the community. In his study of census data from this period, Peter Li reinforces Chan's observations by paying particular attention to gender ratios: "In 1911, among the 27,831 Chinese in Canada, the sex ratio was 2,800 men to 100 women; in 1931, it was 1,240 men to 100 women among the 46,519 Chinese" (2008, 129). That is, women make up less than 1 per cent of the Chinese population in Canada during the exclusion. The effects of this huge gender imbalance was devastating for Chinese families on both sides of the Pacific.

Most of the Chinese migrants in Canada during this period had families but the law prevented these families from being reunited in Canada:

> Not only did the law ban Chinese immigration, it also intentionally disrupted family life and stunted community growth … In 1941 there were 29,033 Chinese men in Canada, over 80 per cent of whom were married with wives and children left behind in China. Enduring this family separation, these "married bachelors" lived alone. A mere handful had the financial means to make a trip to China a few times during the exclusionary years to either marry or visit their wives and children. Whether or not they were Canadian-born or naturalized, they were not allowed to sponsor family members to join them in Canada. (Chan 2017)

This history of exclusion and its shattering effects on Chinese-Canadian families is likely to be familiar to even casual observers of Canadian immigration history. But, through the CI 9 photographs, it is possible to see what a bachelor society looks like at the granular level of individual lives.

Fig. 3.4
"Completion of the Canadian Pacific Railway through the Rockies," 7 November 1885.

Indeed, I want to suggest that the CI 9 photographs should be viewed collectively, *en masse*, as a portrait of the Chinese-Canadian bachelor society. Such a viewing disrupts what has been the more typical depiction of the bachelor society, which is centred on groups of Chinese men, usually in the context of their labour. This includes images of men working on the railway and in lumber camps, such as the images in figures 3.4, 3.5, and 3.6 from the Glenbow Archives.

Fig. 3.5
"Chinese work gang, Canadian Pacific Railway tracks near summit, British Columbia," 1889.

Fig. 3.6
"Interior of city cafe and Chinese restaurant, Lacombe, Alberta," 1900–35.

Fig. 3.7 (opposite)
"Chinese Nationalist League, Fort Macleod, Alberta," ca. 1910.

In addition to these images of Chinese labourers, there are also images of community organizations and social clubs such as hockey teams and the religious associations from this period, including one of the Chinese Nationalist League in Fort Macleod, Alberta, and of the Chinese YMCA Hockey Team in Calgary in 1917.

Even where group portraits did not exist in the first instance, there were composite portraits, such as the one of Chinese men living in Lacombe, Alberta, in figure 3.9.

The Glenbow Archives, where this composite image is housed, notes that "the caption indicates that these are people who live in Lacombe, Canada, and provides a date based on the Chinese year. The photograph is meant to be given to someone as a souvenir."

These group images capture the ways in which Chinese migrants made and found community for each other out of conditions that were otherwise extremely isolated and lonely. Still, focusing on these images as emblematic of a bachelor society risks underestimating the social segregation to which so many Chinese migrants were subjected. Not only were Chinese migrants often segregated from the rest of society, they were also often separated from each other.

Reading the mass of these Chinese head tax photographs collectively as another kind of portrait of the bachelor society allows us to more fully visualize the isolation of Chinese migrants during the head tax and exclusion period. It is not just the absolute volume of these individual images, one

Fig. 3.8
"Hockey team, Chinese YMCA, Calgary, Alberta," ca. 1917.

Chinese man after another, but also the form of the images themselves. As I discuss in chapter 2, the identification photograph exceeds the limitations of its genre. The boundary between a portrait and an identification photograph is often mutable, and, indeed, an examination of Chinese ancestor portraits reveals concordances between honorific and repressive photographs in the context of Chinese portraiture.

Fig. 3.9
"Chinese men's group, Lacombe, Alberta," ca. 1910–35.

Taking up these identification photographs in terms of how they exceed the limitations of the genre means not only seeing beyond their repressive state function, but looking at what they show, at the level of form, about kinship for Chinese migrants of this period. These identification images are overwhelmingly portrayals of isolation. In each one, the subject is caught within the bounds of the frame. Each migrant is cut off from others, shorn of contextualizing and humanizing elements of sociability that the group images gesture towards. Here, in these thousands of identification photographs, the subjects are not visually situated in terms of their work. They are not pictured in the midst of others. Alone, almost always without props such as furniture, books, and other symbols of a place in a social world, the subjects of these images are cut away from each other by the very form of the image. While it is true that identification photographs are, by their very nature, images of individuals cut off from others, the photographs on the CI 9s are particularly notable for their lack of variation and their adherence to the conventions of identity photography established by the mug shot. This consistency distinguishes them from the US identification photographs of Chinese migrants. As Anna Pegler-Gordon observes:

> There was wide variation in the types of photographs submitted to and accepted by the [US] Immigration Bureau. Photographs presented to the Immigration Bureau came in all sizes and shapes: most were rectangular vertical portraits, but some had trimmed corners and others were shaped as arches or ovals. They were placed in various positions on the document: in the upper or lower corners, crammed sideways along the edge, or displayed in the exact center of the paper … The photographs represented a range of portraiture conventions from elaborate studio portraits to simple head shots. They incorporated aspects of Chinese and Western convention, and they presented their subjects standing, seated, facing the camera, or looking to the side. (2009, 44)

This variation in the US Chinese head tax photographs attests to the many ways in which Chinese migrants contested and resisted the constrictions of the demand for photographic identification (48). While Chinese migrants in Canada, as the previous chapter shows, also enacted their own contestations against this regulatory demand, the space in which they did so was much more restrictive. Unlike the US forms that Johnson and Pegler-Gordon examine, there was a clearly demarcated space on each certificate where the identification had to be placed. Only very rarely were there deviations from this spatial rule.

Such exceptions were made for the families of merchants. This can be seen, for example, in the images of the Jung and Chong families (figs. 3.10–3.14).

In this series, the Chong family is pictured in two photographs, both used twice. Together, these two group photographs form a family portrait of a mother and her five children, four daughters and one son. The CI 9s identify the members of this family as follows:

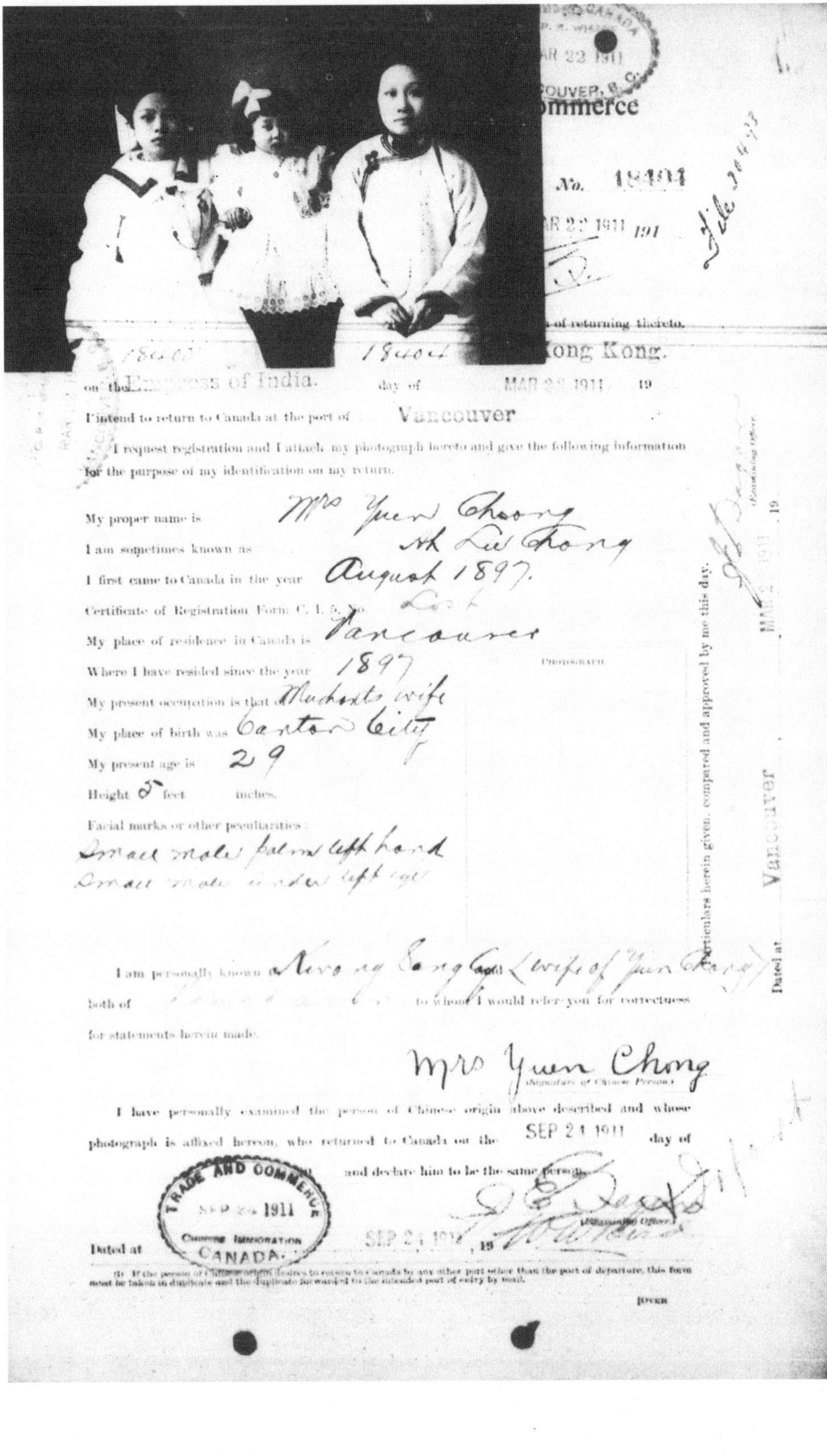

...ommerce

No. 18404

MAR 22 1911 191

File 30473

...of returning thereto.

18403 18404 Hong Kong.

on the Empress of India. day of MAR 22 1911 19

I intend to return to Canada at the port of Vancouver

I request registration and I attach my photograph hereto and give the following information for the purpose of my identification on my return.

My proper name is Mrs Yuen Choong

I am sometimes known as Ah Lee Chong

I first came to Canada in the year August 1897.

Certificate of Registration Form C. I. 5, No. Lost

My place of residence in Canada is Vancouver

Where I have resided since the year 1897

My present occupation is that of Merchant's wife

My place of birth was Canton City

My present age is 29

Height 5 feet inches.

Facial marks or other peculiarities:

Small mole palm left hand

Small mole under left eye

PHOTOGRAPH

I am personally known to Kwong ng Sang Co. (wife of Yuen Chong)

both of to whom I would refer you for correctness for statements herein made.

Mrs Yuen Chong
(Signature of Chinese Person.)

I have personally examined the person of Chinese origin above described and whose photograph is affixed hereon, who returned to Canada on the SEP 21 1911 day of and declare him to be the same person.

(Examining Officer.)

Dated at SEP 21 1911, 19

TRADE AND COMMERCE SEP 21 1911 CHINESE IMMIGRATION CANADA.

(1) If the person of Chinese origin desires to return to Canada by any other port other than the port of departure, this form must be taken in duplicate and the duplicate forwarded to the intended port of entry by mail.

(OVER)

Particulars herein given, compared and approved by me this day.

Dated at Vancouver MAR 22 1911 19

(Examining Officer.)

Fig. 3.10
CI 9 No. 18404,
Reel no. T-6047.

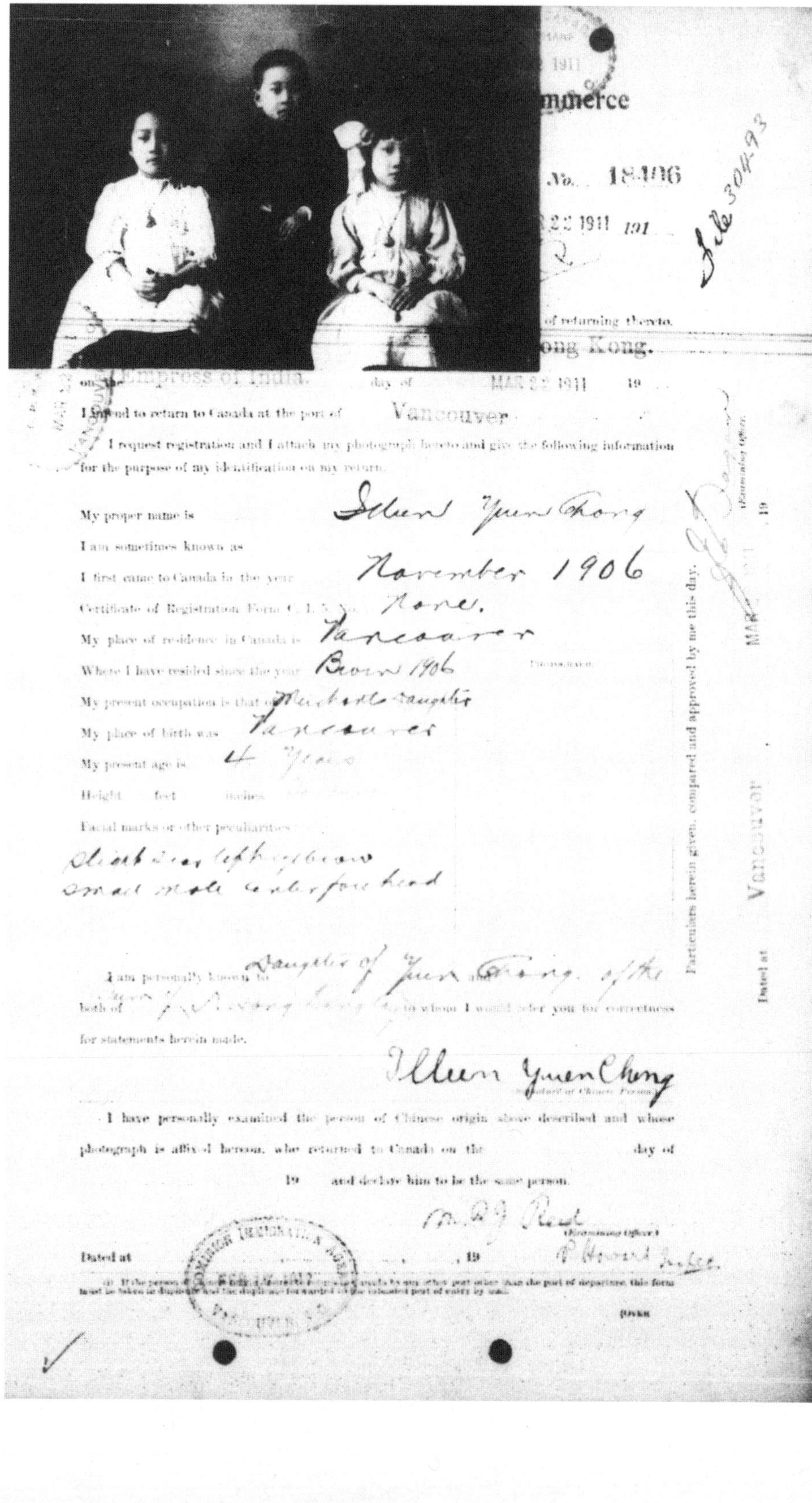

...mmerce

No. 18406

MAR 22 1911 191

File 304-93

...of returning thereto.

...ong Kong.

on the Empress of India. day of MAR 22 1911 19

I intend to return to Canada at the port of Vancouver

I request registration and I attach my photograph hereto and give the following information for the purpose of my identification on my return.

My proper name is Eileen Yuen Chong

I am sometimes known as

I first came to Canada in the year November 1906

Certificate of Registration Form C.I. 5 No. None.

My place of residence in Canada is Vancouver

Where I have resided since the year Born 1906

My present occupation is that of Merchant's daughter

My place of birth was Vancouver

My present age is 4 years

Height feet inches

Facial marks or other peculiarities

Slight scar left eyebrow
small mole under forehead

I am personally known to Daughter of Yuen Chong of the ... both of ... to whom I would refer you for correctness for statements herein made.

Eileen Yuen Chong
(Signature of Chinese Person)

I have personally examined the person of Chinese origin above described and whose photograph is affixed hereto, who returned to Canada on the day of 19 and declare him to be the same person.

M. R. J. Reid
(Examining Officer)

Dated at , 19 P. Howard Insp.

Particulars herein given, compared and approved by me this day. MAR 22 1911 19 (Examining Officer)

Dated at Vancouver

Fig. 3.11
CI 9 No. 18406, Reel no. T-6047.

Fig. 3.12 (opposite)
CI 9 No. 18407, Reel no. T-6047.

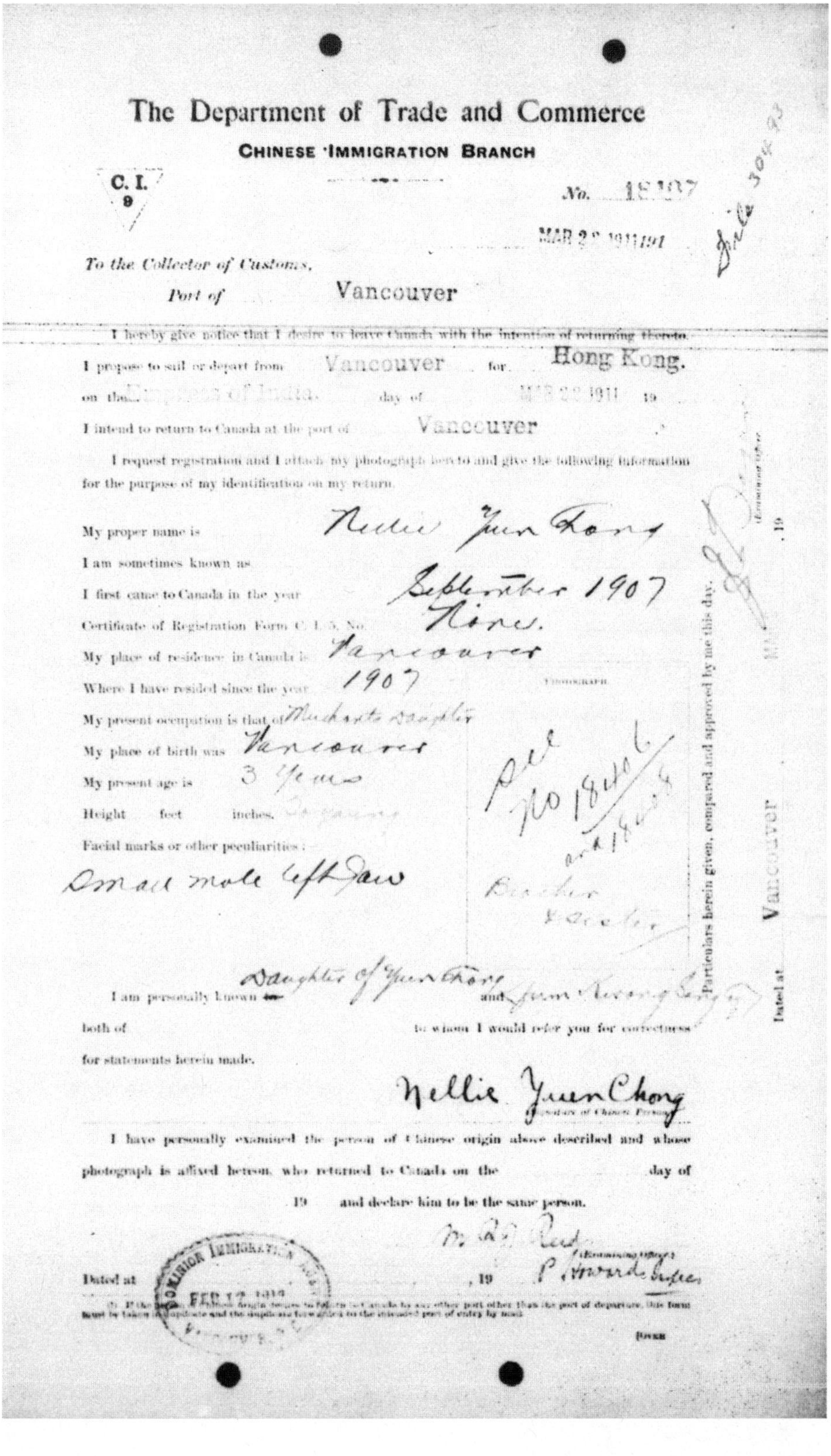

The Department of Trade and Commerce

CHINESE IMMIGRATION BRANCH

C. I. 9

No. 18107

MAR 28 1911 191

File 30493

To the Collector of Customs,

Port of Vancouver

I hereby give notice that I desire to leave Canada with the intention of returning thereto.

I propose to sail or depart from Vancouver for Hong Kong.

on the Empress of India day of MAR 28 1911 19

I intend to return to Canada at the port of Vancouver

I request registration and I attach my photograph hereto and give the following information for the purpose of my identification on my return.

My proper name is Nellie Yuen Kong

I am sometimes known as

I first came to Canada in the year September 1907

Certificate of Registration Form C. I. 5, No. None.

My place of residence in Canada is Vancouver

Where I have resided since the year 1907

My present occupation is that of Merchant's Daughter

My place of birth was Vancouver

My present age is 3 Years

Height feet inches.

Facial marks or other peculiarities:

Small mole left Jaw

PHOTOGRAPH

P.d. No 18406 and 18408 Brother & Sister

I am personally known to Daughter of Yuen Kong and Yuen Kwong Sing

both of to whom I would refer you for correctness for statements herein made.

Nellie Yuen Chong
(Signature of Chinese Person)

I have personally examined the person of Chinese origin above described and whose photograph is affixed hereto, who returned to Canada on the day of 19 and declare him to be the same person.

W. R. Reid
(Examining Officer)

Dated at , 19 P. Howard Insp.

DOMINION IMMIGRATION AGENCY FEB 17 1914 VANCOUVER B.C.

(1) If the person of Chinese origin desires to return to Canada to any other port other than the port of departure, this form must be taken in duplicate and the duplicate forwarded to the intended port of entry by mail.

Particulars herein given, compared and approved by me this day. MAR 19

(Examining Officer)

Dated at Vancouver

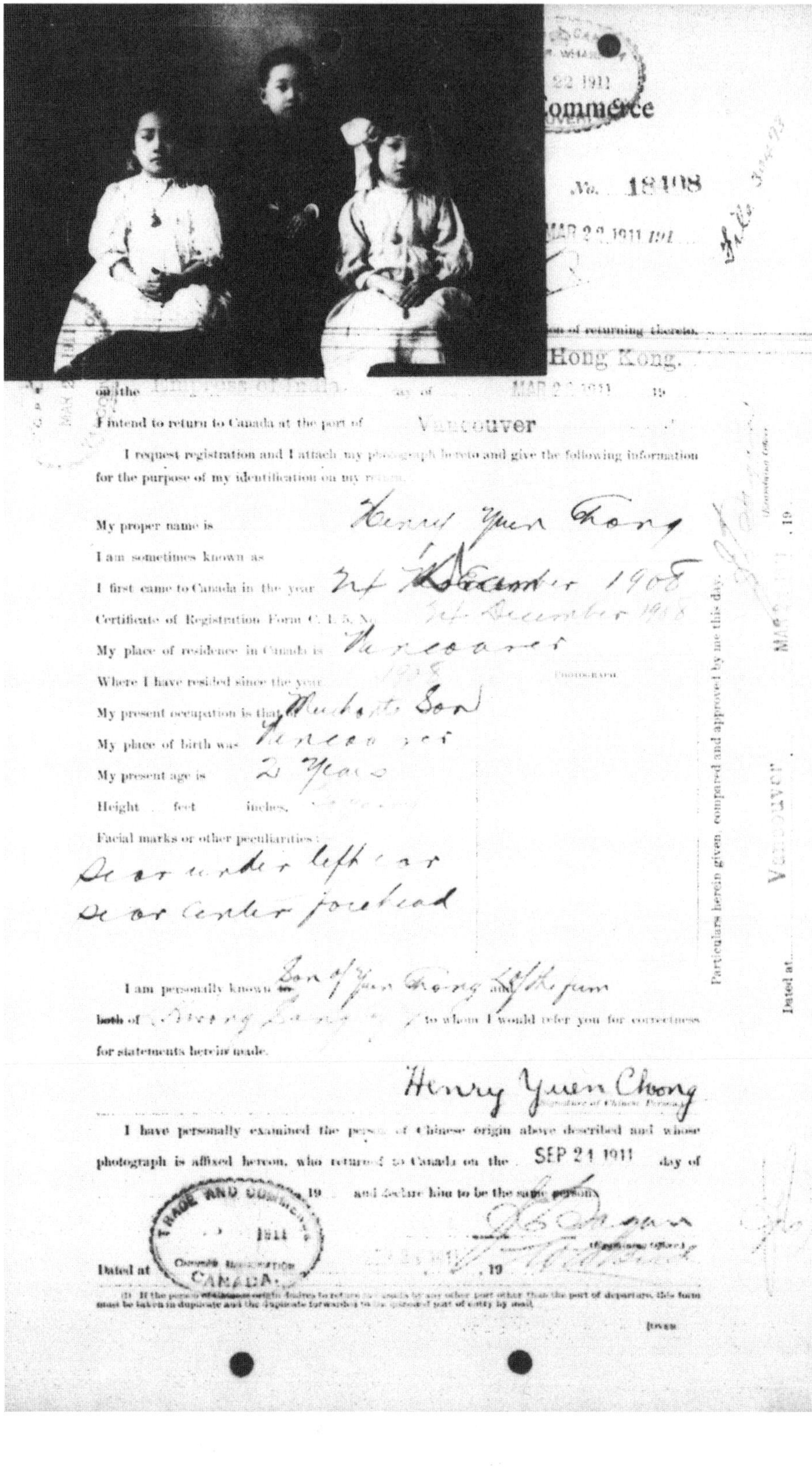

Commerce

No. 18408

MAR 2 ? 1911 191

...on of returning thereto.

Hong Kong.

on the ... day of MAR 2 ? 1911 19

I intend to return to Canada at the port of Vancouver

I request registration and I attach my photograph hereto and give the following information for the purpose of my identification on my return.

My proper name is Henry Yuen Chong

I am sometimes known as

I first came to Canada in the year 1st December 1908

Certificate of Registration Form C. I. 5, No. 1st December 1908

My place of residence in Canada is Vancouver

Where I have resided since the year 1908

My present occupation is that Merchant's Son

My place of birth was Vancouver

My present age is 2 Years

Height feet inches.

Facial marks or other peculiarities:

Scar under left ear

Scar center forehead

I am personally known to Son of Yuen Chong of the firm

both of Wong Lang ... to whom I would refer you for correctness for statements herein made.

Henry Yuen Chong

(Signature of Chinese Person.)

I have personally examined the person of Chinese origin above described and whose photograph is affixed hereon, who returned to Canada on the SEP 21 1911 day of ... 19 ... and declare him to be the same person.

(Controller Officer.)

Dated at ... 19

Particulars herein given compared and approved by me this day.

Dated at Vancouver MAR ... 19

Fig. 3.13
CI 9 No. 18408, Reel no. T-6047.

Fig. 3.14 (opposite)
CI 9 No. 18409, Reel no. T-6047.

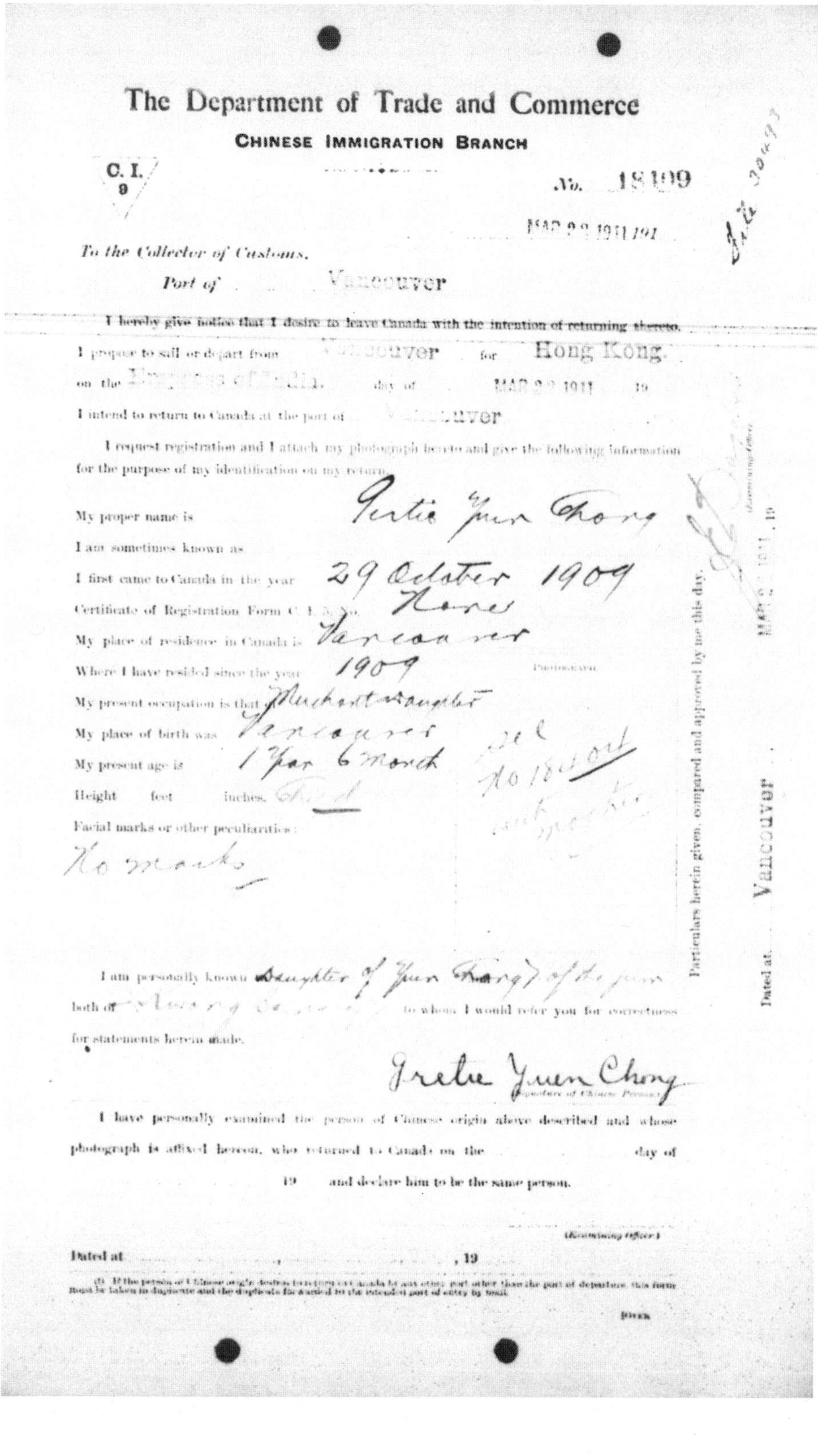

The Department of Trade and Commerce

CHINESE IMMIGRATION BRANCH

C. I. 9

No. 18109

MAR 22 1911 191

To the Collector of Customs,

Port of Vancouver

I hereby give notice that I desire to leave Canada with the intention of returning thereto.

I propose to sail or depart from Vancouver for Hong Kong.

on the Empress of India day of MAR 22 1911 19

I intend to return to Canada at the port of Vancouver

I request registration and I attach my photograph hereto and give the following information for the purpose of my identification on my return.

My proper name is Gertie Yuen Chong

I am sometimes known as

I first came to Canada in the year 29 October 1909

Certificate of Registration Form C. I. 5 No. None

My place of residence in Canada is Vancouver

Where I have resided since the year 1909

My present occupation is that of Merchant daughter

My place of birth was Vancouver

My present age is 1 year 6 month

Height feet inches.

Facial marks or other peculiarities:

No marks

Photograph.

I am personally known Daughter of Yuen Chong of the firm

both of Kwong [illegible] to whom I would refer you for correctness for statements herein made.

Gertie Yuen Chong
(Signature of Chinese Person)

I have personally examined the person of Chinese origin above described and whose photograph is affixed hereon, who returned to Canada on the day of 19 and declare him to be the same person.

(Examining Officer)

Dated at , 19

(1) If the person of Chinese origin desires to return to Canada by any other port other than the port of departure, this form must be taken in duplicate and the duplicate forwarded to the intended port of entry by mail.

Particulars herein given, compared and approved by me this day.

Dated at Vancouver MAR 22 1911 19

(Examining Officer)

CI 9 no. 18404 – Mrs. Yuen Chong, 29
CI 9 no. 18405 – "Fooka" Ella Yuen Chong, 11, daughter
CI 9 no. 18406 – Suen Yuen Chong, 4, daughter
CI 9 no. 18407 – Nellie Yuen Chong, 3, daughter, no photo see 18406, "brother and sister"
CI 9 no. 18408 – Henry Yuen Chong, brother, 2 yrs old
CI 9 no. 18409 – Gertie Yuen Chong, 1 year and 6 months old, no photo see 18404

Even though the whole family is not brought together into a single image, these two photographs of the Chongs allow the viewer to see them as members of a family. No member of the family is pictured alone. And even though a single photograph is used on more than one CI 9, the subjects of the photograph are not subsequently scratched out in order to distinguish one from the other. Instead, the agent who is presented with their certificates engages with their photographs as most viewers of family photographs must – they have to look and try to figure out who each person in the photograph might be. These Chong family portraits thus minimize the harsh effect of the technology of mass capture in that the examiners of their certificates will engage in acts of viewing which demand seeing the people in the photographs as being related to each other.

The CI 9s for this family flout the conventions of the identification photograph in these certificates by either omitting a photograph altogether, or pasting the photograph onto the document such that the photograph obscures some of the writing. On CI 9 18405, the name of the outgoing ship has been completely occluded. While they are not exempted from the requirement for identification photographs, the Chong family is nonetheless permitted to take up a space outside the confines of the identification photograph. That space, with a rectangular outline clearly marked to the right of the certificate, is allowed to be left blank. Instead, appended to the top left corner of the certificate, they are outside of the regulatory frame. Unlike the certificates of Mrs See and Miss Wong Louie Choue from CI 9 nos. 20306 and 20307 (figs. 3.1 and 3.2), the Chong family does not have to submit a separate photograph for each member of the family. Some of the children (Nellie and Gertie) are permitted CI 9s with no photograph at all. The space where the photograph should be on their certificates refers the viewer to another certificate. They are allowed to be seen through their relationships with their mother or brother. While it is rare for any family to be seen in this archive, it is especially rare for the family to be pictured together in group portraits where the relations between one family member and another are clearly identified and acknowledged. Still, the

Chong family is not entirely intact. The father does not appear in either of the two photographs, and the mother does not appear with all five of her children in either photograph.

In contrast, consider the portrait of an intact family, the Jungs, in figure 3.15. As I will show later in my discussion of the Lawsons, a less-privileged Chinese migrant family headed by a man who was neither a merchant nor a diplomat, photographs like the one of the Jungs, where members of a family are pictured together, are the exception rather than the rule. Like the Chong children, the Jung children may travel with certificates that have no photographs at all (figs. 3.16 and 3.17).

In lieu of an identification photograph, the children of this merchant were permitted to simply have their images cross-referenced with their parents' certificates. Instead of having their photographs disfigured and literally crossed out, as was the case with Mrs See and Miss Wong, they are given the grace of a textual reference: "see no 18400/18401." Like the Chongs, their familial relationships are acknowledged with the further note "Father Mother" in the space where the identification photograph should have been. Consolidating their relations as a family, the parents are pictured with their children on their CI 9s.

It is worth noting that even with the privileges afforded this family, their relationships with each other are still often obscured by the diplomatics of the form. In the case of the Jung family, the two children are either not given their father's surname (Jung) or they have a surname (Lin) that they do not share with their father. If not for the note in lieu of the photograph on CI 9 nos. 18402 and 18403 for Lin King and Lin Oy, there would be no way to know that Jung Suk and Mrs Jung Suk of CI 9 nos. 18400 and 18401 are their parents. Without the written note that reads "see no 18400/18401 Father Mother," the only way to understand that Lin King and Lin Oy are the children of the Jungs would be through the sequential ordering of the certificates where the children's certificates follow directly from those of the adults. As my discussion of the Lawson family will show, attending to the numbering of the certificates can reveal family relationships that are otherwise completely invisible within the CI 9s themselves. Kinship relationships are not acknowledged or made evident in the overwhelming majority of the certificates in this archive. Instead, the CI 9 archive separated family members from each other and disavowed the relationships of family members even when they were travelling together.

Most often, the CI 9s capture a group of people who are singled out, specifically and systematically targeted by legislation, and sequestered from the sphere of citizenship because the law permitted and demanded their exclusion. This is not simply the isolation of one group of people from the

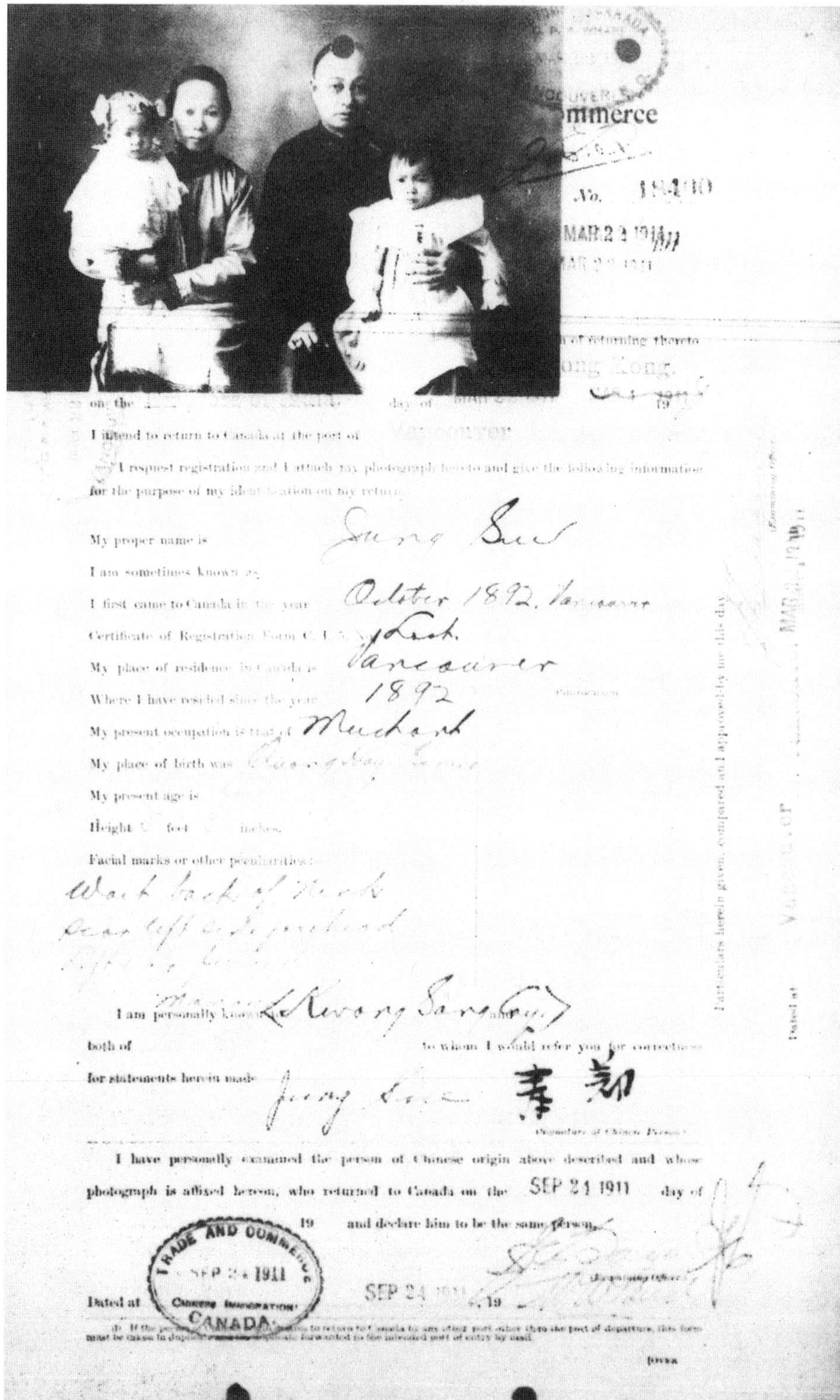

...mmerce

No. 18400

MAR 29 1911

...of returning thereto ...ong Kong.

on the ... day of ... 19...

I intend to return to Canada at the port of Vancouver

I request registration and I attach my photograph hereto and give the following information for the purpose of my identification on my return.

My proper name is Jung Sue

I am sometimes known as

I first came to Canada in the year October 1892, Vancouver

Certificate of Registration Form C. I. 5 No. Lost.

My place of residence in Canada is Vancouver

Where I have resided since the year 1892

My present occupation is that of Merchant

My place of birth was

My present age is

Height ... feet ... inches.

Facial marks or other peculiarities:

Wart back of neck

I am personally known to ... (Kwong Sang ...)

both of ... to whom I would refer you for correctness for statements herein made

Jung Sue

(Signature of Chinese Person)

I have personally examined the person of Chinese origin above described and whose photograph is affixed hereto, who returned to Canada on the SEP 24 1911 day of ... 19... and declare him to be the same person.

TRADE AND COMMERCE SEP 24 1911 CHINESE IMMIGRATION CANADA

Dated at ... SEP 24 1911 19...

(Examining Officer)

[OVER]

Fig. 3.15
CI 9 No. 18400, Reel no. T-6047.

Fig. 3.16 (opposite)
CI 9 No. 18403, Reel no. T-6047.

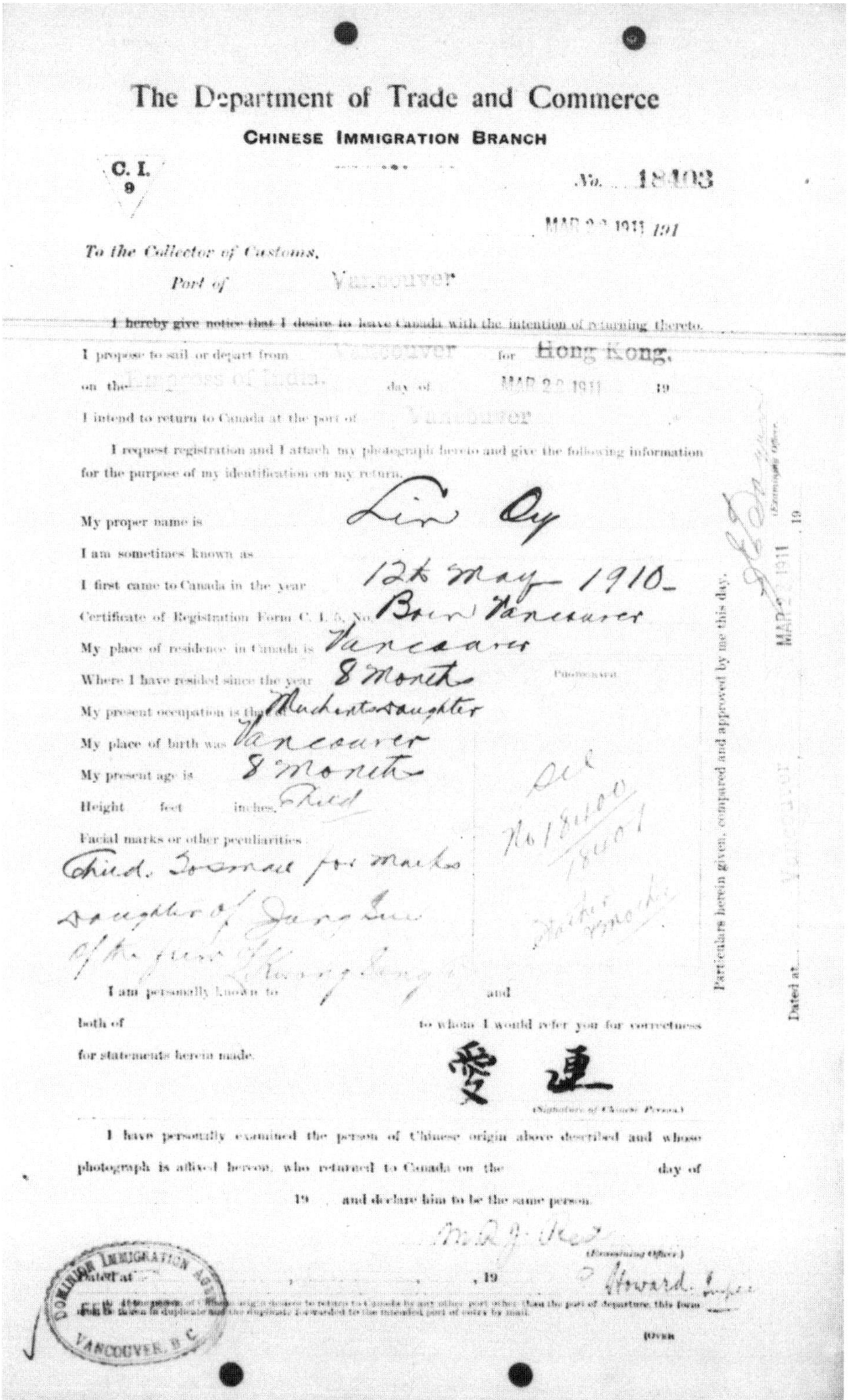

The Department of Trade and Commerce

CHINESE IMMIGRATION BRANCH

C. I. 9

No. 18403

MAR 22 1911 191

To the Collector of Customs,

Port of Vancouver

~~I hereby give notice that I desire to leave Canada with the intention of returning thereto.~~

I propose to sail or depart from Vancouver for Hong Kong,

on the Empress of India. day of MAR 22 1911 19

I intend to return to Canada at the port of Vancouver

I request registration and I attach my photograph hereto and give the following information for the purpose of my identification on my return.

My proper name is Lin Oy

I am sometimes known as

I first came to Canada in the year 12th May 1910

Certificate of Registration Form C. I. 5, No. Born Vancouver

My place of residence in Canada is Vancouver

Where I have resided since the year 8 Months

My present occupation is that Merchant's daughter

My place of birth was Vancouver

My present age is 8 months

Height feet inches. Child

Facial marks or other peculiarities:

Child. Too small for marks

daughter of Jang Lee

of the firm of Kwong Lung

I am personally known to and

both of to whom I would refer you for correctness for statements herein made.

愛連

(Signature of Chinese Person.)

See No 18400 18401

Father mother

Photograph

Particulars herein given, compared and approved by me this day.

MAR 22 1911 19

(Examining Officer.)

Dated at Vancouver

I have personally examined the person of Chinese origin above described and whose photograph is affixed hereon, who returned to Canada on the day of 19 and declare him to be the same person.

(Examining Officer.)

Dated at , 19

Howard. Inspec

If the person of Chinese origin desires to return to Canada by any other port other than the port of departure, this form should be taken in duplicate and the duplicate forwarded to the intended port of entry by mail.

DOMINION IMMIGRATION AGENT VANCOUVER, B.C.

(Over)

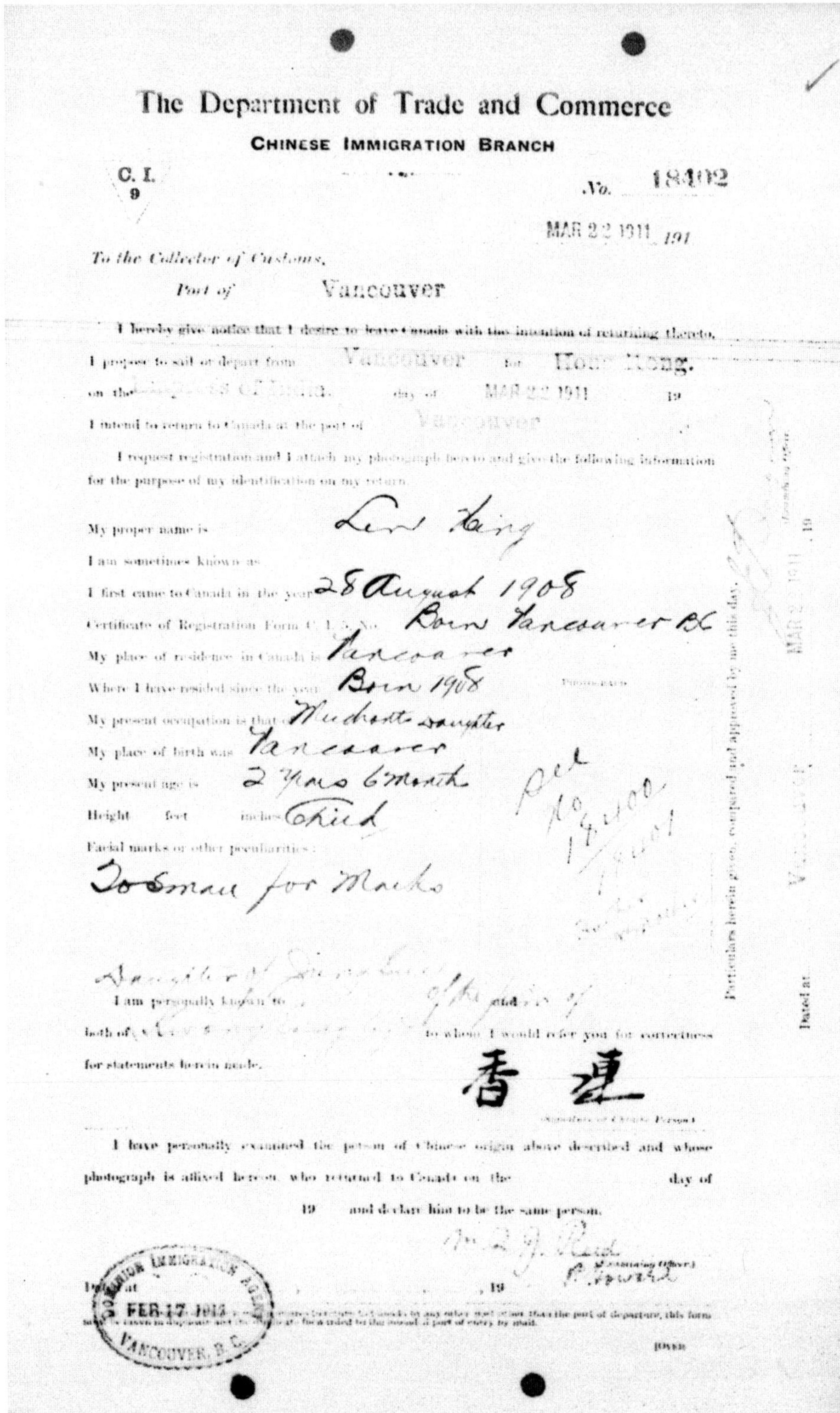

The Department of Trade and Commerce

CHINESE IMMIGRATION BRANCH

C. I. 9

No. 18402

MAR 22 1911 191

To the Collector of Customs,

Port of Vancouver

I hereby give notice that I desire to leave Canada with the intention of returning thereto.

I propose to sail or depart from Vancouver for Hong Kong.

on the Empress of India. day of MAR 22 1911 19

I intend to return to Canada at the port of Vancouver

I request registration and I attach my photograph hereto and give the following information for the purpose of my identification on my return.

My proper name is Lew King

I am sometimes known as

I first came to Canada in the year 28 August 1908

Certificate of Registration Form C. I. 5, No. Born Vancouver BC

My place of residence in Canada is Vancouver

Where I have resided since the year Born 1908

My present occupation is that of Merchants daughter

My place of birth was Vancouver

My present age is 2 years 6 month

Height feet inches Child

Facial marks or other peculiarities:

Too small for marks

Daughter of ...

I am personally known to ... of the ... and ...

both of ... to whom I would refer you for correctness for statements herein made.

香 ...

(Signature of Chinese Person)

I have personally examined the person of Chinese origin above described and whose photograph is affixed hereto, who returned to Canada on the day of 19 and declare him to be the same person.

(Examining Officer)

Dated at 19

DOMINION IMMIGRATION AGENT FEB 17 1914 VANCOUVER, B.C.

Fig. 3.17
CI 9 No. 18402, Reel no. T-6047.

larger society, but also of individual migrants from each other. Viewed as a kind of massive group portrait, the CI 9 photographs offer an image of collective isolation that is compounded by individual isolation. We need to see, or at least try to imagine, the CI 9 photographs *en masse*. We cannot just look at individual photographs and try to piece together, from a representative sample, an image of the group as a whole. I have struggled with this problem throughout my work on this archive.

It is a problem that, in a very different context, Ian Baucom identifies in *Spectres of the Atlantic* as the problem of postcolonial value. The central organizing event in Baucom's book is the *Zong* massacre, an event that I briefly discuss in chapter 1 but which I now want to consider in depth. In 1781, the crew of the *Zong* murdered more than 130 African slaves by throwing them overboard. After a mistake in navigation, the captain of the ship believed that there would not be enough supplies to support all those on board. He calculated that drowning a number of slaves, and then claiming insurance on them as lost cargo, would allow for the journey to remain profitable. The resulting claim and the court battle based on the insurance company's refusal to pay out the claim brought to light some of the horrors of the slave trade and was a signal event in the movement for abolition. For Baucom, the *Zong* massacre sets out a crucial problem of value that remains unresolved in our current moment.

Principally, it is the problem of the singular versus the exemplary. Each of the slaves murdered was singular. Each was an individual person with a specific history and identity. But, in order for their lives to have value in the actuarial sense, all of those differences must be flattened. Each murdered slave must be exemplary of another, an instance of the same kind or type of value. We now live with the legacy of a system of actuarial value that emerged out of, and was refined by, the slave trade. The whole of the insurance industry cannot, Baucom argues, be understood outside of the horrors of transatlantic slavery. This undergirding, the literal insuring of our entire contemporary economy, is problematic not simply because of the legacy of its emergence, but also because it puts into place a system of value that demands the evisceration of difference in the assignation of value. In this system, a life can only be valued insofar as it falls within a set of average values, which necessarily erases individual histories and specificities. For example, my life, insured, can only be valued in the ways in which it is typical within a limited range of controlling factors (age, country of birth, postal code, and so on). Baucom argues that "finance capital and its culture of speculation finds itself at once secured and articulated by that theory and the practice of insurance that exists to reexpress the (after)lives of persons and things not as themselves but as a suppositional, aggregate mode of being in the world. Insurance thus underwrites the hegemony of the average and the typical" (2005, 106). But it is not just the problem of averages that Baucom identifies. To insist upon the opposite, upon the necessity of the singular, is also to relinquish the political power of collectivity. We know about the *Zong* massacre because it was a case of mass murder. It did not draw public outrage because *one* slave had been thrown overboard. It comes to us because many people were murdered. It is a problem that persists. We live in the wake, as Christina Sharpe posits, of "the disaster of Black subjection" (2016, 5). The Black Lives Matter movement would not exist if one, singular, Black person had been killed by police. There would be no political movement over the unbearable but still individualized loss of Tamir Rice, or Eric Garner, or Sandra Bland, or Michael Brown. It is a movement because, in the United States in this moment in history, Black men are three and a half times more likely to be killed by police than white men. Thus, the problem of the singular versus the exemplary is also one of political weight. To insist on the singular is to also give up on the weight of the patterns, of the mass of an event, the profound collectivities formed out of the relationship between one tragedy and another.

In the fifth chapter of his book, Baucom tries to address this problem by turning to Gayatri Spivak's *A Critique of Postcolonial Reason*. For Baucom, Spivak "stages the undecidability of the singular and the obligation of decision as a challenge: 'Please decide …'" (2005, 166). Our choice is to decide what kind of truth the *Zong* massacre reveals. On the one hand, it "speaks to the episystemic truth of a global, worldly, situation." That is, "to read the *Zong* as symptomatic, exemplary, typical of something larger, more abstract, and more total, to read it … as something *worth* reading, *worth* uncovering, *worthwhile*, because the utterly singular history it assembles can be seen to find its general equivalent in the history of the modern, is to risk grounding the value of such a way of reading in the very value form whose speculative and catastrophic triumphs this event brings to light." Or, on the other hand, is the *Zong* massacre "something that maintains its cryptic silence, something singular and unverifiable" (168)? That is, is it something so unique that any truth it holds belongs solely to its own place in history, that there is no equivalent to it, that it is not a symptom or a shard of something larger? In wrestling with these questions, Baucom notes that Spivak deconstructs the binary of the choice that has to be made, but it is still a choice. Please, decide, she asks.

This choice, between that which is exemplary and that which is singular, has haunted me. On the one hand, I want to attend to, and honour, each life on each certificate. Even if the subject's identity might be, on some level, falsified. There is still someone there behind that number, that photograph, those details of residency and occupation. There is a desire to uncover as much of the story of each person on each certificate as possible. Indeed, such an investigation can yield enormous rewards: there are deeply complex and illuminating histories behind each certificate. But I do not want to lose sight of the ways in which these certificates, taken together, also matter. It is the *mass* of these documents that reveals so much about the devastation of this system of exclusion, as well as the resilience of the people who were subjected to its strictures.

Portrait of the Kinship of the Passage

How, then, to think of more than 40,000 certificates? How to see them and understand them as a collectivity? As a vast system of relation? Their number is not so vast as to exceed the capability of the human imagination. 40,000 is a number that can be imagined. For example, there are about that many full-time students at the university where I work. At the same time, I cannot ask you, the reader, to look at each and every CI 9 as part of the process of reading this book. Still, I want you to look at them collectively, all 40,000 of them, as a larger portrait of the devastating effects of the head tax. That is not possible within the scope of this book.

Although it is an imperfect solution, I would like to show you a "portrait" of one form of relation that emerges in the CI 9 archive: the kinship of the passage. The bonds of the passage formed in the holds of the ship have been a fulcrum of diaspora studies. For Paul Gilroy, the ship, and by extension the relationships emerging in its hold, form a "chronotope" of Black slavery:

> I have settled on the image of ships in motion across the spaces between Europe, America, Africa, and the Caribbean as a central organising symbol for this enterprise and as my starting point. The image of the ship – a living, microcultural, micro-political system in motion – is especially important for historical and theoretical reasons … Ships immediately focus attention on the middle passage, on the various projects for redemptive return to an African homeland, on the circulation of ideas and activists as well as the movement of key cultural and political artifacts: tracts, books, gramophone records, and choirs. (1995, 4)

For Vijay Mishra (1996), the hold of the ships that carried indentured Indian workers across the Pacific made possible the emergence of the *jahaji bhai*, or ship brotherhood. Writing of the way in which the colonial process of documenting the disembarkation of Indian coolies was in itself a process of the reformation of kinship and relation, Mishra writes movingly of the passage as a rebirth, reinvention, and entry into history:

> There was a collective drama as one post was left for another. Labourers waded through knee-deep water after reaching the lagoons on lifebuoys. The repetitive nature of this disembarkation meant that people could refer to it as a moment of origin or genesis in the new land. Apart from the bonding possibilities of this act, the colonial documentation of the event meant that for the first time Indian subalterns became historical subjects. Since … their names, their villages, their castes and their parents' names were recorded on emigration passes this motley crowd entered for the first time the regulative history of the Empire. Yet there is no subaltern Marlow who has recounted the first encounter with these outposts of Empire, even though scattered and fragmented oral accounts of some indentured labourers have survived in folk stories and songs. All that remained was the memory of the passage and a loss that could only be sustained through the categories of myth. The sailing ship (and after 1880 the steamship) became as important a site for the purposes of legitimation as the motherland itself. The bonds created through the *jahaji bhai* ('ship-brotherhood') confraternity led to social configurations that were not unlike those of the village networks in India, but much more radical because this was the first space in which the Indian labourers had to face the reality of losing caste as a consequence of crossing the *kalapani*, the black sea. (429–30)

Of course, this ship brotherhood was also a sisterhood. As Miriam Pirbhai notes in "The Jahaji-Bhain Principle," there was ship sisterhood that reworks the singularity of the fraternal experience Mishra depicts. Still, both Pirbhai and Mishra locate the experience of the passage, of the collective displacement, centrally in the construction of new forms of relation in diaspora.

In a reverse journey that remains nonetheless tied to the diasporic connection that Gilroy, Mishra, and Pirbhai uncover, the CI 9 archive shows the destruction and reformation of kinship relations in the journey away from the site of diasporic rupture. In the CI 9s, we can follow connections formed by migrants who are engaging in a doubled return – back to a putative "home" across the Pacific, and then, often, again to their lives in Canada. Where Mishra and Gilroy understand the shipboard passage from the space of origin as one in which diasporic subjects emerge out of the trauma of dispersal, the *Oanfa* portraits (collated as a "collective portrait" in the endpapers to this book) show diasporic subjects who are ostensibly returning "home." But, the homes to which they might return – and it is, of course, speculation that they are returning home – cannot be the same homes that they left behind. As each of their certificates reveal, they have been away too long for these homes to have stayed the same. Most migrants were away for many years. What is more, the restrictions of the Chinese Immigration Act meant that they could not be away from Canada for more than two years at a time if they wished to be readmitted. So the homes to which they were returning, if they were indeed returning home, were provisional. If the ship brotherhood and sisterhood of the voyage out is fundamentally a kinship borne of collective trauma, this passage of return cannot undo that harm. It may offer repair or alleviate the ache of losing family and intimacy, but it is not a reversal. It does not unmake the bonds that were formed on the passage out and the subjectivities forged out of the trauma of that experience.

Still, the bonds formed on the ship, crossing back eastward across the Pacific, should not be dismissed. The migrants aboard are not subject to the initial trauma of dispersal, but this crossing carries its own pain. Every person who has ever tried to return home knows this pain. Deep in your body, you know that there is no return. The home that you have left is no longer. The relations you had are ruptured. There may be repair, and there will be a different home, but the pain of those losses forges its own bond. Each ship in the CI 9 archive carries a community of migrants bound by the processes of mass capture where relationships and connections between people are broken, formed, and reformed. Later in this chapter I will show, in detail, the process of destruction and reconstruction of one family enfolded into this archive. But first, let me pause and ask you to consider with me the ship itself as a site of relation and kinship. In approaching the ship as a space of kinship, I am wagering a response to the question of postcolonial value that Baucom and Spivak pose. I cannot choose between the singular and the exemplary. I do not wish to choose. Instead, let us consider just one ship as both singular and exemplary.

I have created an online album displaying the CI 9s for every certificate-carrying passenger on the SS *Oanfa*, which departed from Victoria, British Columbia on 14 October 1911. These are CI 9 nos. 17903 to 18190. There are 286 migrants that have been issued CI 9s on this ship. To visit what I am calling the "*Oanfa* album," please see the open access edition of this book.

To look at the certificate and photograph of everyone on this ship is to see how each migrant is singular and exemplary. No one person on this ship is like another, and yet each one is also so much like the other. Bound by a process of mass capture that defined them by their exclusion from the state, and then bound again by the bonds of a passage across the Pacific Ocean, each migrant on this ship must be seen at least twice. Seen once, he or she is an individual with a specific history. Seen again, they are also borne on a trans-oceanic kinship bound to each other for the duration of the experience of the passage.

In asking for the collectivity of these 286 photographs to be seen together as a way to envision kinship, I am calling for a rethinking of the family album. In *Suspended Conversations* Martha Langford observes that "family has always begged explanation, and the 'family album' does too" (2001, 99). In this sense, I want to assume the role of the "compiler" of this family album and use the remainder of this chapter to offer what Langford calls "the oral scaffolding" (23) for the *Oanfa* album. I will point to pictures and tell you about the connections between them. "The album is an instrument of collective show and tell," writes Langford (20); let us look at how these CI 9s function as a collective. Even though no one on this ship is pictured together in the album, there are relations between all of them that matter. These photographs of Chinese migrants aboard the *Oanfa* depart from the way in which families have been represented but I argue that they are, taken together, a portrait of kinship forged out of the diasporic experience of a passage and the histories of racism that bound them through this process of mass capture.

Regarding the photographs from these 286 CI 9 certificates as a kind of collective family portrait is one way to decolonize family photographs in the manner outlined by Andrea Doucet. In her discussion of decolonizing family photographs, Doucet argues for taking up "non-representational" approaches where "a shift to nonrepresentation means thinking about the dialogic and performative character of narratives and how they are made and remade within relational webs and relational ontologies" (2018, 19). Decolonizing the family photograph is grounded in the shift from knowing by looking at something to knowing through the intimacies of engaging with the images' materiality. For mass capture, this material is not necessarily about physically handling the photographs themselves – an act which is, as the coda to this book will discuss, nearly impossible – but rather about materiality in terms of the conditions of the object's production. For the CI 9s, this materiality is about taking into account the persecution that has led to the production of these photographs on these forms.

Considered as a whole, the 286 photographs of CI 9 holders on the *Oanfa* is a collective portrait emerging out of persecution. Seeing these photographs as tied to one to another, we can break down the ways in which these men, women, and children were visually siloed. We can see through the persecution of their isolation. Kept apart from one another, denied the intimacy of being pictured together, these are images of mass capture as a denial of kinship. Viewing them together is itself a radical act of picturing what mass capture could not fully do. The people on this ship did have relationships; they were bound by feelings of kinship, of ship brotherhood and sisterhood. We have to look for these intimacies despite the conditions of their persecution. For McAllister, persecution means "actions taken against a group that restricts or denies their freedom to participate in society and maintain and develop their identities, cultures, and political institutions. The ability to record, save, and transmit information about their lives is impeded through laws such as censorship, destruction, or confiscation of their records, poor institutional funding, public hostility, and hate crimes: recall the Black Loyalist Heritage Centre in Birchtow, which was burnt down in 2006" (2018, 169n2). McAllister's definition points to the role of private and public records in the persecution of a community. The CI 9 records persist despite the families that were ruptured by the laws of which the CI 9 system is a part. In seeing the *Oanfa* photographs collectively, we counter some of the state's attempts to deny these migrants a sense of kinship. In her examination of Japanese-Canadian family photographs, Namiko Kunimoto argues that family photographs taken under conditions of persecution "allowed a space of intimacy between the image and the subject, a space denied in political propaganda and the official documentary photographs of Japanese Canadians ... Photographs by government officials most often represent Japanese internees as an anonymous, powerless group – a problematic representation that personal photography works against" (2004, 142). While the CI 9 photographs were not directly produced by the state, their use by the state effected a refusal of feelings of kinship that viewing them collectively restores.

This restoration through envisioning kinship across the forms and regulations that divide does ask the viewer to look at the idea of kinship and family non-representationally. It asks for a way to see family by shifting what a representation of a family should look like. But this shift poses a different kind of ethical question, one that Doucet draws from Cate Sandilands: "'How can the recognition of the limits of representation coexist with the desire to include – represent – other voices more fully?'" (2018, 19). In response to this question, I ask for the inclusion of this shipboard brotherhood and sisterhood to be understood as a representation of family photography. To find family in the wake of the devastation of legislative practices that deliberately sought to separate families from each other means looking for representations that are non-representative. Following Gillian Rose (2010), Doucet notes that "social, public, and cultural narratives of family photos have widened to include how particular kinds of 'family photographs are entering public circulation' and 'public spaces of display,' thus changing the conceptual meanings of both *family* photographs and intimacies" (2018, 19). While Rose and Doucet discuss contemporary family photography, their embrace of the need to change what we think of as family photography, and of the intimacies in those images, resonates with my call to think of the *Oanfa* photographs as a collective portrait, and as an envisioning of the feeling of kinship.

Looking at identification photographs in aggregate, as a collective portrait spanning the berths of single ship, also allows for a different understanding of the relationship between these photographs and vernacular photography. Like conventional family photographs, identification photographs are part of a genre of photography known as "vernacular photographs." Geoffrey Batchen writes of vernacular photographs as "tending to be made in vast numbers by anonymous, amateur, working-class, and sometimes even collective hands or, worse, by crass commercial profiteers … they muck up the story of great masters and transcendent aesthetic achievements, and disrupt its smooth European-American prejudice" (2002, 57–8). Annette Kuhn applies this idea to family photographs in particular when she argues for the critical value of these images: "As commonplace material artifacts, family photographs and albums contain meanings, and also seem infinitely capable of generating new ones at the point at which photography and memory work meet" (2007, 285). Expanding the idea of the family photograph or family album to a collection of 286 identification photographs of migrants aboard a ship reveals the necessity of memory work for looking at these photographs. Engaging with them non-representationally, as Doucet advises, allows a view into intimacy and feelings of kinship that would otherwise be invisible. Adopting a "nonrepresentational approach to family photographs … attends to images as a set of practices whose content and meanings are in turn made within social practices, including specific research practices wherein the photos are viewed and discussed" (Doucet 2018, 11). Examining the CI 9 photographs as part of a practice addresses the ways in which families are not obviously represented in these images and allows for a way of envisioning kinship non-representationally. While identification photographs and family photographs might both easily fall under the concept of the vernacular photography, they are not often thought of together. Doing so now, thinking of identification as a route to kinship, is one way to see through the persecution of mass capture.

Even though the CI 9 archive is overwhelmingly one of people separated from their families, it is also a site for understanding how the relationships formed on board a ship offer a view of relation grounded in the experience of diaspora. These migrants are bound by the experience of the passage "home." Though the CI 9s are visual representations of social isolation and the systematic rupture of families, the *Oanfa* portraits collectively outline the twofold nature – destruction but also formation – of mass capture's effect on kinship and relation.

Rupture, Relation, and the Lawson Family on the *Oanfa*

Head tax and exclusion legislation systematically denied thousands of families the opportunity to be together, but there are some conventional families that can be found in this archive. The Lawsons were one such family and they happened to have been aboard the *Oanfa*. However, as I will show, even conventional families – where such families are defined as configured by a father, mother, and children – must be envisioned outside the conventions of both family and family photography.

Tucked in the midst of the CI 9 certificates of passengers on the SS *Oanfa* in 1911, you will find a family portrait that may not, at first, look like a family portrait (figs. 3.18–3.22). Here, in numerical sequence and as identified by the names written on their certificates, are: James J. Lawson, aged thirty-four, CI 9 no. 17938; Mrs J.J. Lawson, aged twenty-four, CI 9 no. 17939; James Ying Choury, aged five, CI 9 no. 17940; Jane Lawson, aged six, CI 9 no. 17941; and Ethel Lawson, aged three, CI 9 no. 17942.

Unlike the Chong family discussed earlier in this chapter, the members of this family are not pictured together. Indeed, it is not immediately obvious that they are a family at all. On the basis of the information on the certificate alone, James Ying Choury would not seem to be a member of the Lawson family. Jane and Ethel share a surname with James J. Lawson and Mrs Lawson. There is much to say about Mrs Lawson, but let me first unfold the relationships between the members of the family pictured here. From the deployment of the honorific "Mrs," and her proximity to James J. Lawson in the sequencing of the certificates, it seems almost certain that Mr and Mrs Lawson are married to each other. The surname also offers a strong indication that Jane and Ethel are the children of Mr and Mrs James J. Lawson. Again, unlike the Chongs, the Lawson children are not afforded the privilege of being identified in terms of their familial relation to each other. There are no scripts pointing to them as sisters or daughters. Without more information (and there is more, but not here), we can only guess that the two Lawson girls are the daughters of Mr and Mrs Lawson. But what to do with the fact that each Lawson is identified with a different geographic location? Mr Lawson's place of residence appears to be "Hillborg"? Mrs Lawson is not given a place of residence and is identified geographically only by place of birth: Hamilton. On Jane's certificate, there is only

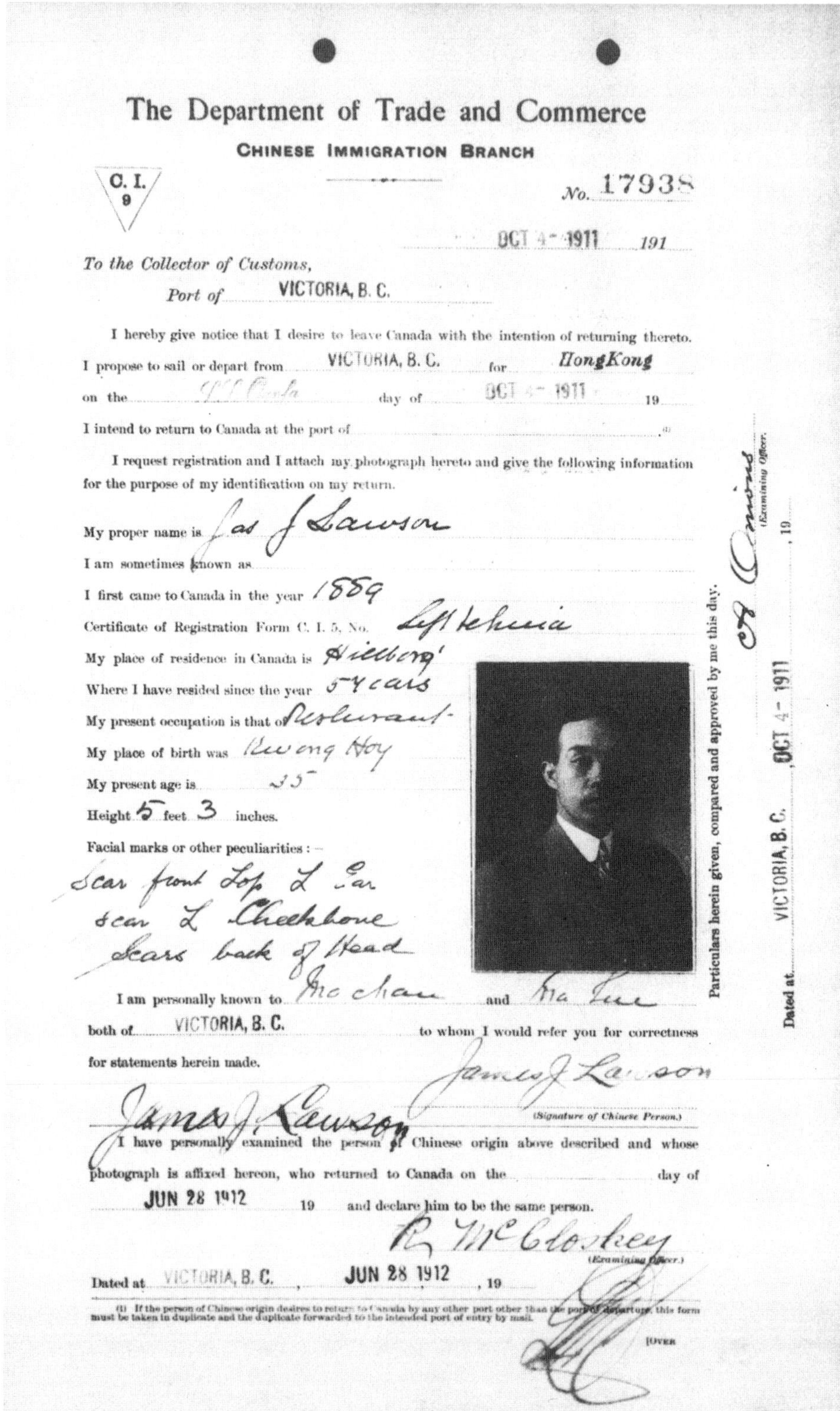

The Department of Trade and Commerce

CHINESE IMMIGRATION BRANCH

C. I. 9

No. 17938

OCT 4 1911 191

To the Collector of Customs,

Port of VICTORIA, B. C.

I hereby give notice that I desire to leave Canada with the intention of returning thereto.

I propose to sail or depart from VICTORIA, B. C. for HongKong

on the [illegible] day of OCT 4 1911 19

I intend to return to Canada at the port of (1)

I request registration and I attach my photograph hereto and give the following information for the purpose of my identification on my return.

My proper name is Jas J Lawson

I am sometimes known as

I first came to Canada in the year 1889

Certificate of Registration Form C. I. 5, No. Left Victoria

My place of residence in Canada is Hillberg

Where I have resided since the year 5 years

My present occupation is that of Restaurant

My place of birth was Kwong Hoy

My present age is 35

Height 5 feet 3 inches.

Facial marks or other peculiarities:—

Scar front top L ear
Scar L Cheekbone
Scars back of Head

I am personally known to Mc Chan and Ma Lee

both of VICTORIA, B. C. to whom I would refer you for correctness for statements herein made.

James J Lawson

(Signature of Chinese Person.)

Particulars herein given, compared and approved by me this day.

[illegible]

(Examining Officer.)

Dated at VICTORIA, B. C., OCT 4 1911, 19

James J. Lawson

I have personally examined the person of Chinese origin above described and whose photograph is affixed hereon, who returned to Canada on the day of JUN 28 1912 19 and declare him to be the same person.

R McCloskey

(Examining Officer.)

Dated at VICTORIA, B. C., JUN 28 1912, 19

(1) If the person of Chinese origin desires to return to Canada by any other port other than the port of departure, this form must be taken in duplicate and the duplicate forwarded to the intended port of entry by mail.

[OVER

Fig. 3.18
CI 9 No. 17938, Reel no. T-6038.

Fig. 3.19 (opposite)
CI 9 No. 17939, Reel no. T-6038.

The Department of Trade and Commerce

CHINESE IMMIGRATION BRANCH

C. I. 9

No. 17939

OCT 4 – 1911 191

To the Collector of Customs,

Port of VICTORIA, B. C.

I hereby give notice that I desire to leave Canada with the intention of returning thereto.

I propose to sail or depart from VICTORIA, B. C. for HongKong

on the S.S. Canfa day of OCT 4 – 1911 19

I intend to return to Canada at the port of (1)

I request registration and I attach my photograph hereto and give the following information for the purpose of my identification on my return.

My proper name is Mrs J J Lawson

I am sometimes known as

I first came to Canada in the year

Certificate of Registration Form C. I. 5, No.

My place of residence in Canada is

Where I have resided since the year

My present occupation is that of housewife

My place of birth was Hamilton

My present age is 24

Height 5 feet 0 inches.

Facial marks or other peculiarities :—

Small Mole R Cheek

(Hamilton Ont)

White Lady

I am personally known to — and —

both of VICTORIA, B. C. to whom I would refer you for correctness for statements herein made.

Mrs Mary J J. Lawson Mrs J. J. Lawson (Signature of Chinese Person.)

I have personally examined the person of Chinese origin above described and whose photograph is affixed hereon, who returned to Canada on the day of JUN 28 1912 19 and declare him to be the same person.

R McCloskey (Examining Officer.)

Dated at VICTORIA, B. C., JUN 28 1912, 19

(1) If the person of Chinese origin desires to return to Canada by any other port other than the port of departure this form must be taken in duplicate and the duplicate forwarded to the intended port of entry by mail.

[OVER

Particulars herein given, compared and approved by me this day.

Dated at VICTORIA, B. C. OCT 4 – 1911, 19

(Examining Officer.)

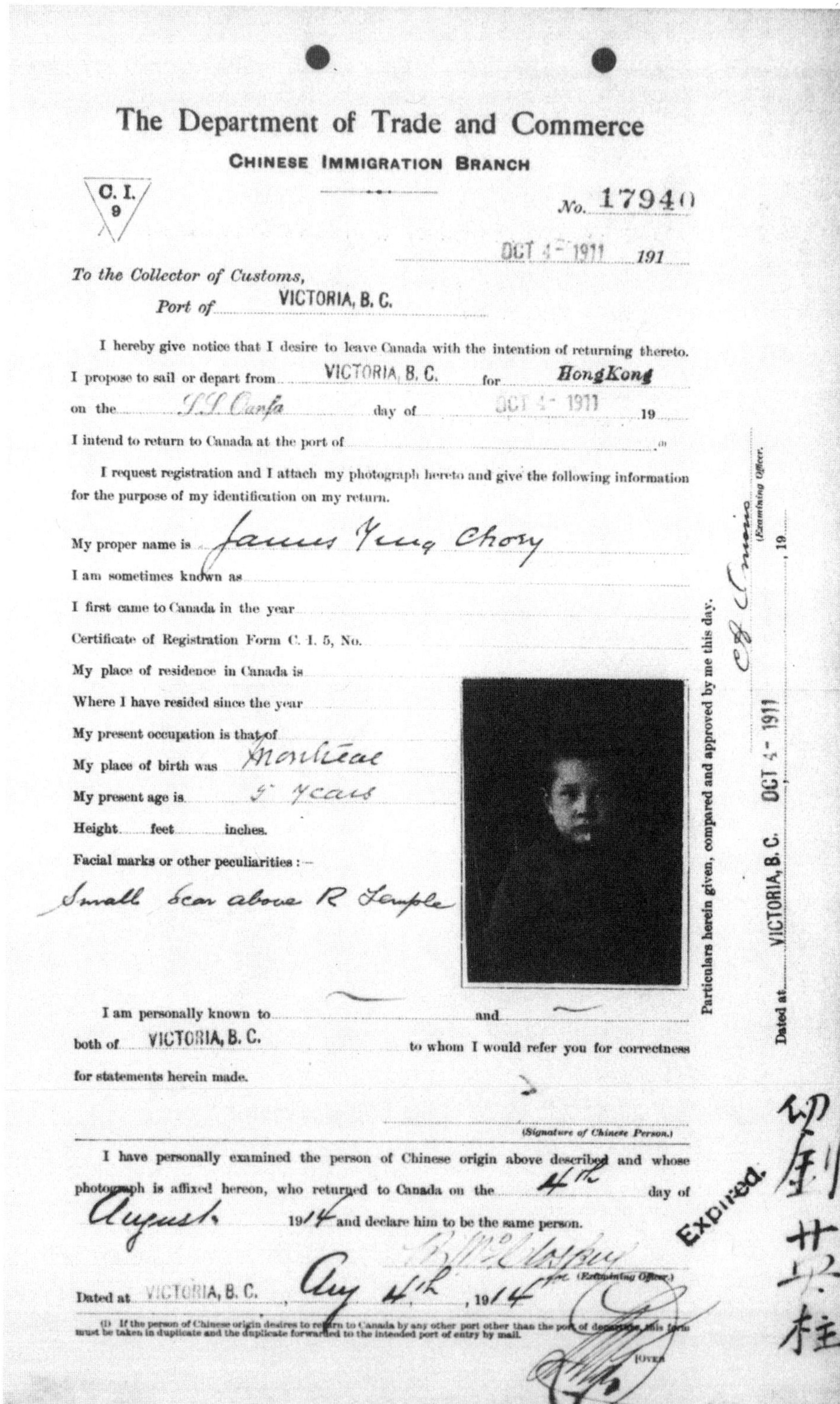

The Department of Trade and Commerce

CHINESE IMMIGRATION BRANCH

C. I. 9

No. 17940

OCT 4 1911 191

To the Collector of Customs,

Port of VICTORIA, B. C.

I hereby give notice that I desire to leave Canada with the intention of returning thereto.

I propose to sail or depart from VICTORIA, B. C. for HongKong

on the S.S. Oanfa day of OCT 4 1911 19

I intend to return to Canada at the port of

I request registration and I attach my photograph hereto and give the following information for the purpose of my identification on my return.

My proper name is James Yung Chory

I am sometimes known as

I first came to Canada in the year

Certificate of Registration Form C. I. 5, No.

My place of residence in Canada is

Where I have resided since the year

My present occupation is that of

My place of birth was Montreal

My present age is 5 years

Height feet inches.

Facial marks or other peculiarities:—

Small Scar above R Temple

I am personally known to and

both of VICTORIA, B. C. to whom I would refer you for correctness for statements herein made.

(Signature of Chinese Person.)

劉其柱

I have personally examined the person of Chinese origin above described and whose photograph is affixed hereon, who returned to Canada on the 4th day of August 1914 and declare him to be the same person.

Dated at VICTORIA, B. C., Aug 4th, 1914 (Examining Officer.)

(1) If the person of Chinese origin desires to return to Canada by any other port other than the port of departure, this form must be taken in duplicate and the duplicate forwarded to the intended port of entry by mail.

(OVER)

Expired.

Particulars herein given, compared and approved by me this day.

Dated at VICTORIA, B. C. OCT 4 1911, 19 (Examining Officer.)

Fig. 3.20
CI 9 No. 17940, Reel no. T-6038.

Fig. 3.21 (opposite)
CI 9 No. 17941, Reel no. T-6038.

The Department of Trade and Commerce

CHINESE IMMIGRATION BRANCH

C. I. 9

No. 17941

OCT 4 - 1911 191

To the Collector of Customs,

Port of VICTORIA, B. C.

I hereby give notice that I desire to leave Canada with the intention of returning thereto.

I propose to sail or depart from VICTORIA, B. C. for HongKong

on the [illegible] day of OCT 4 - 1911 19

I intend to return to Canada at the port of (1)

I request registration and I attach my photograph hereto and give the following information for the purpose of my identification on my return.

My proper name is Jane Lawson

I am sometimes known as

I first came to Canada in the year

Certificate of Registration Form C. I. 5, No.

My place of residence in Canada is

Where I have resided since the year

My present occupation is that of Toronto

My place of birth was 6 years

My present age is

Height feet inches.

Facial marks or other peculiarities :—

No Description

I am personally known to ~ and ~

both of VICTORIA, B. C. to whom I would refer you for correctness for statements herein made.

(Signature of Chinese Person.)

Particulars herein given, compared and approved by me this day.

[illegible] (Examining Officer.)

Dated at VICTORIA, B. C. OCT 4 - 1911, 19

I have personally examined the person of Chinese origin above described and whose photograph is affixed hereon, who returned to Canada on the 4th day of Aug. 1914 19 and declare him to be the same person.

R. McCloskey (Examining Officer.)

Dated at VICTORIA, B. C. Aug 4th, 1914

Expired.

(1) If the person of Chinese origin desires to return to Canada by any other port other than the port of departure, this form must be taken in duplicate and the duplicate forwarded to the intended port of entry by mail.

The Department of Trade and Commerce

CHINESE IMMIGRATION BRANCH

C. I. 9

No. 17942

OCT 4- 1911 191

To the Collector of Customs,

Port of VICTORIA, B. C.

I hereby give notice that I desire to leave Canada with the intention of returning thereto.

I propose to sail or depart from VICTORIA, B. C. for HongKong

on the S.S. Oanla day of OCT 4- 1911 19

I intend to return to Canada at the port of (1)

I request registration and I attach my photograph hereto and give the following information for the purpose of my identification on my return.

My proper name is Ethel Lawson

I am sometimes known as

I first came to Canada in the year

Certificate of Registration Form C. I. 5, No.

My place of residence in Canada is

Where I have resided since the year

My present occupation is that of

My place of birth was Hellbay

My present age is 3 years

Height feet inches.

Facial marks or other peculiarities :—

No Description

I am personally known to ~ and ~

both of VICTORIA, B. C. to whom I would refer you for correctness for statements herein made.

(Signature of Chinese Person.)

Particulars herein given, compared and approved by me this day.

Dated at VICTORIA, B. C. OCT 4- 1911, 19

(Examining Officer.)

I have personally examined the person of Chinese origin above described and whose photograph is affixed hereon, who returned to Canada on the day of JUN 28 1912 19 and declare him to be the same person.

R. McCloskey (Examining Officer.)

Dated at VICTORIA, B. C., JUN 28 1912, 19

(1) If the person of Chinese origin desires to return to Canada by any other port other than the port of departure, this form must be taken in duplicate and the duplicate forwarded to the intended port of entry by mail.

[OVER

Fig. 3.22
CI 9 No. 17942,
Reel no. T-6038.

"Toronto" written next to the line for "present occupation." Presuming that Toronto is not an occupation and that the agent meant to write this on a different line, Toronto could either be her place of birth or her place of residence. On Ethel's certificate, a place that looks like "Hellbay" is listed as her place of residence. Four people, seemingly travelling together and sharing one surname, but not one clearly identifiable place of residence among them.

And what to do with five-year-old James Ying Choury, who does not share a surname and seems to have no place of residence but only a place of birth, "Montreal"? I will return to James.

First, let me sort through the relationship between Mr and Mrs Lawson, and Jane and Ethel. In order to find this relationship, we have to go outside of the CI 9 archive and into birth and marriage records. According to the record of Jane Lawson's birth shown in figure 3.23, she is indeed the daughter of James J. Lawson, as listed on line 44. From this record, we now also

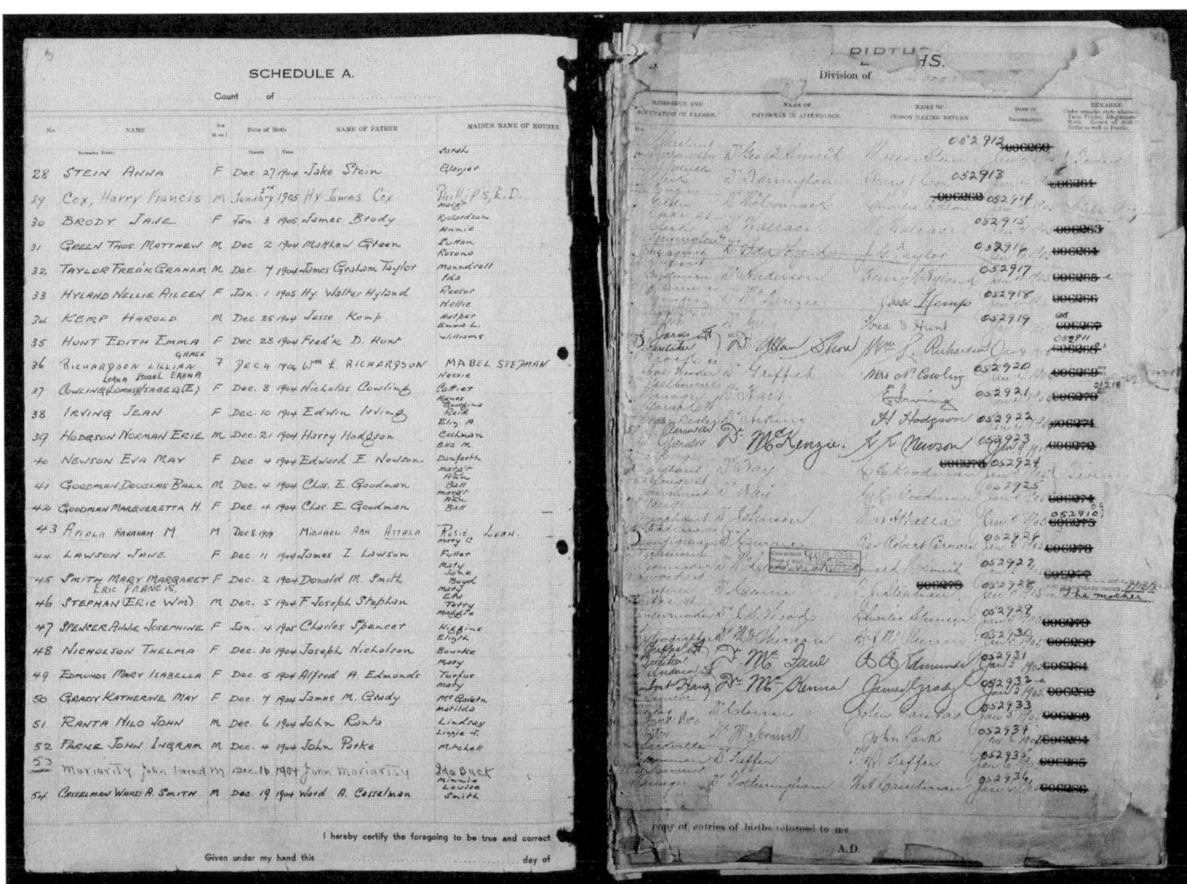

Fig. 3.23
Jane Lawson's record of birth, 11 December 1904, Toronto, York, Ontario, Canada.

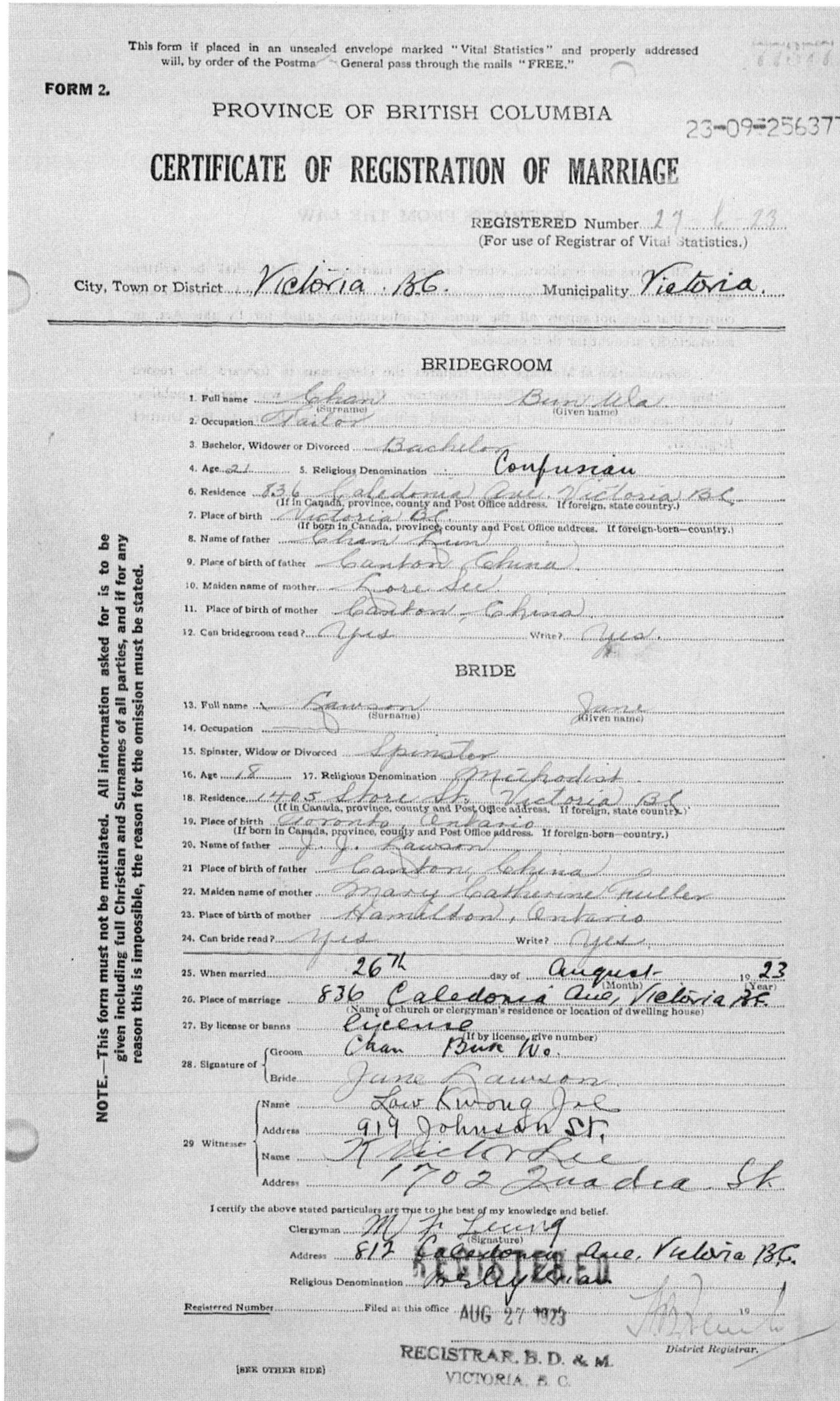

This form if placed in an unsealed envelope marked "Vital Statistics" and properly addressed will, by order of the Postmaster General pass through the mails "FREE."

FORM 2.

PROVINCE OF BRITISH COLUMBIA

23-09-256377

CERTIFICATE OF REGISTRATION OF MARRIAGE

REGISTERED Number 27 6 23
(For use of Registrar of Vital Statistics.)

City, Town or District Victoria B.C. Municipality Victoria.

BRIDEGROOM

1. Full name Chan (Surname) Bun Wa (Given name)
2. Occupation Tailor
3. Bachelor, Widower or Divorced Bachelor
4. Age 21 5. Religious Denomination Confusian
6. Residence 836 Caledonia Ave. Victoria B.C. (If in Canada, province, county and Post Office address. If foreign, state country.)
7. Place of birth Victoria B.C. (If born in Canada, province, county and Post Office address. If foreign-born—country.)
8. Name of father Chan Lum
9. Place of birth of father Canton China
10. Maiden name of mother Lore See
11. Place of birth of mother Canton, China
12. Can bridegroom read? Yes Write? Yes

BRIDE

13. Full name Lawson (Surname) Jane (Given name)
14. Occupation —
15. Spinster, Widow or Divorced Spinster
16. Age 18 17. Religious Denomination Methodist
18. Residence 1405 Store St. Victoria B.C. (If in Canada, province, county and Post Office address. If foreign, state country.)
19. Place of birth Toronto, Ontario (If born in Canada, province, county and Post Office address. If foreign-born—country.)
20. Name of father J. J. Lawson
21. Place of birth of father Canton, China
22. Maiden name of mother Mary Catherine Fuller
23. Place of birth of mother Hamilton, Ontario
24. Can bride read? Yes Write? Yes

25. When married 26th day of August (Month) 19 23 (Year)
26. Place of marriage 836 Caledonia Ave, Victoria B.C. (Name of church or clergyman's residence or location of dwelling house)
27. By license or banns License (If by license, give number)
28. Signature of Groom Chan Bun Wo; Bride Jane Lawson
29. Witnesses Name Law Kwong Joe; Address 919 Johnson St.; Name K. Victor Lee; Address 1702 Quadra St.

I certify the above stated particulars are true to the best of my knowledge and belief.

Clergyman M. J. Leung (Signature)
Address 812 Caledonia Ave. Victoria B.C.
Religious Denomination Wesleyan

REGISTERED

Registered Number .... Filed at this office AUG 27 1923 19
District Registrar.

REGISTRAR. B. D. & M.
VICTORIA, B. C.

(SEE OTHER SIDE)

NOTE.—This form must not be mutilated. All information asked for is to be given including full Christian and Surnames of all parties, and if for any reason this is impossible, the reason for the omission must be stated.

Fig. 3.24
Jane Lawson and Bun Wa Chan's marriage certificate, 26 August 1923, Victoria, British Columbia, Canada.

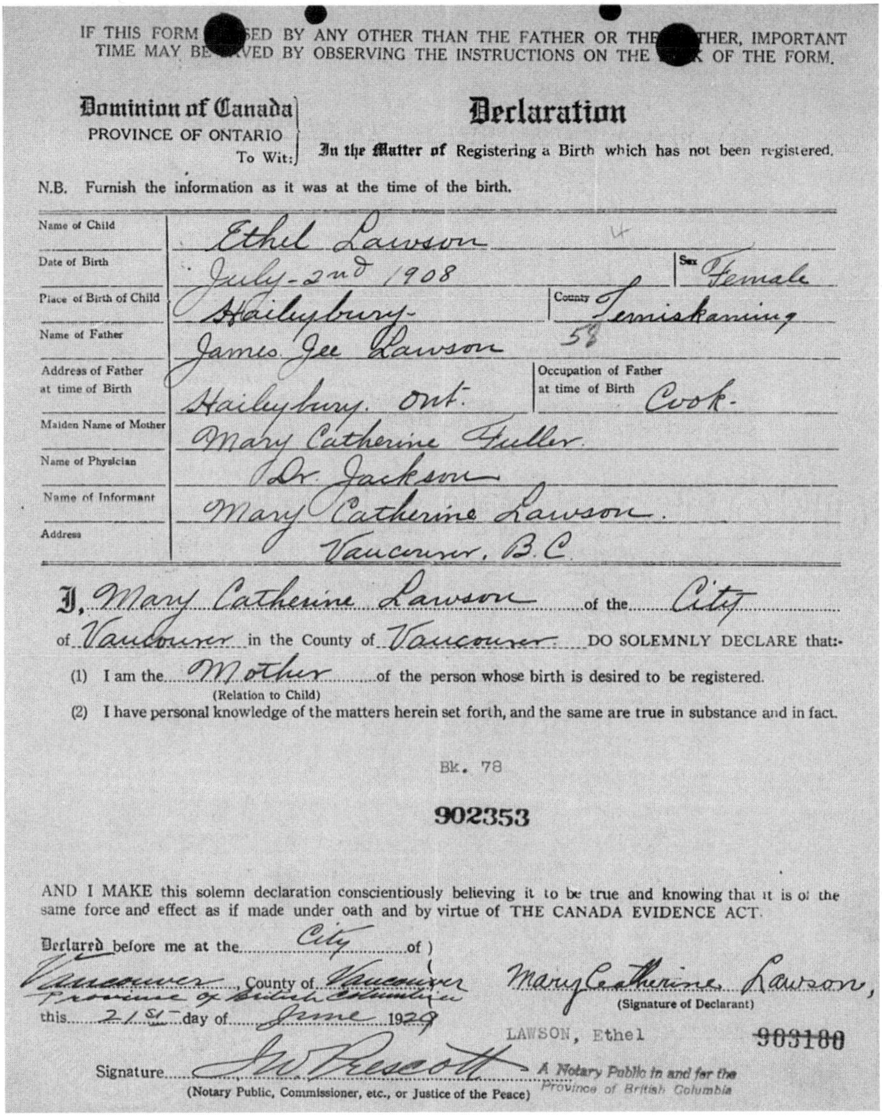

IF THIS FORM [illegible]SED BY ANY OTHER THAN THE FATHER OR THE [illegible]THER, IMPORTANT TIME MAY BE [illegible]VED BY OBSERVING THE INSTRUCTIONS ON THE [illegible] OF THE FORM.

Dominion of Canada
PROVINCE OF ONTARIO
To Wit:

Declaration

In the Matter of Registering a Birth which has not been registered.

N.B. Furnish the information as it was at the time of the birth.

Name of Child	Ethel Lawson
Date of Birth	July-2nd 1908
Sex	Female
Place of Birth of Child	Haileybury-
County	Temiskaming
Name of Father	James Jee Lawson 58
Address of Father at time of Birth	Haileybury. Ont.
Occupation of Father at time of Birth	Cook-
Maiden Name of Mother	Mary Catherine Fuller.
Name of Physician	Dr. Jackson
Name of Informant	Mary Catherine Lawson.
Address	Vancouver, B.C.

I, Mary Catherine Lawson of the City of Vancouver in the County of Vancouver DO SOLEMNLY DECLARE that:-

(1) I am the Mother (Relation to Child) of the person whose birth is desired to be registered.

(2) I have personal knowledge of the matters herein set forth, and the same are true in substance and in fact.

Bk. 78

902353

AND I MAKE this solemn declaration conscientiously believing it to be true and knowing that it is of the same force and effect as if made under oath and by virtue of THE CANADA EVIDENCE ACT.

Declared before me at the City of Vancouver, County of Vancouver, Province of British Columbia this 21st day of June 1929

Mary Catherine Lawson, (Signature of Declarant)

LAWSON, Ethel 903180

Signature J W Prescott A Notary Public in and for the Province of British Columbia
(Notary Public, Commissioner, etc., or Justice of the Peace)

Fig. 3.25
Ethel Lawson's birth certificate, 2 July 1908, Haileybury, Timiskaming, Ontario, Canada.

have Mrs Lawson's maiden name: "Mary C. Fuller." This information can be further corroborated by Jane Lawson's marriage certificate (fig. 3.24), from which we learn that she was born in Toronto, that her mother's full name is "Mary Catherine Fuller," and that Mrs James J. Lawson (née Mary Catherine Fuller) was born in Hamilton, Ontario.

Ethel Lawson's birth certificate uncovers the mystery behind the terrible handwriting that obscures her place of residence and that of her father: not Hellbay or Hillborg but Haileybury, Ontario (fig. 3.25).

Name:	Mary Savage
Sex:	Female
Husband:	James Jee Lawson
Son:	James Ying Choury Lawson

Other information in the record of James Ying Choury Lawson
from British Columbia Death Registrations

Name:	James Ying Choury Lawson
Event Type:	Death
Event Date:	04 Jun 1970
Event Place:	North Vancouver, British Columbia, Canada
Gender:	Male
Age:	64
Marital Status:	Married
Birth Date:	18 Jan 1906
Birth Year (Estimated):	1906
Birthplace:	Montreal, Quebec
Father's Name:	James Jee Lawson
Mother's Name:	Mary Savage
Spouse's Name:	Mae Bunn

Fig. 3.26
James Ying Choury Lawson's record of death.

Now, James Ying Choury. As a five-year-old, he could not have been travelling unaccompanied. The numerical sequencing of his CI 9 suggests that he travelled with the Lawsons. But nothing about his name, nor his unlisted place of residence, nor his listed place of birth (Montreal) connects him to the Lawsons, who, we now know, resided in the town of Haileybury where James J. Lawson worked as a cook and where Ethel was born, and who were also connected to Hamilton, where Mrs James J. Lawson (née Mary Catherine Fuller) and Jane were born. However, James Ying Choury's record of death shows that his father was indeed James J. Lawson (fig. 3.26).

In this record James Ying Choury is given the Lawson surname, and here, we also learn the name of his mother, "Mary Savage." Was James a half-brother to Ethel and Jane? No. We have to look even further to find the truth of his familial relationship. Mary Savage's obituary in the 25 January 1950 edition of the *Vancouver Sun* reads in full:

> SAVAGE – Passed away suddenly Jan. 23, Mary Catherine (nee Fuller), beloved wife of John Savage, 407 Nelson St., in her 62nd year. Survived also by 6 daughters, Mrs. Jan Chan, Mrs. Victoria Long, Mrs. Edna Savage Chew, Mrs. Beth Malbeuf of Vancouver, Mrs. Ethel Jayne of Philadelphia, Mrs. Pearl Fletcher and 1 son, Mrs. James Lawson of New York; also 28 grandchildren and 3 great-grandchildren. Funeral service, Thursday, Jan. 26, at 1:30pm., from Armstrong & Co., Chapel of Flowers, 304 Dunleavy Ave., Rev. H. R. Whitehead officiating. Internment, Forest Lawn Memorial park.

Now we know that Mary Catherine Savage was also Mary Catherine Fuller, and that James Ying Choury is her son and brother to Ethel and Jane. By the time she died, she had remarried and John Savage was her husband. But the CI 9 certificates for this family do not make any of these relationships clear. Looking only at CI 9 nos. 17938, 17939, 17940, 17941, and 17942, the relationships between the members of this family are obscure at best. There is more to say about the Lawson family and their journey on the *Oanfa*, but before I go on, I want to emphasize how the mass capture process itself has fractured this family. These certificates show how the Chinese Immigration Act, along with other forms of legislative and social discrimination, worked to isolate this family from each other and from the communities in which they lived. This family would have suffered particular pressure because Mary Fuller was not Chinese.

When Mary Fuller boarded the *Oanfa*, she did so at a time of moral panic over contact between white women and Chinese men in Canada. As Karen Drubinsky and Adam Givertz argue, there was a "campaign to construct Chinese men as sexual villains [that] involved the interaction of several historical processes, namely, the making and remaking of sexuality and the relatedness of gender, class, and race" where "the connection between these is illuminated in the fabrication of the Chinese man as simultaneously degraded labourer and a debaucher of young White girls" (2003, 72). White masculinity defined itself through this twinned process of degrading and sexualizing Chinese men: "the image of Chinese men entrapping White women was crucial to the formation of Anglo-Canadian male identity, and certainly also reinforced already existing concerns among White male labourers about economic competition" (ibid.). This consolidation of Anglo-Canadian masculinity culminates in a series of what are known as "White Women's Labour Laws" enacted across Canada. While Saskatchewan led the way, passing An Act to Prevent Employment of Female Labour in Certain Capacities in 1912, British Columbia, Manitoba, and Ontario followed suit over the next seven years modelling their statutes on Saskatchewan's (Backhouse 2004, 346).

These statutes were explicitly racist in their targeting of Asian men. For example, the Saskatchewan statute reads, "No person shall employ in any capacity any white woman or girl or permit any white woman or girl to reside or lodge in or to work in or, save as a *bona fide* customer in a public apartment thereof only, to frequent any restaurant, laundry or other place of business or amusement owned, kept or managed by any Japanese, Chinaman or Oriental person" (quoted in Backhouse 1994, 136). This law also inaugurates whiteness as a legal concept in Canada: "While the property of 'whiteness' was clearly a definable asset from which all manner of privilege and power flowed, it tended to disappear in legal terminology. The 'white women's labour bill' marks the first overt racialization of 'whiteness' in Canadian law" (Backhouse 2004, 360). In codifying whiteness this way, these laws show some of the ways whiteness defines itself through its engagement with Asianness.

While the racist impulse of these laws is undeniable, a careful examination of the enactment and enforcement (or lack thereof) of this legislation illuminates a much more complex picture of the relationship of whiteness to Chineseness. Interestingly, Ontario's version of this statute "never received royal assent but remained amidst the statutes of [1914] as an unproclaimed bill. But when Ontario's statute law was collected and rationalized in 1927 in a single bill, the *Revised Statutes of Ontario*, the unproclaimed bill, because of a technical error, became law" (Drubinsky and Givertz 2003, 249n46). The law did not go unchallenged. The Chinese consul general wrote, in September 1928, to W.H. Price, the attorney general of Ontario, to protest the law, and "a group of 69 [white] waitresses petitioned the Lieutenant-Governor of Ontario requesting that he rescind the legislation, stating that they were well satisfied with their employment. Ultimately, the act was amended under the *Statute Law Amendment Act* [1929] to return it to its unproclaimed state" (ibid.). The Statute Law Amendment Act (1929) was passed to read:

> Section 30 of *The Factory, Shop and Office Building Act* is repealed and the following substituted therefor:
>
> 30. (1) No Chinese person shall employ in any capacity or have under his direction or control any female white person in any factory, restaurant or laundry.
>
> (2) Subsection 1 shall not come into force until a day to be named by the Lieutenant-Governor by his Proclamation.

The date for the proclamation was never named, so Ontario's prohibition of the employment of white women by Chinese men was left in a kind of legal purgatory, passed by the legislature but not in force. This move allowed the government to placate those who demanded that it take action to prevent the mixing of white women and Chinese men, while at the same time ensuring that the law itself was impotent. The moral panic may have been widespread, but its manifestation in the form of labour laws was not something that the government of Ontario actually had a genuine desire to enforce. That the province bothered to amend the accidental proclamation of the law in 1928 through a separate piece of legislation strongly suggests that the state had little appetite for this law as a law.

Despite the racism impelling the moral panic of this period, the passing but unproclaiming of Ontario's laws about white women's interactions with Chinese men gives some indication of the complexities attendant upon Mary Fuller's relationship with James Jee Lawson. Indeed, the law was unproclaimed not once, but twice. That it was never made enforceable, that the government of Ontario went to the length of amending the statute in 1929 to undo the accidental proclamation of this law in 1928, suggests that

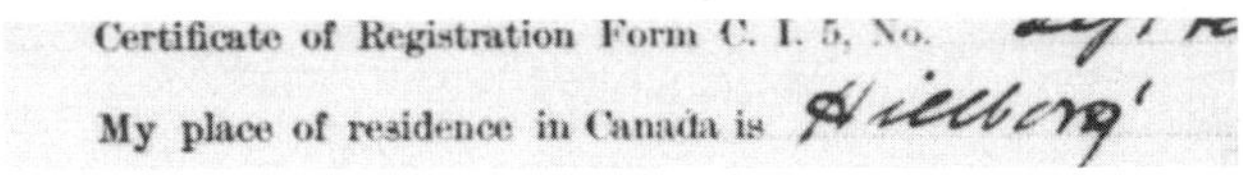
Certificate of Registration Form C. I. 5, No.
My place of residence in Canada is

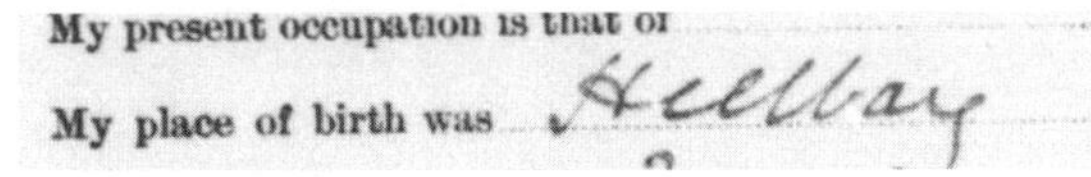
My present occupation is that of
My place of birth was

Fig. 3.27
CI 9 no 17938 [zoom on place of residence for James J. Lawson], Reel no. T-6038.

Fig. 3.28
CI 9 no 17942 [zoom on place of birth for Ethel Lawson], Reel no. T-6038.

the moral panic was not so widespread. The laws' contorted history shows that Mary's marriage to James, while not typical, was perhaps not wholly reviled; despite antagonism, there may have been more space for their relationship in Ontario rather than Saskatchewan or Manitoba. I have discussed these laws at some length because they are the clearest laws where the relations between white women and Chinese men were governed by legislation, which speaks to the social atmosphere. Of course, it is not necessarily the case that these laws, unenforceable though they were, necessarily applied to Lawsons. Although James J. Lawson identifies as working in a restaurant on his CI 9, and gives his occupation as "cook" on Ethel's birth certificate (fig. 3.25), it is not obvious that Mary Fuller ever worked in the restaurants – or, even if she did, that she worked where James cooked. But let me return to the CI 9s themselves.

Separated from each other by the diplomatics of the CI 9 certificate where no one member of the family could name their relationship with another member of the family, James, Mary, James Jr, Jane, and Ethel are isolated from each other. They are scattered across geographies with each member of the family identified with a different town or city. Even when they are noted as living in the same place, as with the James J. Lawson and Ethel Lawson, the carelessness of the handwritten entries still makes it look as if they did not. Look again at James J. Lawson's place of residence as compared to that of Ethel's place of birth (figs. 3.27 and 3.28). It is only through further research in other archives that the scribbled locations on both certificates can be uncovered as "Haileybury." And despite being able to place Ethel with her father there, the certificates still leave all the other members of the family strewn across multiple towns and cities. The geographical information pertaining to each member of the family on the form actually works against seeing these five people as members of a single family.

Two of the Lawsons, Mary Fuller and James Ying Choury, are particularly cleaved from their families in these CI 9s. The CI 9s deny them relation to the family of their birth. Let me discuss the case of the younger James first. The use of names works most cruelly against James Ying Choury. Why was he not permitted to also be known by the surname he shares with his father? It is only his certificate's place in the sequence that hints that he travelled with the other Lawsons. Knowing his proper surname allows us to find him again in the CI 9 archive. A decade later, on

THE DEPARTMENT OF IMMIGRATION AND COLONIZATION

CHINESE IMMIGRATION BRANCH

File 24097

C. I. 9

No. 0307

FEB 11 1921 19....

To the Controller of Chinese Immigration,

Port of Vancouver

I hereby give notice that I desire to leave Canada with the intention of returning thereto.

I propose to sail or depart from Vancouver for Hong Kong

on the Katori Maru day of FEB 14 1921 19

I intend to return to Canada at the port of Vancouver

I request registration and I attach my photograph hereto and give the following information for the purpose of my identification on my return.

My proper name is James Lawson

I am sometimes known as

I first came to Canada in the year Native born ,1906.Jan.18th

My place of residence in Canada is Victoria, B.C.

Where I have resided since the year 4 years

Birth Cert. to be produced later

Certificate of Registration Form C. I. 5 No.

My present occupation is that of School-boy

My place of birth was Montreal,P.Q.

My present age is 15

Height 5 feet 1½ inches.

Facial marks or other peculiarities:—

Scar r. eyebrow

Light scar over r. eyebrow

Small scar inner cor. r. eye

I am personally known to James Jee Lawson(father)

both of Victoria to whom I would refer you for correctness of statements herein made.

桂英劉

(Lau Ying Quai)

(Signature of Chinese Person.)

Particulars and photograph hereon shown compared with applicant and approved by me this day.

H Crump for Controller

Dated at Vancouver FEB 11 1921 19

I have personally examined the person of Chinese origin who claims to be the person above described and whose photograph is affixed hereon, who returned to Canada on the Empress of Australia day of 19 , and declare him to be the same person.

MAR 12 1924 VANCOUVER, B.C.

H Crump for (Controller)

Dated at 19

[OVER.]

CI44 # 5624

Fig. 3.29
CI 9 No. 0307, Reel no. T-6052.

14 February 1921, he leaves from the Port of Vancouver. He has more scars. He signs his name in Chinese. This choice to write his Chinese name instead of his anglicized name is particularly notable given that his father, James Jee, never writes his name in Chinese. Indeed, we only know this family's surname in Chinese, 劉 or Lau, because the younger James insists upon being known as such, at least in the moment of self-naming that is the signature on the form.

Knowing his surname, that he is not only James Ying Choury but also James Lawson, allows us to learn about the life he led. His obituary in the 15 June 1970 edition of the *Vancouver Sun* reveals that he was "a printer by trade, working as a compositor and proofreader for the Pacific Press," and that he was a leader in the Boy Scout movement who received the "highest award given to Boy Scout organizers shortly before his death June 4." He was married to Mae Bunn when he died, but had previously been married to Ann Chung. His wedding to Ann Chung in 1935 was reported in the Boston papers with the headline, "Chinese Bride and Bridegroom Married at Methodist Church."

CI 9 no. 0307 opens up the life of James Y.C. Lawson. Here, at least, he is given and gives his proper surname, in Chinese and English. Here, his date and place of birth. Here, his place of residence from the years 1917–21. Here, at last, his father is clearly identified. But the CI 9s still leave the identity of his mother a mystery. Alone, without genealogical research, the CI 9s do not reveal his relationship to Mary Fuller.

Mrs Lawson, Mary Catherine Fuller, is torn from her family in a different way than her son. Married to James Jee Lawson, the CI 9 removes her from the family she had before this marriage. CI 9 no. 17939 reveals how a white woman would become Chinese in the eyes of the state. There are no laws that explicitly demand this transformation, but the effect of bureaucratic regulation effectively made her Chinese. Where other white people could travel in and out of Canada without a CI 9, without providing an identification photograph and having their identity documents filed for future suspicion upon their return to Canada, Mary Fuller, despite being a native-born Canadian from Hamilton, Ontario, was treated like any other working-class Chinese person. Even the privileges of her race did not earn her the right to be pictured with her family. Her Chinese affiliation is emphasized by the donning of explicitly non-Western clothes in her identification photograph. Indeed, her CI 9 is full of conflict in terms of racial identifications. Her place of birth is written twice on the form. Once it appears where it should, on the blank space next to the line reading, "My place of birth was." Then, as if it needed to be underscored, it is written again in the space reserved for "Facial marks and other peculiarities." In

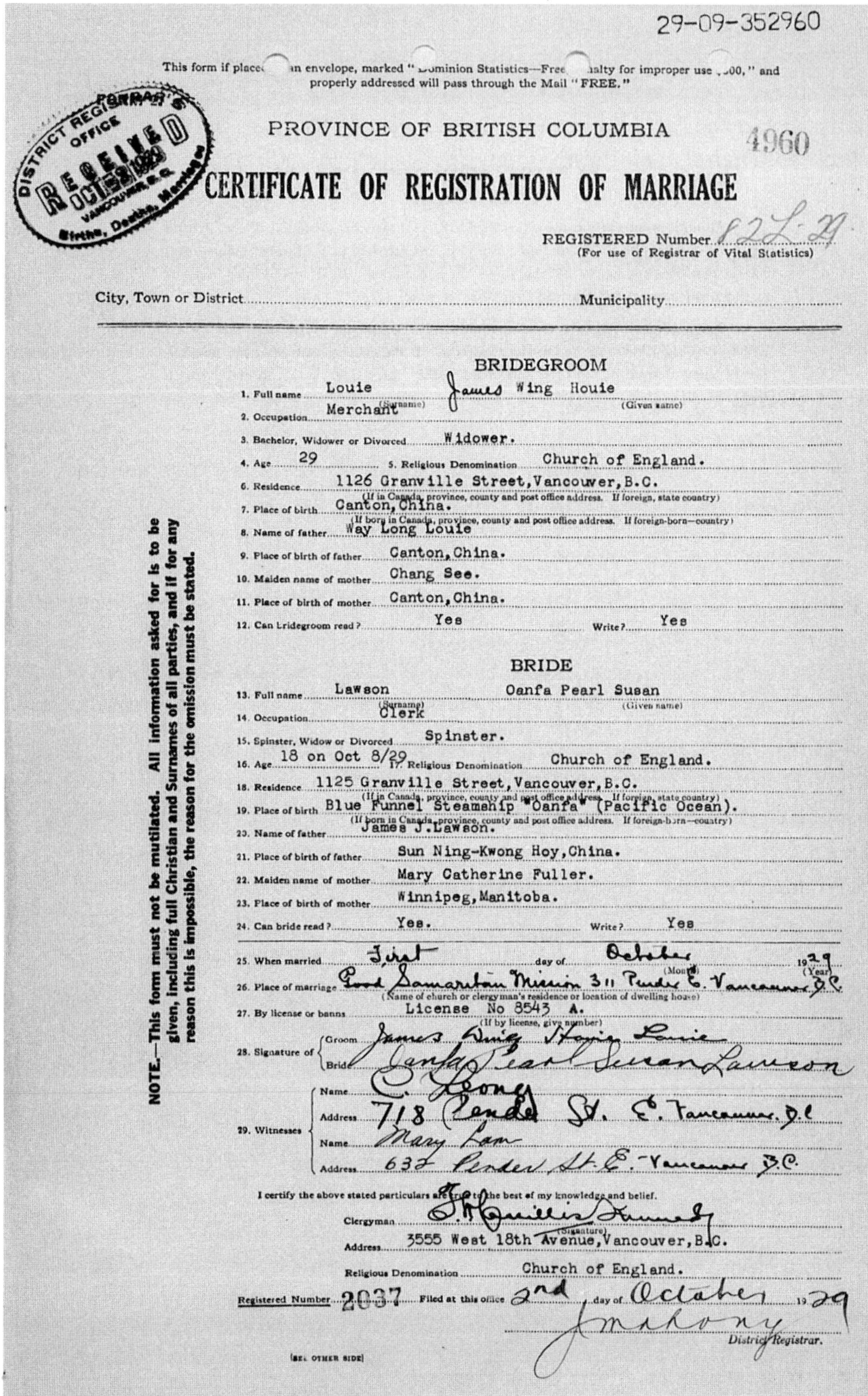

29-09-352960

This form if placed in an envelope, marked "Dominion Statistics—Free. Penalty for improper use $..00," and properly addressed will pass through the Mail "FREE."

DISTRICT REGISTRAR'S OFFICE RECEIVED OCT 2 1929 VANCOUVER, B.C. Births, Deaths, Marriages

PROVINCE OF BRITISH COLUMBIA 4960

CERTIFICATE OF REGISTRATION OF MARRIAGE

REGISTERED Number 82L-29
(For use of Registrar of Vital Statistics)

City, Town or District .... Municipality ....

BRIDEGROOM

1. Full name Louie (Surname) James Wing Houie (Given name)
2. Occupation Merchant
3. Bachelor, Widower or Divorced Widower.
4. Age 29 5. Religious Denomination Church of England.
6. Residence 1126 Granville Street, Vancouver, B.C. (If in Canada, province, county and post office address. If foreign, state country)
7. Place of birth Canton, China. (If born in Canada, province, county and post office address. If foreign-born—country)
8. Name of father Way Long Louie
9. Place of birth of father Canton, China.
10. Maiden name of mother Chang See.
11. Place of birth of mother Canton, China.
12. Can bridegroom read? Yes Write? Yes

BRIDE

13. Full name Lawson (Surname) Oanfa Pearl Susan (Given name)
14. Occupation Clerk
15. Spinster, Widow or Divorced Spinster.
16. Age 18 on Oct 8/29 17. Religious Denomination Church of England.
18. Residence 1125 Granville Street, Vancouver, B.C. (If in Canada, province, county and post office address. If foreign, state country)
19. Place of birth Blue Funnel Steamship "Oanfa" (Pacific Ocean). (If born in Canada, province, county and post office address. If foreign-born—country)
20. Name of father James J. Lawson.
21. Place of birth of father Sun Ning-Kwong Hoy, China.
22. Maiden name of mother Mary Catherine Fuller.
23. Place of birth of mother Winnipeg, Manitoba.
24. Can bride read? Yes. Write? Yes

25. When married First day of October (Month) 1929 (Year)
26. Place of marriage Good Samaritan Mission 311 Pender E. Vancouver B.C. (Name of church or clergyman's residence or location of dwelling house)
27. By license or banns License No 8543 A. (If by license, give number)
28. Signature of Groom James Wing Houie Louie
Bride Oanfa Pearl Susan Lawson
29. Witnesses Name C. Leong
Address 718 Pender St. E. Vancouver B.C.
Name Mary Lam
Address 637 Pender St. E. Vancouver B.C.

I certify the above stated particulars are true to the best of my knowledge and belief.

Clergyman [illegible] (Signature)
Address 3555 West 18th Avenue, Vancouver, B.C.
Religious Denomination Church of England.

Registered Number 2037 Filed at this office 2nd day of October 1929
J. Mahony District Registrar.

(SEE OTHER SIDE)

NOTE.—This form must not be mutilated. All information asked for is to be given, including full Christian and Surnames of all parties, and if for any reason this is impossible, the reason for the omission must be stated.

Fig. 3.30
Pearl Oanfa Susan's marriage certificate.

parentheses under the notation "small mole r cheek" are the words, "Hamilton, Ont," and underneath that, "White Lady." Her Hamilton roots and her whiteness are doubly emphasized. But her relationship to her husband, despite the fact that she is identified only by his name, is not. Thus, she is "Mrs JJ Lawson," but there are only cursory dashes in the space where she could have been identified as having ties to her husband, or anyone at all. She is not "personally known" to anyone according to her CI 9, even though the agent could surely have written in this space that she is the wife of the migrant identified on CI 9 no. 17938.

There is another family connection hidden in Mrs Lawson's CI 9 of 1911. She is pregnant at the time this photograph was taken. She will give birth to Pearl Oanfa Susan Lawson aboard the *Oanfa*. Pearl's marriage certificate reveals her unseen presence on Mrs Lawson's 1911 photograph (fig. 3.30). Pearl's place of birth is given as "Bluc Funnel Steam ship 'Oanfa' (Pacific Ocean)." She is an eighteen-year-old "spinster" when she marries in 1929. On this certificate, her father is James J. Lawson and her mother is Mary Catherine Fuller. Pearl's marriage certificate notes that her mother, Mary, was born in Winnipeg; Mary Fuller has, until now, been identified as being from Hamilton. But Mary had also been in Winnipeg. Indeed, a 1912 travel document notes that James Jee Lawson lived in Winnipeg for six years, beginning in 1896, and then moved to Haileybury. It seems likely that he met Mary in Winnipeg.

There are two more children of James Jee Lawson and Mary Fuller who are not pictured: Mamie Lawson and Victoria Lawson. According to the record of her death, Mamie lived for less than six months (fig. 3.31). This record shows that she was born to James Lawson and Mary Fuller in Haileybury, on 24 March 1910. She died on 14 September 1910. Less than a year later, in October 1911, James and Mary will have gathered up their remaining children, Ethel, Jane, and James Jr, and sailed for Hong Kong on the *Oanfa*. Pearl Oanfa Susan would be born aboard this ship.

Victoria is registered with Pearl Oanfa Susan when they return to Canada with Mary Fuller and James Lawson on the SS *Protesilaus* on 4 August 1914. The girls' entry into Canada is recorded in the 5 September 1914 General Register of Chinese Immigration (fig. 3.32). Pearl is three years old when she arrives in Canada. Victoria is six months old. The register confirms again that Pearl was born at sea on the SS *Oanfa* and that Victoria was born in Medan-Deli, Sumatra. Medan-Deli was a trading centre for tobacco developed by Dutch trading companies in partnership with the Sultanate of Deli. There were thousands of Chinese migrants living and working there at the time and it is notable that, in this General Register notation, Victoria and Pearl are each recorded as being a "Merchant's daughter." Since leaving

Schedule D.

DEATHS

County of (2) Nipissing Division of (1) Haileybury

	Surname first.	Surname first.	Surname first.
FULL NAME of Deceased. Initials only not accepted. 3*	[illegible]	3. Rooney Robt [illegible]	3. [illegible]
Sex, and Race. 4.	F.	4. M.	4. F.
Date of Death. 5.	Sept 4/10	5. Sept 13/10	5. Sept 14/10
Date of Birth. 6.	Oct 20/1887	6. Aug 14/10	6. [illegible]
Age and Place of Birth. 7.	22 yrs 10 mos 15 days Douglas	7. Haileybury	7. Hby
Place of Death, City, Town, Village, or Concession and Lot. If in Hospital, give name, how long Deceased was an inmate, and former or usual place of residence. 8.	Haileybury	8. do	8. do
Occupation. 9		9.	9.
Single, Widowed, or Divorced. 10.	020997	10. 020998	10. 020999
Full Name of Father. 11.	James P. Smith	11. Robt [illegible] Rooney	11. James J. [illegible]
Birthplace of Father. 12.	Canada	12. [illegible]	12. [illegible]
Maiden Name of Mother. 13.		13. [illegible]	13. Mary E. [illegible]
Birthplace of Mother. 14.		14. Muskoka	14. Hamilton Ont.
Name of Physician who attended Deceased. 15.	F. H. Hughes	15. F. F. Jackson	15. F. F. Jackson
Certified by	[illegible]	[illegible] Rooney	James J. [illegible]
Address	Haileybury	Hby	Hby
Date 16.	Sept 6/10	16. Sept 14/10	16. Sept 14/10

	Medical Certificate of Death. I hereby certify that I attended the deceased.	Medical Certificate of Death. I hereby certify that I attended the deceased.	Medical Certificate of Death. I hereby certify that I attended the deceased.
Name.	[illegible]	Rooney [illegible]	[illegible]
From	19	[illegible] 1910	Sept 8 1910
To	19	Sept 13 1910	" 13 1910
That I last saw h........ alive on	19	" 13 1910	" 13 1910
That the Death occurred on	Sept 4 1910	" 13 1910	" 14 1910
CAUSE OF DEATH. Primary.	Tuberculosis	General debility	Whooping Cough
Duration.		from Birth	?
Immediate.			General debility
Duration.	[illegible]		
Physician's name.	F. H. Hughes	F. F. Jackson	F. F. Jackson
Address.	Haileybury	Haileybury	Haileybury
Date.	Sept 6/10	Sept 14/10	Sept 14/10
Remarks.			

I hereby certify the foregoing to be the true and correct entries of all Deaths returned to me for the quarter ending SEP 30 1910 A.D. 19

Given under my hand, this OCT 1 1910 day of 19

Division Registrar of TOWN OF HAILEYBURY.

*N.B.—The reference numbers given are those found in Form C, to assist in transcribing.

Canada in 1911, James Jee Lawson has risen from being a cook to a merchant. Neither Victoria nor Pearl have CI 9s. They were born abroad and had not been in Canada before. Mary Fuller's CI 9 shows that she returned on the same date as Pearl and Victoria, 4 August 1914 (fig. 3.33).

This CI 9 shows Mary having departed from Victoria on 26 August 1913. She sailed with James and Ethel. James's CI 9 for the same departure is pictured in figure 3.34, and Ethel's CI 9, travelling with her parents, is pictured in figure 3.35.

Here, Ethel is five years old. Her previous CI 9, no 17942, issued when she departed in 1911 on the *Oanfa*, shows that she returned to Canada, with both her parents, on 28 June 1912. They did not return with Pearl, James Jr, and Jane on this trip. The family would be reunited and return to Canada together, with two new additions, Pearl and Victoria, on 4 August 1914. James Jee Lawson and Mary Fuller had to get back to Canada before their CI 9s expired (two years after the date of issue). They brought Ethel but, for reasons we cannot know, took the risk of leaving three of their children

Fig. 3.31 (opposite) Mamie Lawson's record of death, 14 September 1910, Haileybury, Nipissing, Ontario.

Fig. 3.32 Victoria and Pearl Susan Oanfa Lawson in the 5 September 1914 General Register of Chinese Immigration.

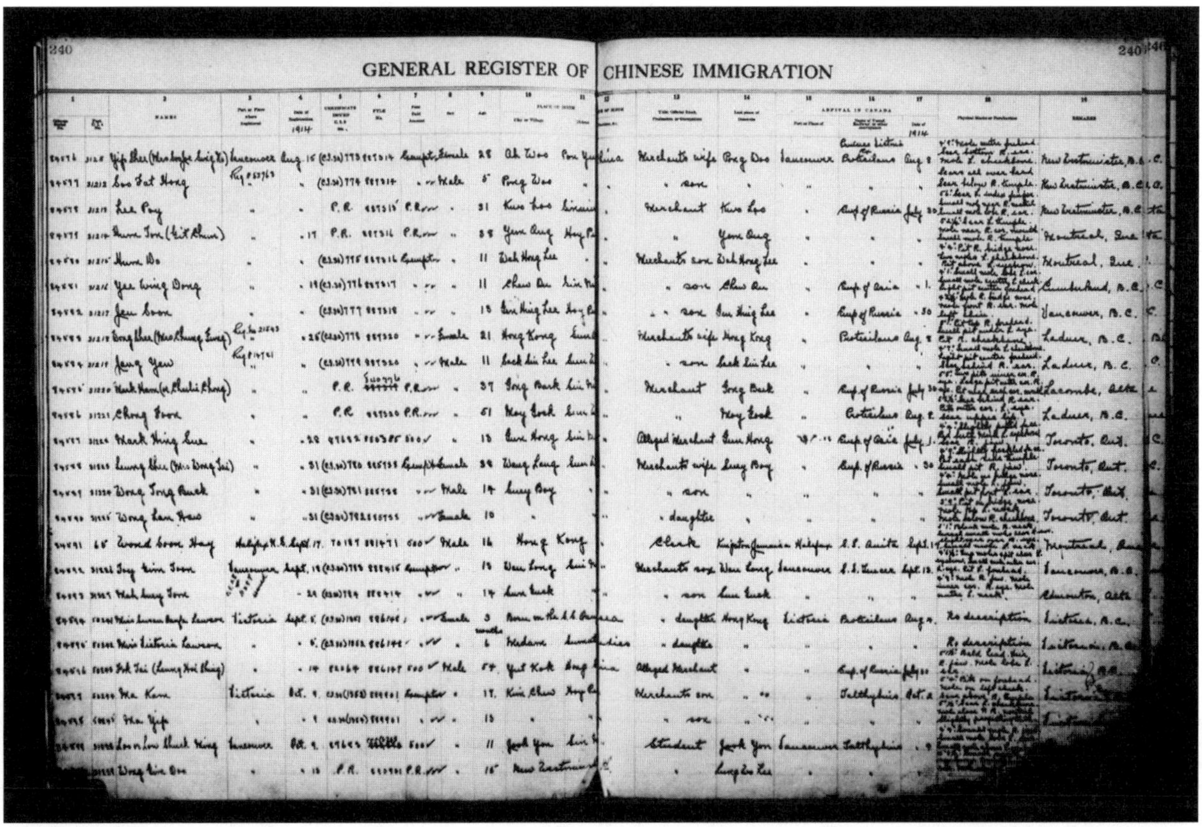
240

GENERAL REGISTER OF CHINESE IMMIGRATION

240

THE DEPARTMENT OF THE INTERIOR.

CHINESE IMMIGRATION BRANCH.

C. I. 9

No. 00016

AUG 26 1913 191

To the Collector of Customs,

Port of VICTORIA, B. C.

I hereby give notice that I desire to leave Canada with the intention of returning thereto. I propose to sail or depart from VICTORIA, B. C. for HongKong on the YOKOHAMA MARU day of AUG 26 1913 191

I intend to return to Canada at the port of

I request registration and I attach my photograph hereto and give the following information for the purpose of my identification on my return.

My proper name is Mrs. Mary Catherine Lawson

I am sometimes known as

I first came to Canada in the year Born in Canada (Hamilton)

My place of residence in Canada is Victoria

Where I have resided since the year 1887

Certificate of Registration Form C. I. 5 No.

My present occupation is that of Housewife

My place of birth was Hamilton. Ont

My present age is 26

Height 4 feet 11 inches.

Facial marks or other peculiarities :—

mole right cheek

I am personally known to Miss Maggie Smith (Oriental home)

both of VICTORIA, B. C. to whom I would refer you for correctness of statements herein made.

Mrs Mary Catherine Lawson
(Signature of Chinese Person.)

I have personally examined the person of Chinese origin who claims to be the person above described and whose photograph is affixed hereon (2), who returned to Canada on the day of AUG 191 and declare him to be the same person.

R. McCloskey
(Controller.)

Dated at VICTORIA, B. C. AUG 191

(1) If the person of Chinese origin desires to return to Canada by any other port, other than the port of departure, this form must be taken in duplicate and the duplicate forwarded to the intended port of entry by mail.
(2) The initials of the Controller should be affixed in ink so that a portion thereof overlaps the photograph.

[OVER.]

Particulars and photograph herein shown compared with applicant and approved by me this day of 191 Controller.

Dated at VICTORIA, B. C. AUG 26 1913

Mrs Mary Catherine Lawson

Fig. 3.33
CI 9 No. 00016,
Reel no. T-6046.

Fig. 3.34 (opposite)
CI 9 No. 22432,
Reel no. T-6041.

THE DEPARTMENT OF THE INTERIOR.

CHINESE IMMIGRATION BRANCH.

C. I. 9

No. 22432

AUG 26 1913 *191*

To the Collector of Customs,

Port of VICTORIA, B. C.

I hereby give notice that I desire to leave Canada with the intention of returning thereto. I propose to sail or depart from VICTORIA, B. C. for *HongKong* on the YOKOHAMA MARU day of AUG 26 1913 191

I intend to return to Canada at the port of (1)

I request registration and I attach my photograph hereto and give the following information for the purpose of my identification on my return.

My proper name is James Jee Lawson

I am sometimes known as Low. Sew

I first came to Canada in the year 1898

My place of residence in Canada is Victoria

Where I have resided since the year 1 Year

Certificate of Registration Form C. I. 5, No. 20029

My present occupation is that of Restaurant

My place of birth was Kwong Hoy

My present age is 37

Height 5 feet 3 inches.

Facial marks or other peculiarities:—

Scar outer corner R eye brow

" L. Temple

M. L eye lid

I am personally known to Ma Chan and Ma Sue both of VICTORIA, B. C. to whom I would refer you for correctness of statements herein made.

James Jee Lawson
(Signature of Chinese Person.)

Particulars and photograph hereon shown compared with applicant and approved by me this day. A. Mondich, 191 , Controller.

Dated at VICTORIA, B. C. AUG 26 1913

J. J. Lawson

I have personally examined the person of Chinese origin who claims to be the person above described and whose photograph is affixed hereon, (2) who returned to Canada on the day of AUG 4 1914 191 , and declare him to be the same person.

B. W. McCloskey
(Controller.)

Dated at VICTORIA, B. C., AUG 4 1914, 191

(1) If the person of Chinese origin desires to return to Canada by any other port other than the port of departure, this form must be taken in duplicate and the duplicate forwarded to the intended port of entry by mail.

(2) The initials of the Controller should be affixed in ink so that a portion thereof overlaps the photograph.

[OVER]

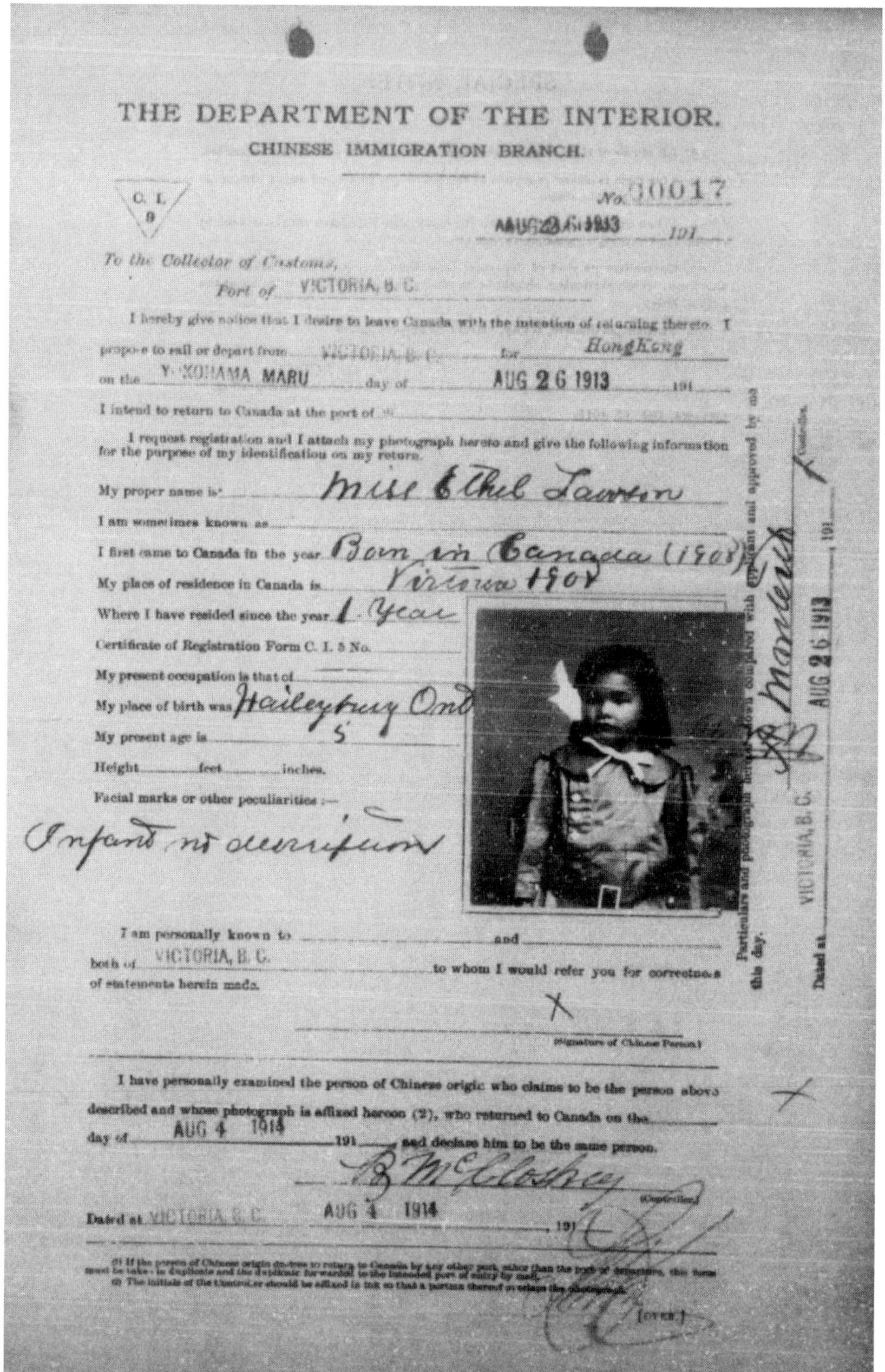

THE DEPARTMENT OF THE INTERIOR.

CHINESE IMMIGRATION BRANCH.

C. I. 9

No. 00017

AUG 26 1913 191

To the Collector of Customs,

Port of VICTORIA, B. C.

I hereby give notice that I desire to leave Canada with the intention of returning thereto. I propose to sail or depart from VICTORIA, B. C. for HongKong on the YOKOHAMA MARU day of AUG 26 1913 191

I intend to return to Canada at the port of

I request registration and I attach my photograph hereto and give the following information for the purpose of my identification on my return.

My proper name is Miss Ethel Lawson

I am sometimes known as

I first came to Canada in the year Born in Canada (1908)

My place of residence in Canada is Victoria 1908

Where I have resided since the year 1 Year

Certificate of Registration Form C. I. 5 No.

My present occupation is that of ——

My place of birth was Haileybury Ont

My present age is 5

Height feet inches.

Facial marks or other peculiarities :—

Infant no description

I am personally known to and both of VICTORIA, B. C. to whom I would refer you for correctness of statements herein made.

X

(Signature of Chinese Person)

Particulars and photograph herein have been compared with [illegible] and approved by me this day. B. Manderick Controller.

Dated at VICTORIA, B. C. AUG 26 1913 191

I have personally examined the person of Chinese origin who claims to be the person above described and whose photograph is affixed hereon (2), who returned to Canada on the AUG 4 1914 day of 191 and declare him to be the same person.

R. McCloskey (Controller)

Dated at VICTORIA, B. C. AUG 4 1914 191

(1) If the person of Chinese origin desires to return to Canada by any other port, other than the port of departure, this form must be taken in duplicate and the duplicate forwarded to the intended port of entry by mail.
(2) The initials of the Controller should be affixed in ink so that a portion thereof overlaps the photograph.

[OVER.]

Fig. 3.35
CI 9 No. 00017,
Reel no. T-6046.

behind. Pearl, James, and Jane would not rejoin the family until their journey to Canada in 1914. Indeed, the CI 9s that had been issued to James and Jane in 1911 had both already expired and been clearly marked as such. Fortunately, they were readmitted despite the expiration of their CI 9s.

There is still one more member of the Lawson family in the CI 9 archive. When James Ying Choury Lawson departed from the Port of Vancouver on 14 February 1921 aboard the *Katori Maru*, he did so with four-year-old Bert Lawson (fig. 3.36). On CI 9 no. 0308, in the space where Bert is to provide the names of people to whom he is "personally known," James Jee Lawson is identified as Bert's father. Here, yet another geographic location to add to the complex map of places where the Lawsons have resided. Bert is born in Port Alberni, British Columbia. The identity of his mother is still a mystery. James Ying Choury Lawson and Bert Lawson sailed on the same ship but they did so without their parents and sisters. There are no CI 9s for a 14 February 1921 departure for James Jee Lawson, or Mrs Lawson, or for Ethel, Jane, Victoria, and Susan Pearl Oanfa.

Bert sails out with his older brother but the boys do not return together. James Ying Choury's 1921 CI 9 notes that he returned to Canada on the *Empress of Australia* on 24 March 1924. Bert returns after only five months, on 29 July 1921 on the SS *Tyndarius*. There is no record of who accompanied him on this return journey. He would have just turned five. James Jee Lawson and Mary Catherine Fuller (and it is not necessarily the case that she is Bert's mother – especially given that her obituary states that she had four daughters and only one son) were not recorded as having left Canada that year.

Bert resurfaces in the CI 9 archive two years later (fig. 3.37). He sailed out of the Port of Victoria on 30 August 1923 on the *President McKinley*. At this point in the records, the CI 9s for native-born Chinese children began to be filed separately from those of adults. He was not travelling with any of the other Lawson children, since there are no CI 9s issued for them departing at the same time. Nor are there any records of James Jee Lawson departing Canada on this ship on this day. Mrs Lawson née Fuller is not recorded as leaving Canada at this time.

There is much that remains a mystery about this little boy. Certainly, he had traversed the Pacific Ocean twice by the time he was seven years old. He did so without his father. His mother is also absent on these ships and in these records. There is no indication that he returned to Canada after leaving in 1923.

So much hovers on the edge of sadness for me about Bert Lawson. In this archive, he is the most peripheral, a small boy both times he appears. A minor detail that reveals a great deal about how Bert was torn away from

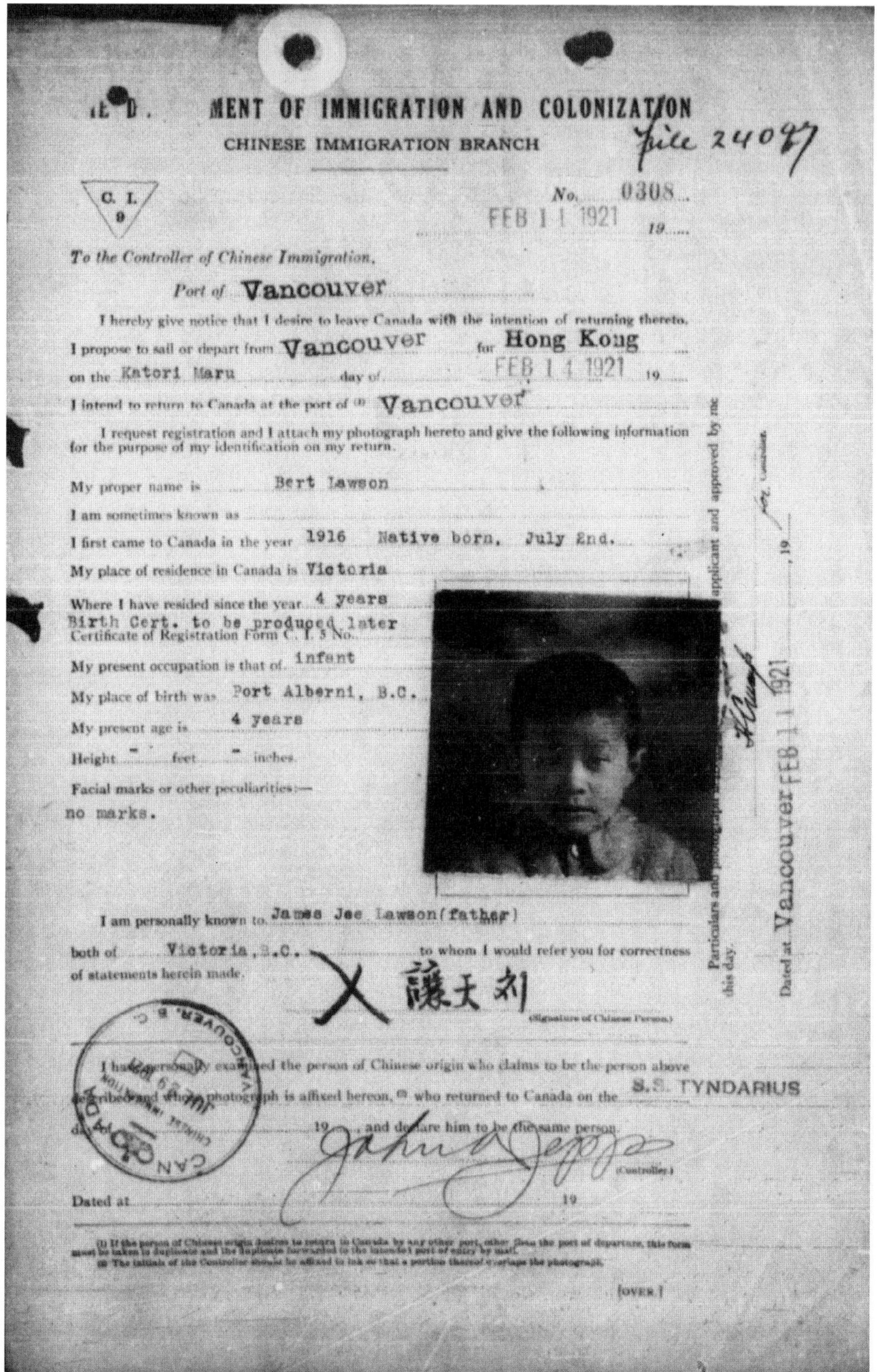

DEPARTMENT OF IMMIGRATION AND COLONIZATION

CHINESE IMMIGRATION BRANCH

File 24097

C. I. 9

No. 0308

FEB 11 1921 19....

To the Controller of Chinese Immigration,

Port of Vancouver

I hereby give notice that I desire to leave Canada with the intention of returning thereto.

I propose to sail or depart from Vancouver for Hong Kong

on the Katori Maru day of FEB 11 1921 19

I intend to return to Canada at the port of (1) Vancouver

I request registration and I attach my photograph hereto and give the following information for the purpose of my identification on my return.

My proper name is Bert Lawson

I am sometimes known as

I first came to Canada in the year 1916 Native born, July 2nd.

My place of residence in Canada is Victoria

Where I have resided since the year 4 years

Birth Cert. to be produced later

Certificate of Registration Form C. I. 5 No.

My present occupation is that of infant

My place of birth was Port Alberni, B.C.

My present age is 4 years

Height - feet - inches

Facial marks or other peculiarities:—

no marks.

I am personally known to James Jee Lawson (father)

both of Victoria, B.C. to whom I would refer you for correctness of statements herein made.

X 劉天藤

(Signature of Chinese Person)

Particulars and photograph examined and approved by me this day. Dated at Vancouver FEB 11 1921

I have personally examined the person of Chinese origin who claims to be the person above described and whose photograph is affixed hereon, (2) who returned to Canada on the S.S. TYNDARIUS day of 19...., and declare him to be the same person.

(Controller)

Dated at 19

(1) If the person of Chinese origin desires to return to Canada by any other port, other than the port of departure, this form must be taken in duplicate and the duplicate forwarded to the intended port of entry by mail.

(2) The initials of the Controller should be affixed in ink so that a portion thereof overlaps the photograph.

[OVER]

Fig. 3.36
CI 9 No. 0308, Reel no. T-6046.

Fig. 3.37 (opposite)
CI 9 No. 809, Reel no. T-6046.

File #29898

THE DEPARTMENT OF IMMIGRATION AND COLONIZATION

CHINESE IMMIGRATION BRANCH

C. I. 9

No. 809

AUG 30 1923 19

To the Controller of Chinese Immigration,

Port of ....

I hereby give notice that I desire to leave Canada with the intention of returning thereto.

I propose to sail or depart from .... for ....

on the President McKinley day of AUG 30 1923 19

I intend to return to Canada at the port of [1] ....

I request registration and I attach my photograph hereto and give the following information for the purpose of my identification on my return.

My proper name is Bert Lawson

I am sometimes known as En Yong

I first came to Canada in the year July 2nd 1916

My place of residence in Canada is Victoria BC

Where I have resided since the year 1916

Certificate of Registration Form C. I. 5 No. Pt.Alberni Birth Certificate April 8/21

My present occupation is that of Child

My place of birth was Port Alberni

My present age is 7 yrs

Height 3 feet 6½ inches.

Facial marks or other peculiarities:—

Mole left cheek

Small pit above right ear

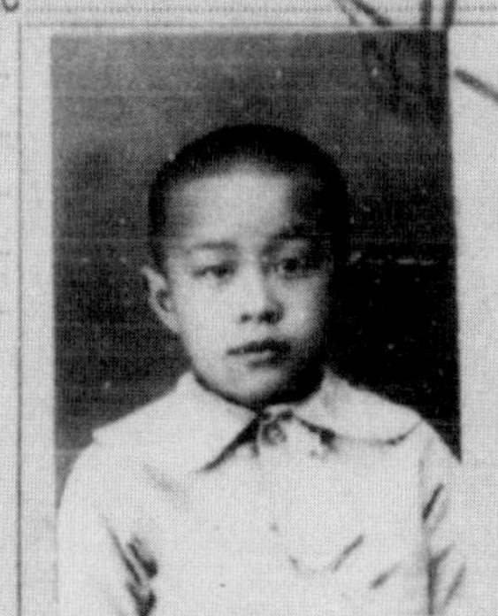

I am personally known to Father and Mother

both of Victoria to whom I would refer you for correctness of statements herein made.

刘天譲

(Signature of Chinese Person.)

Particulars and photograph hereon shown compared with applicant and approved by me this day.

S. N. Reid

Dated at VICTORIA, B. C. AUG 29 1923, 19

I have personally examined the person of Chinese origin who claims to be the person above described and whose photograph is affixed hereon, [2] who returned to Canada on the .... day of .... 19 ...., and declare him to be the same person.

(Controller.)

Dated at .... 19 ....

---

(1) If the person of Chinese origin desires to return to Canada by any other port, other than the port of departure, this form must be taken in duplicate and the duplicate forwarded to the intended port of entry by mail.

(2) The initials of the Controller should be affixed in ink so that a portion thereof overlaps the photograph.

C.I. 44 # 20015

[OVER.]

what he knew: in 1921, even at the age of five, Bert had been taught to write his name in Chinese. Not only that, but he signs his name following the conventions of Chinese script with his surname, 劉, or "Lau," written first from right to left. Two years later, when he leaves Canada seemingly for the final time, he still signs his name in Chinese, but has reversed the script. He has written his name with his surname first from left to right. Over the passage of two years, Bert Lawson consistently chooses to identify himself by signing his name in Chinese. In contrast, his father, James Jee Lawson, never signs his name in Chinese. But as he has aged, Bert has also become more Canadian. He has started to write from left to right instead of right to left. He is caught between two systems of writing, and two systems of identification (his name, and the CI 9 document). Sailing back and forth across the Pacific twice in two years, Bert is displaced again and again.

Strikingly, in the Lawson family, it is the sons who are cut away from family most forcefully by the cruel logic of the CI 9 forms. James and Bert are denied in different ways. James's CI 9 takes away from him a surname that would have connected him to his father and his mother. Bert is allowed his father's surname, but not the company of either one of his parents when he crosses the ocean four times as a young child. Bert is granted a connection to his father on a line in the form where he is identified as being "personally known" to his father, James Jee Lawson. But in both cases, the idea of the family is shorn from these boys. As Spillers understands, "'family,' as we practice and understand it 'in the West' – the *vertical* transfer of a bloodline, of a patronymic, of titles and entitlements, of real estate and the prerogatives of 'cold cash,' from *fathers* to *sons* and in the supposedly free exchange of affectional ties between a male and a female of *his* choice – becomes the mythically revered privilege of a free and freed community" (74). The Lawsons were not enslaved. James Lawson has a family. He has a wife of his choosing. He has children. Still, their freedoms were severely limited. The record of their existence as a family reveals a persistent undermining of the fact of this family as a family. The head tax refused the sons access to the patronymic; it denied the transfer of titles and entitlements between fathers and sons. James Ying Choury does not appear to have a father or a mother until his re-emergence as James Lawson on CI 9 no. 0307 in 1921 (fig. 3.29). Bert's patrilineage is permitted but only when he is separated from his father by dint of a long journey. Spillers argues that "captive persons were *forced* into patterns of *dispersal*" (75). The family that the Lawsons make is both their own and not their own. Their separations, either by the careless entry of a line on a form, or by the fact of a physical separation to which the form bears witness, are part of a larger pattern by which Chinese migrants lost their families repeatedly.

For the Lawsons, the CI 9s tell a story of making and remaking, of a family in near constant motion attempting to stay ahead of restrictions on their movements. Returning to the first set of CI 9s for the Lawsons, recording their departure aboard the *Oanfa* in 1911, we can see a family portrait within what I have argued is a larger portrait of the kinship of the ship itself. This family travelled together on that ship. But even a cursory look at their 1911 certificates already indicates how difficult it is to envision family and kinship in these certificates. To rely solely on the information contained in those 1911 CI 9s would have uncovered only part of the family that had been together on the *Oanfa*. James Ying Choury would seem to be, based on just his CI 9, a stranger child who was, at best, travelling in the company of the Lawson family. Susan Pearl Oanfa is not in the picture but had been present in that first photograph of Mrs Lawson. Finding this family demanded seeing beyond the CI 9s and looking for other evidence of their relatedness. Mass capture bound them together, as it did with every other Chinese migrant on the *Oanfa* in 1911, but it also visually fractures them. Siloed by their certificates, each member of the family has been cut away from the other.

White Women, Chinese Subjects

I want to conclude this chapter on looking for kinship in the CI 9 certificates by examining one more family travelling together aboard the *Oanfa* in 1911 (figs. 3.38 and 3.39). Here, on CI 9 no. 18001, is Mrs Fred Lun, or Lum, or Lau – without the Chinese ideogram for the name, it is hard to definitively decipher the handwriting. She is from Kingston, England. She is a housewife who was twenty-eight years old when she boarded the *Oanfa*. In the space for noting "facial marks and peculiarities," the agent has written, "Scar under R Jaw" and "White Lady."

Although nothing on the CI 9 explicitly identifies the six-year-old boy in the subsequent certificate as her son, based on the surname it seems possible that Raymon Fred Lun, Lum, or Lau is travelling with his mother. He was born in Niagara Falls and has "brown spots" all over his nose. Nobody is identified as being "personally known" to him. Neither the certificate before 18001 nor the one following 18002 identifies a man who could be the father. CI 9 no. 18000 is for Lee Shei who claims to have been residing in and working as a labourer in Victoria for the last eleven years. CI 9 no. 18003 is for Jong Mou, who had been working as a farmer in Ashcroft, British Columbia for seven years prior to boarding the *Oanfa*.

Like the case of Mary Fuller, Mrs Lun does not enter this archive with any record of her maiden name. She can only be known here by her mar-

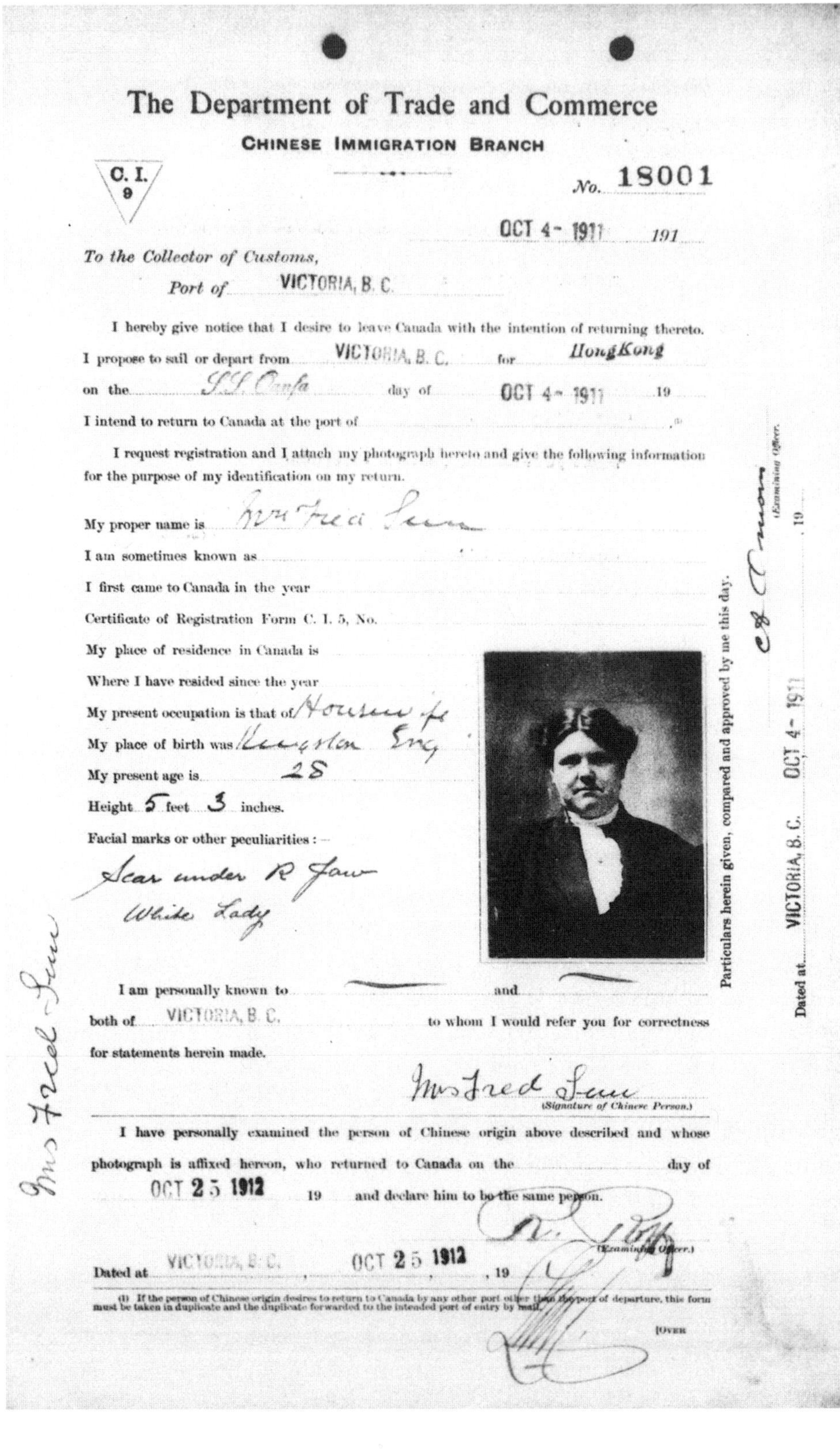

The Department of Trade and Commerce

CHINESE IMMIGRATION BRANCH

C. I. 9

No. 18001

OCT 4 - 1911 191

To the Collector of Customs,

Port of VICTORIA, B. C.

I hereby give notice that I desire to leave Canada with the intention of returning thereto.

I propose to sail or depart from VICTORIA, B. C. for HongKong

on the S.S. Oanfa day of OCT 4 - 1911 19

I intend to return to Canada at the port of (1)

I request registration and I attach my photograph hereto and give the following information for the purpose of my identification on my return.

My proper name is Mrs Fred Sam

I am sometimes known as

I first came to Canada in the year

Certificate of Registration Form C. I. 5, No.

My place of residence in Canada is

Where I have resided since the year

My present occupation is that of Housewife

My place of birth was Kingston Eng

My present age is 28

Height 5 feet 3 inches.

Facial marks or other peculiarities: –

Scar under R Jaw

White Lady

I am personally known to —— and ——

both of VICTORIA, B. C. to whom I would refer you for correctness for statements herein made.

Mrs Fred Sam

(Signature of Chinese Person.)

Particulars herein given, compared and approved by me this day.

Dated at VICTORIA, B. C. OCT 4 - 1911 19

(Examining Officer.)

I have personally examined the person of Chinese origin above described and whose photograph is affixed hereon, who returned to Canada on the day of OCT 25 1912 19 and declare him to be the same person.

(Examining Officer.)

Dated at VICTORIA, B. C., OCT 25 1912, 19

(1) If the person of Chinese origin desires to return to Canada by any other port other than the port of departure, this form must be taken in duplicate and the duplicate forwarded to the intended port of entry by mail.

[OVER

Mrs Fred Sam

Fig. 3.38
CI 9 No. 18001,
Reel no. T-6039.

Fig. 3.39 (opposite)
CI 9 No. 18002,
Reel no. T-6039.

The Department of Trade and Commerce

CHINESE IMMIGRATION BRANCH

C. I. 9

No. 18002

OCT 4 - 1911 191

To the Collector of Customs,

Port of VICTORIA, B. C.

I hereby give notice that I desire to leave Canada with the intention of returning thereto.

I propose to sail or depart from VICTORIA, B. C. for *Hong Kong*

on the S.S. Empress day of OCT 4 - 1911 19

I intend to return to Canada at the port of (1)

I request registration and I attach my photograph hereto and give the following information for the purpose of my identification on my return.

My proper name is Raymon Tea Lau

I am sometimes known as

I first came to Canada in the year

Certificate of Registration Form C. I. 5, No.

My place of residence in Canada is

Where I have resided since the year

My present occupation is that of

My place of birth was Niagara Falls

My present age is 6 years

Height feet inches.

Facial marks or other peculiarities :—

Brown spots all over nose

Particulars herein given, compared and approved by me this day.

Dated at VICTORIA, B. C. OCT 4 - 1911 19

(Examining Officer.)

I am personally known to and

both of VICTORIA, B. C. to whom I would refer you for correctness for statements herein made.

(Signature of Chinese Person.)

I have personally examined the person of Chinese origin above described and whose photograph is affixed hereon, who returned to Canada on the day 19 and declare him to be the same person.

Expired

(Examining Officer.)

Dated at VICTORIA, B. C. , 19

(1) If the person of Chinese origin desires to return to Canada by any other port other than the port of departure, this form must be taken in duplicate and the duplicate forwarded to the intended port of entry by mail.

[OVER

ried name. Again, as with the Lawsons, the information on the certificates ties mother and child, but also separates them. The only geographic location on hers is Kingston, England, and the only geographic location on his is Niagara Falls. The photographs on CI 9 nos. 18001 and 18002 offer the possibility of familial relation at the same time that they deny it. In this double movement, of connection and the denial of connection, these two photographs resonate with Kunimoto's reading of how the family photograph "entices but ultimately denies contact: reunion is offered but never actualized" (2004, 133). Although the identification photographs of Mrs Lun and Raymon Lun do not constitute a family photograph in the conventional sense, as I have been arguing, seeing them together does offer a portrait of togetherness for a group of people who were systematically denied so many forms of intimacy and familial relation. Still, even here, there is only the possibility of a reunion, of a mother and a child together.

Almost as soon as we can make out their togetherness, we are also left with the fact of their separation. Mrs Lun's CI 9 notes that she returned to Canada on 25 October 1912. Raymon Lun's CI 9 gives no return date. His certificate is stamped "expired." She came back but he did not. Again, a family whose separation can be parsed through the cool objectivity of date and expiration stamps. There was a little boy who travelled with a woman who was most likely his mother. They were together. And then they were not. These certificates record their attachment and their separation.

Mrs Lun's CI 9 is also another record of the bureaucratic transformation of a white woman into a Chinese subject. Such a transformation has already happened with Mrs James Jee Lawson on CI 9 no. 17939. Now, with CI 9 no. 18001, it becomes clear that this subjection of white women to the legislative regime of the Chinese Immigration Act is not a one-off. Both women are clearly identified as white. Both are definitely subjected to the legal demand that stipulated that Chinese migrants had to register through the CI 9 certificate system, before departing Canada. Such demands were not made of any other group of people living in Canada at this time. Canadian-born white women like Mary Fuller, or women from England like Mrs Lun, should have been exempt from this legislative demand. Yet, as CI 9 nos. 17939 and 18001 make clear, they had to register and provide an identification photograph like any other Chinese migrant. The CI 9s for white women in this archive are evidence of the extent to which white women who married Chinese men were treated as though they were Chinese. Their punishment for the families that they chose to make was to be swept into the net of mass capture.

To be clear, there is absolutely nothing in any Canadian statute that specifies that a white woman who marries a Chinese man should suddenly have to give up her whiteness. Still, this treatment of white women such as Mary Fuller and Mrs Lun echoes the "marrying out" rules that governed the identity of women under the Indian Act. Beginning in 1851 and lasting until these provisions were amended by the passage of Bill C-31 in 1985, the Indian Act deemed that non-Indigenous women who married Indigenous men would be considered "status" Indians. Relatedly, Indigenous women who married non-Indigenous men would lose their status under the provisions of the Indian Act, as would their children. Even though the Chinese Immigration Act never discusses the Chinese status of white women who marry Chinese men, CI 9 nos. 17939 and 18001 make very clear that white women married to Chinese men would be considered Chinese whenever they wished to travel outside of Canada with the intention of returning. They were considered to have "married out" not by statute, but by being captured within a process of exclusion that was blandly bureaucratic (complete this form, provide this identification photograph) and devastatingly regulatory. Because they were considered Chinese, there were restrictions placed on their movements. They had to return to Canada within two years of departure, and, as you can see from the return stamps on their forms, both women meticulously observed this regulation by returning before two years were up – even if it meant leaving again very soon to find children they had left behind (as was the case with Mary Fuller).

The CI 9s for white women, women who are explicitly identified as white and yet classified as Chinese by virtue of marriage to Chinese men, illuminate the way in which the mass capture of Chinese migrants also had consequences white Canadians. It makes visible a practice that had, until Mary Fuller and Mrs Lun surfaced in this archive, been unknown. Envisioning kinship under the conditions of mass capture uncovers the reach of the CI 9 system and how it captured whiteness in ways that were both gendered and racialized. As the textual material on the CI 9 certificates for Mary Fuller and Mrs Lun reveals, this system underwent all manner of contortions in order to mark these women as Chinese while also insisting upon their whiteness.

The position of white women marked as Chinese in the CI 9 archive also shows the complexities of the relationship between kinship and citizenship for Chinese migrants in Canada. With naturalization only accessible to some rare wealthy merchants, Chinese people in Canada could not be citizens until the repeal of the Chinese Immigration Act in 1947. By marrying Chinese men, Mary Fuller and Mrs Lun enter an in-between sphere where they may have been able to vote, but were unable to travel with their families without being marked as Chinese. They are very much, in Judith Butler's terms, people whose "ontological status as legal subjects is suspended. These are not lives that are being genocidally destroyed, but neither are they being entered into the life of the legitimate community in which standards of recognition permit for an attainment of humanness" (2000, 81). Following Butler's reading of citizenship and kinship through the figure of Antigone, these women's access to "*citizenship demands a partial repudiation of the kinship relations that bring the male citizen into being*" (12). Mary Fuller and Mrs Lun are even farther removed than the figure of the gendered citizen in Butler's discussion, because their kinship relations do not produce citizens. Their sons and daughters, as evidenced by the CI 9s they carried, were considered Chinese and did not have access to full citizenship in Canada. Mary Fuller and Mrs Lun both sailed on the *Oanfa* carrying CI 9s that signalled the Chineseness they acquired through marriage. We do not know if they were permitted into the parts of the ship reserved for white passengers or if they had to remain with others bearing CI 9s. Did their whiteness register differently at sea? At some point during that transpacific journey, they must have met. We cannot know what they might have said to each other, but we know that they share something in the papers they carried.

As a ship carrying migrants from Canada across the Pacific Ocean, the *Oanfa* is both typical and, as this chapter shows, exceptional. On this ship, as with so many others that are part of the CI 9 archive, the journey would have forged connections that were not there before, while also consolidating relationships that existed prior to its departure from port. In her discussion of family photography in China and its relationship to history, Laura Wexler writes: "Photographs have a privileged relation to memory, which brings issues of recollection to the forefront of every photographic image. As theorist after theorist has demonstrated, photographs draw us into what we know so that we can recognize what we have forgotten, or refused to see" (2011, 9). Although Wexler's argument emerges out of her research on the circulation of family photography in contemporary China, her discussion can be expanded from the function of memory within a single family to its function within the nation and the diaspora. The photographs of families in the CI 9 collection feature only a handful of people, but they nonetheless demand their beholders to consider that which has been forgotten or discounted, particularly in terms of the destructiveness of the policies of racial exclusion.

The CI 9 certificates demand a different envisioning of kinship than that of a conventional family photograph where members of a family are pictured together in a single frame. Here, kinship is formed despite the devastating denial of intimacy that the Chinese Immigration Act encodes through its restrictions on the entry of Chinese of migrants and the regulations governing their mobility. We can see families fractured both visually, through the visual siloes of their identification photographs, and physically, in the records of their movements. This chapter looks for kinship despite laws and regulations that actively separated Chinese migrants from their families. Seeing through this persecution and into the bonds of the shipboard journey, and looking for families whose connections have been lost or obscured, is the task of envisioning kinship for *Mass Capture*.

CHAPTER FOUR

MASS CAPTURE AND THE GRAMMARS OF PERSISTENT REPRESENTATION

Mass capture is a double formation that is both documentary and corporeal. As I outline in chapter 1, mass capture works through the capture of information and bodies, and one form of capture informs and shapes the other. There is no mass capture of Chinese migrants during the period of the head tax and exclusion (1885–1947) without the information apprehended in the once-blank spaces of the CI 9 certificates, and the bodies of the migrants caught within the hold of the ship, and the labour contracts that left them indebted and further ensnared. Yet, as chapter 2 shows, this capture was never total. There is no necessary correlation between the person the certificate claims to represent, and the actual person holding the certificate. Indeed, the absence of a discernible relationship between the anglicized and Chinese names on so many certificates suggests that such a lack of correlation is more commonplace. Although this argument opens up a way to see how Chinese migrants may have turned the CI 9 system against itself, I recognize that it also works against a major part of the argument that I present in chapter 3. In that chapter, I argued for the need to see each certificate as representative of a life. For example, in my discussion of the photographs of the Chinese passengers on the *Oanfa*, I asked readers to think of each certificate as representing a life and a member of the kinship network of the diasporic passage experienced by those on board that ship. Thus, after questioning the capacity of the CI 9 to represent a life, I insist that it does.

This apparent contradiction reveals a larger problem regarding the authenticity or veracity of the CI 9s themselves. In this chapter, I will address the problem of the realness of these documents, and of the people they purport to represent, by turning to the study of diplomatics, a branch of archival research that emerges in the medieval era but has more recently taken on new dimensions through the work of Luciana Duranti. Citing Peter Herde, Duranti offers the very general definition of diplomatics as "'the study of documents'" (1989, 14). Throughout this book, I have looked closely at the people caught in these documents, and the processes of their capture, but I have not yet examined the CI 9s as forms in themselves. Building on the work of Duranti, this chapter takes up the problem of the form itself as an object of study. Such a turn resolves the contradiction of the CI 9 as both that which does and does not represent the lives of the people caught within its frame.

The CI 9s do represent the life of a migrant, but these certificates do not always represent the particular life of the person carrying that particular certificate. A diplomatic analysis will show how to understand the truth of these documents *as documents*. It will also show how an examination of the CI 9 as a document allows us to see more clearly the lives that are captured on the document. While it may seem in tension with my commitment to honour the lives of the people who have been subjected to the processes of mass capture in the CI 9 system, I suggest that focusing on the document instead of the person represented by it actually allows for a return to the corporeal consequences of mass capture. As I will outline in the next section, the certificates attempt to capture a specific kind of truth about each migrant, but what they capture instead is the truth of a process. The CI 9s do not document people. Rather, they document a process that attempted to document people.

The move from person to process is not a shift away from the people who have been subjected to mass capture. It is a move towards understanding more clearly the process of their subjection. As chapter 2 shows, the CI 9s are not a perfect record of each and every Chinese migrant who ever registered an outward journey with the intention of returning to Canada. The records are flawed, not least because of the ingenuity of migrants who may themselves have exploited the system's weaknesses. Because of these flaws, the CI 9s are not always a reliable genealogical resource. Certainly, many people have already found the CI 9s to be a tremendous resource for finding traces of their relatives. I have no doubt that many more will continue to find these certificates to be a resource for ancestry research. As I have shown with the Lawson family in chapter 3, the CI 9s used in tandem with other resources – such as birth and death registries, newspaper obituaries, and the General Register of Chinese Immigration – can yield a rich portrait of a family through several generations. Nevertheless, unlike the Lawsons, there are thousands of migrants whose presence in this archive will yield little further knowledge.

For example, the baby, "Miss Wong Louie Youe," in CI 9 no. 20306 (fig. 3.1 in chapter 3) is recorded in this archive, but she is more lost than found. Her birth was not recorded in Canadian registries. Her name on the CI 9 may or may not have been correctly noted. We cannot find her parents. The woman who holds her in the photograph, Mrs Hom See, is also a mystery. But these losses, the information gaps around these women, do not invalidate the truth of their presence in this archive. Understanding their presence as central to the process of mass capture is one way to attend to what remains real about these documents. There was a baby. She was here. Her CI 9 may not be telling the truth of her identity, but it does incontrovertibly tell us that she was subjected to a process that has, in Vijay Mishra's phrasing, "entered for the first time the regulative history of Empire" (1996, 429). Here, she becomes a subject of history. It does not matter whether she is who the certificate claims. She is here before us now. Despite the loss of her family, the loss of the records that would allow us to find them, her presence persists on this form and in this documentary process.

These documents are representations of the activity of mass capture, the processes to which people were subjected and how these processes made people into subjects of history. Miss Wong Louie Youe enters history because of a discriminatory system of information capture that attempted to make her known to the state. We may not know much about Miss Wong herself, but the document that claims to represent her is richly telling. It tells us that even babies who could neither speak nor write were subjects of mass capture. It tells us that some children were separated from their families and that this separation is plain to see in the documentary record itself. More than anything, it tells us that the CI 9 system was a series of actions and activities indifferently applied to many different people, and that this application enables a persistence of presence. A diplomatic turn will illuminate the workings of this persistence.

Diplomatics as Persistent Representation

Diplomatics is a field of archival study that emerged in the medieval period in response to a rise in the forgeries of administrative-legal documents. It rose in tandem with paleography and, as noted by Duranti (who is widely credited with spearheading the application of diplomatics beyond medieval studies), forgeries did not become a widespread problem until documents were separated from the places where they were kept:

> The problem of distinguishing genuine documents from forgeries was present in the earliest periods of documentation, but until the sixth century no attempt was made to devise criteria for the identification of forgeries. Even legislators did not demonstrate interest in the issue, basically because of the legal principle commonly accepted

in the ancient world that authenticity is not an intrinsic character of documents but is accorded to them by the fact of their preservation in a designated place, a temple, public office, treasury, or archives. This principle was open to abuse. Eventually, people began to present forgeries to designated records offices to lend them authenticity. Therefore, practical rules to recognize them were introduced in Justinian's civil code (*Corpus iuris civilus*) and later in a number of Paper *Decretales*. (1989, 12)

When documents did not travel, when their authenticity could be guaranteed by their immobility, the issue of authenticity did not arise. It is only when documents began to move, when they were presented to places of juridical or legal import rather than being consulted in those places, that forgeries became a problem. This linking of mobility with suspicion will emerge again in chapter 5 in my discussion of the rise of the passport in relation to the CI 9. For now, it is sufficient to note that the mobility of documents, much like the mobility of people, instigates suspicion.

The movement of documents necessitates their doubling. Appropriately for CI 9s, which begin their lives as doubled documents, diplomatics is etymologically rooted in the idea of doubling:

> Both the words diplomacy and diplomatics have their root in the Greek verb *diploo* (διπλό), meaning "I double" or "I fold," which gave birth to the word *diploma* (δίπλωμα), meaning "doubled" or "folded." In classic antiquity, the word diploma referred to documents written on two tablets attached with a hinge and called diptych; and, during the Roman Imperial period, to specific types of documents issued by the Emperor or the Senate, such as the decrees conferring privileges of citizenship and marriage on soldiers who had served their time. In time, diploma came to mean a deed issued by a sovereign authority, and was extended to include generally all documents issued in solemn form. (1989, 12)

Understanding the CI 9s as a problem of diplomatics locates the problem of their authenticity squarely within their existence as documents that were presented and exchanged in the course of travel, and which were, by their very nature, doubled and folded into the documentary apparatus of the state.

Crucially, diplomatics enables us to disentangle the ways in which the CI 9s can be both authentic as documents, and potentially inauthentic in terms of the people they purport to identify or represent. Duranti draws out the differences between diplomatic authenticity, legal authenticity, and historical authenticity. For her, these three types of authenticity can be totally independent of each other. "*Diplomatic authenticity* does not coincide with *legal authenticity*, even if they both can lead to an attribution of *historical authenticity* in a judicial dispute." For example, a "Papal brief which does not contain the expression 'datum ... sub anulo piscatoris' may be legally and historically authentic, but it is diplomatically inauthentic" (1989, 17). Such distinctions are helpful for understanding how any particular CI 9 might be authentic in terms of its diplomatics because all the necessary signatures, countersignatures, and other verifying marks are present. It can also be legally authentic in that it will afford its bearer the right to return to Canada. But, as in the case of Wong Lim Foon on CI 9 no. 22711, discussed in chapter 2, a CI 9 can be historically false because the certificate does not accurately represent the identity of the man it claims to identify.

This differentiation between the diplomatic, legal, and historical authenticity of a document offers a way to understand how each CI 9 is representative of a life, yet not necessarily representative of the specific life that it claims to represent. The CI 9s remain legally authentic in that they "bear witness on their own because of the intervention, during or after their creation, of a representative of a public authority guaranteeing their genuineness" (Duranti 1989, 17). They are also diplomatically authentic documents in that they "were written according to the practice of the time and place indicated in the text, and signed with the name(s) of the person(s) competent to create them" (ibid.). Indeed, the CI 9s in this collection are almost uniformly diplomatically authentic. I have yet to find one that does not include the requisite signatures. The rules to which they had to conform vary slightly over the years, but they are remarkably consistent in their observance of the demands of the form itself. The blanks spaces are filled out. The photographs are attached. The signatures of the migrants are either included or an "x" or a thumbprint is given by those who could not write their own names. But, in terms of their accuracy as documents representing the history of a particular person, they start to fall apart for all the reasons that I outlined in chapters 2 and 3. The agents recording the information did not speak Chinese and relied on translators. There was no consistent system for anglicizing Chinese names. There was no differentiation between surname and given name. The state used the exact same set of numbers for certificates of migrants leaving from Victoria and those leaving from Vancouver, resulting in the existence of thousands of certificates that share a numerical identifier. There were literally two of every certificate number, each representing an entirely different person departing from a different port on a different ship. Thus, Wong Lim Foon had a double. CI 9 no. 22711 also belonged to Ing Yong Lan (figs. 2.2 and 2.4 in chapter 2). Or, in the case of the Lawsons, James Ying Choury on CI 9 no. 17940 was not given his father's surname and would have been lost to the family, in terms of the records, had it not been for the numerical sequencing of the certificates (fig. 3.20 in chapter 3).

Even though so much of my research has resulted in finding examples where the state failed in its attempt to identify and track each Chinese migrant who ever wanted to temporarily leave Canada, I have also never lost my sense that a given certificate truly does represent a life. In each case, at least one person was issued that certificate and carried it on his or her person. A photograph attached to a CI 9 is an image of a real person. Again, it matters less to me whether or not that photograph is of the person it claims to identify. For the person who is looking for a great-great-grandfather, I hope that it is. But I also do not want to discount the value of these images on the grounds that they may not correspond with the identity of the person on the certificate. As Elizabeth Edwards argues, "it is not what a photograph is of in purely evidential terms that should primarily concern us, but the context in which it is embedded" (2001, 88). The context of the CI 9 demands a way of seeing these images and these documents as more than just the sum of their evidentiary parts. Taken together in their context, the images on these documents uncover the complexity of a process of capture that almost always worked as a process, but often failed as a system. These failures are to be celebrated. Capture was not, and was never, total. That does not mean that the process itself should not be examined. And it certainly does not mean that the presence of these thousands and thousands of migrants, caught within what Leigh Raiford in a very different context calls the "luminous glare" of the state, should not be valued (2013, 1).

Indeed, it is the persistence of the presence of the men, women, and children in these certificates that has held me. This persistence also has a place in diplomatics, in what Geoffrey Yeo calls "persistent representations" (2007, 342). Yeo comes to his theory of the archival record as a persistent representation out of his dissatisfaction with understanding archival records as either evidence or information. Instead, he argues that archival records should be understood as "*persistent representations of activities*" (ibid.). Building from literary theory on representation, and particularly that of W.J.T. Mitchell, Yeo argues that "records have persistence." As he points out, not all representations are persistent: "The reflection in the pond, the reading on the speedometer of a car, the unsaved document residing only in a computer's temporary memory are not persistent." In contrast, "a persistent representation is one with the capacity to endure beyond the immediate circumstance leading to its creation. Persistence need not imply survival without limit of time. Records may not last forever and decisions may be made to destroy them. But records are persistent in the sense that they endure beyond the temporal ending of the activities they represent. Their durability gives them the potential to be shared and passed on across space and time" (2007, 337). This conception of the archival record as a persistent representation encompasses both the letter and the spirit of what I want to hold in the CI 9s. The latter persist as representations of the actions of a state that engaged in processes of mass capture in order to make and remake, again and again, these migrants as non-citizens. But they also persist as the indelible presence of people whose gazes have endured the destruction of lives and families, even the destruction of the original records themselves. The people on these certificates look back at us across space and time and challenge their viewers to look away.

Taking Yeo's conception at a remove, understanding the CI 9s as persistent representations is not only a way of distinguishing their value as both evidence and information, but also a way to embrace the endurance of the lives captured in these certificates. Yes, these certificates do represent the activities of a state-sponsored process of mass capture. However, they are more than that. To think of the CI 9s as the representation of a process is also to take up these certificates as a record of what it took to endure this process.

On every CI 9 is a persistent representation of endurance. Take, for example, just one of the many CI 9s that records the presence of a Chinese migrant living and working in Canada for decades. According to the certificate in figure 4.1, Kong Hong, CI 9 no. 15842, first came to Canada in 1885, which was the first year of Chinese Immigration Act. It is not clear whether he lived in one of the parts of Vancouver that were at various times known as Strathcona, or in the town of Strathcona near Edmonton, Alberta. The latter seems more likely as many certificates list Vancouver as a place of residence and other Vancouver neighbourhoods are not listed as separate geographical entities on these forms. He would have been among the first to pay the head tax, but there is no evidence of this payment because his CI 5 has been lost. On 3 October 1910, when he sailed for Hong Kong on the SS *Antilochus*, he is recorded as being thirty-three years old. That means that he would have arrived in Canada at the age of eight. Was he born in Canada but did not have the opportunity to record this fact on the form because there is no line to indicate place of birth? The CI 9 does not tell us. But it does tell us that he worked in a restaurant, that he

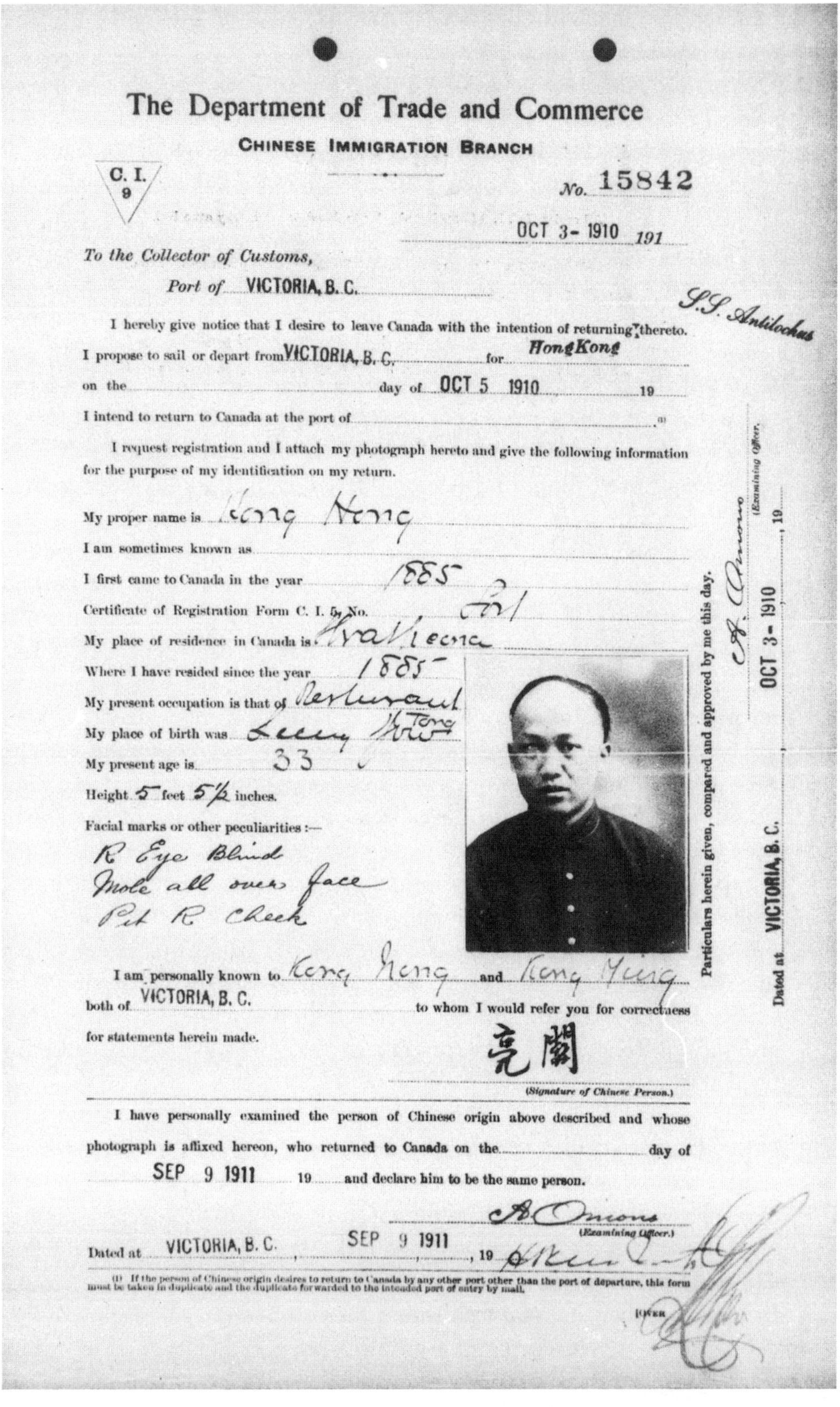
The Department of Trade and Commerce

CHINESE IMMIGRATION BRANCH

C. I. 9

No. 15842

OCT 3- 1910 191

To the Collector of Customs,

Port of VICTORIA, B. C.

S.S. Antilochus

I hereby give notice that I desire to leave Canada with the intention of returning thereto.

I propose to sail or depart from VICTORIA, B. C. for HongKong

on the .... day of OCT 5 1910 19

I intend to return to Canada at the port of ....(1)

I request registration and I attach my photograph hereto and give the following information for the purpose of my identification on my return.

My proper name is Kong Heng

I am sometimes known as

I first came to Canada in the year 1885

Certificate of Registration Form C. I. 5, No. Col

My place of residence in Canada is Strathcona

Where I have resided since the year 1885

My present occupation is that of Restaurant

My place of birth was Leong Tong Shui

My present age is 33

Height 5 feet 5½ inches.

Facial marks or other peculiarities:—

R Eye Blind
Mole all over face
Pit R Cheek

I am personally known to Kong Heng and Kong Ying

both of VICTORIA, B. C. to whom I would refer you for correctness for statements herein made.

亮關

(*Signature of Chinese Person.*)

Particulars herein given, compared and approved by me this day. A. Onions (*Examining Officer.*)

Dated at VICTORIA, B. C. OCT 3- 1910, 19

I have personally examined the person of Chinese origin above described and whose photograph is affixed hereon, who returned to Canada on the .... day of SEP 9 1911 19 and declare him to be the same person.

A. Onions (*Examining Officer.*)

Dated at VICTORIA, B. C. SEP 9 1911, 19

(1) If the person of Chinese origin desires to return to Canada by any other port other than the port of departure, this form must be taken in duplicate and the duplicate forwarded to the intended port of entry by mail.

[OVER

Fig. 4.1
CI 9 No. 15842,
Reel no. T-6038.

returned to Canada less than a year after he left, on 9 September 1911, and that he was blind in the right eye.

What did Kong Hong endure? What must it have been like to live in a small prairie town for so many years? When did he lose the use of his right eye? What did this disability mean for how he made his way in a country that was inhospitable to him, at a time when he would have been frequently targeted by white working-class labourers who saw him as a threat to their livelihoods? As I note throughout this book, the details of each life that are recorded on the CI 9s also often pose as many questions as they answer.

Even if only some of the information on this certificate is true, it is a record of the persistence of Kong Hong's presence. The exact dates and years might not be correct, but the general parameters of his time in Canada still indicate that he was not a tourist or visitor. He was not passing through or visiting for a few months or even a couple years: he had been here for decades. He might have been born here. In Yeo's terms, this CI 9 is representationally persistent in that it records activities that endure beyond the instance of the creation of this particular record, and beyond the time of this particular activity (i.e., the tracking of Chinese migrants who left and wished to return to Canada under the auspices of the Chinese Immigration Act). Here, there is the representational persistence of the record as a record, but also a record of the persistence of presence.

These two forms of persistence – the persistent representation and the persistence of presence – work against each other in ways that reveal both the durability of processes of exclusion and the resilience of those who were excluded. Understanding the CI 9 as a persistent representation uncovers the endurance of mass capture – manifested as surveillance in the name of excluding an entire population from access to citizenship – as a process. The certificates are records of a set of activities that clearly target one racial and ethnic group with the sole purpose of their exclusion. But, as records that show the duration of each migrant's tenure in Canada, they also show the endurance of the migrant's refusal to be forced out of a country that they helped to build.

The persistent representation captures a continual attempt on the part of the state to exclude Chinese migrants from Canada. And that very same representation illuminates the persistence of these same migrants' refusal to be removed. More than that, these records show us, at a deeply granular level, how much these migrants could take. We have known generally that Chinese Canadians persisted in their refusal to be forced out of the country, and that they endured tremendous hardship as a result of this endurance. The CI 9s give a sense of just how much could be borne. According to his CI 9, Kong Hong stayed in Strathcona for at least twenty-five years (from 1885 to 1910). For most, if not all, of his life, he grew up, lived, and worked in a country that was profoundly hostile to him.

There are limits to endurance. Kong's CI 9 shows that he did return to Canada. But many did not. There is Mrs Peter Chow, pictured in figure 4.2. She travelled on the same ship as Kong Hong. She is the first Chinese woman to be photographed in the CI 9 archive. Her CI 9 is also a persistent representation and a record of the persistence of her presence. She first came to Canada in 1889. She was seven years old. She arrived as a child in a place that did not want her. She survived the month-long crossing of the Pacific in steerage. She grew up in a country that actively sought to exclude her from having rights of any kind, with the additional burden of being a girl and then a woman enduring the reality of persistent processes of exclusion. She was twenty-eight years old when she left Victoria in 1910.

Her identity is so fully erased that she can only be persistently represented by her husband. Like Mrs J.J. Lawson in chapter 3 (see fig. 3.19), her signature comprises her husband's name. The agent initially recorded her occupation as a housewife, but crossed that out to note that she is a "cook's wife" instead. That revision is telling. She is not the woman of a household, but rather a woman whose presence is tied to the labour of her husband. Her ties to commercial cooking, and not the domestic sphere, must be clarified.

On 5 October 1910, she sailed on the SS *Antilochus* with her husband, Peter Chow. Like his wife, he too has lost his CI 5. There is no record of their payment of the head tax. There is, however, the record of his return to Victoria on 4 September 1911 (five days before Kong Hong). And there is a record of Mrs Peter Chow's refusal to return with him. Her certificate is stamped as expired. She had endured enough.

Grammars of Persistence

Philip Agre's (1994) description of information capture as a grammar of action is particularly useful for its emphasis on the social nature of imposing a grammar onto human activities. Agre's concept makes room for human interpretation and error, for the kinds of eccentricities and innovations that we have already seen at work in the CI 9 system. Even though the system is full of errors, even though it fails in so many ways as a system of surveillance and identification, it is still a systematic treatment where one group of people, working on behalf of the state, subjected another group of people, Chinese migrants, to a system of information capture with the goal of tracking their movements and activities. I have examined some of

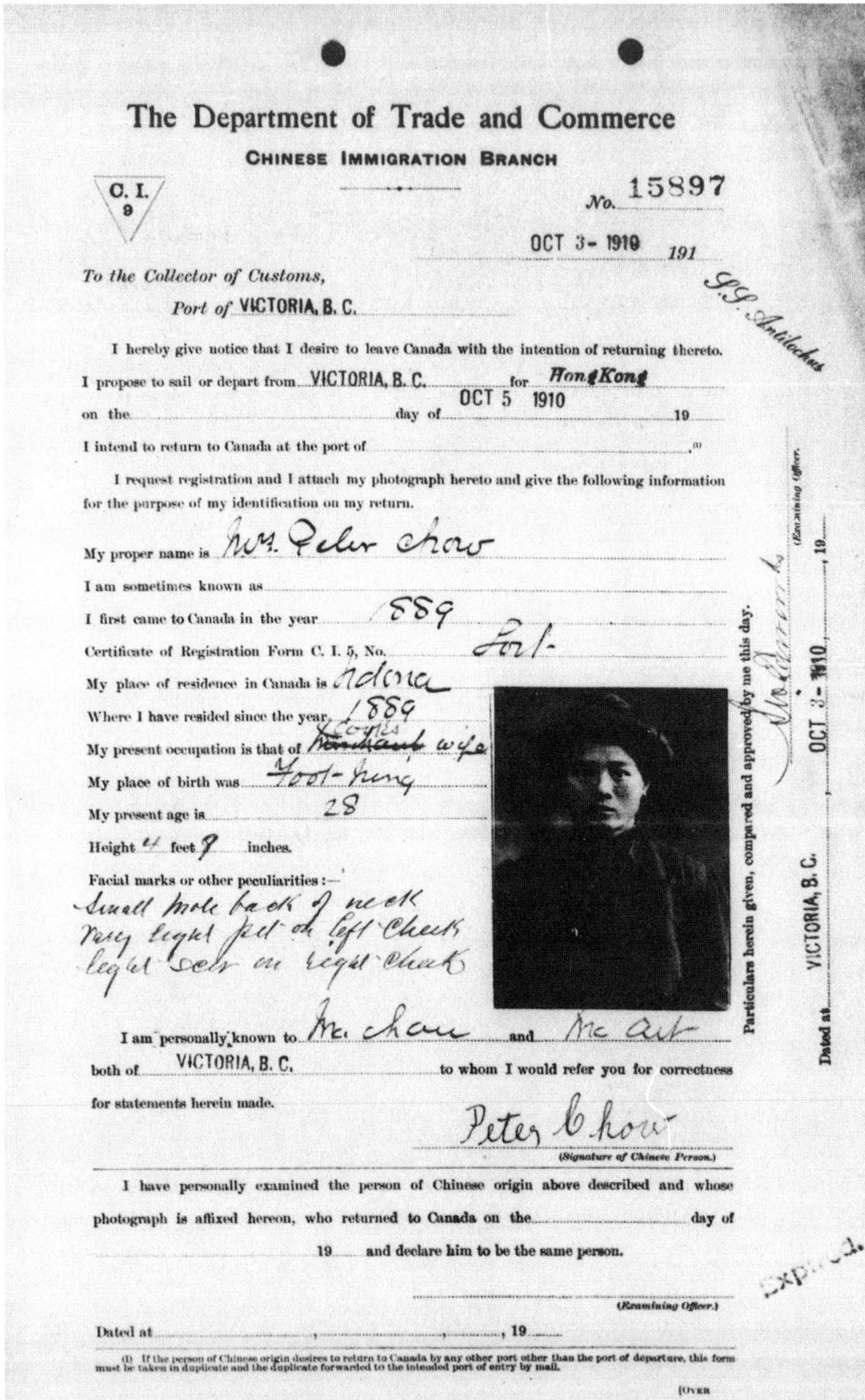

The Department of Trade and Commerce

CHINESE IMMIGRATION BRANCH

C. I. 9

No. 15897

OCT 3- 1910 191

To the Collector of Customs,

Port of VICTORIA, B. C.

S.S. Antilochus

I hereby give notice that I desire to leave Canada with the intention of returning thereto.

I propose to sail or depart from VICTORIA, B. C. for Hong Kong

on the OCT 5 1910 day of 19

I intend to return to Canada at the port of (1)

I request registration and I attach my photograph hereto and give the following information for the purpose of my identification on my return.

My proper name is Mrs. Peter Chow

I am sometimes known as

I first came to Canada in the year 1889

Certificate of Registration Form C. I. 5, No. Lost

My place of residence in Canada is Victoria

Where I have resided since the year 1889

My present occupation is that of Merchant Cook's wife

My place of birth was Yoot-Ning

My present age is 28

Height 4 feet 9 inches.

Facial marks or other peculiarities:— Small mole back of neck very light pit on left cheek light scar on right cheek

I am personally known to Mr. Chow and Mr. Ait

both of VICTORIA, B. C. to whom I would refer you for correctness for statements herein made.

Peter Chow
(Signature of Chinese Person.)

Particulars herein given, compared and approved by me this day.

Dated at VICTORIA, B. C. OCT 3- 1910, 19

(Examining Officer.)

I have personally examined the person of Chinese origin above described and whose photograph is affixed hereon, who returned to Canada on the day of 19 and declare him to be the same person.

(Examining Officer.)

Dated at , , 19

(1) If the person of Chinese origin desires to return to Canada by any other port other than the port of departure, this form must be taken in duplicate and the duplicate forwarded to the intended port of entry by mail.

[OVER

Expired.

Fig. 4.2
CI 9 No. 15897,
Reel no. T-6038.

Fig. 4.3 (opposite)
CI 9 No. 15898,
Reel no. T-6038.

The Department of Trade and Commerce

CHINESE IMMIGRATION BRANCH

C. I. 9

No. 15898

OCT 3- 1910 191

To the Collector of Customs,

Port of VICTORIA, B. C.

S.S. Antilochus

I hereby give notice that I desire to leave Canada with the intention of returning thereto.

I propose to sail or depart from VICTORIA, B. C. for Hong Kong

on the .... day of OCT 5 1910 19

I intend to return to Canada at the port of .... (1)

I request registration and I attach my photograph hereto and give the following information for the purpose of my identification on my return.

My proper name is Gelir Chow

I am sometimes known as

I first came to Canada in the year 1890

Certificate of Registration Form C. I. 5, No. Lost

My place of residence in Canada is Victoria

Where I have resided since the year 1890

My present occupation is that of Cook

My place of birth was Fook Ning

My present age is 32

Height 5 feet 3½ inches.

Facial marks or other peculiarities:—

Large scar front top left ear

Scar under chin

Scar left cheek bone

I am personally known to Ma Lee and Mc Chau

both of VICTORIA, B. C. to whom I would refer you for correctness for statements herein made.

周發喜 P. Chow

(*Signature of Chinese Person.*)

Particulars herein given, compared and approved by me this day.

(*Examining Officer.*)

Dated at VICTORIA, B. C. OCT 3- 1910, 19

I have personally examined the person of Chinese origin above described and whose photograph is affixed hereon, who returned to Canada on the .... day of SEP -4 1911 19 and declare him to be the same person.

(*Examining Officer.*)

Dated at VICTORIA, B. C., SEP -4 1911, 19

(1) If the person of Chinese origin desires to return to Canada by any other port other than the port of departure, this form must be taken in duplicate and the duplicate forwarded to the intended port of entry by mail.

the ways that the CI 9 system is vulnerable to error in chapters 2 and 3, and I tried to read some of these errors as more than mere mistakes, but rather as instances of ingenuity, resilience, and resistance on the part of Chinese migrants. These errors and resistances do not mitigate the fact that the CI 9s were a system of capture. Using Agre's concept of grammars of action allows for an understanding of capture as a technology with social and ideological implications. As he argues,

> no matter how thoroughly the capture process is controlled, it is impossible, short perhaps of total mechanization of a given form of activity, to remove the elements of interpretation, strategy, and institutional dynamics. This is not to say that capture is impossible; to the contrary, numerous impressive examples already exist. The point, rather, is that capture is never purely technical but always sociotechnical in nature. If a capture system "works," then what is working is a larger sociopolitical structure, not just a technical system (Bowers, 1992). And if the capture process is guided by some notion of the "discovery" of a preexisting grammar, then this notion and its functioning should be understood in political terms as an ideology. (1994, 112)

As any habitual user of social media can see, Agre's recognition of the imbrication of the social with the technical in matters of information capture is prescient and accurate. It may seem obvious to us now that we so frequently use technology as a platform for social engagement and community, but it is still worth explicitly recognizing that technology does not exist in a vacuum divorced from social relation. Long before millions of people in the twenty-first century managed their social lives with a technology founded on a virtual "book" of faces, the CI 9s organized the lives of Chinese migrants based on physical books of their faces. Agre's recognition of the foundationally social nature of technologies of capture uncovers the political and ideological foundations of grammars of action. The CI 9s are not merely a grammar. They do not merely describe replicable interactivities of humans and machines. They are put into place to make "discoverable" captive subjects in ways that are deeply grounded in a politics of exclusion and an ideology of racism.

Within these grammars of actions, there is persistence. Although, in the previous two chapters, I have read for instances of resistance in the slips and errors and potential deceptions riddled all through the system, I also want to recognize that resistance can take an even quieter form. Reading into the dates of arrival on so many of these certificates, a new collective portrait emerges of practices of refusal and persistence. Here, the refusal to be forced out. Here, the persistence of those who endured hardship upon hardship. Unwittingly, the CI 9s capture this refusal and this persistence. Even though grammars of action were directed towards the capture of Chinese migrants for the purposes of exclusion founded on racist motivations, they are also a place to look for that which the system did not mean to show: the quiet dignity of people who endured and persisted.

The grammar of persistence leverages grammars of action. If the latter are intended, in the case of the CI 9s, to capture migrant bodies, the former exists within the cramped space of that capture in order to transform it. The photographs themselves, despite being the product of a repressive state demand, become a site for the grammar of persistence. In this other turn to grammar, the visual grammar of the migrant caught in the photographic frame, I am guided by Tina Campt's reading of what she identifies as the "tense grammar" of people photographed for the purposes of their own subjugation. For Campt, the tension of stasis, the work of holding still and refusing to be moved, is a crucial part of the power of these images. In this, they share a capacity of refusal alongside the passport photographs of African Caribbean migrants to the United Kingdom, which, as Campt notes in an interview with Kevin Coleman, register "as a refusal to embrace the limitations of the category of containment produced by the genre of the passport photo itself" (Coleman 2018, 214). These photographs encompass "practices of refusal" (Campt 2017, 41). They refuse to be contained by the photographic genre of the identification photograph. They demand to be seen, and heard, in ways that far exceed and undermine their original function.

They demand to be seen *and* heard because, as Campt reminds us, there is no such thing as an absolutely silent photograph. Instead, there are quiet images. Quietness must not be mistaken for silence. It has, as Campt insists, a frequency. It hums. We have to listen for it. As Campt tells Coleman, quiet images are differently telling than "spectacular images or images that make grand statements." She says that we must think "about how to attune our attention to the undercurrents of images." Instead of "complete silence," she "believe[s] there are quiet moments and that those quiet moments are dense and require us to unpack them in complex and nuanced ways" (Coleman 2018, 210). To hear the quiet of an image is to "engage the affective registers of the image," and those registers allow us to "apprehend in these photos … the ways the individuals are challenging the government's capacity to refuse their capacity to relocate at will. So, here again, we see them refusing the refusal of the state" (214). This practice of refusing refusal reverberates throughout the CI 9 photographic archive. In the faces of these thousands of migrants there is a refusal of the state's refusal to count them out. They are captured, but they are not captive.

What is more, there is a complex beauty in these images of the mass captured. Describing her reaction to the ethnographic photographs of South African women who had been brought to the Eastern Cape to build farms, Campt writes: "I'm conflicted by the beauty I see in them, perplexed by the quiet introspection they so hauntingly depict. I see images of black women with dignity and stature … Yet viewed in their historical and institutional context, they witness a transliteration of beauty into racialized cultural categories and confront us with a vulnerability that also frames each of these women's photographic presentations" (2017, 50). I have also experienced this tension in my work with the CI 9 photographs. For me, they are haunting not only because of the repression they depict, but also because I do see beauty, strength, and dignity in them. Campt resolves this tension between the beautiful and the repressive by turning to Darieck Scott's work on "'muscular tension' for theorizing an alternate vision of black futurity and possibility": Scott's theorization shows how "muscular tension constitutes a state of black powerfulness in the midst of debility, a form of resistance expressed through a refusal to accept or acquiesce to defeat" (ibid.). Campt's reading of refusal in the tense stillness in photographs made for the purposes of colonization and imperial expansion opens up a way to see the CI 9 photographs as engaging in similar practices. The practices of refusal in the CI 9s are not identical to those of the South African women in the Eastern Cape. I acknowledge the crucial differences between the experiences of Black subjection and slavery, and that of the Chinese migrants caught in the CI 9 archive. I also, as I discuss in chapter 1, seek out the possibility of intersections and affinities between Black slavery and Asian indenture, between Black subjection and the Chinese migrants captured in the CI 9 archive.

In the quiet of the CI 9 photographs, there is a tense grammar of stasis, not stillness. For Campt, stasis demands seeing beyond stillness, demands feeling:

> Engaging in these portraits [of South African women] as stasis rather than stillness means that, rather than motionlessness, what we see is an effortful equilibrium achieved through a labored balancing of opposing forces and flows. These images require us to do more than just *see* stasis, for they capture unvisible forms of motion held in tense suspension. Their stasis registers beyond what we see, like the vibrations that form the fundamental basis of sonic frequency … Their stasis requires us to listen to the infrasonic frequencies of images that register through feeling rather than vision or audible sound. (Campt 2017, 52)

Campt's analysis helps me to finally understand my own deeply affective relation to the CI 9 archives. I have been studying them for nearly a decade. It is hard for me to look at them for very long without weeping. What they hold at bay and what they make so visible is a legacy of decades of subjection to deep inequity and unmasked racism. Mrs Peter Chow enters our field of vision looking straight into the camera. Her eyes are clear and open wide. Her mouth held still, the corners only slightly turned downward. How much strength must it take to maintain so much impassivity in the face of the undisguised contempt and discrimination to which she, and every other Chinese migrant in this archive, had been subjected? Such stillness is a labour. It demands exertion. Unlike the triumphant photographs of the completion of the Canadian Pacific Railway, where Chinese labour is clearly visible even if displaced by the spectacle of white men driving in the ceremonial last spike, the CI 9 photographs are images of deep exertion, and of labour that cannot be clearly seen. No one is holding a pick-axe in these images. Indeed, often these photographs are images of exertion's opposite. They might seem, at first glance, to capture an instance of repose. But it would be a mistake to miss the energy put into repose – to mistake stasis for stillness. Mrs Peter Chow does not hold still. She must actively hold herself in. Refusing refusal can be quiet work, but it is still work. It is a labour that demands a tense grammar of every mass captured body.

There is a visual economy to the extractive labour demands of settler colonization. Such an economy might sometimes be spectacularly visible. For example, the photographic history of Chinese labour on display in images of railway gangs (see figs. 3.4 and 3.5 in chapter 3). There is no labour on display in the CI 9 photographs, but that does not mean that there is no work happening in these images. The refusal of spectacle, the quiet positioning of the self as contained against containment, is also part of the labour captured by photographic legacies of colonial expansion. As Adrian De Leon understands with respect to the intertwining of the visuality of labour and colonialism, small acts should not be overlooked; we must, instead, develop "reading practices that recognize small-scale negotiations around the camera" so that "we can observe emergent labor politics that take place within this visual economy" (2018, 77). De Leon writes about colonial photography in the Philippines and how it works to "separate culture from economy and thus deny the political economy of Cordillerans and sovereignty claims to their land" (ibid.). Although the CI 9 photographs function very differently, in that they are made to track the movements of Chinese migrants rather than the extraction of their labour, they share an affinity with the colonial photography of De Leon's study: they are a visual record of the intersection of racialized labour and photography taken as a key element of the scaffold of settler colonization.

The persistent grammar of the CI 9 photographs is a visual grammar that works against mass capture's sociotechnical grammar of action. Agre's grammars of actions show us how human-machine interactions are codified as units of replicability so that, in the case of CI 9s, information can be captured for the purposes of producing non-citizen subjects. Campt's tense grammar illuminates the tremendous labour that is at the core of how we can understand De Leon's "small-scale negotiations" that are part of the practices of refusal in colonial photography. These two grammars are different but connected. One is a grammar of capture, the other of resistance. In the final part of this chapter, I want to examine one more iteration of grammar and persistence in the CI 9s: the language on the actual certificates.

Persistent Tension

While the previous section uses Campt's idea of tense grammar to track the positioning of bodies in and against the frame of colonial photography, I now want to follow another form of tension on the CI 9s constituted by the grammar of the certificate itself. There is a persistent tension in every CI 9: the language demands forms of self-declaration or confession that are simultaneously working to flatten or, in some cases, completely erase the identity of the self-declaring subject. On each certificate, there is a series of self-declarations that deny selfhood. The language of the certificate is written in the first person, but the person making these declarations is only one out of at least three people actually authoring the form. In order to fill in the blanks of each certificate, there must be in place the Chinese migrant who provides the information, the customs agent who enters the information, and the interpreter who tells the agent what to write. Should the migrant return to Canada, then there would be the additional entries of the agent at the port of re-entry and, again, the interpreter providing the actual evidence necessary for permitting re-entry. Even in the case of those migrants such as Mrs Peter Chow who apparently did not return to Canada, there is a persistent tension in the grammar of the certificate itself. This tension resides in a contradiction of authorship. What Mrs Chow says of herself is not necessarily what is recorded on the certificate. And even if the information on the certificate perfectly corresponds with what Mrs Chow gives as the details of her life, there remains the tension of a migrant declaring oneself to be something in the first person but doing so at a doubled remove, through the intermediating hand of the agent and the interpreter.

Look again at Mrs Peter Chow's CI 9 (fig. 4.2). Transcribing the text of the certificate, her identification details would read as follows:

> To the Collector of Customs, Port of *Victoria, B.C.*
>
> I hereby give notice that I desire to leave Canada with the intention of returning thereto. I propose to sail or depart from the *Port of Victoria, B.C.* for Hong Kong on the [blank] day of *Oct 5 1910*. I intend to return to Canada at the port of [blank].
>
> I request registration and I attach thereby my photograph hereto and give the following information for the purpose of my identification on my return.
>
> My proper name is *Mrs. Peter Chow*
> I am sometimes known as [blank]
> I first came to Canada in the year *1889*
> Certificate of Registration From C.I. 5, No. *Lost*
> My place of residence is *Victoria*
> Where I have resided since *1889*
> My present occupation is that of ~~*Merchant's*~~ *Cook's Wife*
> My place of birth was *Foot-Ning*
> My present age is *28*
> Height *4* feet *9* inches
> Facial marks or other peculiarities: --
> *Small mole back of neck*
> *Very light pit on left cheek*
> *light scar on right cheek*
>
> I am personally known to *Ma Chau* and *Ma Art* both of *Victoria, B.C.* to whom I would refer you to for corrections for statements herein made.
>
> *Mrs. Peter Chow*
> (Signature of Chinese Person.)

In this transcription, I have italicized all the words on the certificate that were filled into the pre-existing blanks, but italicization does not, of course, give you a sense of the range of hands at work in completing each blank. First, there are the handwritten and typographic scripts. "*Victoria, B.C.*" and the date, "*Oct 5 1910*," are clearly inserted through a pre-set stamp.

Who authors these entries? Whose handwriting is on these certificates? The answers are in the secretary of state's annual Civil Service List – a compendium of the name of every person, from chief controller to janitor, employed by the federal civil service, along with the date of their appointment, their date of birth, and their annual salary. The CI 9 entries were authored by agents who were officially called examining officers by the Department of Customs. Because the vast majority of migrants entered and exited Canada from either Victoria or Vancouver, the examining officers at those two branches would have been the ones largely responsible for nearly every entry in the CI 9 archive. The Civil Service List does note the employment of a Chinese interpreter in Montreal as well as in Vancouver and Victoria, but the number of certificates generated out of central and eastern Canada does not compare with those created and filed in British Columbia. Note that the examining officers who sign off on each certificate are employed by a different department of the federal government (Customs) than the one actually responsible for Chinese immigration (the Department of Trade and Commerce). The Civil Service List for 1910, the year of Mrs Peter Chow's CI 9, clearly identifies the collector of customs, to whom the CI 9 is addressed in the first instance, and the interpreter, who is all but invisible on the form, as employed by the Chinese Immigration branch of the Department of Trade and Commerce (*Sessional* 1910, 54). That same list classifies all the examining officers under the Department of Customs (129–31). I am belabouring the fact that the certificate's institutional address is different from that of its authorship because it is another form of tension in the certificate. One department is the addressee and archival home of the certificate. An entirely different department enters the information captured on it.

The text that is filled in on each CI 9 is a complex form of collaborative authorship involving the migrant, an interpreter, and the examining officer. The latter's hand is the most visible on the certificate. For example, next to Mrs Peter Chow's photograph is the signature of the examining officer, Samuel Wesley Edwards. According the 1910 *Sessional Papers of the Dominion of Canada* (which publishes the secretary of state's Civil Service List), Edwards was born in 1858, which meant that he was fifty-two years old when he would have signed off on Mrs Peter Chow's identification photograph. He had been appointed to the position since 1904 and earned $950 per annum in this role (*Sessional* 1910, 130). Edwards would have been aided in his work by Lee Mong Kow, the sole interpreter employed at the Victoria office of the Department of Trade and Commerce. Lee had held this position since November 1889. He was forty-nine years old when he would have interpreted Mrs Chow's answers for Edwards. He was younger than Edwards but earned significantly more money, $1,200 per year (54). Given the racism of this time, it may be surprising that a Chinese person could earn more than his white colleagues, but it is important to remember that the interpreter positions, unlike all of the other staff positions in this office, were political appointments. From my study of all the salaries in the Civil Service List for 1910, it becomes clear that the examining officer is one of the most poorly paid positions. The only people who earned less were a handful of "preventative officers" who were paid $650 a year for their work. The men who were charged with the responsibility of examining and verifying the identity and information for the Chinese migrants captured on each CI 9s were themselves some of the least valued members of the federal civil service.

Remuneration aside, and returning to the question of authorship, the information recorded on the CI 9s can thus be said to have three "authors": the examining officer, the Chinese interpreter, and the Chinese migrant. In this scene of tripled authorship, the role of the interpreter is key. As Lisa Mar argues, "enforcement of the head tax depended on Chinese collaborators, which deeply affected its character. Interpreters handled most communications between arriving immigrants and Anglo officials" (2010, 23). Given the important role of interpreters for the construction of the CI 9s, and their invisibility on the forms themselves, I want to offer a brief portrait of the curious position that interpreters held and then look more closely at the man who would have interpreted the answers given on the CI 9s I have discussed in this chapter.

The interpreters held considerable power over the fates of Chinese migrants. Aside from the interpreters, none of the officials that a Chinese migrant would deal with would have spoken any Chinese. The vast majority of migrants spoke little to no English. Such a situation rendered the Chinese interpreters both potential advocates for migrants and collaborators with the state. These positions were political appointments and they were often held by a single person in a given office for many years. Given the power accorded to interpreters, corruption or abuse of the position is inevitable. Mar gives the example of Yip On, who served for decades as the interpreter for the Vancouver branch of the Department of Trade and Commerce. In 1908, Mar reports that a Chinese merchant named Lum Ching, who had resided in British Columbia for twenty-nine years, attempted to re-enter Canada after a visit to China. "Yip On denied all evidence of Lum's merchant status and naturalized citizenship [something that was available to merchants]. Yip On detained Lum until he paid the $500 head tax as if he were a newly arrived Chinese laborer" (2010, 24–5). Mar notes that it was harder to re-enter Canada than to enter for the first time, and, "like Lum, a great many Chinese returning from visits to China struggled to prove their identities" (25). Interpreters worked within a nexus of power and interest from Canadian political parties, corporations, Chinese communities, and trade networks in Hong Kong and China.

The man who interpreted Mrs Peter Chow's answers to Examining Officer Edwards was Lee Mong Kow. He was the sole interpreter for the

Fig. 4.4
Lee Mong Kow and his family. Victoria, British Columbia.

Victoria branch of the Department of Trade and Commerce for thirty-one years. He was a prominent member of the Chinese-Canadian community and was also highly regarded in the Anglo-European community. Under the title "A Remarkable Canadian Chinaman," the 1 May 1909 issue of *MacLean's* published a photograph of Lee Mong Kow alongside a flattering profile written by R.B. Bennett (who would eventually become Conservative prime minister from 1930 to 1935) (fig. 4.4).

Lee is on the right, pictured with his mother, his wife, and their five children. Unlike the fractured portrait of the Lawsons that I assembled in chapter 3, here is a family portrait that follows the conventions of most normative family photography. All the members of the family are together in a single frame. Their relative importance is signalled by their position in the photograph. In this case, Lee's mother, the matriarch, is at the centre of the frame. She holds in her lap the youngest member of the family so that the image is anchored by the force of familial history and the promise of its future. Lee Mong Kow and his wife Seto Chang Ann flank the family. More than the opulence of their clothing, the photograph reinforces the Lee family's stature by the simple fact that the whole family can be depicted together. This photograph was published one year before he would take down the particulars of Mrs Peter Chow's identity for her CI 9. Bennett's article commends Lee's service to the crown: "As might be expected, he makes enemies of his countrymen and it is not uncommon for those who are interested in the immigration of coolie labor and who have been frustrated in their designs by the wit of the Chinese interpreter to charge wrongdoing on his part. But, after 10 years of service, it has not yet been shown that he ever acted dishonestly and Lee Mong Kow commands wide respect" (1909, 67). After covering some of Lee's biographical information (his past as the son of a merchant, a house that he bought in the fashionable Victoria neighbourhood called "the Gorge"), Bennett closes the profile by asserting that Lee is the ideal type of Chinese immigrant, not least because he has assimilated so well. "While conservative, Lee Mong Kow is only natural, for few of us change from the style and customs to which we have been accustomed, and after all he comes nearer to being a 'white' man than many a Caucasian. If all Oriental immigrants were such as he, the 'yellow peril' would not be the problem that it is feared in America" (67). Contrary to Lee's representation in the popular press, Mar observes that his record is not entirely immaculate. There was evidence of his misconduct in a *habeas corpus* case relating to an alleged prostitute in 1901 (2010, 143n17), and business records that show he ran an illegal gambling den (2010, 62). Lee held tremendous power not least because of the length of his tenure in the busiest port of departure for Chinese migrants in Canada. It is no exaggeration to say that he controlled the fates of thousands of Chinese migrants.

Given the discrepancy of power between Mrs Peter Chow and Lee Mong Kow, it is hard to imagine that her encounter with him would have been without tension. Like every Chinese migrant who appeared before him, she needed something from him, which he could choose not to provide. Edwards, as the examining officer, may have written the information on the certificate and signed his name to it, but Lee told him what to write. Lee's power is especially insidious in that his hand is nowhere visible on the certificate. Edwards signs. Mrs Peter Chow signs. But not Lee Mong Kow. His name is not on this certificate. It is not on any of them other than his own.

The CI 9 in figure 4.5 records Lee's permanent departure from Canada. He had finally left his position as an interpreter and, according to his

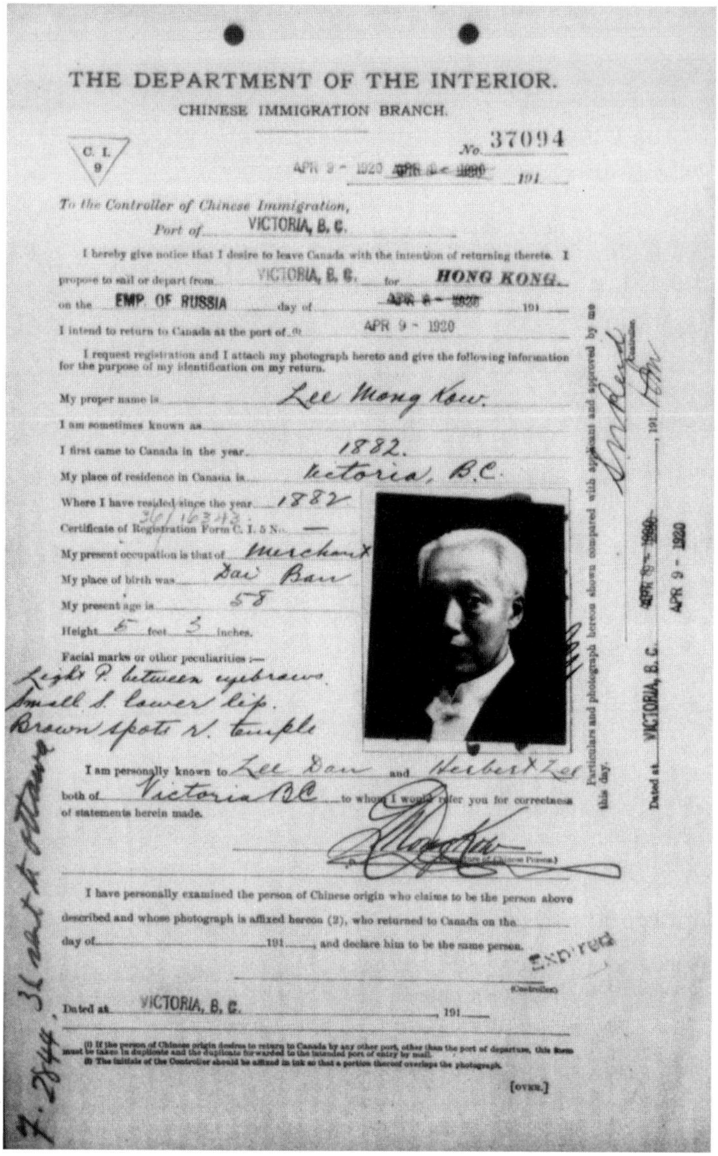

THE DEPARTMENT OF THE INTERIOR.
CHINESE IMMIGRATION BRANCH.

C. I. 9

No. 37094

APR 9 - 1920 APR 8 - 1920 191

To the Controller of Chinese Immigration,
Port of VICTORIA, B. C.

I hereby give notice that I desire to leave Canada with the intention of returning thereto. I propose to sail or depart from VICTORIA, B. C. for HONG KONG on the EMP. OF RUSSIA day of APR 8 - 1920 191

I intend to return to Canada at the port of APR 9 - 1920

I request registration and I attach my photograph hereto and give the following information for the purpose of my identification on my return.

My proper name is Lee Mong Kow.
I am sometimes known as
I first came to Canada in the year 1882.
My place of residence in Canada is Victoria, B.C.
Where I have resided since the year 1882
Certificate of Registration Form C. I. 5 No. 36/16343 —
My present occupation is that of Merchant
My place of birth was Dai Bau
My present age is 58
Height 5 feet 3 inches.
Facial marks or other peculiarities:—
Light P. between eyebrows.
Small S. lower lip.
Brown spots r. temple

I am personally known to Lee Dan and Herbert Lee both of Victoria BC to whom I would refer you for correctness of statements herein made.

Lee Mong Kow

I have personally examined the person of Chinese origin who claims to be the person above described and whose photograph is affixed hereon (2), who returned to Canada on the day of 191 , and declare him to be the same person.

Expired

(Controller)

Dated at VICTORIA, B. C. 191

Particulars and photograph hereon shown compared with applicant and approved by me this day.

Dated at VICTORIA, B. C. APR 9 - 1920 APR 9 - 1920

7.2844. 36 ... Ottawa

[over.]

Fig. 4.5
CI 9 No. 37094, Reel no. T-6045.

entry in the *Dictionary of Canadian Biography*, he took up a position as the Chinese agent for the Canadian Pacific Ocean Services Limited (Stanley 1921–30). Prior to CI 9 no. 37094, Lee Mong Kow's name is invisible in the CI 9 archive even though his words are recorded on tens of thousands of certificates. It is only on CI 9 no. 37094 that we can see, via his signature, his handwriting, or at least what we are told is his handwriting, for the first and last time. Lee's CI 9 might be the one that is most free of the tension that riddles the others. He was a man for whom the tensions of the invisible authorial relationship between interpreter, migrant, and examining officer had been radically reduced. Not for him the uncertainty of wondering if the interpreter would faithfully and favourably transmit the information provided by the migrant. Unlike Mrs Peter Chow, Lee was a true collaborator in the text of his certificate.

As the handwriting on the certificates makes clear, even in the case of Lee Mong Kow it is not the subject of the certificate who inscribes its content. The inscription is done by proxy on his behalf. Despite the immediacy of the language of the first-person voice on each certificate, the CI 9 is a document of persistent tensions in the discrepancy between the grammar of its declarations and the practices by which those declarations are made. Mass capture on the CI 9 demands that the migrant answer a series of questions about their identity. Each answer is translated and written down (or, in later years, typed). Almost every certificate involves two proxies, the interpreter and examining officer. The language of the certificate attempts to obscure these two proxies, these two removes from the subject of the certificate itself. What is more, the language of the certificate is relentlessly personal in its insistence on the first-person pronoun: my name is; my occupation is; I came to Canada in; I am personally known to. This tension between the first-person declaratives and the third-person interferences literally written all over the form itself persists.

It is no accident that diplomatics shares an etymological root with diplomacy. Diplomatics, the study of documents and the processes of establishing their authenticity, comes to matter when people and documents start to move around more. Diplomacy, as Duranti notes, comes from the French word "*diplomatie* [and] refers to the art of conducting international negotiations which result in the compilation and exchange of documents, namely diplomas" (1989, 12). The increasing need for documents to speak for others through processes of cross-border exchange sheds a different light on the CI 9 as a type of diplomatic process. Indeed, as I will show in the next chapter, the CI 9 resembles a passport insofar as it guarantees the bearer's right to return to the country of issuance. A passport tells the agent that the bearer has the right to return to the nation from which the passport originates. A passport does not guarantee the bearer the right to leave a country; it guarantees the right to return. Of course, in the case of the CI 9, the bearer is being guaranteed the right to return to a nation-state that insists on excluding them. In the next chapter I will think through the contradiction of treating Chinese migrants as though they were citizens only for the purposes of re-entry. As I will show, the CI 9s anticipate the demands of the contemporary passport.

On a passport, the bearer does not speak. The document speaks on behalf of the head of the nation-state which issued it, to the person (usually a border agent or official) the passport is presented to. The bearer has no role, no voice, in that conversation. In contrast, on the CI 9, the bearer is compelled to speak by virtue of the language of the form. That speaking, as this chapter shows, is rife with tension. Despite the repressive functions of this document, and the ways in which it nakedly attempts to make a racial other knowable through grammars of action that constitute mass capture, there are a host of alternate and tense grammars that actively refuse captivity. In the identification photographs that refuse to be contained by their genre, in the tension of the authorship of each CI 9, there is what Campt knows is stasis and not stillness. Hold still, these certificates demand. Holding still, the subjects of these certificates reveal the resilience of their refusal. In listening to the image of the identification photographs on each CI 9, we can come closer to hearing the long history of the refusal to be refused.

CHAPTER FIVE
ANTICIPATING CITIZENSHIP AND MASS CAPTURE

Over the course of the last four chapters, *Mass Capture* has outlined the ways in which processes of surveillance as capture produce the figure of the non-citizen. Throughout this book, I have been arguing that the non-citizen is not simply *there*. The non-citizen must be constructed and produced by processes designed to systematize and flatten their subjectivity into traceable and trackable units. However, thus far, this book has only considered these migrants as non-citizens. In this chapter, I want to adjust the focus and think about how the people captured in the CI 9s were also potential citizens.

This shift moves the discussion of the mass captured away from negation, what they were not, and into the realm of potentiality, what they could be. They were not citizens. Until the repeal of the Chinese Immigration Act in May 1947, there was little likelihood of their ever achieving citizenship. But the fact that they could not be citizens does not mean that they might not have wanted to be, that they might not have dreamt of such privileges, that such dreams might not have informed their comportment and self-portrayal in these documents. Even though such thinking is speculative, I want to insist on the importance of understanding the potentiality of citizenship locked within the experience of mass capture. To think of these Chinese migrants only as non-citizens, and not as future citizens, risks missing what they can tell us about citizenship itself.

As I have argued, because of the elaborate bureaucracy and documentation attendant upon their production, the Chinese head tax certificates are an incredibly rich resource for considerations of citizenship and migration. The consistent expressionlessness of these photographs reveals the conjoined demands for emotional neutrality and a stable visual identity for diasporic subjects who are between states – between China and Canada, between migrant and citizen. These certificates foretell the eventual demand for identification photographs from anyone who wished to cross a border. In drawing a relationship between identity, emotion, and citizenship, this chapter theorizes anticipation as a key mode of agency.

Non-citizens anticipate citizenship. Rather than understanding this anticipation as one that is solely defined by privation where the non-citizen is constantly wanting that which the citizen already has, I want to consider how this anticipation can itself be agential. Anticipation is an affect, but also a mode of agency. Anticipation responds to the conditions of possibility, however narrow and even impossible those possibilities might be, and capitalizes on them. Anticipation channels desire. Just because Chinese migrants were denied citizenship does not mean that they did not want it. The expression of desire is necessarily complex for those who want seemingly impossible things. Think about a moment when you wanted something that was wildly out of reach. Think about wanting something as fundamental as freedom from discrimination on the basis of race and country of origin. Such desires are not easily stamped out. They burn quietly. Anticipation looks ahead to what could be and responds to those possibilities.

What does anticipation look like? How does one read for anticipation in a photograph? In thousands of photographs? How to see anticipation when there was no place for the expression of the desire for something as unlikely as citizenship? As anyone who has ever wanted something seemingly impossible will know, the more powerful the desire, the quieter its expression. However, as Tina Campt's discussion of "quiet photography" reveals, learning to listen to an image yields a different kind of encounter with the identification photograph. There is, as Campt recognizes, a hum in these silences. In her description of seeing the vernacular images of the *Gulu Art Studio* installation at the Walther Collection (identification photographs where the face of each subject had been stamped out), Campt positions a complex form of quietude as a modality of the photographic encounter: "As soon as I entered the gallery, it was clear that quiet was the most appropriate modality for encountering the installation. But its quietude was anything but simple. It was the kind of quiet that is in no way an absence. It is fulsome and expressive. Restless, awkward, and unsettling, it is a form of quiet where gnawing questions simmer and send one searching for more complicated answers" (2017, 18). Campt's exhortation for us to listen to the photograph, and particularly to quiet photographs such as identification photographs, opens up a way to understand the affective resonance of the CI 9 photographs. Even though these photographs are overwhelmingly emotionally flat or neutral, Campt's work allows me see, and hear, more than just the lack of emotional expression on the surface of these images.

It is absolutely the case that the vast majority of the CI 9 photographs capture subjects who seem to express no emotion. As a document that reinforces the subject's connection to the state, and as a photograph that draws upon honorific traditions of portraiture, the head tax certificate indexes a fascinating historical juncture that illuminates the complexity of diasporic subjectivity. These photographs reveal diasporic subjects for whom the CI 9 certificates are the only way to prove their right to return to the Canada in the event of a temporary absence.

Chinese migrants' access to citizenship in Canada was non-existent prior to 1947 and uncertain post-1947. Canadian citizenship is, itself, a relatively new entity. The Citizenship Act of Canada was passed in January 1947. Before then, there were no Canadian citizens. After, Chinese migrants living in Canada could apply for naturalization, but the decision to allow for naturalization would have been made by a provincial court judge (acting on behalf of the federal government) who would determine whether or not the petitioner would make a good citizen. Thus, successful and well-established merchants had better chances for successful applications, but even these were not assured. After the repeal of the Chinese Immigration Act in 1947, Chinese migrants in Canada still "registered out" with CI 9s in order to ensure their re-entry into Canada. We have CI 9s dating well into 1953. Throughout the later CI 9 years, Chinese migrants in Canada existed precariously. Often not yet citizens, they relied on the CI 9 system to document their rights as almost-citizens. As the CI 9s of the Lawson children discussed in chapter 3 show, even Chinese people born in Canada were not exempt from the necessity of registering out, and thus from subjection to the process of mass capture.

Mass capture was a persistent process of excluding Chinese migrants from the sphere of citizenship, but these certificates nonetheless reveal the future of citizenship itself. The diasporic subjects of these photographs anticipate not only what a citizen should look like, but also what they should feel like. Although the injunction against expressing emotion in identification photographs for passports has become naturalized, this chapter examines the ways in which this naturalization of emotional neutrality is intimately bound with the visual documentation of Chinese immigrants in the early part of the twentieth century. The archive of identification photographs captured in these certificates indicates and foreshadows the exigencies of citizenship itself.

For the mass captured, there is an inescapable link between mobility and citizenship. As the next section will elaborate, the history of passports is one of suspicion levelled against anyone who did not want to stay in place. The connection between mobility and suspicion, and the rise of the demand for documents as a response to this suspicion, precedes the CI 9 and continues to inform state responses to migrant mobilities. Even as I write this, the discourse of hysteria levelled at "migrant caravans" continues apace. The migrant is, by definition, a person who is on the move and who cannot stay in the place where they once were. And it is mobility itself that triggers the mechanisms of state suspicion.

Suspect Mobilities

While mobility and suspicion are not so closely connected in the current historical moment, where a sign of cosmopolitanism is partially defined by a surfeit of mobility, it was and still sometimes is the case that being on the move is a cause for state suspicion. It is a suspicion emerging from anxieties over the difficult task of identification – from the difficulty of knowing with certitude that a person is who they claim to be. As Simon Cole notes in his discussion of the sixteenth-century case of Martin Guerre, where attempts were made to determine the identity of a potential impostor through the sworn but contradictory testimony of over 150 villagers (even comparing his feet with the lasts of another man's shoes), identification only became a problem when people started moving around. "From a modern perspective, it is tempting to assume that premodern courts lacked a method of identification because they lacked know-how … But, in fact, early modern societies were not desperately seeking some means of identifying people because, for the most part, it was unnecessary. Most people *were* known in their small local communities. Many lived their whole lives without ever leaving the vicinity of the village … Martin Guerre posed a problem of identification precisely because he had been 'snatched from the known context of fields and family' for eight years" (2001, 7). Cole's point regarding the problem of identification as a phenomenon specifically tied to migration and movement has strong resonances for thinking about the use of identification photography for diasporic subjects.

Identification documents are, by their very nature, demanded where there is cause, imagined or otherwise, for suspicion. They must be produced when there is some doubt, some need for evidence, of the person and the identity they claim. As the history of the passport reveals, it is a document of skepticism rather than recognition. John Torpey observes that in 1791, with the victories of the revolution still fresh, the French National Assembly voted to abolish passport controls in favour of cosmopolitanism and freedom of movement (1999, 27). But only a year later, passport controls were reinstated and increasingly refined, thus laying the foundation for the contemporary passport. Torpey argues that the invention of the passport emerged as a response by an increasingly suspicious state to enemies that it saw everywhere but could not easily mark. The document served as a means of regulating mobility, a notice of the bearer's right to return to the country of issuance: "Just as the passport constitutes *prima facie* evidence that the issuing country will take in the bearer if he or she is denied entry into or expelled from the destination country, the document constitutes *prima facie* evidence of a claim to the issuing country. In the end, therefore, passports are necessary *and sufficient* not for gaining entry to another country but only for returning to one's country of origin" (164). The passport does not guarantee its bearer the right to enter a particular country – that is what visas are for – but rather the right to return to the country that issued the document. Well into the twentieth century, the passport was understood to be a punitive document, such that "the 1921 conference of the International Parliamentary Union in Stockholm expressed its condemnation of the passport system and called for greater freedom of movement" (27). While the passport may seem relatively benign, indeed desirable, in the contemporary period, the consolidation of its usage attests to a long history of state suspicion levelled with particular acuity against anyone who does not want to stay put.

Indeed, documentary mass capture depends upon subjects in motion. Wendy Chun works through Agre's thinking and arrives at a particularly stunning observation connecting capture with mobility: "in order for something to be captured, it must be in motion. There must be a change of state; things must be updated in order to be registered" (2016, 60). A person or thing can only be captured when in motion. Stay still, and you will be invisible to the technology of capture. As Chun points out, "in a capture system, the base unit is an action, or change of state, rather than an entire person" (ibid.). The logic of capture is premised on change or motion. It does not need the whole person; it only needs to apprehend the fact of that person's movement or change of state. Your social media applications, for example, capture you when you make a move, when you report a change in your "status," post an update, or even passively scroll a newsfeed. These changes do not have to be big. They can be tiny, and so incremental as to appear like no change at all (just opening the application, or only "creeping" and never posting). Nevertheless, capture, as Chun so brilliantly reveals, only works when there is movement on some scale. Insofar as it is premised on motion, the logic of capture is, fundamentally, the logic of the CI 9 system. Torpey's discussion of the rise of regulations against nomads in France in 1912 reveals the ways in which being on the move is itself criminalized. As he observes of the intent of the *carnet des nomades*, the state wanted to "insure that these wanderers would have a precise and 'immutable' identity, even if this necessitated imposing a new one upon them" (2000, 108). As I show in chapter 2, many Chinese migrants did find themselves with new identities as a result of the CI 9 system.

Whatever the identities imposed and adopted would be, mass capture is only levelled against those who do not want to remain in place. In this sense, the logic of capture, as Chun identifies, is fundamentally hostile to diaspora. Diaspora is itself premised on movement. What is more, the CI 9 system was only necessary because these migrants wished to be in motion. It is a system that punishes those who will not relinquish their desire to be mobile. They sought to cross a border and cross back. If the migrant chose to never leave Canada, no CI 9 would have been generated for them. They would have been invisible in this system.

In the head tax certificates, the use of photography for the identification of explicitly racialized subjects marks a departure from the consolidation of other identification technologies in the British Empire. Before the inclusion of photographs in passport documents, fingerprinting, for example, was relied on to verify identity. Cole observes that fingerprinting, initiated by Sir William James Herschel, came to be used in mid-nineteenth-century India to resolve the problem of differentiating between racial subjects: written descriptions of brown hair and brown eyes were all but useless to colonial administrators (2001, 65). As Cole recounts, Herschel initiated fingerprinting in India in 1858 because he was frustrated by what he saw as rampant pension fraud, where one person would claim another person's identity to collect their pension. For Herschel, fingerprinting was a means of differentiating one colonized subject from another. "Fingerprinting in India, then, began as a technique for civil, not criminal, identification" (ibid.). This account also reveals fingerprinting as a technique for identification circumscribed by a particular local space, and not for identifying subjects moving across localities.

In the transition from fingerprinting in British colonial India to photographic identification for Chinese migrants elsewhere in the empire, Canada, we can track the difference in the anxieties of colonial bureaucracies attending to a local, fixed population, versus a mobile, diasporic one. In the space of diaspora or migrancy, where power has to pin down a subject between states, it is photography and not fingerprinting that becomes the standard for identification.

The introduction of the passport photo was one attempt at maintaining the fidelity between the traveller and her passport. According to Torpey, a man named Richebourg claimed to have introduced the idea of the passport photograph in an 1854 article in *La Lumière* (1999, 172n62). Mark Salter's investigations into the archives of the British Passport Office reveal that photographs became a standard requirement for British passports as of 1916, when Form A was revised and "we see the first issuance of a passport in a recognizable form: a folded sheet of cardboard, not paper, that included the coat of arms of the country, a photograph of the bearer, and an official standardized message from the secretary of state for foreign affairs" (2003, 28). Azoulay posits that "the camera modified the way in which individuals are governed and the extent of their participation in the forms of governance" (2008, 89). With the introduction of the photographic requirement on passports, the camera modified the governance of individual movement along the lines of identification invented not for tracking travellers, but rather for tracking criminals.

As I note in chapter 2, the protocols of the passport photograph share something with those of another set of identification photos, the mugshot. Recalling her assertion of a civil contract of photography where the photograph constitutes a "statement," Azoulay's suggestion of photography's construction as an "*énoncé*" evokes the notorious *portrait parlé* (spoken portrait) developed by Alphonse Bertillon in the nineteenth century. With his development of anthropometry, where the human body could be measured and broken down into a series of written codes, Bertillon standardized the identification photographs of criminals and denoted them as *portraits parlés*, portraits that spoke so that they could "be read in many cities, provinces, across jurisdictions" (Cole 2001, 43). The passport photograph does not communicate "an electric body of speed, transmitted telegraphically" the way that Bertillon's mugshots did (Matsuda quoted in Cole 2001, 43). It was never broken down with such precision. Nevertheless, it calls to mind the burden of identification photos to speak; to announce and respond to the question insinuated but not asked about the truth of one's identity, the fidelity of one's appearance with that of the image on the document; to declare *prima facie* that one is who one claims to be.

And yet, photography can fail. Chapter 2 showed that even a system as elaborate as the CI 9s can fall significantly short in terms of identification. Nearly a century later, the case of Suaad Hagi Mohamud illustrates the tenuousness of the relationship between one's identity and one's identity documents. In the summer of 2009, Mohamud was stranded in Kenya because various governmental bodies insisted on the lack of correspondence between her and her identifying documents. Despite several pieces of Canadian identification in her wallet, including her driver's licence, border officials in Kenya declared that her lips did not resemble those in her passport photograph. When her passport was sent to the Canadian consulate in Nairobi, they immediately declared her an "impostor" and voided her passport. She asked to be fingerprinted but there were no prior prints with which to make a comparison. Eventually, she was permitted to undergo DNA testing, which finally proved that she was indeed the person that she declared herself to be. Mohamud's case highlights the precarious nature of photographic identification. The fidelity of the photograph to the person is constantly under erosion, not only with the passage of time – news reports of Mohamud's case repeatedly noted that her passport photograph was four years old – but also due to the instabilities of photographic representation as such. As theorists of photography know, there is more reason to suspect photography's representation of reality than to trust it. Mohamud's appeal for fingerprinting and other biometric information poses questions about the use of photographic identification as opposed to other technologies of identification. Of course, the insistence upon the passport itself suggests a certain faith in the notion that people are who their documents declare them to be. "With the widespread use of a similar passport," Salter notes, "the examination at the border came to be centered on whether *documents* – rather than the traveler herself – were in order" (2003, 28).

The process that we have now normalized – where we present ourselves at national borders and hand over our passports for inspection, allowing the document to speak for who we are, never once uttering our own names to the agent at the gate of entry – hearkens to this moment when the Canadian state privileged the Chinese migrants' CI 9 numbers above any other item of identification information. The question of who this person might be is resolved by a careful examination of the document, and how well that document corresponds with the one already on file, rather than any scrutiny of the person themselves. As Craig Robertson observes, the passport photograph offered the "promise to deliver accurate identification … based in a faith in the mechanical reproduction of the camera over the lingering subjectivity of the written physical description" (2010, 81). The passport signals a "collapsing of identity into identification" that emerges with particular clarity in the case of the state's attempt to control and regulate racialized bodies at the border, which brought about, for example, the Chinese exclusion laws in the United States and Canada (245).

As the next section will show, identity is collapsed into identification with special acuteness for racialized bodies, but also for the feelings of racialized bodies. Identification photography demands the evacuation of emotion. Identifying a citizen and distinguishing the citizen from the non-citizen turns on the expression of emotion.

The Impossibility of the Feeling Citizen

If you have recently had your passport photo taken in Canada, the United Kingdom, or the United States, you may recall a curious injunction against emotional expression. For a photograph to be acceptable for use on a passport, it must, in addition to following many specifications for lighting, composition, and background, portray its subject as an emotionally empty one. The federal department Passport Canada specifies: "Applicant must show a neutral facial expression (no smiling, mouth closed) and look straight at the camera." The UK's Identity and Passport Service requires the subject of a passport photograph to have a "neutral facial expression" with the "mouth closed (no grinning, frowning or raised eyebrows)." Similarly, the US Department of State's guidelines for acceptable passport photos insist: "The subject's expression should be natural, with both eyes open. Please refer to the photographs found on this website for acceptable facial expressions." The "acceptable" facial expressions reveal no emotion. A natural countenance is depicted as being completely without feeling. That is, it is not natural at all. It exposes a citizen-subject caught and composed for identification purposes. This subject is neither angry, happy, sad, disgusted, nor even particularly present.

One might argue that the instructions for the passport photo are about security and biometrics and the urgency of the task of recognition. That might be the case, although it bears mentioning that almost everyone I know has, at one time or another, disparaged the lack of resemblance between their passport photo and the way they normally look. And it is doubtful that, in the uneasy moment of the encounter with a border patrol officer, any one of us looks as indifferent as our passport photos make us out to be. Whether or not these acceptably neutral and "natural" facial expressions allow for easier identification, they do indicate more than just what a citizen is supposed to look like, but what being a citizen should *feel* like. The injunction against emotion in the passport photograph projects the way in which the ideal citizen, in the eyes of the state, is an emotionally neutral one. Indeed, the photographs that identify us as citizens must be without emotion because they are themselves a vestigial reminder of the fraught relationship between emotion and citizenship.

The foreclosure of emotion in a passport photograph, the identity document that ties a person to a nation, illuminates a contradiction between feeling and citizenship. On the one hand, as these instructions for the passport photographs suggest, emotion obscures the identity of the citizen. On the other, as I will discuss later, emotion, or the capacity for it, is very much a part of the conception of the modern citizen. The migrants captured in the CI 9 photographs lay bare the problem of emotion at the heart of contemporary citizenship.

Critics such as Susan Maslan and Giorgio Agamben, through their analyses of the 1789 *Déclaration de droits de l'homme et du citoyen*, or Declaration of the Rights of Man and Citizen, have shown how citizenship is antithetical to feeling. Examining the pre-history of what she calls modern citizenship (citizenship in the wake of eighteenth-century European political movements), Maslan argues that modern citizenship attempts to resolve a foundational divide between the "human" and the "citizen" upon which the early modern models of citizenship depend: "If we think that 'human' and 'citizen' are or *should be* corresponding and harmoniously continuous categories it is because we think in the wake of the 1789 Declaration. In the early modern political imagination, to be a citizen meant to cease to be human. This is the legacy that the Declaration tries to overcome and that it conceals … and so the new Republic turned to – or better yet, invented – the language of universalism to repress and resolve the tensions it can neither dissipate nor acknowledge" (2004, 372). As Agamben notes, the discontinuity of the human and the citizen "is implicit, after all, in the ambiguity of the very title of the 1789 *Déclaration de droits de l'homme et du citoyen*, in which it is unclear whether the two terms are to name two distinct realities or whether they are to form, instead, a hendiadys in which the first term is actually always already contained in the second" (2000, 190). This division of human from citizen was delineated along the lines of feeling in opposition to reason: "despite commonplace assumptions about the Enlightenment, the primary qualification for inclusion within the category of the human was the capacity to feel, not the capacity to reason" (Maslan 2004, 358). Thus a duality is established where humans feel but citizens must think.

While critics such as Mona Ozouf note the prevalence of the sentiment of patriotism during this period, I would suggest that there is nonetheless an important difference between an unthinking sentiment such as patriotism, and the complexities of feeling that Maslan associates with the category of the human. Rei Terada identifies this difference as "self-differentiality" (2003, 156). Regarding the zombies in George Romero's films, she notes that "Romero's living dead are notoriously undivided, they are needs and compulsions … They don't think twice about anything; they are pure intentionality, directional in one direction at a time. A living system is self-differential; only self-differential entities – 'texts' – feel" (ibid.). Terada uses this argument for self-differentiality to articulate the ways in which the purportedly postmodern death of the subject is actually the inauguration of feeling, because emotion requires expression which in turn requires an understanding of difference and interpretation. Her argument clarifies the difference between the undivided intentionality of a sentiment such as patriotism and the divided differentiality of feeling.

In "Citizenship, Diaspora and the Bonds of Affect," I argue that the demand for emotional neutrality on contemporary passport photographs, despite the ostensible rationale regarding ease of identification, indicates how the ideal citizen should look and feel. The relationship between emotion and citizenship is predicated on the question of the humanity of the citizen subject. Maslan's argument breaks the familiar Greek to Roman to French to American narrative of citizenship's progression as a concept. Her examination of pre-modern citizenship in relation to the legacy of the French Revolution, an event closely connected to modern conceptions of citizenship, reveals a deeply uneasy relationship between the universal claims of citizenship and the exclusions of its practice.

In a historical moment when more people move around more than ever before, these claims have become more frequent and more fraught. As Cole notes of the crisis engendered by the urbanization movements in nineteenth-century Europe, "People in modern cities might not be who they claimed to be. They could be anyone; they could come from anywhere. Nineteenth century society shifted from a closely hierarchical society of ranks and orders, in which everyone knew his or her place and the place of others, into what … Michael Ignatieff has called a 'society of strangers'" (2001, 9). The status of the stranger, the foreigner, stands in tension with that of a community whose integrity is, as Benedict Anderson famously suggests, imaginary. The diasporic subject's difference challenges the homogenizing stipulations of national citizenship and illuminates the contradictions of citizenship. These are contradictions that turn on feeling. Citizenship is both bonded by affect and, in the instance of its visual manifestation through the passport photograph, hindered by it. The injunction against emotion in passport photos projects a fantasy of a passive, transparent, and readable national subject.

The figure of the foreigner poses a distinct challenge to this fantasy, in that the foreigner's subjectivity cannot be easily assimilated into this discourse of citizenship. Torpey's recognition, through the work of Gérard Noiriel, of the problem of the "foreigner" suggests a strong connection between the idea of Man and the notion of the foreigner located within the founding of the 1789 Declaration itself: "Noiriel has written that the modern conception of the 'foreigner' came into being with the French Revolution as a result of the elimination of feudal privileges on 4 August 1789, which formally created a national community of French citizens. This Act was, however, in inherent and insoluble tension with the Declaration of the Rights of Man and Citizen, which proclaimed equality of all *individuals* and thus tended to promote the rights of foreigners as such" (Torpey 2000, 28). This tension between the rights of Man and the rights of the community of citizens does not simply lie in that classic liberal problem of individual desire set against communal need. Rather, the tension can be located in the problem of the rights of the foreigner, coded as individual Man, which pose a threat to the rights of the citizen.

Arguing for a sharper understanding of the chasm between the figure of Man and the figure of the citizen in contemporary understandings of citizenship, Maslan also draws attention to the foreignness of the figure of Man and suggests how this figure is indeed racialized. As she observes, the very title of the 1789 *Déclaration des droits de l'Homme et du Citoyen* indicates that the continuity between the figure of the human and that of the citizen cannot be taken for granted.

> The authors of the Declaration understood that they were in the process of elaborating two distinct kinds of rights: rights proper to an individual *outside* of any constituted political body – that is, in the language of the eighteenth century, natural rights – and rights proper to a member of an organized political body or state. It would appear, then, that natural rights are those that belong to man and political and civil rights are those at the disposal of the citizen. Asian and Africans, both favorite French examples of oppressed peoples, would be recognized by the Declaration not as citizens of France, of course, but rather in their capacity as *men* – a title which confers upon them a body of rights that must be acknowledged and recognized by all other human beings. (2004, 360)

This split in the Declaration allowed for the recognition of the humanity of oppressed racial others such as Asians and Africans, but it also explicitly denied them any kind of obvious access to the rights and privileges of citizenship, creating a divide between human and citizen.

As the need to mediate that divide became more pressing, it was feeling and emotion that were pressed into service. As Maslan observes, the Marquis de Lafayette argued that the declaration should "*dire ce que tout le monde sait, ce que tout le monde sent*" (2004, 358). The world should not only know but also feel these foundations of contemporary citizenship. The capacity to feel thus became just as indicative of humanity as the capacity to reason (and perhaps even more so). The physical fact of being human came to matter less in the *ancien régime* than emotional aspects of human existence: "Sentimentalizing the 'human' of human rights implied a shift from bodies and their sufferings, to persons and their unhappinesses, from biology to the mental and emotional cognates of physical suffering" (Maslan 2006, 80). Emotion and affect could negotiate the chasm between the human and the citizen. However, the reliance upon emotion and feeling to humanize the figure of the citizen depends upon the idea that emotions are an indication of human subjectivity.

With reference to subjectivity, Rei Terada notes the fallacy of what she calls the "expressive hypothesis" where "the claim that emotion requires a subject – thus we can see we're subjects, since we have emotions – creates the illusion of subjectivity rather than showing evidence of it" (2003, 11). It has become conventional, as Terada notes, to think of emotion as something "lifted from a depth to a surface" through the mechanism of expression. Expression "serves as the distracting white handkerchief" which naturalizes the logic of the expressive hypothesis (ibid.). This white handkerchief also distracts from the role of representation in feeling: "We are not ourselves without representations that mediate us, and it is through these representations emotions get felt" (21). For Terada, the death of the subject ascribed to contemporary postmodern theory does not mean the death of feeling. On the contrary, the death of the subject initiates feeling.

The dream of a feeling citizen cannot hide the monstrous anti-human heart of the original citizen subject. Terada shows us that feeling is not a guarantee of subjectivity. On the contrary, emotions can indicate the death of the subject and real subjectivity can be an indication of monstrosity. As she wryly observes of Romero's zombies, they seem to "emblematize postmodern subjectivity" because "everyone knows that if there's one thing dead subjects don't have, it's emotion" (2003, 156). However, she points out that the opposite is actually the case: "Romero's living dead are notably undivided about their desires, or rather … their desires are undivided" (ibid.). As a "well-known counterillustration," she offers the case of the replicants in Ridley Scott's *Blade Runner*: "In the film … the explicitly sentimental moment for the replicant played by Sean Young – the one time she cries – is the moment when she discovers that she's a replicant, whose memories are not her own. We assume she had feelings before, but reserving the sight of her tears for this occasion dramatizes the fact that destroying the illusion of subjectivity does not destroy emotion, that on the contrary, emotion is the sign of the absence of that illusion" (157). "Unlike replicants," Terada argues, "zombies don't experience themselves as though they were someone else" (ibid.). Terada's deeply provocative description of the feeling dead subject, the replicant who experiences herself as though she were someone else, reveals the alienation of the unfeeling photographed citizen and, specifically, the problem of the diasporic citizen. Insofar as diaspora is a state of dislocation where one becomes located through a process of experiencing one's home – the site of one's identity – as though it were someone else's, there is some resonance between the replicant of Terada's example and the person in diaspora. In diaspora, the notion of identity as something that might be grounded in an idea of home is highly mediated through representation and narrative. As Vijay Mishra understands, "it is becoming increasingly obvious that the narrative of the damaged home … takes its exemplary form in what may be called diasporas, and especially in diasporas of colour, those migrant communities that do not quite fit into the nation-state's barely concealed preference for the narrative of assimilation" (1996, 112). It has become something of a convention in diaspora studies to talk about the ways in which "home" does not exist except in memory, as a representation, and a problematically misremembered one at that. And part of that convention involves the tragic moment of recognizing that the diasporic person's home is not what they thought it was, that it exists as a fantasy or unreality which can be shattered, and which renders the diasporic home something that can only be experienced as though it belonged to someone else.

Indeed, not only does the diasporic subject share something with the replicant, but the figure of man-citizen promoted by the *ancien régime* recalls the living dead in their unwavering and undivided desires. Through the work of Elisabeth G. Sledziewski, Maslan points out that "the desire to create the unified man-citizen, a subject who would *feel* his ties and obligations of citizenship as a part of his interiority just as he would understand his familial and amical bonds as part of his civic participation, was a central motive force in the creation of revolutionary legislation" (Maslan 2006, 75). The citizen is expected to feel unwaveringly bound to home and country in such a way that the idea of home does not contradict the idea of national belonging. In contrast, the diasporic subject becomes a citizen knowing that they become unified with the nation at the expense of distancing themselves from themselves. They must experience their home as though it was someone else's, and themselves as though they were someone else, as though there were no contradictions between being diasporic and being a citizen.

Feeling does not mediate the divide between human and citizen. It exposes it. Diasporas take up the dream of the feeling citizen not as a way of burying or resolving the divide between humanity and citizenship, but rather as a way of engaging it. What will save citizenship from the monstrosity of real subjectivity will be a recognition of the distance between the diasporic subject and the citizen – a recognition of the mediation necessary for those in diaspora to become a citizen. The moment of breaking the illusion of some kind of naturalized continuity between the diaspora and citizenship is not so unlike the moment in which the replicant recognizes the death of her subjectivity. It is what makes her less, and not more, monstrous.

Given the explicit references to racialized others such as Asians and Africans that Maslan points to in "The Anti-Human," racism constitutes at least one source of the divide between human and citizen in the French declaration. It made clear that one could be human in the eyes of the declaration, but not a citizen. The case of the Haitian revolution and Toussaint L'Ouverture's mistaken belief in his own access to citizenship makes this exclusion clear. Recognizing the divide between the person in diaspora and the citizen is an acknowledgment of the racism embedded within the concept of citizenship. To become a citizen, one must let go of one's particularity, suspend it, so as to become part of something more general, more universal. The moment when a diasporic subject must choose to side with the generalizing principles of citizenship and to let go of the specificity of diaspora is an uneasy one. It is also a moment in which one can see the racism attendant upon citizenship.

In the CI 9 photographs, Chinese migrants must try to look like someone who should be granted one of the signature rights of citizenship – the right of return – while also being targeted because of their particularity. In order to read for emotion in these photographs, it is useful to look at the history of the photographic capture of emotional expression. Charles Darwin's *The Expression of Emotion in Man and Animals* ([1889] 1998) was the first book to publish photographs of emotional expression as evidence for a scientific theory of affect. As Philip Prodger notes in his essay "Photography and *The Expression of Emotions*," Darwin's book "was one of the first scientific books ever published with photographic illustrations" and it thus "played a major role in bringing photographic evidence to the scientific world" (2009, 400–1). For Darwin, photography would allow people to see emotions that were otherwise too fleeting. What is more, in this book, Darwin established a convention that is still in place whereby photographers and cinematographers (think of the close-up) regard the face as the locus of human emotional expression. If Darwin had focused on some other part of the body (hands, for instance) or insisted on reading for emotion in the body as a whole, we would now have a very different set of visual conventions for visualizing emotional expression. But that was not the case. In terms of animals such as dogs and cats, Darwin's work did examine images of emotion as more wholly corporeal, and his analysis likewise engaged more fully with the whole body of the animal. However, setting aside the long-standing debate about whether or not the facial expression of emotion is innate and universal across cultures, Darwin anchors his study on the face and the connection between facial expression and emotion.

Let me bring the work of Darwin into dialogue with that of Terada by considering this implication: if emotion lies in its representation, then the face must be one of the most powerful mediums of emotional expression. The passport photograph and the CI 9 portraits suggest that there is indeed a strong possibility for the expressive potentiality of the face to expose the contradictions of citizenship. Not only is Darwin's study of the face resonant for thinking about emotion and expression, the very process by which he arrived at the visual evidence for his thesis also recalls the fine line between humanity and monstrosity. It is a process that in and of itself is richly suggestive of the contradictions of citizenship.

Darwin's study relied upon a number of photographs of various facial expressions taken by Oscar Rejlander, James Crichton Browne, George Charles Wallich, Adolph Diedrich Kindermann, and Guillaume-Benjamin Duchenne de Boulogne. It is in Duchenne's photographs that the line between humanity and monstrosity becomes most thin. By this, I do not mean that the subject of Duchenne's photographs was a monster, but rather that Duchenne's subject breaks down the divide between human and non-human if the former is, as Maslan suggests, distinguished by the capacity for emotion.

The Duchenne photographs in Darwin's book are of a man who has lost the capacity to move the muscles in this face. Because, as Prodger points out, Darwin was particularly interested in capturing "the ephemeral movements of facial muscles for analysis" (2009, 403), the photographs of Duchenne's patient were ideal for Darwin's analysis. The man who could not express emotion was a patient at La Salpêtrière hospital upon whom a number of electrical experiments were being carried out. The patient "suffered from an anaesthetic condition of the face, which made it possible to stimulate individual groups of his facial muscles without causing involuntary response among others. It was as if, Duchenne chillingly remarked, he were '"working with a still irritable cadaver"' (quoted in Prodger 2009, 405). Because photographic processes had not accelerated enough to capture the emotions Darwin wanted to reveal, Duchenne's plates froze "the activity of his subjects long enough to accommodate the lengthy exposure times necessitated by photographic technology" (2009, 405). That is, in order to illustrate emotion, Darwin had to turn to images of a man who had lost the capacity to express emotion, who was a cadaver-like zombie requiring electrical stimulation to show emotion.

That some of the most exemplary images of emotional expression in Darwin's work relied upon a figure whose face had lost feeling recalls that other ideally emotional void figure, the contemporary citizen. Now that photographic technology has accelerated to the point where a whole range of nuances of expression can be captured, there is no small irony in the demand for an image of citizenship that must hold any of those emotions at bay long enough for the citizen to adopt the expression of Duchenne's patient prior to being prodded and manipulated by electrical stimulation.

The demand for emotional neutrality in the passport photograph encapsulates the contradiction of citizenship even as the CI 9 photographs illuminate them. As I have been arguing, the contradiction of citizenship lies in being both diasporic and a citizen where the diasporic subject's divided feelings for "home" challenge citizenship's demand for a subject whose feelings are undivided. This contradiction emerges from the demand for the capacity to feel, despite the injunction against emotion in the very document that identifies one as a citizen. The representation of the racialized subject in an identification photograph calls attention to the dangers of misrecognition and the instability of the connection between the photograph and its subject.

For the viewer, any identification photograph poses the silent question: Is that you? The request for an identification photograph is also always a question of one's identity. It is a demand for proof even before the question is asked. As Terada's work emphasizes, feeling alone will not make human subjects more human, and so feeling alone cannot mediate the contradictions between citizenship and humanity embedded within the origins of contemporary citizenship. Perhaps only when the distance between the human and the citizen can be recognized in that alienating moment of experiencing oneself as though one were somebody else, and experiencing one's home as though it were somebody else's, will citizenship come close to fully embracing the bonds of affect.

CODA
SHAME ABOUT THAT MICROFILM

For *Mass Capture*, microfilm is everything. The thousands of documents upon which this book is based exist only as microfilm. As was the practice in "preservation microfilming," the originals were destroyed. They can be remembered but only as the result of their destruction. This paradox of their material memorialization raises questions about the relationship between microfilm and photography. When I first began to present papers on the CI 9s, papers that focused on what I saw as the incredible power of the identification photographs attached to each certificate, I was invariably asked by astute listeners about the existence of the originals. Did they exist? Could I detach the photograph from the certificate in order to look for the stamp of a photography studio, or other information that might further illuminate the ways in which these images were produced and circulated? Were there photographic negatives? My answers were always a disappointment. No, I did not think there were any originals. Yes, I was still hopeful that some might emerge. No, I have never touched an original CI 9, and could not even imagine what riches might lie on the other side of the photograph, much less in the materiality of negatives.

In terms of its claim to be a project about the relationship between photography and citizenship, the loss of the original certificates cast, for me, an air of fraudulence over the entire enterprise. Could this really be a discussion of photography when there were no physical photographs at the core of the investigation? The question seems less about what might or might not count as a photograph than about the kinds of expectations and desires that attend to critical work on photography. So much of that work demands looking in ways that are deeply tactile. The present work attends to the image as object. It takes up other ways of looking by looking deeply, askew, and all around. Archival work in particular involves a deep-seated desire for what Tina Campt calls "thingyness" (2012, 128). Campt credits Ingrid Pollard with this term, who commented to her: "There's a 'thingyness' to an image … a thingyness you feel incredibly strongly when you work with negatives." For Campt, the thingyness of the photograph enables an engagement that exceeds the seeming limits of two-dimensional visuality. It is no longer just about looking. It has everything to do with – and I borrow from Eve Kosofsky Sedgwick advisedly here – touching feeling. "While the affects of photographs are certainly produced through their visuality," Campt writes, "they also resonate in equally profound ways through their materiality and through the haptics of their thingyness" (ibid.). Campt's claims for the power of thingyness will resonate with anyone who has ever stepped into a humidity-controlled room, slipped on cotton gloves, and picked up a photograph from a time outside of the one that they currently inhabit.

How, then, to understand the affective power of the CI 9 photographs, and their existence as photographs, in the howling absence of their thingyness? There are two moves. First, it is worth exploring the affective materiality of microfilm itself. Second, we also need to attend to the curious distinction between microfilm and photography. Let me take up the latter move before turning to the former.

Microfilm and photography emerged into the world simultaneously. As Jonathan Auerbach and Lisa Gitelman point out, "The first 'microphotography,' as the medium was long called, was done in England in 1839; the same year Louis Daguerre first made photographic reproduction practical" (2007, 748). Auerbach and Gitelman distinguish microfilm from photography, marking the birth of the microphotograph as separate from, albeit temporally adjacent to, the daguerreotype. This distinction is curious and is repeated throughout discussions of microfilm history, including Frederic Luther's (1959) *Microfilm: A History, 1839–1900*. Even though both technologies relied on nearly identical apparatuses and processes – camera, film, development – the scholarship on microfilm tends to emphasize its distinctiveness from photography rather than its alikeness.

Not only does microfilm circulate as separate from photography, it also occupies a position that situates it as alternately the salvation of, or purely supplemental to, photography. For example, in "A Positive Approach to Negatives," Ruth B. Kerns identifies microfilm as the technology that saves photographs when she talks about the experience of the special collections and archives at George Mason University preserving nearly 9,000 deteriorating photographic negatives – mostly materials from the Library of Congress Federal Theatre Project, which had been one of the four Works Progress Administration (WPA) projects launched during the Depression. Among preservation archivists, microfilm is still the medium of choice despite the many, many moves towards digitization. It is an incredibly stable technology with an established track record of longevity. High-quality microfilm, produced with silver-halide development processes, will last in excess of five hundred years. It is hard to imagine any digital platform that can reliably make such a claim.

Outside the circles of preservation archivists, microfilm may not typically circulate as a technology of photographic salvation, but its function as supplementary is not a surprise. As Allardyce Nicholl notes, "microfilm has been used up to the present as a supplement, not as a fundamental basis. We have been accustomed, as individual scholars, to turn to microfilm only when the particular library in which we are working does not possess a copy of some particular text we require; similarly, many libraries have endeavoured to make their collections complete by obtaining photographic copies of excessively rare (perhaps even unique) exemplars elsewhere" (1953, 62). Nicholl writes as a Shakespearean who must work with texts that are always at risk of disintegration, but his point regarding the format's secondary or supplementary nature highlights an enduring attitude to microfilm. The microfilm is a copy. It contains, seemingly, none of the aura of the original. It is the medium of second choice. No scholar, given the choice, would choose to work with microfilm over the original. And, unlike digital images – which do seem to offer some genuine advantages over the original even in their portability and searchability – microfilm is frustratingly analogue yet stripped of the pleasures of the analogic object. Its thingyness eludes us because it registers first as cumbersome, awkward, and, dare I say, vaguely shameful. I will say more about these affective registers of microfilm later. For now, let me note that it was not always the case that microfilm would function as a supplement, as a copy of a copy, as that source of last resort, turned to only when all else has failed or been destroyed. Indeed, microfilm was once glamorous.

Microfilm came into the world as a jewel: microphotographs were inserted into jewels for Queen Victoria (Luther 1959, 27). At what must be the height of microfilm's claim to glamour, it was central to practices of espionage, both real and filmic. Rebecca Lemov observes the unique anxieties engendered by microfilm in her description of the 1943 noir detective film *Sherlock Holmes in Washington*: "Passed from a dying British secret agent to an American debutante, its tiny texts ended up stored in her 'V for Victory' matchbook, where they sat, hidden in plain sight, producing anxiety in the audience every time someone lit up a cigarette" (2015, 88). Similarly, in their consideration of the microfilm and the Cold War containment narrative, Auerbach and Gitelman discuss Cary Grant's memorable line to Eva Marie Saint in Hitchcock's *North By Northwest* (1959): "I see you've got the pumpkin" (2007, 745). Grant refers not to a squash but to a figurine stuffed with microfilm of state secrets, which the spies must now carry across "the brows and necklines of Mount Rushmore," staging the way in which the state intersects with the microfilm on scales that are both gargantuan and intimately diminutive. While Auerbach and Gitelman are absolutely right to suggest that microfilm "graphically dramatizes questions of scale" (746), it is their observation about the paradox of microfilm's relationship to memory that helps me to think through the CI 9 photographs and the construction of non-citizenship.

Microfilm preserved the CI 9s and it was also the reason for their destruction. The final lines of the LAC descriptive record for the CI 9s reads: "These records were filmed by the Department under microfilm authority M6-62 in 1963 from originals which were then destroyed. Many of the images are of poor quality." Microfilm authority M6-62 – even the name, both austere and seemingly arbitrary, suggests the contradictory nature of the imperative it contains – was responsible for the simultaneous safeguarding and obliteration of hundreds of thousands of original records relating to immigration, including "juvenile report cards" (reports of children sent to Canada by various agencies), ships manifests, individual entry forms for settlers arriving between 1919 and 1924, records of migrants entering Canada from 1865 to 1961, and, of course, the CI 9s. As Auerbach and Gitelman understand, "microfilm simultaneously promised preservation and destruction, security and risk. Under the emerging technocratic aegis of professional librarianship, 'preservation microfilming' came to mean destroying original documents in order to preserve them on film, a practice that continues today" (2007, 749). This paradox is not unique to microfilm. Anne Carson would remind us that the earliest practices of technologies of memory, dating to Simonides's invention of the art of memory itself, were deeply attuned to the ways in which memory demands forgetting and loss: "Remembering brings the absent into the present, connects what is lost to what is here. Remembering draws attention to the lostness and is made possible by emotions of space that open backward into a void" (2002, 38). That memory necessitates destruction is not new, but the connection between this paradox and the nation-state is uniquely modern, and here microfilm shines. With reference to Susan Stewart's work on the miniature, Auerbach and Gitelman note that the metaphors for miniaturization that tended to herald the advantages of microfilm – "'The whole archives of a nation might be packed away in a snuffbox'" – function as "prosaic celebrations of microfilm reduction ratios [that] work by emphasizing contrasts in scale between bourgeois interiority on the one hand and the national public on the other. They recur as triumphal images of domestication and preservation directed at the public record, safeguarding made all the more imperative by the threat of war" (2007, 748). Thus, in *Sherlock Holmes Goes to Washington*, it is significant that, in addition to the anxieties about the microfilm being obliterated in an unknowing puff of cigarette smoke, it is the secret of the state itself that is at risk. Storing these secrets right next to the very incendiary device that could destroy them, a device that is literally imprinted with the promise of the victory of the state, perfectly encapsulates the way in which microfilm is poised at the intersection of the wildly, gigantically public (Mount Rushmore! V for Victory!) and the terribly intimate and secretive. Here, the secret of bourgeois interiority plays out against the very public history of the trafficking of the secrets of the state.

Notably, these are secrets that must be mediated through a machine. Microfilm can only be read with the aid of mechanical intervention. Even safeguarded from accidental incineration and ferried across the face of national monuments, microfilm is useless without a microfilm reader. The paradox of its function as a technology of memory is thus further compounded by its reliance upon a secondary technology of reading, one that highlights the absurdity of microfilm as a medium of secrecy: in order to be read, the microfilm must literally be blown up, and it can only be blown up with the aid of outside intervention. The anxiety telegraphed by *Sherlock Holmes Goes to Washington* extends far beyond the possibility of the microfilm's destruction ignited by every puff of cigarette smoke. It reaches into the compromises engendered by the success of a secret transmission. Even when the secrets have been safely deposited, they must be threaded through a machine, shot through with light, and enlarged to the point where a safe and private viewing will only be notional. The intimacy of the microfilm lies in its promise to always betray the secrets that it holds.

Although they are far removed from the allure of noir detective films and the thrills of Hitchcock, the CI 9s do, in their positioning of that which is both remembered and forgotten, preserved and destroyed, reveal something about the secretive intimacy, and betrayals, of the state. It wanted and needed these migrants at the same time that it had to engineer a massive system of bureaucracy to make known their supposed expendability. This system begins in the legislated racism and discrimination of the head tax enshrined in the multiple iterations of the Chinese Immigration Act between 1885 and 1947, but its execution lies in the technologies and mechanisms of the certificates themselves. In their original form and function, the CI 9s make visible the secret of a state that wanted Chinese migrants even though it hated them. In their current material form, preserved and destroyed as several thousand metres of microfilm neatly spooled in the beige metal drawers of the third floor of Library and Archives Canada, they make manifest the way in which public histories are rife with secrets that perpetually threaten to undo the foundations of the state. Unspooling the microfilm one certificate at a time, the CI 9s reveal again and again and again (and again several thousand times) the ways in which the achievement of contemporary Canadian citizenship rests upon the perpetual construction of non-citizens.

This construction has a materiality. I want to turn now to the thingyness of microfilm through a consideration of its affective registers. In doing so, I want to return to the sense of fraudulence that attended my early presentations on the CI 9s. That worry exceeded the usual stuff of impostor syndrome. There was, I now realize, a sense of shame that I experienced at not being able to give the "right" answers about these images as photographic objects. And it was a shame that persisted even when I learned that I would never be able to give the right answers, because the original CI 9s had all been destroyed. As the magnitude of the destruction of the original CI 9s really began to sink in, this sense of shame telescoped outward well beyond my own personal scholarly dilemmas, towards the problem of national memory.

Shame, as Elizabeth Povinelli and Elspeth Probyn understand, is deeply political. More than that, shame can be central to the construction of citizenship and national belonging. As Povinelli so powerfully outlines in her essay on the political uses of shame and *Mabo v. Queensland (No. 2)*, a decision of the High Court of Australia that recognized native title for the first time, "the fantasy of shame and reparation created an experience of intimacy – intimate holding, intimate understanding, intimate knowledge – between those who control the access to and those excluded from critical rights" (1998, 598). In its decision, the court demanded an engagement with a national sense of shame around the issue of Indigenous land rights: "The High Court's claim in *Mabo* that the common law was shamed by its own history and an international gaze should be placed within the context of these other contemporary national mortifications" (597). In this affective move, the court also put into motion a rhetoric of national shame that was quickly co-opted by right-wing political interests claiming to be ashamed (for example) of the ways in which Australia buckled to international pressure. This discourse revealed "how institutions are claimed to have feelings and how these feeling institutions translate liberation struggles against them into their own legitimation" (598). As I have previously argued with respect to the connection between the inauguration of the Canadian Citizenship Act on 1 January 1947 and the repeal of the Chinese Immigration Act a few months later, citizenship does not emerge free of the baggage of national history.[1] The parliamentary debates in the months

1 Please see "Redress Revisited: Citizenship and the Chinese Canadian Head Tax" (Cho 2013).

leading up to the repeal of the Chinese Immigration Act, and thus the end of the era of Chinese head tax and exclusion, were completely bound by precisely the same kinds of considerations that Povinelli tracks in relation to *Mabo*. Broadly speaking, a majority of parliamentarians began to struggle with the realization that the explicit racism embedded within the Chinese Immigration Act was no longer compatible with the vision of Canadian and Canadian citizenship domestically, and also internationally. It is not an exaggeration to say, after reading the text of the debates in the Canadian House of Commons in the months between January and May 1947, that shame was one of the primary motivations for granting Chinese people access to Canadian citizenship.

The connection between the uses and abuses of this national shame and the CI 9s specifically can be found at the intersection of interiority and publicity that microfilm so perfectly inhabits. As a central part of the mechanism of mass capture that constructed Chinese migrants as non-citizens, the CI 9s reveal not just the shameful secret of a state that ruthlessly exploited thousands of people by harnessing their labour and putting in place legislation that would leave them separated from families and communities for most of their lives. While this story of the effects of the head tax and exclusion on Chinese families is well known, the CI 9s open up individual stories and experiences of exclusion. Here, in each certificate, we can read the details of an existence in Canada that tells of years, often decades, separated from family and loved ones. We can track histories of violence in the scars and other identifying marks recorded by customs agents. Even though we know that these men laboured alone and in terrible conditions for decades, the CI 9s put a literal face to that loneliness and those conditions.

However, there can be a productivity to this shame and it lies in the thingyness of the CI 9 as microfilm. Here, I am coming full circle. Where I began with some sense of shame over the fact that all of the primary materials for this book exist only as microfilm, I want to now close with a more complex understanding of shame as something that is not only about bad feelings. I want to bring that complexity to a way of understanding the thingyness of microfilm, and of the CI 9 microfilms in particular.

In the case of the CI 9s, the entire geography and physical architecture of Library and Archives Canada serves only to amplify this shame. The building sits at the end of the nation's most geographically symbolic streets. Its immediate neighbour is the Supreme Court of Canada and, next to the courthouse, Parliament Hill itself. That is, the archives are housed in a location that signals their importance as being adjacent to, and second only to, the highest court of the nation and the seat of national governance.

Once inside Library and Archives Canada, researchers undergo all the rituals of divestment central to the experience of any archival visit. Your personal belongings must be placed in a locker. You are permitted to carry in only materials that can fit into a clear plastic pouch issued by security. No pens. In order to access the CI 9s, you must ascend the marble steps of the building to the third floor. You will first walk past a beautiful reading room that is flooded with light from a wall of windows overlooking the Ottawa River. There will be serious-looking people doing what you think of as real archival work in this room. They will be at the tables, boxes of precious materials neatly stacked around them. They will be wearing gloves. You will look at them with longing, knowing that, for the length of this research trip, the only time you will spend in this beautiful room will be when you take a break to check email. You keep walking into a room full of long flat metal filing cabinets. There will still be windows here, and the view of the river is still spectacular, but you know that this is only the room where you pull at the smoothly greased bearings of drawers containing reels T-6038 to T-6046. You take three or four reels to start and proceed to the next room. In this one the blinds are always drawn. There will be a clerk who gives you a perfunctory nod. There will be rows and rows of machines. You will have your pick. You are almost never alone – one or two unfortunate others will also be bent over these machines – but you often wonder why you can't do work that allows you to be in the serious and beautiful room.

This acknowledgment of the strange shamefulness of the whole experience of an archival trip devoted solely to the supplementariness of microfilm forced me to consider why I was so devoted to a project whose central materials were a source of disappointment, frustration, and, yes, shame.

Of course, the CI 9s are profoundly important. Of course, as this book argues, they make visible the relationship between photography, surveillance, and the construction of non-citizens. But beyond this obvious importance, there is also a simple, straightforward, and intense interest. From the moment when I first saw these certificates in 2009, I could not take my eyes off them. I could not stop looking. As Elspeth Probyn charts in *Blush*, the relationship between looking, interest, and the productivity of shame runs deep.

> Someone looks at you with interest and you begin to be interested, only to realize she's looking at someone else. Or, as [Silvan] Tomkins notes, "One starts to smile but found one was smiling at a stranger." If you're interested in and care about the interest of others, you spend much of your life blushing. Conversely, if you don't care, then attempts to shame won't move you. Shame highlights different levels

> of interest … interest is the key to understanding shame, and shame reminds us with urgency what we are interested in. Shame reminds us of the promises we keep to ourselves. (2005, x)

Probyn's account tracks the quiet, almost often erotic, charge of shame. Fittingly, this account turns upon looking and, more specifically, upon the misdirected look. What is more, this misdirected look emerges only because the observer thought she was the object of attention. She thinks that interest has been directed at her, which excites her interest, and then, blushing, she realizes that her interest has been misplaced. Probyn outlines the strange circuit of shame wherein its subject must be initially passive. This economy of interest, where the subject of shame is doubly shameful not only because she has misplaced her interested gaze, but also because she was brought to interest through the mistaken belief in herself as an object of interest, perfectly models my own encounters with academic research itself in a broad sense, and this project in particular. As I confess in the preface, I wasn't looking at all for this stuff. It found me. In my case, I owe a debt to Johanna Mizgala, the archivist who, in 2009, first handed me a CD-R (speaking of outdated technologies of memory) of over two thousand CI 9s that archivists at Library and Archives Canada had scanned in their own time. It was actually handed to me. I was just minding my own business when this research came along. But when I started to look, I realized that I was looking at it all wrong.

Where for Probyn shame comes from misperceiving oneself as an object of interest, the CI 9s pose a converse problem. Even though they demand to be looked at, and to be examined in great detail, it would be a mistake to overlook the way in which they look out at those looking at them. As I have noted throughout my analysis of these certificates, without fail and in the absence of a formal demand, the people in these photographs are all photographed facing squarely into the camera. As I argue in chapter 5, they anticipated the demands of identification photography for citizens long before such demands existed. I have, in other words, considered the way in which the subjects of the photographs can be looked at. But these are not subjects who are content to be observed. They look back. They look back in ways that unsettle, that haunt, and that commit the full force of their interest.

In suggesting that part of the productivity of the shame of these photographs lies in the way that their subjects look back at those looking at them, I gesture, only partly in jest, to the old Scooby Doo joke about the painting with the moving eyes. That gag turns upon the idea of being unknowingly watched by something that is itself meant to be looked at, and the secret animation of the animate. However, this is a trick of the eye. The painting does not move. No part of the painting (eyeballs or otherwise) moves. The direction of the viewer, and of the perception point of the painting, does not actually move the painting. As researchers in the field of optical perception note in their analysis of perception and paintings, "the pointing direction is invariant, and it is always orthogonal to the picture plane (as an object in pictorial space), exactly as the painter painted it" (Koenderink et al. 2004, 527). The perception that the eyes in the painting move tells us more about those who do the looking than that which is being looked at. This is the story of the CI 9 photographs. They seem to tell us so much about their subjects, but an equally important story is the one they tell us about the need of the state to look, and to look so obsessively, at those it works so hard to exclude from the sphere of citizenship.

Shame, as Probyn teaches us, comes from mistaken interests. For *Mass Capture*, these photographs are not simply a record of the shameful treatment of their subjects by a state that accepted decades of their labour while shamelessly denying them access to citizenship on the basis of race. The CI 9 photographs also inject the shame of mistaking, and misreading, the interest of the subjects into those who will look at them. From the immigration agent who first formally encountered these photographs, to the mid-twentieth-century librarians who destroyed the original documents in the name of committing them to national memory, to contemporary researchers like me who have been so fortunate to have been held captive by their complexity, the CI 9 photographs compel because there are so many ways to mistake their interest.

APPENDIX A
CHINESE IMMIGRATION CERTIFICATES

The following is a provisional list of Chinese Immigration certificates used throughout the years of the Chinese Immigration Act (1885–1947). It is compiled by the Vancouver Public Library and is drawn from a provisional list drafted by Library and Archives Canada in 1987.

CI Certificates

Form number	*Title of description*	*Dates in use*	*Purpose and contents*
CI 1	"Special Reports Required by Law to be Made by the Master of Any Vessel Bringing Chinese Immigrants to Canada"	Before 1911 – after 1911	The Chinese Immigration Act of 1885 (c.71 s.6) required the master of a ship to list the names and birthplaces of crew members, and the names, birthplaces, occupations, and last places of domicile of Chinese passengers.
CI 2	"Bill of Health"	Before 1911 – after 1911	This certified good health on vessels bringing Chinese passengers into port. The certification was made by port quarantine officers.
CI 3	"Controller's Warrant for the Landing of Chinese Immigrants"	Before 1911 – after 1911	This authorized a ship master to land Chinese immigrants.
CI 7	Unknown	(?) – before 1911	Unknown
CI 8	"Report of Transactions under the Chinese Immigration Act"	Before 1910 – after 1947	This was a monthly report of certificates issued and other transactions carried out under the Chinese Immigration Act. It was forwarded by the collectors of customs who handled Chinese immigration cases.
CI 9 (Nfld.)	Out-registration certificate	1906–1950	This form was used to document individuals leaving Newfoundland temporarily. It was similar to the CI 9 issued by Canadian immigration authorities. There are no known examples. Out-registrations were recorded in a ledger called the Newfoundland Register of Arrivals and Outward Registrations.

/continued

Form number	*Title of description*	*Dates in use*	*Purpose and contents*
CI 10	"Certificate Issued by the Government of the Dominion of Canada to *[name]*, a Chinese Person About to Go to the United States"	Before 1911 – after 1911	The CI 10 was issued to Chinese persons wishing to visit the US and return to Canada. Usually these persons were exempt from head tax. CI 10s were issued only at Vancouver, Victoria, and Ottawa. They recorded detailed identifying information for each individual.
CI 11	"Report of Chinese and Other Passengers Landed from or Reported at the Port of *[name]*"	Before 1911 – after 1911	This was a statistical report of numbers of Chinese persons landed from steamships, according to class (e.g., exempt, head tax payers, CI 9 returnees, etc.)
CI 12	Unknown	Ceased before 1911	Unknown
CI 13	Unknown	Ceased before 1911	Unknown
CI 14	Unknown	Ceased before 1911	Unknown
CI 15	CI 5 register	Before 1911 – after 1911	These were large registers of CI 5 forms received and issued.
CI 16	"Requisition for Chinese Certificates"	In or before 1910 – after 1910	This form was used to request blank CI 5 certificate forms to be used for specific ship arrivals. The CI 16 was used only at Vancouver and Victoria.
CI 17	Untitled	In or before 1910 – after 1910	This was a "Confidential" form, used to record the results of an examination of a person claiming to be a merchant or other person exempt from paying head tax.
CI 18	"Form for Son's Examination"	Around 1910 – in order after 1921	This was a "Confidential" form, used to record the results of an examination of a person claiming to be the son of a merchant or other person exempt from paying head tax. Various versions were used.
CI 18	"Form for Father's Examination"	Around 1910 – in order after 1921	This was a "Confidential" form, used to record the results of an examination of a person claiming to be the parent of a merchant or other person exempt from paying head tax. Various versions were used.
CI 19	Unknown	Ceased before 1911	Unknown
CI 20	File jacket	In or after 1893 – 1911	This was a file jacket or folder for the Chinese Immigration Service, issued by the Department of Trade and Commerce.
CI 21	Release certificate	In or before 1910 – after 1910	This certificate released a Chinese person who had been detained and whose right to enter Canada had been established.

Form number	*Title of description*	*Dates in use*	*Purpose and contents*
CI 22	"Report of Chinese Outwards"	In or before 1910 – after 1911	A list of Chinese persons leaving Canada by ship who had passed across Canada in transit to and from foreign countries. It was submitted by the shipmaster.
CI 23	"Special Chinese Manifest"	Unknown	This form listed Chinese persons travelling across Canada by train, in transit to another country. It was issued in accordance with R.S.C. 1906, c.95, s.7 and Chinese immigration regulations.
CI 24	"Records of Chinese Exempts"	Before 1910 – after 1910	This was a monthly report submitted by ports of entry which tabulated the numbers of different classes of exempt persons and overstays.
CI 25	Temporary head tax receipt	Unknown	A temporary receipt for payment of head tax. It was cancelled when the CI 5 was issued.
CI 26	Unknown	Unknown	Unknown
CI 27	Unknown	Unknown	Unknown
CI 29	Untitled affadavit for application to replace lost CI 5	Around 1912 to around 1947(?)	This affadavit provided detailed identifying information, as well as a photograph and references. It was used to support applications for CI 28s, which replaced lost CI 5s.
CI 31	Unknown	Unknown	Unknown
CI 32	Unknown	Unknown	Unknown
CI 33	Unknown	Unknown	Unknown
CI 34	Unknown	Unknown	Unknown
CI 35	Untitled application form for a CI 36 certificate	Before 1916 – after 1916	This form was used to apply for a CI 36 certificate, which was a substitute for CI 5 certificates issued without photos.
CI 37	Unknown	Unknown	Unknown
CI 38	Unknown	Unknown	Unknown
CI 39	Unknown	Unknown	Unknown
CI 40	"Investigation Made into the Standing as a Chinese Merchant of *[name]*"	Around 1911 – after 1914	This form was used to document the investigation of persons claiming exemption from paying head tax based on the fact that they were a merchant. The form recorded names of partners, amounts invested, location and description of business premises, turnover, and merchandise.

/continued

Form number	*Title of description*	*Dates in use*	*Purpose and contents*
CI 41	Unknown	Unknown	Unknown
CI 43	Unknown	Unknown	Unknown
CI 47	Unknown	Unknown	Unknown
CI 48	Unknown	Unknown	Unknown
CI 49	Unknown	Unknown	Unknown
CI 50	Untitled certificate issued to temporary Chinese visitors	After 1912 – around 1947	This was issued to Chinese temporarily admitted to Canada by minister's permit under the Chinese Immigration Act of 1923, s.9. Those admitted included diplomats, merchants, servants, entertainers, doctors, teachers, scholars, clergymen, students, and tourists. Two versions were used.

Source: "Chinese Immigration Certificates." Vancouver Public Library. http://guides.vpl.ca/ccg/ChineseImmigrationCertificates.

APPENDIX B
CI 9 FINDING AID NOTE

There are three digital repositories where CI 9s can be found: Library and Archives Canada; Canadiana; and the Mass Capture repository at York University.

This appendix is a brief guide to searching for CI 9s in each repository. Please note that you may want to search for the same information in all three repositories and, as I describe below, each one will yield slightly different information.

CI 9s at Library and Archives Canada (LAC)

The largest and most comprehensive collection of Chinese immigration certificates can be found here. The CI 9s are part of a larger group of Chinese immigration records held by Library and Archives Canada. LAC offers a concise description of these records and how they are organized in the "Immigrants from China, 1885–1949" section of their website.

All of the Chinese immigration records in LAC can be accessed through a database: https://www.bac-lac.gc.ca/eng/discover/immigration/immigration-records/immigrants-china-1885-1949/Pages/search.aspx.

The search screen on this database allows you to search by three fields of information:

- Name
- Date of Registration
- Certificate Number

As LAC notes on their description of this database: "Names were input as they appear in the register; no distinction was made between given name(s) and surname. Try searching by surname only."

This database gives researchers access not only to CI 9s, but to all Chinese immigration records held by LAC. Searching in this database will yield results for the General Registers of Chinese Immigration, 1885–1949, and any surviving certificates including CI 5s, CI 6s, and, of course, CI 9s.

Here is some further information about using each of these three search fields.

Name. Because there were no standards for anglicizing Chinese names, and because surnames and given names were often switched around, there is considerable inconsistency in the names that are recorded. One form of anglicization may have been used for many different Chinese names. For example, 于, 余, and 俞 will likely have been written as "Yu." Additionally, try different ways of spelling the name. For example, for "Yu," try also "Yue," "You," and even "Yee." Despite these inconsistences, if you are looking for a particular person, and you do not have information for the other two search fields, searching by name is a very good place to start and can yield accurate results.

Date of Registration. You do not need to know the exact date of registration and, indeed, unless you are holding an actual immigration certificate in hand, it is unlikely that you will have this information. However, inputting a year of registration can be very helpful for narrowing results. For example, putting "Yu" into the search field under "name" generates over 2,000 results that include names such as "Yuen," Yum," and "Yunt" in either the surname or given name fields. However, adding a year, "1913," limits the results to 800. If you know that the person you are searching for would have arrived in Canada around a particular year, it is well worth trying to limit the search by that year, and the years adjacent to it.

Certificate Number. If you have a certificate number, that is ideal. It can be the number for any certificates in Appendix A. For example, if you have the number of a person's CI 5, and if they had given their CI 5 number when they registered to leave Canada, putting that into the search field will also give you their CI 9.

Canadiana

Library and Archives Canada (LAC) contracted Canadiana (now part of the Canadian Research Knowledge Network) to digitize the CI 9s on its behalf. Canadiana has the complete digital collection of CI 9s on a website dedicated to these materials: https://heritage.canadiana.ca/view/oocihm.lac_mikan_161413.

The Canadiana holdings organize the CI 9s by microfilm reel number. Here is what you will find in each reel:

Vancouver departures
T-6047 – Sept 1910 to Jan 1912 – CI 9 no. 17286 to 20110
T-6048 – Jan 1911 to Oct 1913 – CI 9 no. 20111 to 22899

T-6049 – Oct 1913 to July 1916 – CI 9 no. 22900 to 27772
T-6051 – Nov 1917 to July 1919 – CI 9 no. 28650 to 31399
T-6052 – June 1915 to Sept 1929 – CI 9 no. 1 to 03240

Victoria departures
T-6038 – Sept 1910 to Oct 1911 – CI 9 no. 15701 to 18099
T-6039 – Oct 1911 to Oct 1912 – CI 9 no. 10100 to 21100
T-6040 – Oct 1912 to March 1914 – CI 9 no. 21101 to 23800
T-6041 – March 1914 to Dec 1914 – CI 9 no. 23801 to 26500
T-6042 – Dec 1914 to Oct 1915 – CI 9 no. 26501 to 29200
T-6043 – Oct 1915 to Nov 1916 – CI 9 no. 24201 to 31700
T-6044 – Nov 1916 to Oct 1918 – CI 9 no. 31701 to 34400
T-6045 – Oct 1918 to April 1920 – CI 9 no. 34401 to 37100
T-6046 – May 1913 to July 1952 – CI 9 no. 00001 to 2375

Each reel has its own hyperlink. When you access the reel, you will be shown each certificate in that reel in numerical order. There are approximately 2,500–3,000 certificates in each reel.

As with the microfilm reels themselves, there is no nominal index for the certificates in the Canadiana repository. You cannot search this repository by the name of the migrant. You can only find a certificate by reading each certificate in the reel. Each reel is organized by date of issue and, as a result, often also by ship, since migrants departing on the same date usually did so on the same ship.

However, despite these limitations, and even if you have found the certificate that you are looking for in the LAC database, there are still very good reasons for looking at the same certificate in the Canadiana repository. Because the certificates in the Canadiana repository can be accessed, digitally, in a way that is similar to how you would have found them by searching a microfilm reel, you will be able to see certificates that are adjacent to one another.

As I show in chapter 3 in my discussion of the Lawson family, examining which certificates came after others was the only way to be able to see this family in the CI 9 archive. The Lawsons travelled as a family of five but they were not pictured together anywhere in this archive. However, seeing their certificates in sequence will allow you to see the migrants who travelled together at the same time and on the same ship. Indeed, looking at the CI 9s in the Canadiana repository is the best way to find Chinese migrants via the ship they boarded.

There is currently no way to search by ship in any of the existing repositories or databases. However, in the Canadiana repository, the certificates are organized de facto by ship and departure date, because that is the order in which the certificates were originally issued and filed. Scrolling through the certificates in sequential order allows researchers to see migrants who travelled together.

The Canadiana repository also gives researchers digital access to the certificates in reels T-6046 and T-6052. These reels contain the CI 9s of "native-born" Chinese migrants. Because of this classification, there are more certificates belonging to women and children on these reels than any of the others.

Mass Capture Repository

As described in the preface, *Mass Capture* re-digitized thousands of CI 9s. Because the Canadiana repository was digitized in batches using a semi-automated process, the image quality is not optimal. *Mass Capture* re-digitized the certificates in the following reels:

T-6038
T-6039
T-6040
T-6041
T-6042
T-6043
T-6044
T-6045
T-6047
T-6048
T-6049
T-6050
T-6052

My project could not re-digitize all of the reels because of varying access restrictions and privacy concerns relating to some of the reels over the years that my research team worked on them. Some access restrictions are still in place even at the time of this writing.

Of the three repositories outlined in this appendix, the Mass Capture repository is the least comprehensive; however, this repository offers the highest quality images versions of the certificates it contains. Each certificate in the Mass Capture repository is digitized by a professional photographer who captured each one frame by frame. After they were photographed, each certificate in this repository was also given extensive post-production treatment where the levels, sharpness, contrast, and brightness were all manually adjusted to render the best possible image.

Additional Resources

While the CI 9s contain a tremendous amount of information, there are additional resources that can help researchers follow the connections suggested in these certificates. As the discussion of the Lawson family in chapter 3 shows, cross-referencing the information found on the CI 9s with census records, genealogical search portals, and archival newspapers can generate a much fuller picture of the people captured in these certificates. Sometimes, as was the case with my search for the woman and the baby discussed at the beginning of chapter 3 (figs. 3.1 and 3.2), or the first Chinese woman photographed in this archive (fig. 4.2) discussed in chapter 4, these additional resources did not shed further light. Particularly in the cases where the migrant did not return to Canada, searching additional resources will yield very little.

REFERENCES

Agamben, Giorgio. 2000. *Means without End: Notes on Politics.* Edited by Vincenzo Binetti and Cesare Casarino. Minneapolis: University of Minnesota Press.

– 2008. "No to Biopolitical Tattooing." Translated by Stuart J. Murray. *Communication and Critical/Cultural Studies* 5 (2): 201–2. doi:10.1080/14791420802027452.

Agre, Philip E. 1994. "Surveillance and Capture: Two Models of Privacy." *The Information Society* 10 (2): 101–27. doi:10.1080/01972243.1994.9960162.

– 1998. "Beyond the Mirror World: Privacy and the Representational Practices of Computing." In *Technology and Privacy: The New Landscape*, edited by Phillip E. Agre and Marc Rotenberg, 29–62. Cambridge, MA: MIT Press.

Auerbach, Jonathan, and Lisa Gitelman. 2007. "Microfilm, Containment, and the Cold War." *Media, Culture and Communication* 19 (3): 745–68.

Azoulay, Ariella. 2008. *The Civil Contract of Photography.* Cambridge, MA: Zone Books.

Backhouse, Constance. 1994. *Colour-Coded: A Legal History of Racism in Canada, 1900–1950.* Toronto, ON: University of Toronto Press.

– 2004. "White Women's Labour Laws." *Law and History Review* 14 (2): 315–68. doi:10.2307/743786.

Bajorek, Jennifer. 2010. "Photography and National Memory: Senegal about 1960." *History of Photography* 34 (2): 158–69.

Bamford, Andrew J., Ara Monadjem, Maria Diekmann, and Ian C.W. Hardy. 2009. "Development of Non-explosive-based Methods for Mass Capture of Vultures." *South African Journal of Wildlife Research* 39 (2): 202–8.

Barker, Elton. 2009. *Entering the Agon: Dissent and Authority in Homer, Historiography, and Tragedy.* Oxford: Oxford University Press.

Barron, Laurie. 1988. "The Indian Pass System in the Canadian West: 1882–1935." *Prairie Forum* 18: 25–42.

Batchen, Geoffrey. 2002. *Each Wild Idea: Writing, Photography, History.* Cambridge, MA: MIT Press.

Baucom, Ian. 2005. *Specters of the Atlantic: Finance Capital, Slavery, and the Philosophy of History.* Durham, NC: Duke University Press.

Bennett, B. 1974. "Study of Passes for Indians to Leave Their Reserves." Prepared for the Treaties and Historical Research Centre, University of Saskatchewan.

Bennett, R.B. 1909. "A Remarkable Canadian Chinaman." *Maclean's* (May): 65–8.

Bhandar, Davina. 2004. "Renormalizing Citizenship and Life in Fortress America." *Citizenship Studies* 8 (3): 261–78.

Bittarello, Maria. 2007. "The Teucer Paradigm." CLC *Web: Comparative Literature and Culture* 9 (3): 1–9.

Bothwell, Robert. 1994. "Foreign Relations and Defense Policy." *Canadian History: A Reader's Guide. Volume 2: Confederation to the Present.* Edited by Doug Owram. Toronto, ON: University of Toronto Press.

Browne, Simone. 2015. *Dark Matters: On the Surveillance of Blackness.* Durham, NC: Duke University Press.

Cadava, Eduardo. 2004. "The Guano of History." In *Cities without Citizens*, edited by Eduardo Cadava and Aaron Levy, 137–66. Philadelphia, PA: Slought Foundation.

Campbell, Persia. 1923. *Chinese Coolie Emigration to Canada.* London: King.

Canada. 1885. *Report of the Royal Commission on Chinese Immigration.* https://epe.lac-bac.gc.ca/100/200/301/pco-bcp/commissions-ef/chapleau1885-eng/chapleau1885-eng.htm.

– 1902. *Report of the Royal Commission on Chinese and Japanese Immigration.* Ottawa, ON: S.E. Dawson. https://catalog.hathitrust.org/Record/100767886.

– 1911. *Report of Mr. Justice Murphy, Royal Commissioner Appointed to Investigate Alleged Chinese Frauds and Opium Smuggling on the Pacific Coast, 1910–11.* https://epe.lac-bac.gc.ca/100/200/301/pco-bcp/commissions-ef/murphy1913-eng/murphy1913-eng.htm.

Carson, Anne. 2002. *Economy of the Unlost (Reading Simonides of Keos with Paul Celan).* Princeton, NJ: Princeton University Press.

Caswell, Michelle. 2014. *Archiving the Unspeakable: Silence, Memory, and the Photographic Record in Cambodia.* Madison: University of Wisconsin Press.

Chan, Arlene. 2017. "Chinese Immigration Act." *The Canadian Encyclopedia.* https://www.thecanadianencyclopedia.ca/en/article/chinese-immigration-act.

Cho, Lily. 2002. "Rereading Head Tax Racism: Redress, Stereotype, and Antiracist Critical Practice." *Essays on Canadian Writing* 75: 62–84.

– 2013. "Redress Revisited: Citizenship and the Chinese Canadian Head Tax." In *Reconciling Canada: Historical Injustices and the Contemporary Culture of Redress*, edited by Jennifer Henderson and Pauline Wakeham, 87–99. Toronto, ON: University of Toronto Press.

– 2014. "Anticipating Citizenship: Chinese Head Tax Photographs." In *Feeling Photography*, edited by Elspeth Brown and Thy Phu, 158–80. Durham, NC: Duke University Press.

Choi, Sze Hang. 2017. *The Remarkable Hybrid Maritime World of Hong Kong and the West River Region in the Late Qing Period.* Leiden, Netherlands: Brill Publishers.

Chow, Rew. 2012. *Entanglements, or Transmedial Thinking about Capture.* Durham, NC: Duke University Press.

Chun, Wendy H.K. 2016. *Updating to Remain the Same: Habitual New Media.* Cambridge, MA: MIT Press.

Clement, Catherine. 2019. *Chinatown through a Wide Lens: The Photographs of Yucho Chow.* Vancouver: Chinese Canadian Historical Society of British Columbia.

Cole, Simon A. 2001. *Suspect Identities: A History of Fingerprinting and Criminal Identification.* Cambridge, MA: Harvard University Press.

Coleman, Kevin. 2018. "Practices of Refusal in Images: An Interview with Tina M. Campt." *Radical History Review* 132: 209–19.

Daschuk, James. 2013. *Clearing the Plains: Disease, Politics of Starvation, and the Loss of Aboriginal Life.* Regina, SK: University of Regina Press.

De Leon, Adrian. 2018. "Working the Kodak Zone: The Labor Relations of Race and Photography in the Chilippine Cordilleras, 1887–1914." *Radical History Review* 132: 68–95.

Delgado, Lourdes. 2017. "Mugshot's Bias: A Semantic History of Guilt." *Photography and Culture* 10 (3): 215–32.

Derrida, Jacques, and Eric Prenowitz. 1995. "Archive Fever: A Freudian Impression." *Diacritics* 25 (2): 9–63.

Dominion of Canada. 1910. *Sessional Papers of the Dominion of Canada 1910.* Ottawa, ON.

Doucet, Andrea. 2018. "Decolonizing Family Photographs: Ecological Imaginaries and Nonrepresentational Ethnographies." *Journal of Contemporary Ethnography* 47 (6): 729–57.

Dubinsky, Karen, and Adam Givertz. 2003. "'It Was Only a Matter of Passion': Masculinity and Sexual Danger." In *Gendered Pasts: Historical Essays in Femininity and Masculinity in Canada*, edited by Kathryn McPherson, Cecilia Morgan, and Nancy M. Forestell, 65–79. Toronto, ON: University of Toronto Press.

Duranti, Luciana. 1989. "Diplomatics: New Uses for an Old Science." *Archivaria* 28: 7–27.

Dyzenhaus, David, and Mayo Moran. 2005. *Calling Power to Account: Law, Reparations and the Chinese Canadian Head Tax Case.* Toronto, ON: University of Toronto Press.

Ebbott, Mary. 2003. *Imagining Illegitimacy in Classical Greek Literature.* Lanham, MD: Lexington Books.

Edwards, Elizabeth. *Raw Histories: Photographs, Anthropology, and Museums.* Oxford: Berg.

Eng, David L. 2010. *The Feeling of Kinship: Queer Liberalism and the Racialization of Intimacy.* Durham, NC: Duke University Press.

Finn, Jonathan. 2009. *Capturing the Criminal Image: From Mug Shot to Surveillance Society.* Minneapolis: University of Minnesota Press.

Gilroy, Paul. 1995. *The Black Atlantic: Modernity and Double-Consciousness.* Cambridge, MA: Harvard University Press.

Glissant, Edouard. 1997. *Poetics of Relation.* Translated by Betsy Wing. Ann Arbor: University of Michigan Press.

Gooch, F.G. 1953. "Techniques for Mass Capture of Flightless Blue and Lesser Snow Geese." *Journal of Wildlife Management* 17: 460–5.

Gu, Yi. 2013. "What's In a Name? Photography and the Reinvention of Visual Truth in China, 1840–1911." *The Art Bulletin* 95 (1): 120–38.

Hu-Duhart, Evelyn. 1994. "Chinese Coolie Labor in Cuba in the Nineteenth Century: Free Labor of Neoslavery." *Contributions in Black Studies* 12, article 5.

Isin, Engin. 2002. *Being Political: Genealogies of Citizenship*. Minneapolis: University of Minnesota Press.

Johnson, LiLi. 2017. "Paper Family Photography: Photography and the State in the Era of Chinese Exclusion (1882–1943)." *Photography and Culture* 10 (2): 105–19. doi:10.1080/17514517.2017.1327567.

Kelley, Ninette, and Michael Trebilcock. 2010. *Making of the Mosaic: A History of Canadian Immigration Policy*. Toronto, ON: University of Toronto Press.

Kindlmann, Peter. 2000. "Philip Agre's Mind." *Red Rocket Eater News*. http://wtf.tw/ref/agre.html.

Koenderink, Jan J., Andrea J. van Doorn, Astrid M.L. Kappers, and James T. Todd. 2004. "Pointing Out of the Picture." *Perception* 33: 513–30. doi:10.1068/p3454.

Koeselleck, Reinhart. 2004. *Futures Past: On the Semantics of Historical Time*. Translated by Keith Tribe. New York: Columbia University Press.

Kuhn, Annette. 2007. "Photography and Cultural Memory: A Methodological Exploration." *Visual Studies* 22 (3): 283–92.

Kumlertsakul, Pad. 2017. "Chinese Labour Corps on the Western Front." *The National Archives Blog*, 18 January. https://blog.nationalarchives.gov.uk/chinese-labour-corps-western-front-2/.

Kunimoto, Namiko. 2004. "Intimate Archives: Japanese-Canadian Family Photography, 1939–1949." *Art History* 27 (1): 129–55.

Lemov, Rebecca. 2015. *Database of Dreams: The Lost Quest to Catalogue Humanity*. New Haven, CT: Yale University Press.

Li, Peter. 2008. "Reconciling with History: The Chinese-Canadian Head Tax Redress." *Journal of Chinese Overseas* 4 (1): 127–40.

Library Archives Canada (LAC). 2020. "Thematic Guides – Canadian Immigration since Confederation and the Department of External Affairs." https://www.bac-lac.gc.ca/eng/discover/immigration/Pages/thematic-guides-canadian-immigration.aspx.

Look Lai, Walton. 2004. *Indentured Labor, Caribbean Sugar: Chinese and Indian Migrants to the British West Indies, 1838–1918*. Baltimore, MD: Johns Hopkins University Press.

Lowe, Lisa. 2015. *The Intimacies of Four Continents*. Durham, NC: Duke University Press.

Luff, P., D. Frohlich, and G.N. Gilbert. 1990. "Computers and Conversation." In *Computers and People*. London: Academic Press.

Lum, Julia. 2017. "'Familial Looking': Chinese Canadian Vernacular Photography of the Exclusion Period (1923–1967)." *Visual Studies* 32 (2): 112–23. doi:10.1080/1472586X.2017.1326838.

Lynch, Jennifer. 2012a. *Face Off: Law Enforcement Use of Face Recognition Technology*. San Francisco, CA: Electronic Frontier Foundation.

– 2012b. "What Facial Recognition Means for Privacy and Civil Liberties." Written testimony for Senate Committee on the Judiciary Subcommittee on Privacy, Technology, and the Law. https://www.eff.org/document/testimony-jennifer-lynch-senate-committee-judiciary-subcommittee-privacy-technology-and-law.

Madokoro, Laura. 2016. *Elusive Refuge: Chinese Migrants in the Cold War.* Cambridge, MA: Harvard University Press.

Mamers, Danielle Taschereau. 2017. "Settler Colonial Ways of Seeing: Documentary and Governance of Indigenous Life in Canada and Its Disruption." PhD diss., University of Western Ontario. https://ir.lib.uwo.ca/etd/4651.

Mar, Lisa. 2010. *Brokering Belonging: Chinese in Canada's Exclusion Era, 1885–1945.* Toronto, ON: University of Toronto Press.

Marien, Mary W. 2002. *Photography: A Cultural History.* 2nd ed. London: Laurence King.

Marshall, Y.M. 1987. "Maori Mass Capture of Freshwater Eels: An Ethnoarchaeological Reconstruction of Prehistoric Subsistence and Social Behaviour." *New Zealand Journal of Archaeology* 9: 55–79.

Maslan, Susan. 2004. "The Anti-Human: Man and Citizen before the Declaration of the Rights of Man and of the Citizen." *South Atlantic Quarterly* 103 (2–3): 357–74.

– 2006. "The Dream of the Feeling Citizen: Law and Emotion in Corneille and Montesquieu." *SubStance* 35 (1): 69–84.

Mawani, Renisa. 2010. *Colonial Proximities: Crossracial Encounters and Juridical Truth in British Columbia.* Vancouver: University of British Columbia Press.

McAllister, Kirsten E. 2018. "Family Photography and Persecuted Communities: Methodological Challenges." *Canadian Review of Sociology/Revue canadienne de sociologie*, 55: 166–89. doi:10.1111/cars.12188.

Meagher, Arnold J. 2008. *The Coolie Trade: The Traffic in Chinese Laborers to Latin America.* Bloomington, IN: Xlibris.

Merolli, Jessica. 2016. "Manufacturing Desire and Producing (Non-)citizens: Integration Exams in Canada, the UK and Netherlands." *Citizenship Studies* 20 (8): 957–72. doi:10.1080/13621025.2016.1229192.

Mishra, Vijay. 1996. "The Diasporic Imaginary: Theorizing the Indian Diaspora." *Textual Practice* 10 (3): 421–47.

Mongia, Radhika V. 2003. "A History of the Passport." In *After the Imperial Turn: Thinking with and through the Nation*, edited by Antoinette Burton, 196–214. Durham, NC: Duke University Press.

Mullaney, Thomas S. 2018. *The Chinese Typewriter: A History.* Cambridge, MA: MIT Press.

Müller, Benjamin. 2004. "(Dis)qualified Bodies: Securitization, Citizenship, and 'Identity Management.'" *Citizenship Studies* 8 (3): 279–94.

Ngai, Sianne. 2007. *Ugly Feelings.* Cambridge, MA: Harvard University Press.

Nicoll, Allardyce. 1953. "The 'Basic' Use of Microfilm." *PMLA* 68 (4): 62–6.

Norton-Kyshe, J.W. 1898. *History of the Laws and Courts of Hong Kong.* 1971 reprint. Cambridge: Cambridge University Press.

Pan, J.Y.C., and J.M. Tenenbaum. 1991. "An Intelligent Agent Framework for Enterprise Integration." *IEEE Transactions on Systems Man and Cybernetics* 21 (6): 1391–408.

Pegler-Gordon, Anna. 2009. *In Sight of America: Photography and the Development of U.S. Immigration Policy*. Berkeley: University of California Press.

Phillips, David J. 1998. "Cryptography, Secrets, and the Structuring of Trust." In *Technology and Privacy: The New Landscape*, edited by Phillip E. Agre and Marc Rotenberg, 243–76. Cambridge, MA: MIT Press.

Pinney, Christopher. 2003. "Introduction: 'How the Other Half …'" *Photography's Other Histories*, edited by Christopher Pinney and Nicolas Peterson, 1–16. Durham, NC: Duke University Press.

Phu, Thy. 2011. *Picturing Model Citizens: Civility in Asian American Visual Culture*. Philadelphia, PA: Temple University Press.

Povinelli, Elizabeth A. 1998. "The State of Shame: Australian Multiculturalism and the Crisis of Indigenous Citizenship." *Critical Inquiry* 24 (2): 575–610.

Probyn, Elspeth. 2005. *Blush: Faces of Shame*. Minneapolis: University of Minnesota Press.

Prodger, Philip. 2009. "Photography and the Expression of Emotions." In *The Expression of Emotion in Man and Animals* [1890], by Charles Darwin, edited by Paul Ekman. Oxford: Oxford University Press.

Pugliese, Joseph. 2010. *Biometrics: Bodies, Technologies, Biopolitics*. New York: Routledge.

Raiford, Leigh. 2013. *Imprisoned in a Luminous Glare: Photography and the African American Freedom Struggle*. Chapel Hill: University of North Carolina Press.

Robertson, Craig. 2010. *The Passport in America: The History of a Document*. New York: Oxford University Press.

Rosenthal, Caitlin. 2018. *Accounting for Slavery: Masters and Management*. Cambridge, MA: Harvard University Press.

Roy, Patricia. 2007. *The Triumph of Citizenship: The Japanese and Chinese in Canada, 1941–67*. Vancouver: University of British Columbia Press.

Royal Commission on Chinese Immigration. 1885. *Report of the Royal Commission on Chinese Immigration: Report and Evidence*. Ottawa, ON.

Rule, J., and P. Attewell. 1989. "What Do Computers Do?" *Social Problems* 36 (3): 225–41.

Salter, Mark B. 2003. *Rights of Passage: The Passport in International Relations*. Boulder, CO: Lynne Rienner.

Sekula, Allan. 1986. "The Body and the Archive." *October* 39: 3–64.

Shachar, Ayelet. 2009. *The Birthright Lottery: Citizenship and Global Inequality*. Cambridge, MA: Harvard University Press.

Sharpe, Christina. 2016. *In the Wake: On Blackness and Being*. Durham, NC: Duke University Press.

Sheehan, Tanya. 2014. "Looking Pleasant, Feeling White: The Social Politics of the Photographic Smile." In *Feeling Photography*, edited by Elspeth H. Brown and Thy Phu, 127–57. Durham, NC: Duke University Press.

Smith, Keith. 2009. *Liberalism, Surveillance, and Resistance: Indigenous Communities in Western Canada, 1877–1927*. Athabasca: Athabasca University Press.

Smuts, G.L., I.J. Whyte, and W. Dearlove. 1977. "A Mass Capture Technique for Lions." *African Journal of Ecology* 15 (1): 81–7.

Spillers, Hortense. 1987. "Mama's Baby, Papa's Maybe: An American Grammar Book." *Diacritics* 17 (2): 64–81. doi:10.2307/464747.

Stanley, Timothy J. 1921–30. "Lee Mong Kow." *Dictionary of Canadian Biography*, vol. 15. http://www.biographi.ca/en/bio/lee_mong_kow_15E.html.

Stoler, Ann Laura. 2008. *Along the Archival Grain: Epistemic Anxieties and Colonial Common Sense*. Princeton, NJ: Princeton University Press.

Strassler, Karen. 2010. *Refracted Visions: Popular Photography and National Modernity in Java*. Durham, NC: Duke University Press.

Stuart, Jan. 2005. "The Face in Life and Death: Mimesis and Chinese Ancestor Portraits." In *Body and Face in Chinese Visual Culture*, edited by Wu Hung and Katherine R. Tsang, 197–228. Cambridge, MA: Harvard University Asia Center.

Tagg, John. 1988. *The Burden of Representation: Essays on Photographies and Histories*. New York: Springer Publishing.

– 2009. *The Disciplinary Frame: Photographic Truths and the Capture of Meaning*. Minneapolis: University of Minnesota Press.

Terada, Rei. 2003. *Feeling in Theory: Emotion after the "Death of the Subject."* Cambridge, MA: Harvard University Press.

Torpey, John. 2000. *The Invention of the Passport: Surveillance, Citizenship and the State*. Cambridge: Cambridge University Press.

United Nations. 2006. "The Rights of Non-citizens." *Office of the United Nations High Commissioner for Human Rights*. New York and Geneva: United Nations.

Vismann, Cornelia. 2008. *Files: Law and Media Technology*. Translated by Geoffrey Winthrop-Young. Stanford, CA: Stanford University Press.

Volpp, Leti. 2007. "The Culture of Citizenship." *Theoretical Inquiries in Law* 8 (2): 571–602. doi:https://doi.org/10.2202/1565-3404.1161.

– 2014. "Civility and the Undocumented Alien." *Civility, Legality, and Justice in America*, edited by Austin Sarat, 69–106. Cambridge: Cambridge University Press.

– 2015. "The Indigenous as Alien." *UC Irvine Law Review* 5 (2): 289–326.

Wagner, Jonathan. 2006. *History of Migration from Germany to Canada*. Vancouver: University of British Columbia Press.

Wexler, Laura. 2011. "'The Bridge Connecting Them to Ourselves': Childhood, Photography and Memory in Contemporary China." *The Journal of the History of Childhood and Youth* 4 (1): 3–10.

Williams, Alex. 2015. *The Pass System*. Dir. Alex Williams. Toronto: Vtape.

Williams, Frederick Benton. 1896. *Of Many Seas: The Life and Exploits of a Yankee Sailor*. New York: MacMillan.

Williams, Raymond. 1977. *Marxism and Literature*. Oxford: Oxford University Press.

Wu, Hung. "Inventing a 'Chinese' Portrait Style in Early Photography." In *Brush and Shutter: Early Photography in China*, edited by Jeffrey W. Cody and Frances Terpak, 69–90. Los Angeles, CA: Getty Research Institute.

Wue, Roberta. 2005. "Essentially Chinese: The Chinese Portrait Subject in Nineteenth-Century Photography." In *Body and Face in Chinese Visual Culture*, edited by Wu Hung and Katherine R. Tsang, 257–82. Cambridge, MA: Harvard University Asia Center.

Yeo, Geoffrey. 2007. "Concepts of Record (1): Evidence, Information, and Persistent Representations." *The American Archivist* 70 (2): 315–43.

INDEX